COMPUTER PROGRAMMING FOR GRAPHICAL DISPLAYS

COMPUTER PROGRAMMING FOR GRAPHICAL DISPLAYS

Daniel L. Ryan

Clemson University

Brooks/Cole Engineering Division
Monterey, California 93940

Brooks/Cole Engineering Division
A Division of Wadsworth, Inc.

Printed in the United States of America

10 9 8 7 6 5 4 3 2 1

Library of Congress Cataloging in Publication Data

Ryan, Daniel L., 1941–
      Computer programming for graphical displays.

      Bibliography: p.
      Includes index.
      1. Computer graphics.   2. Electronic digital com-
puters—Programming.   I. Title.
T385.R926 1983   001.64'43   82-22624
ISBN 0-534-01357-0

Subject Editor: Ray Kingman
Manuscript Editor: Susan Weisberg
Production: Ron Newcomer & Associates, San Francisco, California
Interior Design: Ron Newcomer
Cover Design: Debbie Wunsch
Illustrations: Irene Imfeld
Typesetting: Typothetae
Production Services Manager: Stacey C. Sawyer

CONTENTS

1   INTRODUCTION   1

A Multigraphic Approach, 2

Graphic Decision-Making Aids, 3

Data-Base Management Systems, 6

COM (Computer-Output-Microfilm), 8

Review Problems, 9

2   WORKING TERMINOLOGY   13

Review Problems, 25

3   ENGINEERING DRAWING AND DRAFTING APPLICATIONS   29

Computer-Assisted Graphics (CAG), 30

Computer-Aided Drafting and Design (CADD), 33

Computer-Aided Design (CAD), 39

Review Problems, 46

4   PREPARING ENGINEERING GRAPHICS DISPLAYS   55

Using FORTRAN 77, 55

Structured Program Operation, 57

Providing Display Lists for Structured Programs, 66

Loading and Executing Structured Programs, 70

Review Problems, 82

5   COMPUTER GRAPHICS HARDWARE   87

Programming Computer Graphics Hardware, 87

Direct-Display Devices, 88

CRT (Cathode Ray Tube), 88

DVST (Direct-View Storage Tube), 98

Pen Plotters, 107

Graphics Tablets, 120

Hard-Copy Devices, 124

Review Problems, 125

6   PROGRAMMING GRAPHICAL ROUTINES   129

2-D Geometric Constructions, 129

Transformations, 147

3-D Picture Graphics, 157

Review Problems, 161

7   USING HARDWARE AND SOFTWARE SUCCESSFULLY   165

Hardware Architecture, 165

Software Architecture, 174

Review Problems, 220

8   PROGRAMMING ANIMATION   223

3-D Coordinate Systems and Wireforms, 226

3-D Transformation Packages, 231

Surface Description and Shading, 239

Review Problems, 242

9   PROGRAMMING SIMULATION TECHNIQUES   253

Hidden-Line Removal During Rotation, 257

Surface Shading During Rotation, 263

Data Structures for Simulation Displays, 265

Review Problems, 271

10   PROGRAMMING SURVEY   279

Freeing Drafting Tasks and Time, 280

Improving Drafting Productivity, 283

Programming Improvement for Display Hardware, 287

Computer-Aided Design and Analysis, 290

Final Review Problems, 291

APPENDIX   293

      A.1 CUPID1, 293

      A.2 CUPID2, 318

      A.3 CUPID3, 328

BIBLIOGRAPHY   333

INDEX   335

PREFACE

Computer programming for graphical displays is a technique used by professional engineers, designers, and draftspersons to produce a wide range of engineering documentation. This book presents the technique in a way that both present and future professionals can learn with ease. No previous experience is necessary; anyone with interest can study the material in each chapter and work the review problems. Terminology is defined before it is used. The review problems and answers test and reinforce the reader's understanding of certain concepts, then give the answer for reinforcement.

No special computers, languages, or other requirements are needed to use this book. It is a logical approach to organizing computer graphic outputs so that programs can be written in a common language. Because the book is so basic in its approach, the reader will need to do further study in situations calling for specific output to a particular piece of hardware. The approach to programming is general; in other words, the reader will understand how to organize instructions for all CRTs, but will not be introduced to how these instructions apply, for example, to an IBM 3350. However, the general instruction on CRTs should be helpful when a particular model like the 3350 is used.

Similarly, no computer language is used at the expense of another. Problems are solved at the structure level when a plan for organizing the graphics output is created. The computer instructions may be written in APL, BASIC, PL1, FORTRAN IV, WATERLOO FORTRAN, FORTRAN 77, or any other language best suited to the available host computer. The computer used in this book is a large-scale digital computer; however, any size digital computer may be used. Graphical displays may be produced by micro-, mini-, or maxi-computers; the subject matter is independent of the size of the computer. Common types of digital output device are discussed in this book. To fully understand how to output graphical shapes, the reader must have a plotter, CRT, DVST, printer-plotter, or some other device to test the concepts presented in the last chapters.

Computer Programming for Graphical Displays presents a highly organized and simplified approach to solving several complex problems facing today's engineers: how to get more out of the digital computer; how to produce drawings in a meaningful way; and how to produce programs that generate needed documents. I wrote this text after developing several other works: *Principles of Drafting* (1967); *Automated Drafting and Design Notes* (1977); *Computer-Aided Graphics and Design* (1979); and *Computer-Aided Kinetics for Machine Design* (1981). A sequence of courses I developed at Clemson University made apparent the need for a programming book for draftspersons, designers, and engineers.

I wish to thank all those persons who read and reread the various versions of the manuscript during the last three years. I offer special thanks to those who worked the many problems contained in this book; their efforts in finding and correcting misunderstandings, errors, and ambiguities are greatly appreciated. I also wish to thank Mr. Charles Brack of Gerber Scientific Instrument Company for his assistance in providing the industrial photographs and detailed explanations of graphic workstations.

Daniel L. Ryan

COMPUTER PROGRAMMING FOR GRAPHICAL DISPLAYS

1
INTRODUCTION

If you are a draftsperson, graphic artist, or detailer working in an office that has just ordered a computer, this chapter may be the most important section of any book you have ever read. It will address many of your fundamental concerns about working with a computer. Will the computer put you out of work? Will you know how to use it without programming experience? How fast can programming be learned? How difficult is it? These are but a few of the many questions that will be answered throughout this chapter and the book as a whole.

Many books, magazine articles, and manuals have been written about computer programming and its role in modernizing drafting practices. The majority of these writings fall into two groups: those that try to justify computers used in drafting offices, and those that try to ridicule the use of a computer to replace a human worker. This chapter falls squarely between the two groups. The computer should be an aid to the draftsperson to make the workplace more productive. The most important thing to remember about computer programming for graphical displays is that the human controls what happens, *not the computer*. This book's energetic approach to computer programming always places the human first. In a human/computer relationship the human directs the machine.

The widespread use of computer graphics by designers and engineers was built on the principle of letting the human do the design (thinking) and letting the machine carry out the drafting work. This book was written for those who will have to program the computer so that drafting sheets can be made. Computer programmers are usually not trained in orthographic projection (three-view relationships), dimensioning techniques, sectioning a drawing, and the like. There is no reason they should be; draftsmen, detailers, and designers do this, and they will continue after the computer arrives. This graphic-type programming is necessary to "bridge the gap" between computer and engineer.

Computer programs consist of written commands, which should be as easy to understand as possible for both the human and the machine (computer). Until now what has been lacking is a programming technique that provides a coupling of the human and the computer. Such programming must not force the designer (human) to change thinking habits, language habits, or the normal time to do basic drawing tasks. In this book the reader can understand how this coupling is possible by carefully studying each of the examples and by working the review problems at the end of each chapter.

A MULTIGRAPHIC APPROACH

Computers have many different uses in an engineering/drafting office. *Computer* is a catch-all word that has been misused by many people. A computer may be digital (works from numbers) or analog (works from voltages). In this book we will work only with digital computers because they are programmed with words, whereas analogs are programmed with circuits wired together. Both types of computer are used in design; drafting work is done on machines that use words and numbers. A computer is also described by size, as a minicomputer, microcomputer, or macrocomputer. The size of the digital computer (mini, micro, macro) makes little difference in learning programming. Big jobs are done on big macrocomputers and little jobs are done on little minicomputers. Microcomputers are usually placed on desk tops and are used to assist the draftsperson or designer with only a portion of the design. Production drawings are usually done by a minicomputer used just for that purpose or by macrocomputers.

In order to do all the work that is required in a drafting office, a multigraphic data (numbers) approach is used. This will allow a programmer to do a drawing detail, label it, and describe it in a set of notes or bill of materials. The procedure for doing all this has already been worked out by the computer manufacturer.

Manufacturers have worked for several decades to develop workstations that are comfortable for the draftsperson to use. The drawing board, called a *data tablet*, looks just like a drawing board. The pencil that is used has a wire running out the end connected to a small box, with an off-and-on switch. If the box is turned on, the tablet sends a board location to the computer when the pencil is touched to the drawing surface. In this manner a draftsperson may send an entire sketch or drawing to the computer. The drawing is sent as a group of numbers, however, not graphic shapes. This group of numbers is called the *data base*; a single number within the data base is called a datum (plural, datums or data). Usually two datums (locations X and Y) are needed to describe a point. Two datums are used along with a signal to control display.

If a data tablet creates data, then something

else must be used to make the drawing. Drawings may be presented on a screen, plotter bed, microfilm, photographic film, or other medium. The important thing is that a signal is sent along with the data (X and Y locations) so that the draftsperson sees points, lines, or spaces. Many different signals are used by different manufacturers. Some use the number 2 or 3, whereas others use the shift N key stroke or up arrow. Draftspersons use these signals to control the presentation of multigraphic data. For example, if the following data were sent to the computer from the data tablet,

```
1.25 1.50 3
4.25 1.50 2
4.25 4.50 2
1.25 4.50 2
1.25 1.50 2
```

a square image three display-units by three display-units would be visible to the draftsperson. The first set of data (1.25 1.50 3) located the three-unit square 1.25 units in X and 1.50 units in Y. The number 3 was used to create a move and not a line. In the remaining data the number 2 at the end of each set meant that a line was displayed.

Data for multigraphic presentations can be produced from the data tablet, typed from a keyboard, sent from another computer, or read from computer storage. For now, the source is not as important as the basic concept that will be used throughout this book: graphical images are produced from numbers called data base. This concept is so simple that many people find it hard to believe. Believe it. The hard part is deciding what the display-unit is. In practice, it is what the manufacturer says it is. The draftsperson must use what is provided. Some cases use an inch, others use a millimeter, and still others use overlapping dots that equal 1/130 of an inch. The programming must take the display-unit size into account.

GRAPHIC DECISION-MAKING AIDS

The display-unit size is just one of several decisions made during the programming for graphical displays. Graphic decision-making aids include the data tablet discussed above and several others. A computer scientist might call these decision-making aids *input devices*, but this would limit them to pieces of equipment. In fact, a decision-making aid might be a pointing device, a display surface, or a section of the computer program written to provide numbers for the digital computer.

The most dynamic example of graphic decision making would be the United States Military SAGE system (Air Defense Against Air Breathing Targets). Although now out of date, the system was a way for digital computers to track and later calculate intercept points for fighters and bombers. This particular development was semiautomatic, relying on a human and a cathode ray tube (CRT) display console to supply inputs the computer was unable to cope with automatically.

It was during SAGE development that the need for graphic decision-making aids became imperative for the digital computer users. Operators needed to decide if the target was a bomber, fighter, or transport plane, and to enter the data. As the traffic was moving, any attempt to type from a keyboard or read a punched card or tape was useless. The operators had to view a graphic display and read a spot flight to recognize a target. This situation prompted the invention of the light pen, which allowed the human operator to simply point at a CRT display and make appropriate decisions.

When these techniques were applied to drafting situations, data-base manipulation became easier. Instead of typing in numbers to represent images, the draftsperson pointed at names representing these images. The names appeared at a convenient place on the CRT screen, usually along the side or bottom of the screen, along a *menu bar*. They looked like this:

```
/ MOVE / DRAW / RECT / CIRCLE / POLYGON / RESET / SET / TURN /
```

When the draftsperson touched the first word (MOVE), the number 3 was assigned to the data base. The second word (DRAW) placed the number 2 after the data base item. The RECT portion of the menu displayed an entire rectangle of pre-programmed size on the screen. CIRCLE displayed a full circle of fixed size on the screen, whereas POLYGON represented a number of equal-sided polygons. RESET and SET were used to display and erase images as desired, and TURN rotated an image on the screen.

In this example the draftsperson placed the light pen (LP) over the word describing the desired action. However, what was sent to the computer was a number, as the program stored in the computer was written to look for a range of numbers. For example:

```
0       10      20      30      42        55      66    75      85
/ MOVE / DRAW / RECT / CIRCLE / POLYGON / RESET / SET / TURN /
```

The menu bar has assigned values along the X direction of:

```
    MOVE  =  0   TO  10
    DRAW  =  10  TO  20
    RECT  =  20  TO  30
  CIRCLE  =  30  TO  42
 POLYGON  =  42  TO  55
   RESET  =  55  TO  66
     SET  =  66  TO  75
    TURN  =  75  TO  85
```

As long as the LP is placed between 0 and 10 display units below the menu bar, the action is a MOVE.

Most computer graphics programs are divided into four main sections:

1. ARITHMETIC . . . . . Statements usually contain an equals sign.
2. CONTROL . . . . Statements are usually IF, GOTO, DO, CONTINUE, STOP, CALL, RETURN.
3. INPUT/OUTPUT . . . Statements take data into a program and display data as graphical images.
4. DECLARATION . . . Statements are usually DIMENSION, COMMON, ALLOCATION, EQUIVALENT.

The section of the program that checks where the LP is pointed is called the *control section*. The light pen uses control statements to check locations and proper actions. In the example menu bar the control section would look like this:

```
IF(LP.GT.0.OR.LP.LT.10) CALL MOVE(IX,IY)
IF(LP.GT.10.OR.LP.LT.20)CALL DRAW(IX,IY)
IF(LP.GT.20.OR.LP.LT.30)CALL RECT(IX,IY)
IF(LP.GT.30.OR.LP.LT.42)CALL CIRCL(IX,IY)
IF(LP.GT.42.OR.LP.LT.55)CALL POLY(IX,IY)
IF(LP.GT.55.OR.LP.LT.66)CALL RESET(IX,IY)
IF(LP.GT.66.OR.LP.LT.75)CALL SET(IX,IY)
IF(LP.GT.75.OR.LP.LT.85)CALL TURN(IX,IY)
IF(LP.LT.0.OR.LP.GT.85)PRINT,'LIGHT PEN IS OFF THE MENU BAR'
PRINT,'LIGHT PEN IS ABOVE THE MENU BAR'
```

The graphical decision box looks like a triangle (see Figure 1-1). The line entering from the top is the pass from the program statement above the first IF statement.

Each IF is a decision that must be answered YES or NO (Figure 1-2). In the case of the first IF statement, the location of the light pen (LP) is tested to see if it is greater than (.GT.) zero or less than (.LT.) ten display units. This test is answered true or false (yes or no). If it is true, the graphical image is called from computer memory and displayed. If it is false, the decision is passed on to the next statement, and so on.

Graphic decision-making aids help the draftsperson select sections of data stored in the computer. In the example just given, the aid was a combination of equipment, programming, and human responses. The human controls the equipment (a pointing device) and writes the program to suit the drafting situation. Menu bars are completely undefined until the user writes the control section of the computer program. When the menu bar appears, anybody can point a light pen at it and select items. To further understand graphic decision-making aids, let us consider how the computer displays the menu bars.

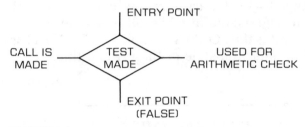

FIGURE 1-1

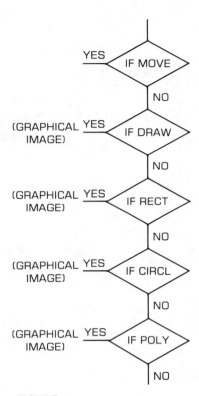

FIGURE 1-2

First, the programmer decides what type of menu bar is desired. A typical problem of this nature is shown in review problem 4 of this chapter. Stop now and work through it to see if you can follow the logic of the control section. Next, an input/output (I/O) section of the program can be written to display the menu bar. I/O sections of programs use various kinds of statements, depending on the manufacturer. No attempt has been made to slant this book toward a single manufacturer, so common I/O will be shown as (see table at right):

To output the menu bar, you use one of the statements from the output list. For example, if the

INPUT	OUTPUT
READ	WRITE
ACCEPT	PRINT
GET	PUT
SEELOC	WHERE

WRITE statement were selected, the program line might look like this:

```
   WRITE(3,99)
99 FORMAT('
 +                 ',//,'/ MOVE / DRAW / ERASE / SAVE / LINE / PL
 +OT / RECT / CIRCLE / POLYGON / DASH /')
```

In this example the WRITE statement has two numbers following it. The first number is the number of the device where the output is to be displayed—in this case, at the bottom of a CRT screen. The second number following the WRITE statement is the FORMAT number. A FORMAT is used to enter the style of the printed line.

DATA-BASE MANAGEMENT SYSTEMS

Two decades have passed since the SAGE system of handling data from a menu bar was first introduced. The drafting operator of today has three techniques available:

1. Read from a CRT current real-time responses from a fast digital computer.
2. Write crudely by pointing with a light pen or other device so that human input will be accepted without coding in computer languages.
3. Real-time feedback response for each input action.

The term *real time* means that a drafting operator can see immediately, in a human language, the result of the input. Data-base management is a technique for gathering pieces of necessary data (numbers) that represent the final drawing. It is also the ability to store, change, and display that data in a variety of different ways. In order to write a section of a graphics program that will manage the data base, the input part of the I/O program is used. The operator chooses one from the I/O list of available statements. It might look like this:

```
     READ(1,10)NPTS
  10 FORMAT(I4)
```

This input statement accepts any value for the storage location NPTS (number of points), as long as it is an integer and is not larger than 9999. Programmers use NPTS or NDATA as a typical storage location to identify the total number of data elements in the data-base listing. To input individual datums into the data base, a control statment and an input statement are used:

```
     DO 100 I=1,NPTS
     READ(1,11) X,Y,IPEN
  11 FORMAT(2,F6.3,I2)
 100 CONTINUE
```

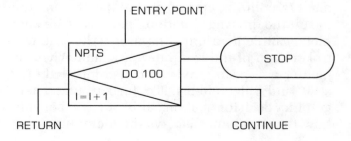

The DO statement uses the NPTS value to read each of the data listings. The READ statement accepts datum entries for X, Y, and IPEN. The FORMAT statement allows two floating-point (real) numbers to be stored in X and Y, as long as they fit into _ _ . _ _ _ number spacings. And IPEN values must be integers not larger than 99. The input technique just used does not store the data anywhere; it just reads and forgets. If a storage technique is desired, then a statement from the declaration portion of a program is used:

```
DIMENSION X(NPTS),Y(NPTS),
IPEN(NPTS)
```

Now if the data are read as:

```
    DO 100 I=1,NPTS
100 READ(1,11) X(I),IPEN(I)
```

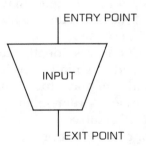

ENTRY POINT

INPUT

EXIT POINT

the data are stored in the dimensioned area X(NPTS), Y(NPTS), and IPEN(NPTS). The DO statement is used to input the data until all items in the data list have been stored.

After the data are stored in the computer as data base, they may be changed in various ways or used to display a graphical image. Changing data is very easy. Suppose that the data base, which represents a graphical image, needs to be moved eight display units to the right. The following ARITHMETIC statements can be used to do that:

```
    DO 55 I=1,NPTS
    X(I)=X(I)+8.
55 CONTINUE
```

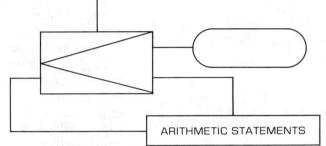

ARITHMETIC STATEMENTS

In this manner graphical images can be moved back and forth in the X direction, or up and down if the Y(I) values are changed.

The remaining data-base management task is displaying the data in a meaningful manner on an output device. Manufacturers of equipment (hardware) and suppliers of programs (software) use several techniques for this. A subprogram technique can be used whereby a CALL statement is inserted in the program to display the data. Subprograms are named whatever the author of the subprogram chooses. Labels such as SHOW, PLOT, TYPE, INITT, or BEGIN could be used; the technique remains the same. Suppose we choose to call the display subprogram DISPLA. The CALL is inserted as:

```
    NPTS=850
    DIMENSION X(NPTS),Y(NPTS), IPEN(NPTS)
    DO 100 I=1,NPTS
100 READ(1,11) X(I),Y(I),IPEN(I)
    DO 55 I=1,NPTS
        CALL DISPLA(X(I),Y(I),IPEN(I))
55 CONTINUE
```

With data base management techniques graphic operators can see immediately what the data base looks like. Changes can be made in 15 seconds or less, and the operator can monitor large data bases (1 million elements). The three principles of graphic reading, writing, and obtaining real-time responses or feedback are the basic ingredients of a data base management system. A manager uses programming sections (arithmetic, control, I/O, and declaration) as shown in the review problems. Stop reading for now and work through problems 6, 7, and 8. These will help you understand data base management systems.

COM (COMPUTER-OUTPUT-MICROFILM)

The graphic decision-making aids and the data base management system we have discussed are seldom a simple combination of commands or sequence of operations. More often questions and answers are necessary. As in the problems of the introductory chapter, the operator begins by making an assumption and seeing what the result will be. As more information becomes available, the operator will try again and gradually converge on a logical solution or logical position that will match the solution. When responses to questions seem to diverge, the operator must change assumptions and try again. These many tries can be stored as computer output. COM techniques have helped match the computer to human processes. Without COM or other storage devices, there was little chance the human could remember the exact thought process at a later time. Now human mental processes do not have to adapt to the machine.

Computer output must be in graphic, readable form. Typical types of output are:

CRT Screen
Plotter page
Photograph image
Microfilm

In the first case, there is only one CRT screen to hold the various tries. In the second, a separate computer process must be used for each page. A device for recording CRT images is the logical method. Either of the photographic methods (listed third and fourth) will speed up the preservation of solution sequences. In the case of microfilm a draftsperson or designer may see each step of the design process by viewing the microfilm on a reader at a later time.

Although COM was ideally suited to static images (described in Chapter 6), it was not suitable for dynamic displays (described in Chapter 8). Most engineers remember the problems worked for the creative design of a product, mechanism, or device that produced motion. The classic textbooks used equations, vector notation, kinematic representation, and any other technique to display the idea of motion. Now the motion itself can be displayed. Simple techniques exist for placing static images together in strip fashion. The resulting frames are then "buffered" to remove any jerk or jump in the picture. And thus we have the Saturday morning cartoons.

This chapter has presented a brief overview of graphic decision-making aids and data base management. The following chapters will go into much more detail about programming in the presentation of multigraphic data.

REVIEW PROBLEMS

1. Using the multigraphic technique described on pages 2–3, prepare a data list for a graphical display image that is located 12 display units in X and 4 display units in Y. The image is composed of three line segments each 10 display units long.

ANSWER

```
12.00   4.00 3
22.00   4.00 2
17.00  12.66 2
12.00   4.00 2
```

2. Prepare a notebook divided into ten sections. Each section will represent the review problems at the end of each chapter in this book. Record the answer for problem 1 above in section 1.1 and so on for each review problem. The notebook should also contain several pages of "coding form," (see Figure 1-3) as well as blank sheets for notes.

3. From your reading of this chapter, list as many applications for computer-aided engineering graphics as you can. Beside each application label the size of computer (micro, mini, or macro) that is used.

ANSWER Varies with background of each reader.

4. Design a menu bar that will appear at the bottom of a CRT screen and have the following actions: MOVE, DRAW, ERASE, SAVE, LINE, PLOT, RECT, CIRCLE, POLYGON, DASH.

ANSWER

```
0      8     16    25    33    41    49    57    67    78    86
/ MOVE / DRAW / ERASE / SAVE / LINE / PLOT / RECT / CIRCLE / POLYGON / DASH /


IF(LP.GT.0.OR.LP.LT.8) CALL MOVE(IX,IY)
IF(LP.GT.8.OR.LP.LT.16)CALL DRAW(IX,IY)
IF(LP.GT.16.OR.LP.LT.25)CALL ERASE
IF(LP.GT.25.OR.LP.LT.33)CALL SAVE
IF(LP.GT.33.OR.LP.LT.41)CALL LINE(IX,IY)
IF(LP.GT.41.OR.LP.LT.49)CALL PLOT(IX,IY,IPEN)
IF(LP.GT.49.OR.LP.LT.57)CALL RECT(IX,IY)
IF(LP.GT.57.OR.LP.LT.67)CALL CIRCL(IX,IY)
IF(LP.GT.67.OR.LP.LT.78)CALL POLY(IX,IY)
IF(LP.GT.78.OR.LP.LT.86)CALL DASH(IX,IY)
IF(LP.LT.0.OR.LP.GT.86) PRINT,'LIGHT PEN IS OFF THE MENU BAR'
PRINT,'LIGHT PEN IS ABOVE THE MENU BAR'
```

5. Write an output statement that will display the menu bar designed in review problem 4.

ANSWER

```
    WRITE(3,98)
98  FORMAT('_____
   +_____',/ /,'/ MOVE / DRAW / ERASE / SAVE / LINE
   +/ PLOT / RECT / CIRCLE / POLYGON / DASH /')
```

6. Write a program section that will read 50 pieces of data (X,Y,IPEN) and list them for the computer-graphics operator.

ANSWER

```
    NPTS=50
    DO 77 I=1,NPTS
    READ(1,10) X,Y,IPEN
10  FORMAT(2F6.3,I2)
    WRITE(3,10)X,Y,IPEN
77  CONTINUE
```

7. Write a program section that will read 850 pieces of data (X,Y,Z) and store them for the computer graphics operator. Provide a storage location for pen controls (IPEN(NPTS)).

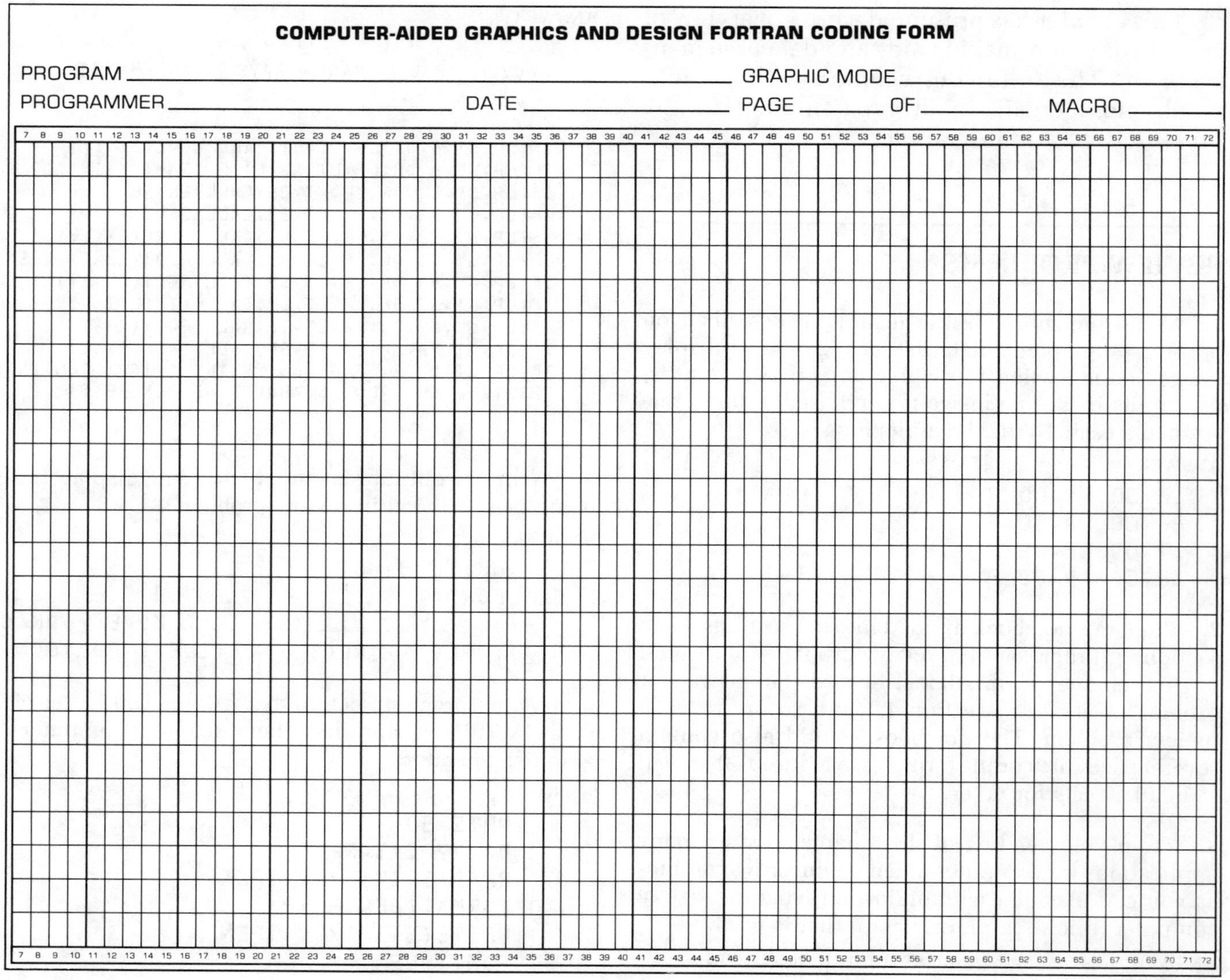

COMPUTER-AIDED GRAPHICS AND DESIGN FORTRAN CODING FORM

PROGRAM ________ GRAPHIC MODE ________

PROGRAMMER ________ DATE ________ PAGE ____ OF ____ MACRO ________

7 8 9 10 11 12 13 14 15 16 17 18 19 20 21 22 23 24 25 26 27 28 29 30 31 32 33 34 35 36 37 38 39 40 41 42 43 44 45 46 47 48 49 50 51 52 53 54 55 56 57 58 59 60 61 62 63 64 65 66 67 68 69 70 71 72

7 8 9 10 11 12 13 14 15 16 17 18 19 20 21 22 23 24 25 26 27 28 29 30 31 32 33 34 35 36 37 38 39 40 41 42 43 44 45 46 47 48 49 50 51 52 53 54 55 56 57 58 59 60 61 62 63 64 65 66 67 68 69 70 71 72

FIGURE 1-3
Example of a computer-aided graphics and design fortran coding form.

ANSWER

```
    NPTS=850
    DIMENSION X(NPTS),Y(NPTS),
    Z(NPTS),IPEN(NPTS)
    DO 66 I=1,NPTS
 66 READ(1,10) X(I),Y(I),Z(I), IPEN(I)
```

8. Write a program section that will take the 850 pieces of data stored in problem 7 and display the X and Y values at a plotter origin of X = 4.75 and Y = 2.5.

ANSWER   Follows the statements of problem 7 as:

```
    CALL DISPLA(4.75,2.5,-3)
    DO 88 J = 1,NPTS
 88 CALL DISPLA(X(J),Y(J),IPEN(J))
C   THE ABOVE PROGRAM SECTION WILL
C   DISPLAY A FRONTAL VIEW OF AN
C   OBJECT DESCRIBED IN X Y AND Z.
```

9. Write a program section that will take the 850 pieces of data stored in problem 7 and display the X and Z values at a plotter origin of X = 4.75 and Y = 9.75.

ANSWER   Follows the statements of problem 8 as:

```
    CALL DISPLA(0.,7.25,-3)
    DO 99 K = 1,NPTS
 99 CALL DISPLA(X(K),Z(K),IPEN(K))
C   THE ABOVE PROGRAM SECTION WILL
C   DISPLAY A TOP (HORIZONTAL) VIEW OF
C   THE SAME OBJECT.
```

10. What is the maximum value for any Y coordinate in the data base used for problem 7, 8, or 9?

ANSWER   The maximum value for Y is 7.25 if the front and top views are touching, less than 7.25 if any space between views is desired.

11. Write a program section that will display the Z and Y values as a right side view.

ANSWER   Follows the statements of problem 9 as:

```
    CALL DISPLA(12.5,-7.25,-3)
    DO 101 L = 1,NPTS
101 CALL DISPLA(Z(L),Y(L),IPEN(L))
C   THIS CODING PLOTS A RIGHT SIDE VIEW.
```

12. What is the maximum value for any X coordinate in the data base used for problems 7, 8, 9, and 11?

ANSWER   The maximum value for X is 12.5 if the front and right sides are touching, less than 12.5 if any space between views is desired.

13. Write a program section that will display the −Z and Y values as a left-side view.

ANSWER   Follows the statements of problem 11 as:

```
    T= -1.
    CALL DISPLA(-14.5, 0.,-3)
    DO 103 M C 1,NPTS
103 CALL DISPLA(Z(M)*T,Y(M),IPEN(M))
C   THIS CODING PLOTS A LEFT SIDE VIEW.
```

14. What is the spacing provided between the frontal and left profile views?

ANSWER   2.0

15. Write a program section that will display the X and −Z as a bottom view.

ANSWER   Follows the statements in problem 13 as:

```
    CALL DISPLA(-2.,-2.,-3)
    DO 105 N = 1,NPTS
105 CALL DISPLA(X(N), Z(N)*T,IPEN(N))
C   THIS PLOTS THE BOTTOM VIEW OF THE SAME OBJECT.
```

16. What is the space between the front and bottom views?

ANSWER   2.0

17. What is the space between the front and right side views if the maximum value of X is 10.5?

ANSWER 2.0

18. What is the space between the front and top views if the maximum value of Y is 5.25?

ANSWER 2.0

19. What would the statement CALL DISPLA(2.75, .5, −3) do if entered after the last statement in the answer to problem 15?

ANSWER Return pen to lower left-hand corner of frontal view.

20. Write a program section that will input 190 pieces of data (X,Y,IPEN), store them, and then MOVE the image 10 display units to the right and up 6 display units. When the move has been completed, display the data base.

ANSWER

```
       NPTS=190
       DIMENSION X(NPTS),Y(NPTS),
       IPEN(NPTS)
       DO 66 I=1,NPTS
   66  READ(1,10) X(I),Y(I),IPEN(I)
   10  FORMAT(2F6.3,I2)
       DO 55 I=1,NPTS
       X(I)=X(I)+10.
   55  Y(I)=Y(I)+6.
       DO 77 I=1,NPTS
       CALL DISPLA(X(I),Y(I),IPEN))
   77  CONTINUE
```

2 WORKING TERMINOLOGY

Computer programming for graphical displays uses a great variety of terms. Some relate to computers, others to programming in the FORTRAN language, and still others to engineering graphics and drafting. Readers may be unfamiliar with some or all of these terms. People studying any new subject need simple terminology whenever possible. Unfortunately, those trying to learn about computers, computer languages, or graphic displays quickly encounter a problem. They must wade through descriptions full of the esoteric and colorful—and often confusing—terms that have evolved with computers. *Real time,* for example, suggests that there may be unreal time somewhere. Slang, technical terms, and phrases used by computer manufacturers all contribute to the problem.

The ultimate example of this confusion is a computer program that selects real phrases and "buzz words" at random and fits them together to make arbitrary sentences. The computer program will produce as many pages of this *cybercrud* as you want. Readers have the baffling feeling that what they are reading almost makes sense, but that the meaning is somehow eluding them. A *cybercrud* terminology synthesizer, shown in Table 2-1, is used by selecting one word from column A, two from column B, and one or more from column C. A subject and verb like "This is a" to start the sentence, and "system" to end the sentence are all that is needed. For instance, try the following combinations: $1 - (6,7) - 3$ will produce the cybercrud sentence "This is a user-oriented sequential access free formatted utility

TABLE 2-1
Cybercrud Terminology

Column A	Column B	Column C
1. user-oriented	1. algorithm	1. display
2. absolute address	2. data based	2. turn-around time
3. bidirectional	3. stand alone	3. utility program
4. asynchronous	4. handshaking	4. block diagram
5. time-sharing	5. hashing	5. von Neumann machine
6. batch-processed	6. sequential access	6. special purpose language
7. bit diddling	7. free formatted	7. information retrieval
8. throughput	8. two-dimensional	8. hardware
9. incremental	9. memory wrapped	9. virtual memory
10. hollerith	10. microcoded	10. automatic drafting

program." Or how about: "I wonder if this is an $4-(9,8)-7$ system? These examples should make you understand the name *cybercrud.*

Fortunately, understanding computer programming for graphical displays does not require more than ordinary language (if you thought Chapter 1 was ordinary). But being able to speak cybercrud is a great help if you run into a computer buff or write equipment justifications. In the following chapters we shall make sure that all terms are defined. If a technical term is used to define a more advanced term, you will be able to find a definition of the simpler term. The remainder of this chapter is devoted to a glossary of the technical terms used in this book. When a term has more than one form, it is defined under its most esoteric-looking form. Acronyms, for instance, are alphabetized and defined under their condensed, rather than their spelled-out forms (DVST, rather than direct view storage tube). This glossary should help you understand the working terminology associated with computers, programming, and graphical displays.

ABSOLUTE DATA Data collections known as data bases can be either absolute or relative. Absolute data are measured from a single origin. Relative data redefine the display origin after each data block is used. The data base in Chapter 1 was considered absolute.

ABSOLUTE POINT OR VECTOR Points are individually addressable positions on the display screen or plotter surface, identified by X and Y coordinate positions. Vectors are line segments drawn from the current pen (plotter) or beam (CRT) position to an absolute point. The end coordinates were defined in Chapter 1 in absolute units relative to the origin of the display device.

ACOUSTIC TABLET A data tablet with strip microphones mounted along two adjacent edges of the tablet to record the sound created by the movement of the stylus on the tablet surface.

ADDRESSABLE POINT The smallest display unit in the CRT or plotter working area that a pen or beam can be sent. These addressable points, or locations, are specified by X and Y coordinates and form a grid over the working area.

ADDRESS REGISTER The address register, found in the display controller hardware, is used to show address (location) of the next instruction.

AIMING SYMBOL A tracking symbol of light projected by the light pen onto the CRT face. It aids in positioning the LP or describing the LP's field of view, as described in Chapter 1. In that case a menu bar was displayed so that the LP could be aimed at the descriptive words.

ALIASING A defect in the display image created by an improper sampling procedure. Raster displays are prone to aliasing. Symptoms include jagged lines, moire circle patterns, and other "glitches" that appear and disappear for no known reason. Glitches are usually @ signs or similar stray characters created by interference in data transmission.

ANIMATION The technique of presenting a sequence of images in rapid succession to create an illusion of motion. Chapter 8 of this book is devoted to animation programming.

ANSI American National Standards Institute.

AREA FILLING The process of modifying pixels within a designated area with a particular color or pattern. Area filling is described in detail later in this book.

ARRANGEMENT OF VIEWS See ORTHOGRAPHIC PROJECTION.

ASCII American Standard Code for Information Interchange.

ASPECT RATIO The height-to-width relationship of a display area.

ATTRIBUTE A characteristic of display item or image, such as color, intensity level, line type, or detectability. Chapter 5 discusses display methods and attributes.

AUXILIARY VIEWS Those display views of an object that are not one of the primary six orthographic views. Auxiliary views are often needed to fully describe an object for manufacture.

AXONOMETRIC PROJECTION In axonometric projection, an object is displayed so three faces or surfaces show in one view. This is accomplished by displaying the object so that its faces are inclined to the surface of the display screen. Wireform objects are often displayed as axonometric projections. Wireform objects are constructed of absolute vectors and displayed as open frames. The terms *wireframe* and *wireform* are interchangable.

BACK VIEW One of the primary orthographic projections. It represents the face turned away from the viewer.

BASE-LINE DIMENSIONING The purpose of base-line dimensioning is to prevent cumulative errors, because each dimension is independent of all others. The base-line, which is called a *part datum*, is usually a common edge or surface for accurate measurement.

BIT A single-digit binary number that can have a value of 0 or 1. Bits are used as maps when a digital memory contains a description of the characteristics of addressable pixels in a raster display. The color or intensity of each pixel is determined by the value of a corresponding set of bits in the bit map. The image created on the screen by the mapping of the bit memory onto the raster display is known as the *bit pattern*.

BLINK A programming technique on a display screen, sometimes implemented in hardware, in which a display image is repeatedly turned off and on. Blinking is used to attract the operator to input data or to do some graphics task.

BOTTOM VIEW One of the primary orthographic projections. It represents the positioning face turned down from the viewer.

BRIGHTNESS A measure of the visual effect of displayed data base. The unit of measure is the foot-lambert, which represents the brightness of a light source.

CALLIGRAPHIC DISPLAY The term *calligraphic* means fine writing; it is descriptive of the higher resolution available to display dots, characters, or vectors. These systems create pictures by moving the electron beam directly from point to point, allowing rapid displays for series of line segments. Motion and quick response to interaction is much more easily implemented in calligraphic than in raster systems because calligraphic needs to process only a few line end points. Calligraphic refresh displays are uniquely suited for applications such as computer-aided design (CAD), for which dynamic motion is desirable or required. The calligraphic refresh display is the most versatile of the CRTs, with such unique features as selective erase in both foreground and background modes.

CELL-ORGANIZED RASTER DISPLAY   In these types of devices the image is constructed by a collection of rectangular characters, each representing a small bit map. Examples are 5 × 7 and 7 × 9.

CHARACTER GENERATOR   The character generator is part of the picture, or circle generator, and accepts and/or interprets character codes from the refresh processor. Then strokes are produced and sent to the line generator for display. Most character generators are capable of creating regular and italicized characters in eight sizes, ranging from .08 cm to 1.88 cm. They also produce subscript and superscript characters approximately two-thirds the full character size. Character generators can be microprogrammed by the user to produce other fonts or special symbols at varying sizes. This ability allows characters to be produced at any orientation (rotation). The character generator has a memory, half of which is preprogrammed to interpret the 128 ASCII characters.

CIRCLE GENERATOR   Sometimes called a *picture generator*, a circle generator produces images to be viewed on the picture display area and manages input/output of the devices. It generates circles and other images by converting digital data into analog signals, which are used to draw line segments on the display. The picture generator consists of three main parts: (1) a refresh and device processor, (2) a character generator, and (3) a line generator.

CLIPPING   A process to ensure that a display image is not generated beyond a predetermined boundary, usually defined by the addressable area on the screen. Clipping may be done by software or hardware.

COMPUTER GRAPHICS   A relatively new and important branch of computer technology in which digital computers prepare and present pictorial output. Computer graphics is well represented by the *A*ssociation for *C*omputing *M*achinery (ACM), *S*pecial *I*nterest *G*roup for *GRAPH*ics (SIGGRAPH). Interactive computer graphics, introduced in Chapter 1, goes one step further in allowing a user to dictate changes and see the results immediately. If computer graphical displays take more than a few seconds, they are considered fast-batch, not interactive (see Chapter 3). The study of computer graphics can be broken down into four major topics: (1) presenting a prepared picture, (2) representing structures to be depicted, (3) preparing a picture of such structures, and (4) interacting with the picture.

COHERENCE   The property of objects in a raster display in which touching pixels or identical pixels in adjacent frames tend to possess similar attributes. Coherence is used later in this book by scan-line algorithms to increase efficiency.

COLOR DISPLAY   Since the number of lines that may be displayed continues to increase with each new raster scan device, color becomes important in helping to distinguish portions of a data base. Until recently the only color techniques adapted to calligraphic displays were frame sequential and beam penetration. The frame-sequential units call for red, green, and blue color filters to alternately pass through the viewer's line of sight on a monochrome CRT. The motion, usually rotation, is extremely rapid, so that each color is in front of the eye at least once per refresh. The display program then synchronizes the rotation of the color filters with the display of lines such that lines that are to appear in a given color are displayed while the color filter is between the eye and the CRT. Frame-sequential color suffers from limited line capacity and difficulty in mixing the colors.

Beam-penetration CRTs have two layers of phosphor, normally red and green. The electron beam voltage is varied to cause the electrons to strike only the inside layer, penetrate to the outside layer, or penetrate midway. Depending on the beam voltage level, the color is red, green, or other colors in the red–green spectrum.

The shadow mask CRT, which was considered limited to raster CRTs, has recently been used in calligraphic CRT construction. Lines may be displayed that light up dots of all three primary colors. These may be in any intensity to form a desired color. Color in calligraphic displays is limited only by the digital host specifications and usually rivals monochrome displays.

COM Computer output to microfilm; discussed in Chapter 1.

CONIC GENERATOR See CIRCLE GENERATOR/PICTURE GENERATOR.

CONTRAST The ratio of the brightness of a display image to the screen background.

CONTROL BALL An input device, in the form of a ball, that can be moved in at least two degrees of freedom. It is used to control the movement of a display item.

CONVERSION TO SCREEN COORDINATES Coordinate data remaining after the clipping process may be of any size and located at any position in the data base. They should be properly scaled (mapped) so that they fill the display area. This area, known as a *viewport*, can be any portion of the viewing region on the screen. If the viewport is a rectangular region aligned with the screen axes, it can be specified by supplying the screen coordinates for its left, right, bottom, and top edges. If the line generator can display lines of varying intensity, a viewport may also specify the intensity limits for the data displayed at the hither and yon boundaries—the *hither and yon intensities*. When the hither and yon intensities are different, the intensity of the displayed picture elements varies between these limits, giving an illusion of depth.

COORDINATES As used in Chapter 1, an ordered set of data values, either absolute or relative, that determines a location on the display area.

CORE SYSTEM The CORE is a standard general-purpose subrouting package established by ACM SIGGRAPH and discussed throughout the later chapters of this book.

CRT Cathode ray tube; an evacuated glass tube in which a beam of electrons is emitted and focused onto a phosphor-coated tube surface. A beam deflection system moves the beam so that an image is traced on the screen.

CURSOR An input aid used and demonstrated in Chapter 5 of this book. Also referred to as *crosshairs*.

CUTTING PLANE See SECTIONS AND CONVENTIONS.

DARK TRACE TUBE A dark trace tube is a type of CRT whose electron beam causes the display surface of the tube to darken rather than brighten. The line images appear against a translucent face (screen).

DATA TABLET The data tablet served as the graphic input device in Chapter 1. The tablet can be used for positioning or pointing to the picture elements by use of a stylus or pen, whose X, Y coordinates are read by the display controller. A cursor may be generated on the display area to indicate the position of the pen on the tablet. This generation may be accomplished automatically by the display processor immediately after the tablet position is read, providing fast response, with no need to interrupt the display controller. In conjunction with a display processor, the tablet and pen can perform the interactive functions usually reserved for such graphic input devices as light pens, joysticks, and function switches.

DEFLECTION TECHNIQUE A deflection technique is used in a refresh calligraphic CRT to display data base without flickering. It is used on a CRT that amplifies the voltages of the electron guns.

DEPTH CUEING A method of simulating depth in the display of a pictorial. One technique modulates the intensity of the line according to its implied distance from the observer. Other techniques use stereo pairs or perspective plotting.

DETAIL DRAWING A computer display consisting of orthographic views, dimensions, centerlines, notes, and other information necessary to manufacture the object described.

DEVICE-INDEPENDENT SOFTWARE Graphic packages often provide "hooks and handles" that may be used to present a uniform interface to get the portability of application programs written in Chapters 3 and 4.

DEVICE DRIVER Program listing written to convert device-independent graphic commands so they might be used on specific output display devices. Device drivers are written for data tablets, control dials, function switches and lights, alphanumeric keyboards, light pens, joysticks, and lighted function buttons. Chapter 6 discusses device drivers.

DIGITAL PLOTTER A plotter (device) whereby the display data base can be moved only in discrete steps and positioned to specific display locations. Many types of plotters are available for graphic ouptut. These plotters may be grouped, by performance and interaction ability, to form a spectrum. At the lower end of this spectrum lie pen-and-ink plotters, in which a computer-driven pen creates a stroke-by-stroke picture. Plotters are unmatched for resolution, but are extremely slow compared to more sophisticated graphic devices.

Next in the spectrum lies the electrostatic dot matrix plotter, which operates by displaying elements of a dot matrix with ink. The pattern of filled and empty elements is assembled to form a picture. A plotter of this type is known as a *raster device* because the engineering drawing is produced as a succession of horizontal lines. The resolution of these plotters is not good, but the time to display is quite fast when compared to a pen plotter.

DIGITIZER An input device that codes graphical images or shapes into digital data. Digitizers are often confused with data tablets until it comes time to pay for one. Digitizers are far more complex and capable of recording X, Y, and Z data, whereas a data tablet is two-dimensional.

DISPLAY The physical hardware device, or the act of presenting the data base as graphical images that are used to draw engineering documents.

DISPLAY BUFFER A storage area. This may be a memory area that holds all display orders and data base (dimension statements) required to generate an engineering drawing.

DISPLAY CODE GENERATOR A software programming technique to generate the display file commands.

DISPLAY CONTROLLER See CIRCLE GENERATOR.

DISPLAY CYCLE The programming sequence needed to regenerate an image once it is on a refresh CRT.

DISPLAY DATA A collection of data intended for display is called a *data base*. After it is processed and displayed, it is called *display data*.

DISPLAY DEVICE A device capable of presenting data base on a display surface is called a *display device*. Chapter 5 of this book is devoted to programming display devices, including drum plotters, flat bed plotters, microfilm recorders, DVSTs and CRTs.

DISPLAY ELEMENT A display element is created by programming a sequence of statements to display a point, line, character, or subpicture display. Subpictures can be either hardware or software generated to form display pictures that will be used in the engineering drawing presentation.

DISPLAY FILE This term is used interchangably with DISPLAY BUFFER.

DISPLAY FOREGROUND Subpictures created by software programming that are subject to change by the program, and are used to display the engineering drawing in an interactive mode.

DISPLAY FRAME Also called a *buffered frame*, a display frame is one set of display images comparable to a frame in a motion picture film. Chapter 8 of this book is devoted to animation.

DISPLAY GENERATOR See CIRCLE GENERATOR.

DISPLAY IMAGE See DISPLAY DATA and DISPLAY ELEMENT.

DISPLAY LIST Graphic commands read and interpreted by the display processor. The display list is created from the graphics program stored in the controller and is used to order the presentation of characters, vectors, and subpictures while manipulating the display registers.

DISPLAY MENU A list of options on a display device that allows the operator to select the next program action by pointing to one or more choices. Also called a *menu bar* (see Chapter 1).

DISPLAY ORDER See DISPLAY LIST.

DISPLAY PANEL Light buttons, function switches, plasma panels, touch tablets, control dials, or the like, associated with display devices.

DISPLAY PROCESSOR A hardware unit that reads operator instructions, data base, and coded information from a host computer. It processes these separate pieces of information and presents them to the display generator.

DITHERING See HALFTONING.

DMA Direct memory access; allows the display processor to act independent of a host computer. It is the transferring of display data to and from host memory without processing on the host computer.

DRAGGING Sometimes called *shifting*, dragging is the translation of a selected subpicture along the path defined by the programmer. In Chapter 1 we shifted (moved) a graphical image along the X direction by entering $X(I) = X(I) + XN$, where XN is any value not clipped by the display area.

DRUM PLOTTER See DIGITAL PLOTTER.

DVST Direct view storage tube; an output device that displays data base as a graphical image. DVSTs are often confused with CRTs. The DVST behaves like a CRT with an extremely long-persistence phosphor, since a line written onto the screen will remain visible for up to an hour before it fades away. The electron beam does not, however, write directly onto the phosphor, but rather charges a fine wire grid mounted behind the face of the screen. The charge left on the grid is continually transferred onto the screen by field electrons. The storage tube has fairly coarse resolution when compared with refersh CRTs, and erasing a line from a drawing causes a momentary flash covering the entire screen. Moreover, portions of the screen cannot be erased selectively, which limits the DVST to graphical applications that are more passive than active.

Important differences exist between DVSTs and CRTs. The DVST has no facility for intensity variation, a feature that was used in depth cueing. A recent development for DVSTs is an ability to display data in "write-thru" mode. Although this is not refresh, it does allow the DVST to be used in applications where refresh displays were formerly required.

ELECTROSTATIC PLOTTER   See DIGITAL PLOTTER.

ERASE   Remove display items from the display area. See CLIPPING.

ESCAPE   A subroutine within the CORE (SIGGRAPH) software known as "hooks and handles" to get to noncore software packages.

EVENT PRIMITIVE   As explained and used throughout this book, an event primitive is an input command that is associated with a device that can be interrupted. The CORE software, for example, uses *pick*, *button*, *stroke*, and *keyboard*.

EXPLODED VIEW   See ZOOM.

EXTENSION LINES   Line images displayed perpendicular to dimension lines at any convenient length so that the reader may read the object that is sized.

FILL   A technique used in raster displays (and demonstrated later in this book). It inserts a group of dots within a designated area described by a SHADE subroutine. Fill is also known as *tone*.

FLASH   See BLINK.

FLAT BED PLOTTER   See DIGITAL PLOTTER.

FLICKER   A condition that exists if the programming is not suitable to refresh the CRT within 1/45 of a second. See DISPLAY CYCLE.

FLOOD GUN   A DVST has a flood gun that issues a flood of electrons. See DVST.

FRAME BUFFER   See DISPLAY BUFFER.

FRONT VIEW   One of the primary orthographic projections. It represents the face turned toward the viewer.

FULL SECTIONS   See SECTIONS AND CONVENTIONS.

GEOMETRIC CONSTRUCTIONS   A collection of graphic subroutines that allow a draftsperson to construct basic geometric elements from a keyboard.

GEOMETRIC MODEL   A geometric model fully defines the coordinates stored in the data structure. Geometric models are described in the finite element modeling section of this book.

GRAPHIC INPUT DEVICE   See CONTROL BALL, DATA TABLET, DISPLAY DEVICE, JOYSTICK, LIGHT PEN, MOUSE, THUMB WHEEL.

GRAPHIC LANGUAGE   Described in the remaining sections of this book.

GRAPHIC OUTPUT MEDIA   For hard copy output media see DIGITAL PLOTTER. Such output is permanent, which can be a disadvantage if any interaction with the engineering drawing process is desired. The CRT has been used since the early development of computers to display non-permanent images. There are three basic types of CRTs: (1) raster scan display, (2) calligraphic refresh display, and (3) color display. These CRTs fall into the performance-interaction spectrum described for digital plotters, but at the high end. All CRTs function basically in the same manner.

GRAPHICS FIELD The area used for plotting images; includes all areas except those reserved for the menu display area.

GRID An orthogonal set of parallel lines usually one pixel high and one pixel wide.

GUIDE LINES Single orthogonal line used for placing lines of lettering for an engineering drawing.

HALFTONING A technique used for three-dimensional graphics. It extends the effective range of intensities for a display by trading off spatial resolution for intensity resolution.

HALOED LINE EFFECT A technique used when a line in three-dimensional space passes in front of another. A gap is produced in the orthographic projection of the more distant line as if an opaque halo surrounded the closer line. When lines or curves on a surface are closer than the halo size, the gaps come together, producing a complete line elimination.

HARD COPY An output device, or a piece of paper produced from that device.

HASP Houston Automatic Spooling Program. Used on IBM graphics systems to aid in job control language (see JCL).

HEDGEHOG Hedgehog displays are wireform, three-dimensional objects without hidden line removal.

HIDDEN LINE A line segment on an engineering drawing that should be obscured from view in a projected plane. In programming for graphical displays these lines may be eliminated or represented as lines with different texture, intensity, or color.

ICON In interactive programming ICON is a symbol used to represent an input command from a menu. In this book we have used ICON(I) to mean a series of commands to represent point connections during animation.

INCREMENTAL VECTOR See RELATIVE VECTOR.

INKING The generation of a continuous line image along the path traced by the input graphic device.

INPUT PRIMITIVE See EVENT PRIMITIVE.

INTERLACE SCAN A television monitor display technqiue to reduce flicker.

JCL Job control language; those statements necessary to enter a computer program and execute it.

JOYSTICK A lever that can be moved to control the movement of one or more display elements. It is used in place of a control ball.

KEYBOARD An event primitive used by CORE programming.

LIGHT BUTTON A light button, usually one of 32 available for preprogramming, operates as a function switch or key.

LIGHT PEN As used in this text, a stylus that detects light within a limited area. It is used with a menu bar for pointing, or it can be used to direct input data for graphic images.

LINEAR TRANSFORMATION Linear transformations (rotation, shifting, scaling) can be described by parameters that indicate the type and degree of transformation. If the transformation parameters are properly arranged into a matrix, a vector of original coordinates can be multiplied by this matrix to give a vector of new coordinates reflecting the desired transformation.

A 4 × 4 matrix can represent any rotation, translation, or change in scale and can be used to transform points representing coordinates. This matrix expression of transformations is used because it is simple and allows the computer to take advantage of the large body of knowledge about matrix arithmetic.

LINE DENSITY   See LINE WEIGHT.

LINE GENERATOR   A line is specified by two end points (X, Y) and (X', Y'). X and Y are usually the present location of the beam or plotter pen, and X' and Y' represent the end of the line to be displayed. The actual movement of the electron beam or pen between the two points is accomplished by a hardware device called a *line generator*. Line generators are also capable of displaying lines with a software program-specified intensity. Where line endpoints are specified by three coordinates (X, Y, Z), the intensity or brightness of lines can appear to trail off in the distance. See DEPTH CUEING.

Line generators can be made to draw lines in a choice of modes and textures, such as blinking, solid, long dashed, short dashed, or a series of colors. Line generators must service more than one type of output device. See GRAPHIC OUTPUT MEDIA.

LINE WEIGHT   The width of the line produced on the engineering drawing.

LISSAJOUS   Two mutually orthogonal sets of curves; can be directly compared to a grid pattern definition. Lissajous figures are used to generate characters and special curved sections.

LOCATOR   A CORE input primitive used to specify position information in a coordinate space.

LP   Light pen.

MACH BANDS   See ALIASING.

MAPPING FUNCTION   See BIT.

MASK   A matrix of binary values, in which a 0 indicates a pixel outside the area, and 1 indicates a pixel inside it. See CRT.

MATRIX-ADDRESSED STORAGE DEVICE   See DVST or PLASMA PANEL.

MATRIX CHARACTER GENERATOR   Used in this book to create characters composed of dots as opposed to stroke characters.

MODE   The current type of operation for a display processor that is determined by the program.

MOIRE PATTERN   See ALIASING.

MOUSE   An input device moved on a data tablet surface to provide data base. A mouse is often used to position a cursor. It may be thought of as an inverted control ball.

MULTIPICTURE SYSTEM   A microprogrammed, general-purpose, interactive computer graphics system. It can display engineering drawings of two- or three-dimensional objects to one or more draftspersons, each independently interacting with the drawing data base.

NESTED SUBPICTURE   A nested subpicture, or subroutine, has the ability to call one subpicture or subroutine from inside another.

ORIGIN   The reference point whose coordinates are all zero.

ORTHOGRAPHIC PROJECTION   A method for presenting an object on an engineering drawing. It has six principal views arranged to present the front, top, bottom, back, right, and left sides in their logical relationships.

OUTPUT PRIMITIVE   The CORE system recognizes the following output primitives: line, text, polyline, marker, and polymarker. Anything that you can see on a display screen.

PAN To pan is to cause a translation of the window in the view plane.

PARAMETERS Data contained in the data base other than X, Y, and Z values. It is used to control pen or beam position or other attributes necessary for display.

PASSIVE GRAPHICS Those forms of graphical presentation that are not interactive or fast-batch.

PERSPECTIVE It is relatively easy to prepare two-dimensional data for display, as shown in Chapter 1. Three-dimensional data may be converted to two dimensions after transformation by simply dropping the depth (Z value). The resulting display would not look realistic since the depth dimension has an enormous effect on the appearance of the horizontal and vertical dimensions. This effect, known as perspective, accounts for the convergence of parallel lines in the distance in real life.

The perspective operation entails computing a point projection of three-dimensional points onto a plane representative of the screen. Perspective can be applied to three-dimensional data by taking advantage of the fact that the perspective transformation is expressable in matrix form. A perspective transformation matrix can be included at the end of the sequence of rotation, shifting, and scale matrices to transform three-dimensional data into a two-dimensional perspective projection.

PFK Program function key. See DEVICE DRIVER.

PICK See EVENT PRIMITIVE.

PIXEL A single picture element in a raster display. A pixel is the smallest displayable spot on the display surface that can be addressed from the data base.

PLASMA PANEL A raster display device consisting of a flat, gas-filled panel containing a grid network of wires. Energized intersections of the grid wires glow and emit light.

PLOTTER See DIGITAL PLOTTER.

RANDOM SCAN See REFRESH DISPLAY.

RASTER A rectangular matrix of pixels is called a raster.

RASTER SCAN DISPLAY The same display CRT used in the commercial television sets. This device functions in a similar manner to the electrostatic dot matrix printer/plotter previously defined (see DIGITAL PLOTTER). A standard television image consists of 480 raster lines. Each line is divided into a number of dots, typically 512. Unlike the electrostatic plotter, the CRT must reproduce the entire drawing each time the image on the phosphor fades, typically 45 times a second. This requires that the raster information be stored in digital form. This quantity of data rapidly becomes rather large, with 245,760 bits of information required for a standard television image of only two intensity levels. Almost 2 million bits of information are required to produce a gray scale image with 256 intensity levels or a color image containing 256 colors.

REFRESH DISPLAY A refresh display uses low-persistence phosphor in the design of the CRT, therefore it must be re-written several times a second or it will fade from the screen. See REFRESH RATE.

REFRESH RATE A refresh rate is usually between 30 and 60 times per second, and re-paints the entire contents of the display screen.

RELATIVE VECTOR Vectors are line segments displayed from the current position to a relative point. Each starting point is assumed to be 0,0. See ABSOLUTE POINT or VECTOR.

ROTATE To turn a display element about an axis on the display screen.

RS232　One of two common types of interfaces between equipment and computers. It uses serial data.

SCALING　Scaling is one of the transformation functions listed earlier and is used to change the size of computer display. Often a CRT image will be enlarged for plotter output.

SCISSORING　Often confused with clipping, scissoring is a process used by the line generator to blank the beam whenever it is moved outside the display area. In clipping, the line value (data) is changed; in scissoring it is saved for later use by the line generator.

SCREEN COORDINATE SYSTEM　A screen coordinate system is typically either integer raster units or fractions between 0 and 1. The DVST contains screen coordinates which if compared with world coordinates would equal 130 for each inch. See DEVICE DRIVER.

SCROLING　The continuous vertical or horizontal movement of the display elements within a viewport. As new information appears at one edge of the viewport, old information disappears at the other edge.

SECTIONS AND CONVENTIONS　Special views of objects to show interior details. Usually the material used for an engineering object is shown along with accepted graphics techniques that deviate from true graphic representation.

SEGMENT　An ordered collection of CORE output primitives defining an image. A segment usually possesses attributes such as visibility and detectability.

SELECTIVE ERASE　The ability to remove one or more specified elements, such as a letter out of a word or a portion of a line segment, without affecting the rest of the display image.

SHADE　A subroutine for the computation of the intensities and/or colors of the surface of a three-dimensional object based on a light source. Chapter 6 of this text has illustrative figures showing the ability to shade an object.

SPLINE　When long sweeping curves have to be input from a large data tablet, ship curves or *splines* are used. Owing to the length of the splines, it is important to hold them in place; therefore "ducks" are used to weight down the spline.

STAIRCASING　One of the forms of ALIASING appearing in a pattern resembling a staircase.

STANDALONE SYSTEM　A graphic system with its own computer.

STEREO VIEWS　This book makes use of two views to represent certain forms of perspective pictorial displays.

STYLUS　A hand-held pointer used to input coordinate data.

TABLET　See DATA TABLET.

TEXT DISPLAY　Almost all graphics applications call for the presentation of alphanumerics on the screen at various times. It is possible to define character shapes in the data base like other drawing images. In fact, this is necessary if characters are to be treated like other drawing objects. If they are to be rotated, clipped, or scaled, then they must be part of the data base. See CHARACTER GENERATOR for the other method of displaying characters.

THUMBWHEEL　A dial or wheel that can be rotated to control the movement of a graphics cursor or to position a graphic subpicture.

TRACKING　The process of moving a predefined symbol across the surface of the display screen with a light pen.

VECTOR GENERATOR   See LINE GENERATOR.

VIEWPORT   A bounded area within the device space that presents the contents of a display window. The viewport may be set to equal the screen size.

WINDOW   In some engineering drawing applications, the data base is displayed in its entirety on the screen. Often, however, only a portion of the data base needs to be seen. The list of data portion of the data base to be seen is called a *window*. Determining what parts of the data list are within the window and what parts are not is a difficult problem. In fact, this determination is so time consuming in programming that it can slow down dynamic displays.

Intelligent programming addresses this windowing problem by performing a visibility check after the transformation stage and draws only visible lines on the display. One such technique, called *Clipping*, entails comparing all lines with the boundaries of a program-specified window superimposed on the data list. Lines or portions of lines outside the window are eliminated, and only visible lines are passed to the screen for display.

WORD   A word is a set of bits that occupies one storage location in the program and is treated by the computer as a unit. Word lengths for graphical display are typically 32 bits.

WORLD COORDINATES   The opposite of *Screen Coordinates*.

WRAP AROUND   Wrap around occurs when a line goes off the right side of the display and reappears on the left. *Scissoring* is used to avoid this problem and save the data. If *Clipping* were used, then the line would become shorter in the data list.

ZOOM   Zoom is the process of scaling all elements of a viewport to give the appearance of having the viewer move toward the graphics. It is often used to isolate a small feature and bring it to fill the screen.

REVIEW PROBLEMS

1.   Using the word-definition approach used throughout this chapter, begin with the first definition on page 14. Underline any term in the definition that is not clear to you.

ANSWER   (example)

ABSOLUTE DATA   Data collections known as *data bases* can be either *absolute* or *relative*. Absolute data are measured from a single *origin*. *Relative* data redefine the *display origin* after each data *block* is used. The *data base* in Chapter 1 was considered *absolute*.

2.   Look up all the underlined words in the rest of Chapter 2 for more information.

ANSWER

data base defined in Chapter 1 and under DIS-PLAY DATA

absolute defined again in ABSOLUTE POINT OR VECTOR

relative not defined in Chapter 1 or 2 _____

absolute data defined several times in Chapter 1 and 2

origin defined under DIGITAL PLOTTER

block not defined again _____

3.   Turn to the index and look up those terms not found in Chapters 1 or 2.

ANSWER

> *relative* used in later chapters to represent transformed data
>
> *block* used in later chapters to mean one row of data listed in the data base

4. Look up terms not found in the index in an ordinary or technical dictionary and write a definition for these.

ANSWER   Varies with reader's background.

5. Continue through the list of terms found in Chapter 2 and repeat review problems 1 through 4.

ANSWER   Varies for each reader.

6. Try the technique of review problems 1 through 5 with a short technical article about programming, graphic displays, or computers.

7. Begin a section of your notes called *new terms*. Whenever you come across an unfamiliar term, add it to the list and write a brief definition as done in this chapter.

8. Review each term listed in Chapter 2. With a light pencil, write the letter "H" after each term that represents computer graphic hardware.

ANSWER

> ACOUSTIC TABLET (H)*
> ADDRESS REGISTER (H)*
> CELL ORGANIZED RASTER DISPLAY (H)*
> COM (H)
> CONTROL BALL (H)
> CRT (H)*
> DARK TRACE TUBE (H)
> DATA TABLET (H)*
> DEVICE DRIVER (H)*
> DIGITAL PLOTTER(H)*
> DIGITIZER (H)*

> DISPLAY BUFFER (H)*
> DISPLAY CONTROLLER (H)*
> DISPLAY DEVICE (H)*
> DISPLAY PANEL (H)*
> DRUM PLOTTER (H)*
> DVST (H)*
> ELECTROSTATIC PLOTTER (H)*
> FLAT BED PLOTTER(H)*
> INPUT DEVICE (H)*
> HARD COPY DEVICE (H)*
> JOYSTICK (H)
> KEYBOARD (H)*
> LIGHT BUTTON (H)*
> LIGHT PEN (H)*
> MOUSE (H)*
> PLASMA PANEL (H)
> STANDALONE SYSTEM (H)*
> THUMBWHEEL (H)*

9. Repeat problem 8 using an asterisk notation for those hardware items at your location.

ANSWER   (example given under problem 8)

10. For those terms remaining in the chapter, use the following code: (S) = software items, (F) = firmware, (DI) = display image, and (EG) = engineering graphics term. Code each of the terms appropriately.

ANSWER   Would appear similar to the listing above for each coded symbol.

11. Repeat problem 9 using the following notation: # = software used, @ = firmware available,] = display image used, & = graphics term understood.

ANSWER   Varies for each reader.

12. In your own words, write a working definition for each of the terms marked by an (*) in problem 9. This should be a "how-to-use-it" at your location. Place this in your notebook.

13. Repeat problem 12 for each of the terms marked by a (#). Place in your notebook.

14. Repeat problem 12 for each of the terms followed by a (@). Place in your notebook.

15. Repeat problem 12 for each of the terms followed by a (]). Place in your notebook.

16. Repeat problem 12 for each of the terms followed by a (&). Place in your notebook.

17. Prepare a list of graphics hardware that can be found at your location that was not included in this chapter. Write a brief description of "how it works" and place in your notebook.

18. Prepare a list of graphics software items at your location that were not included in this chapter.

19. Prepare a list of graphics firmware items at your location.

20. Prepare a list of items commonly used at your location for computer graphics that were not included in this chapter.

3 ENGINEERING DRAWING AND DRAFTING APPLICATIONS

Engineering drawing is the visual language of draftspersons, designers, planners, and others who work for engineers. The engineer makes sketches and notes for the final drawings that will indicate the shape, size, material, and other details of any engineering product from a design idea or an operation sequence, to a fabrication method.

The many different branches of engineering often deal with related parts of the same whole. For example, suppose a new industrial fabrication plant is to be built. The civil engineer is concerned with the site, construction, and material handling of the building; the mechanical engineer is concerned with the air-handling system to be placed inside the building; the electrical engineer is concerned with energy systems involving electrical power, machinery, and communications; the industrial engineer is concerned with the proper placement of equipment and the material handling of the plant; and the chemical engineer is concerned with piping systems for industrial wastes, chemical raw materials, and final products. Depending on the particular plant, other engineers, such as mining, metallurgical, petroleum, or materials engineers, may also be involved. All of these engineers will use engineering drawings at some point in their work. With the aid of digital computers, they now all have access to the same information and can use a uniform style for their drawings. And with modern display equipment all engineers can:

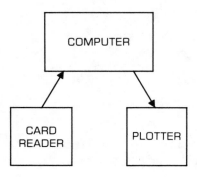

Control the appearance of final drawings

Provide uniform linework and graphic presentation

Work from unlimited geometric shapes

Obtain uniform, neat lettering for drawings

Obtain correct views—such as orthographic, auxiliary, sections, or pictorials—automatically

Get more than one type of dimensioning, tolerance, and interchangeability of parts

Select common fasteners from a computer catalogue listing

Control the working drawing arrangement and choice of drawing types

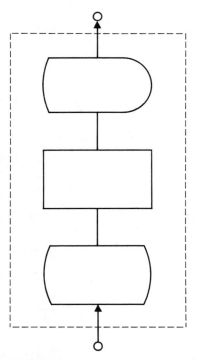

FIGURE 3-2

COMPUTER-ASSISTED GRAPHICS (CAG)

Although one engineering task is the production of final drawings, engineers also use computers in the early formulative stage of design. By providing a method or language that is natural to the set of design problems, computer-assisted graphics puts the user in close touch with the computer processing. The design engineer and digital computer can form a high-speed, highly useful combination.

Graphic reading, writing, and real-time response can be implemented by a CRT and a fairly fast computer. However, to see even more far-reaching effects on information processing, let's give the operator a light pen to use as a writing tool, pointing, or selecting medium, and a keyboard to insert alphanumeric information.

With the general introduction of Chapter 1

and the terms explained in Chapter 2, the programmer is ready to begin simple tasks. A programmer begins the learning process by reading the operations manual for the workstation. It may seem as unnecessary to mention reading the manual as to say a blind person should not drive an automobile, but a lot of operators try to do computer-assisted graphics operations "blind." Because this book does not recommend any type of hardware above any other, we will look at a structured programming approach that can be used to automate the tasks that need to be done.

Structured programming, which became popular in the 1970s, is a universal approach and not particular hardware-dependent programming steps. Therefore, in structured programming, large blocks replace individual language statements. A direct comparison will illustrate this relationship: Figure 3-1 is the HASP version of JCL; Figure 3-2 is the structured approach.

In the HASP-type JCL the task of preparing the workstation to receive program statements or data is cut and dried: prepare the commands on punched cards or terminal statements that are read as separate cards, alert the computer, and drive the plotter or other output device. In the structured approach, by contrast, this task is one large block that can be handled in a variety of ways. Notice that hooks and handles that look like small circles, called *terminal points,* are placed before and after the block. Another operation may be taken from these points or fed into them.

Drafting tasks are blocks composed of arithmetic sequences that are structured to operate as single processors. Structured programming for engineering drawing tasks is analogous to the relatively simple single-minded microprocessor. A microprocessor user enters data, and the processor performs the single drafting task assigned to it. The processor has a single algorithm that follows a well-defined series of steps sandwiched between a single start and a single exit point. The simplest drafting tasks are computations executed in sequence. In order to move a display point on a display surface, for instance, the point is entered as X and Y data locations; to move the display point up, down, left, and right; the processor subtracts or adds to those data. The point may become larger or smaller by multiplication or division. To display lines, planes, and solids, the processor sorts or inverts data matrix or performs exponential functions.

Much of the real power of structured programming is derived from the ability to perform predefined drafting tasks and make the appropriate decisions, such as which task is to be performed next, or whether a particular task is needed. An example is the choice between task A or task B, depending on test condition T. A and B are composed of the necessary statements to complete the task, as shown in Chapter 1. The tasks are stored as subroutines. If T is true, the program may execute block A (subroutine task A); if T is false, the program executes B. The structured programming for this procedure is shown in Figure 3-3. Figure 3-4 is another primitive element of structured programs known as the *selection block*. Note that control to this block can enter the block only at a single point and exit only at one point. However, three tasks can be selected. The tasks are usually coded as −N, O, or +N, where N is the result of the test T.

A different type of decision path is shown in Figure 3-5. The program tests condition T; then, depending on the result, either executes draft-

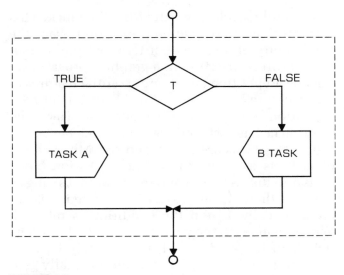

FIGURE 3-3

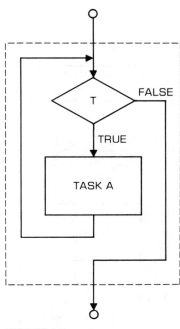

FIGURE 3-5

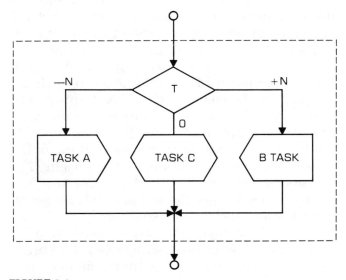

FIGURE 3-4

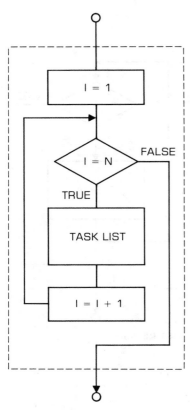

FIGURE 3-6

task A and recycles, or exits from the block. This primitive element called *repetition* has the single-entry and single-exit terminal points that permit direct insertion in a graphics program sequence. Repetition blocks are essential features of all structured programs. An advanced form of repetition is illustrated in Figure 3-6. Here, the drafting task is assigned the value of I. One task is I = 1, two tasks are I = 2, and so forth. The list of tasks is assigned to N. The repetition block adds 1 to the value of I and tests again. As long as I is less than N, the tasks are executed, I is incremented by 1, and the condition is retested. When I equals N, the program exits the loop. The details of initializing and incrementing I and of executing the comparison are automatically generated by the language used, such as FORTRAN or BASIC.

A common drafting task form of repetition occurs when the number of iterations is indefinite, rather than incremental. An example is sectioning a portion of an irregular casting whose shape is defined by an equation. The procedure shown in Figure 3-7 is to initialize Y at some positive value less than the desired number of section lines to be displayed, then test to see if the function of Y in the equation equals X. If this condition is met, the program can display the section lines for the irregular shape. If the condition is not met, Y is increased following the form of the equation and the condition is tested again. The process is continued until the entire area has been sectioned. Once the subroutine is designed, the graphics block can be structured.

All graphic tasks that are defined as algorithms can be expressed with only a few primitive structure elements. A program that uses

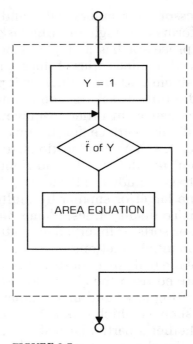

FIGURE 3-7

only these elements will be organized and easy to understand. Page after page of FORTRAN means little to the student, but a structured diagram is meaningful.

Structured programming is *not* flow-charting. Of course, flow-charting is helpful because any structure element may be composed of other elements, implying a nesting of blocks to an arbitrary depth. We can compare unstructured and structured programs using flow-charting with possible decision paths through A then B, through B alone, or through neither A nor B. The unstructured flow chart is shown in Figure 3-8, the structured in Figure 3-9. The unstructured approach may at first appear simpler to write as

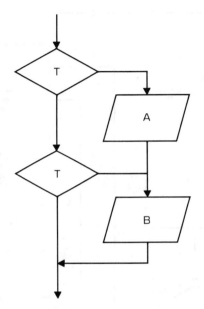

FIGURE 3-8

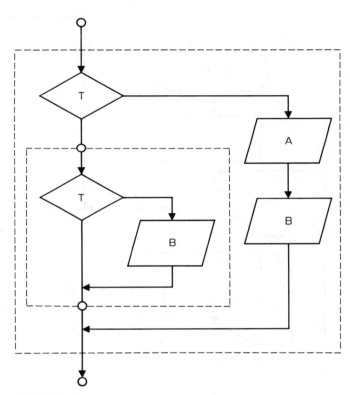

FIGURE 3-9

a program. However, drafting assignments are harder to describe in the unstructured approach. To better understand this we can compare an ACM SIGGRAPH sort-routine, *character strokes*, using both unstructured (Figure 3-10) and structured logic (Figure 3-11). In this case the use of structured programming clearly has the advantage over flow-charted, unstructured programming in a high-level computer language.

When the drafting tasks can be determined, structured programming is the correct choice. In the rest of this book all graphics output is taken from structured programming examples, so we will stress the theory of graphics for computer-aided drafting.

COMPUTER-AIDED DRAFTING AND DESIGN (CADD)

In structured programming each of the common drafting tasks is represented by a rectangular block, which is coded to fit the particular computer that will display the engineering drawing. Table 3-1 lists the common drafting tasks used in computer-aided drafting and design (CADD) to produce an engineering drawing.

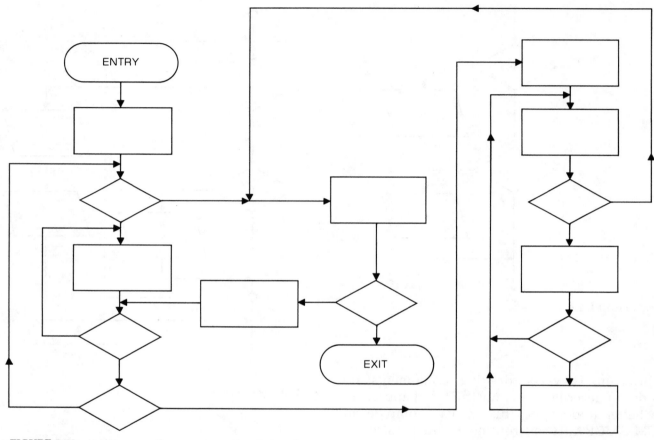

FIGURE 3-10
Unstructured approach.

As an example, suppose an engineering format A from Figure 3-12 is selected for programming. This would require a series of task blocks that display an 8 1/2-by-11-inch drawing sheet with title block and number block. The structured programming would contain three tasks, as shown in Figure 3-13: task 1 is the large rectangular polygon that acts as the sheet border line; task 2 is the frame for the title block; and task 3 is the drawing number block in the upper right-hand corner.

If either the B or the C sheet format were chosen for structuring, a repetitive structure block would be used. In this case the structured approach allows the programmer to think of all the smaller rectangles as a single task. The struc-

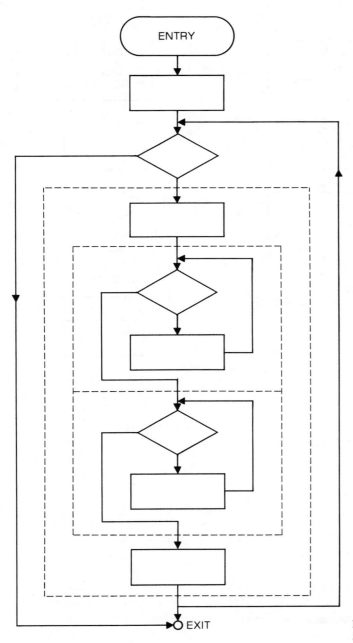

FIGURE 3-11
Structured approach.

TABLE 3-1
Common Drafting Tasks to Be Structured

Task	Structure Block Name
Draw a line	DISPLA
Generate a circle	CIRCLE
Blend geometric shapes together	SMOOT
Create center lines	CNTRL
Create dashed images	DASH
Display dimensions	DIMENS
Divide line images	FACTOR
Generate an ellipse from a circle	DFACT
Use an irregular curve	FIT
Erase images	ERASE
Provide drawing scales	SCALE
Construct polygons	POLY
Provide engineering lettering	LABEL
Build orthographic views	CUPID
Draw hidden lines	DASHL
Display fillets and rounds	FNR
Generate auxiliary views	AUXV
Construct section views	SHADE
Present axonometric objects in pictorial	VANTAG
Present oblique pictorials	VANTAC
Use standard fasteners	FASTNR
Catalog useful parts for working drawings	PARTS

ture block, then, represents the way to program a display of sheet format B or C (Figure 3-14).

At this point the language of the computer program is not important. The coding may be written in BASIC, APL, FORTRAN IV, WATERLOO FORTRAN, FORTRAN 77, or any other language that suits the experience of the particular programmer. The essential point here is that a programmer is also a planner of graphic

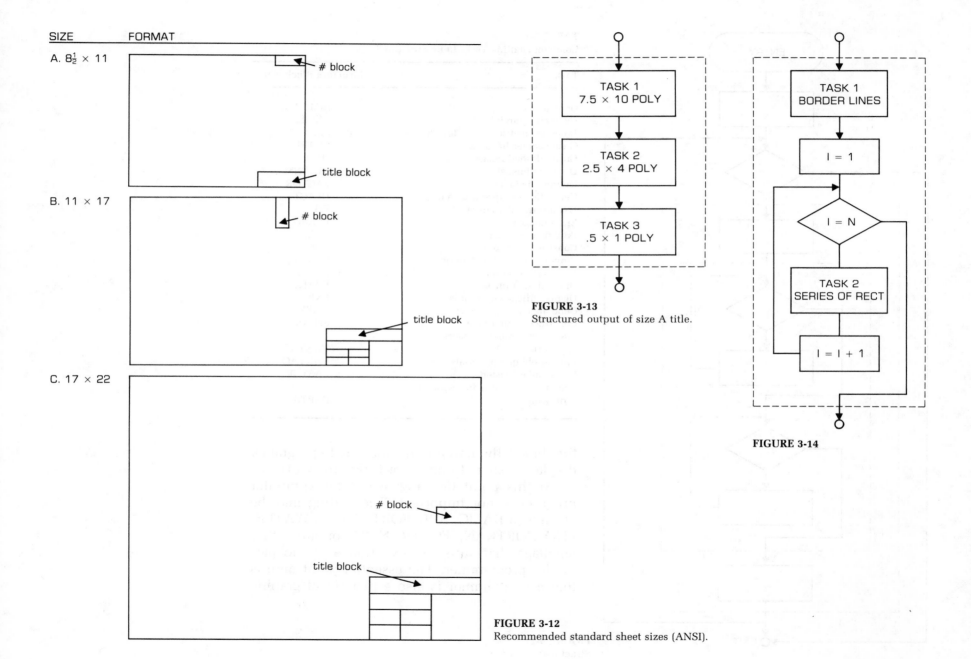

SIZE   FORMAT

A. 8½ × 11   # block   title block

B. 11 × 17   # block   title block

C. 17 × 22   # block   title block

FIGURE 3-12
Recommended standard sheet sizes (ANSI).

TASK 1
7.5 × 10 POLY

TASK 2
2.5 × 4 POLY

TASK 3
.5 × 1 POLY

FIGURE 3-13
Structured output of size A title.

TASK 1
BORDER LINES

I = 1

I = N

TASK 2
SERIES OF RECT

I = I + 1

FIGURE 3-14

shapes that can be used to create an engineering drawing.

Let us now consider the drafting tasks listed in Table 3-1. Symbols are easy to understand at first glance, so structured symbols have been designed for each of the tasks. They may be used in place of the rectangular boxes shown in Figure 3-13, which had to be labeled as to the particular drafting task assigned. Now the planner may use a symbol for easy representation.

Draw a line.   A line symbol is:

It can be used anywhere a single line is displayed in the structured approach.

Generate a circle.   If a circle is to be displayed from the structured block, the symbol used is:

Blend geometric shapes together.   Many times the programmer wishes to generate a smooth curve through several points. If the points exist in the data base, then the planner would use a structure block like:

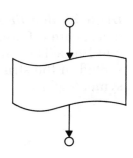

Create center lines.   All circular items displayed from a structured block contain center lines, which locate the center of circles and size or dimension an object. The structure block used is:

Create dashed images. Often it is desirable to represent some graphical images in broken or dashed lines. For this the programmer may use:

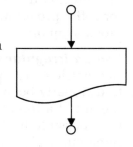

Display dimensions.   In order to place dimensions on an engineering drawing, the programmer uses a combination block that contains the extension lines, arrowheads, dimension lines, and annotation required by this symbol:

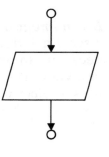

Divide line images.   In some applications, lines are displayed from original data base and then divided. In order to represent this in a structured block, the programmer uses:

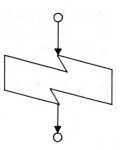

Generate an ellipse from a circle.   Ellipses are displayed by translation of the data base. In other words, if the X data are left alone and the Y data for a circle are reduced, an ellipse with the major diameter parallel to the X direction is displayed. To present this in structured form the programmer uses the block symbol:

Use an irregular curve. Geometric constructions have traditionally been drawn with the aid of a french curve. It is now possible to display the same curves by the use of:

Erase images.   To construct a sectional view, it may be necessary to remove a portion of a view. The programmer uses a selective erase as:

Provide drawing scales. Most engineering drawings are presented at some reduced scale. In order to select a scale, the programmer uses:

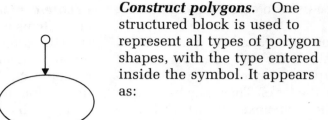

Construct polygons.   One structured block is used to represent all types of polygon shapes, with the type entered inside the symbol. It appears as:

Provide engineering lettering.   No drawing is complete without proper lettering to describe various notes, shapes, dimensions, and descriptions. The programmer may call for lettering by using a special symbol inside a repetition block, as:

Build orthographic views. To represent three-dimensional data base in orthographic views, the programmer uses:

Draw hidden lines.   Dashed objects are different from hidden lines. They are represented in the structured symbology as:

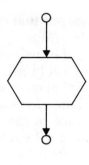

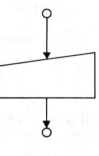

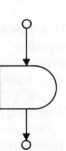

Display fillets and rounds.
To automatically generate rounded corners and filled intersections, the programmer uses:

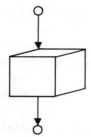

Present oblique pictorials.
In structured planning layouts the subpicture VANTAC is represented by the symbol:

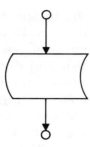

Generate auxiliary views.
Often the six orthographic views known as primary views are not enough to fully describe an object for manufacture. In such cases the programmer can add additional views by using:

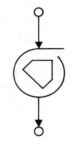

Use standard fasteners.
The use of standard fasteners from a branching subroutine may be shown by:

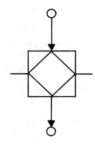

Construct section views.
Sections and conventions can be structured by:

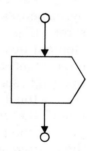

Catalogue useful parts for working drawings. Structured symbols for template parts written to form a stored catalogue look like:

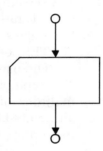

Present axonometric objects in pictorial. In structured planning sequences axonometric views (pictorials) may be presented by the graphics subpicture VANTAG. To write this in symbol form, the planner uses:

COMPUTER-AIDED DESIGN (CAD)

Computer-aided design is a very broad application area used by design engineers from every discipline who want to deal with graphics shapes. Using digital computers without graphic aids has two main limitations:

1. Graphics—especially engineering drawings—is a language all its own. Translating graphics into a computer language before the introduction of structured programming was tedious, error prone, time consuming, and normally more difficult than creating drawings manually.

2. Translating a concept into graphics involves a complex series of intricate steps. The designer must make many individual, and sometimes unrelated, ideas converge into a complete and final design.

Structured programming and modern display hardware have made the design engineer's task somewhat easier by providing the following capabilities:

1. The design engineer deals directly in a visual format rather than in an artificial coding language such as BASIC, APL, FORTRAN IV, WATERLOO FORTRAN, PL1, or FORTRAN 77. The user is a designer, not a programmer. The type of CAD system described in the remainder of this chapter provides a highly automated tool to permit the designer's work to be done faster, more accurately, and more economically.

2. The user of a CAD system proceeds with the design as usual. Now, however, each design step can be evaluated in relation to what has already been drawn. The automated means of producing graphics, called *interactive graphics*, can aid the designer in visualizing design steps.

An interactive graphics system accepts graphic information directly. The engineer enters the information with any of a variety of input devices. In this discussion we will give the engineer a pen and a tablet. The pen is not a light pen and does not touch the CRT surface; it is pressed on the data tablet. Data tablets are available in a number of different sizes depending on the application. In this case a small 11 X 11-inch model will do. When the pen is brought in contact with the surface of the data tablet, it appears to be writing on the face of the CRT. In fact, the pen and tablet are giving instructions to the computer, which in turn is creating a data sequence that causes the tube to respond graphically. In this interaction the programming is *dynamic* because the computer immediately produces a precise picture of what it understood the user to mean.

The user selects from the various options on a menu that displays all of the structured elements described earlier on a grid over the entire CRT screen (Figure 3-15). The designer may select the element desired. When the pen is placed on the data tablet, a small tracking symbol appears on the CRT screen. The designer moves the pen across the tablet to locate the tracking symbol inside the grid display on the CRT screen and presses the pen down on the tablet surface when the desired structured element is located. During the selection process the tracking symbol can move freely back and forth and up and down. Once the pen has been pressed to the data tablet surface, the tracking symbol is frozen in place. When the designer asks for the menu to be displayed again, the tracking symbol from the last time is shown in dotted outline. Once the tracking symbol is moved, the dotted outline is removed from the CRT screen. In this manner the

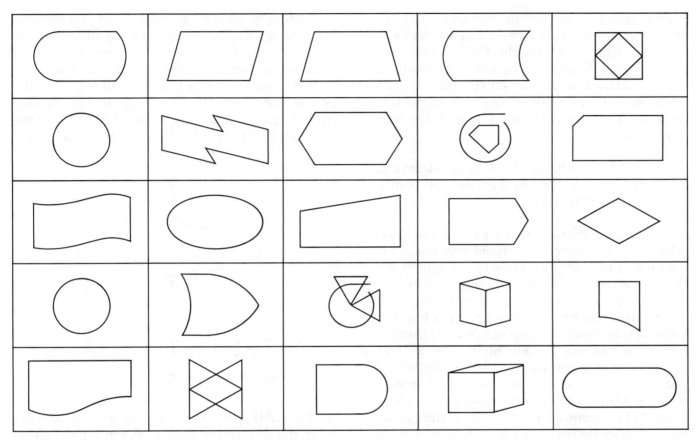

FIGURE 3-15
Menu of structured elements.

designer can keep track of items and the order in which they were used.

To understand how this structured approach is used, let's consider an example. Suppose the designer selects the top left symbol element. When the designer places the pen in the upper left-hand corner of the graphics (data) tablet, the tracking symbol appears in the upper left-hand corner of the CRT screen. When the pen is depressed, the tracking symbol is frozen inside the structure element that is used to draw a line. This action signals the computer to find the procedure called DISPLA, stored in memory. This procedure erases the CRT screen and allows the designer to draw lines on the CRT. When a user draws a line, the system immediately produces a picture of that line on the CRT tube face, showing what the computer did in response to the user's requests from the data tablet. The designer had two requests:

1. Select from a menu the DISPLA structure.
2. Touch the tablet surface for the end points of each line displayed.

The response shown on the face of the CRT is what the computer interpreted the designer to mean; it is not simply a copy of a single input. If the user approves of what the computer presents on the CRT, he continues; if not, any misinterpretation can be immediately corrected. Thus, using this interactive approach, a CAD user has a continual running review of the design and a real-time communication with the digital computer. In this case of engineering lettering for notes real-time interactive display may not be fast enough. For example, the computer must wait for the draftsperson to complete each letter in a character string. In cases such as this, "faster than real-time" is needed to speed up the display time.

When a CAD display programming technique is applied to the structured elements shown on the menu, it uses interactive, real-time computing to either create or revise engineering drawings—the basic starting point for almost all engineering design. In a manual process, the draftsperson uses the T-square and triangle or standard drafting machine to create a horizontal or vertical line. With CAD the user employs the

data tablet to draw such a line. CAD process control tells the digital computer to display only the specified component (straight, vertical, or slant line) no matter how the pen deviates as it is moved across the data tablet. Similarly, a draftsperson can instruct the computer to display curves, circles, and arcs, without tracing the entire path of the specified element, by using this structured element:

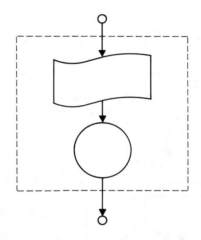

The CAD user can create Figure 3-16 to work with, display, or not display the graphical shape as desired. The CADD user, by contrast, is limited to a tight, structured approach that is coded for later display. The interactive CAD approach, shown in Figure 3-16 is displayed at the time the designer blends the curves to form the final shape (design) of the product. Thus, the CAD user has a choice of two modes (real-time and faster than real-time) in which to operate:

1. Real-time tablet and pen to create design drawings

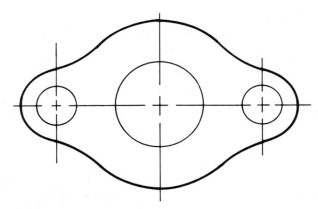

FIGURE 3-16

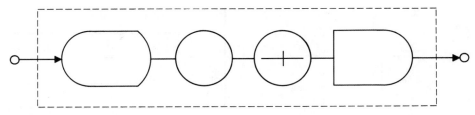

FIGURE 3-17

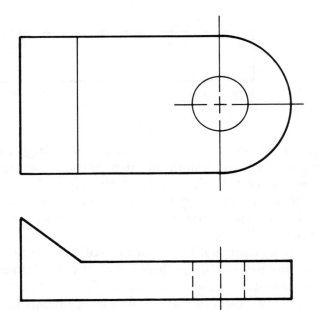

FIGURE 3-18

2. Pen and tablet, like a pointer, to activate controls in the software that define endpoints of lines, centers of circles, and other boundary conditions. The center lines are examples of faster than real time because the CAD user does not want to define each segment in real time. Instead, the image is displayed as a series of line, space, short line, space, line. The entire center line can be handled as one real-time image.

Using the menu for CAD sets these control patterns. The menu consists of all of the structured elements available under CADD, but the CAD method of pointing to a control (structure element) and then interactively building the design image speeds the design drawing to completion. Each of the menu items can be used in this manner, as, for example, Figure 3-17. This will yield the graphic display shown in Figure 3-18. In this example the sequence is: display straight lines, display circle, display center lines, and display hidden lines.

In another case the menu items could be selected as shown in Figure 3-19. This representation will result in the display shown in Figure 3-20. In this example all three views are gener-

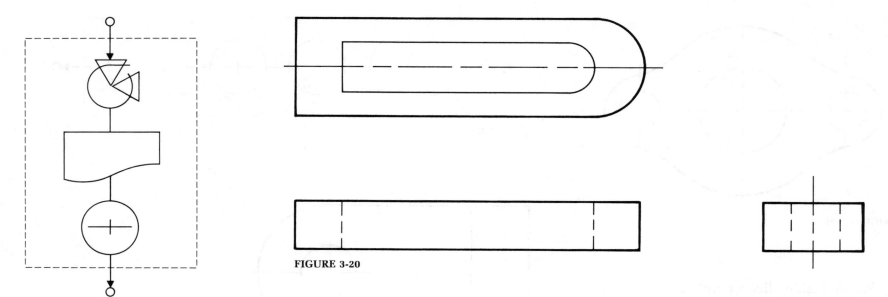

FIGURE 3-19

FIGURE 3-20

ated from three-dimensional data base through an orthogonal view generator. Such automatic three-view generators do not have the capability of placing hidden or center lines. Therefore, the CAD user selects the three-view generator to display object lines.

This displays all the lines as solid; no center lines are present. If the three views supplied from the generator are acceptable, the CAD user may save them, and then edit to remove or change the inside surface representations to dashed lines. The second structure element selected from the menu allows the CAD user to place the hidden lines in the front and side views. The third menu selection will be used to place the center lines.

Proceeding from single views to two-view and three-view displays, and on to dimensioning working views, the following menu selections could display the dimensioned objects shown in

Figure 3-21. The CAD user selects the three-view generator, which displays three views of the object. In this case the top and front views are identical. The CAD user deletes the top view. The side view is symmetrical, so the CAD selects another menu item (the second in the structured program in Figure 3-22) and deletes the left-hand portion of the side view. The same procedure is used to add the hidden lines. Next, the user selects the menu item to display fillets and rounds. The last menu item selected is the automatic dimensioning CAD function, which allows the CAD user to preview the dimensioning of the object being displayed.

Several modifications can be introduced with this same procedure. Suppose the user wished to view the object as a dimensioned pictorial. By selecting the pictorial menu item instead of the three-view generator, the user gets the display

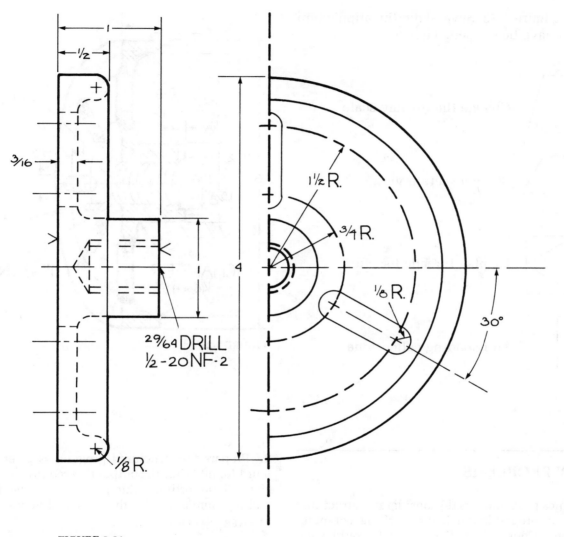

FIGURE 3-21

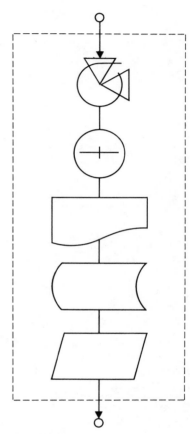

FIGURE 3-22

shown in Figure 3-23. Several modification menu functions have been used. They are:

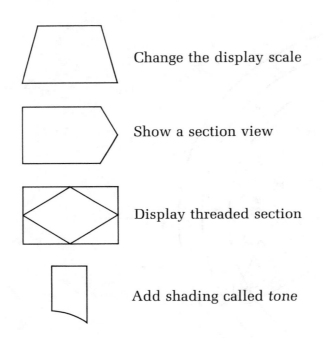

Change the display scale

Show a section view

Display threaded section

Add shading called *tone*

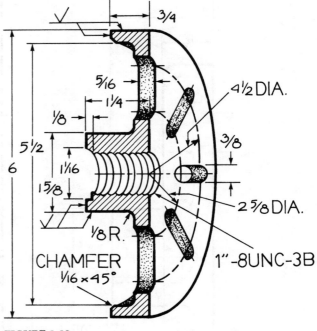

FIGURE 3-23

REVIEW PROBLEMS

1. Graphics programmers do considerable structured planning or programming before writing computer instructions. Construct a diagram that would communicate: (a) prepare proper JCL; (b) output a size B drafting format sheet; and (c) display an orthographic drawing with the data base.

ANSWER   See Figure 3-24.

2. Prepare the structured program as given in problem 1 for (a) a drafting output that requires a size C title sheet; (b) an orthographic projection of the data base; and (c) dimensions for the projected views.

ANSWER   See Figure 3-25.

3. Prepare the same program as outlined in problems 1 and 2 but provide for one or more views to be displayed as an auxiliary view.

ANSWER   See Figure 3-26.

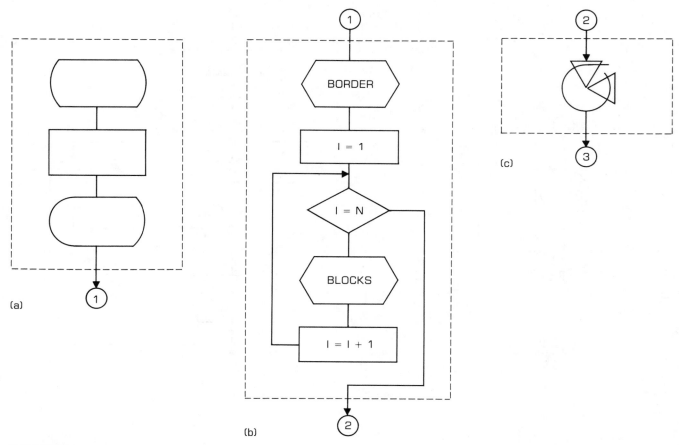

(a)

(b)

(c)

FIGURE 3-24

4. Prepare the same program as outlined in problems 2 and 3, providing for one or more views to be drawn as a section view.

ANSWER See Figure 3-27.

5. Prepare a structured program sequence for the dis-

play of the CAD-generated object shown in Figure 3-28.

6. Prepare a modified program sequence for the graphic image shown in problem 5. Insert the structured block for a right-side view.

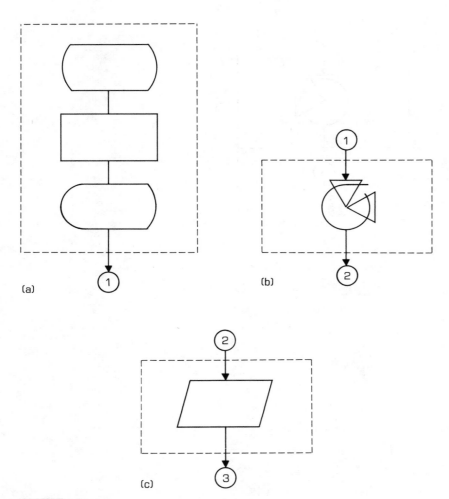

(a)

(b)

(c)

FIGURE 3-25

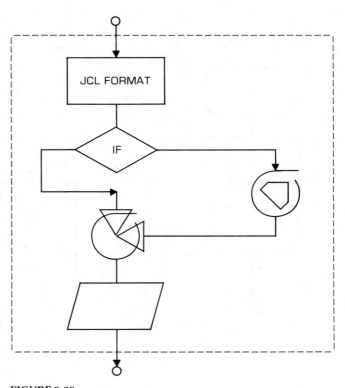

FIGURE 3-26

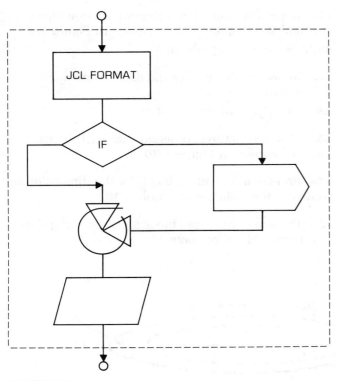

FIGURE 3-27

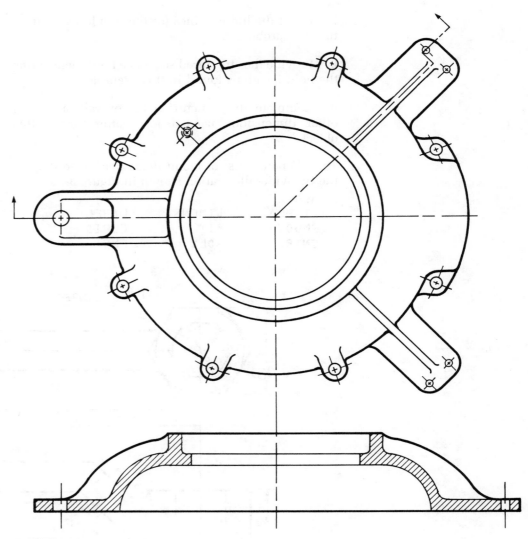

FIGURE 3-28

7. Insert the hidden lines for the profile view structured in problem 6.

8. Provide the structured sequence for dimensioning the hold locations found in this example.

9. Complete the structuring for overall sizes and other dimensions needed for manufacturing this object.

10. Prepare a list of menu items needed to display the two-view illustration shown in Figure 3-29.
ANSWER

DISPLA	DIMENS	LABEL
SMOOT	FIT	CUPID
CNTRL	POLY	FNR

11. Repeat problem 4 and develop section views for A-A and B-B in the example shown in Figure 3-29.
ANSWER Same as problem 4.

12. Repeat problem 5 for the object shown above in the example.
ANSWER See problem 5 response.

13. Plot a structured program that will display the pictorial shown in Figure 3-30.

14. Prepare a structured block for the dimensioning shown in the example of problem 13.

15. Prepare a structured block for the shading shown in the example of problem 13.

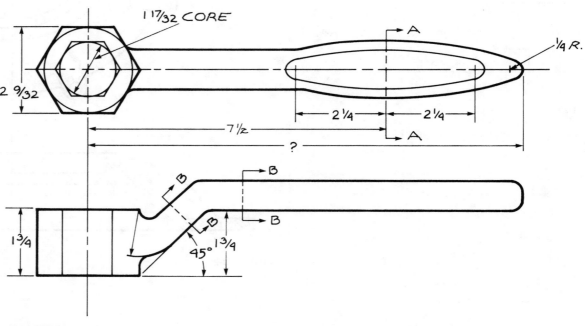

FIGURE 3-29

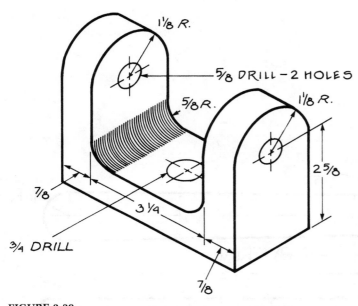

FIGURE 3-30

16. Use the standard fasteners menu item and develop a structured approach for the display shown in Figure 3-31.

17. Insert the american standard unfinished Hexagon Head bolt shown at the top of the example for problem 16 in a working space shown in Figure 3-32.

18. Develop a structured program for the tool design shown in the example in Figure 3-33.

19. Develop a structured program for the cam design shown in Figure 3-34.

20. Develop a structured program for the gear design shown in Figure 3-35.

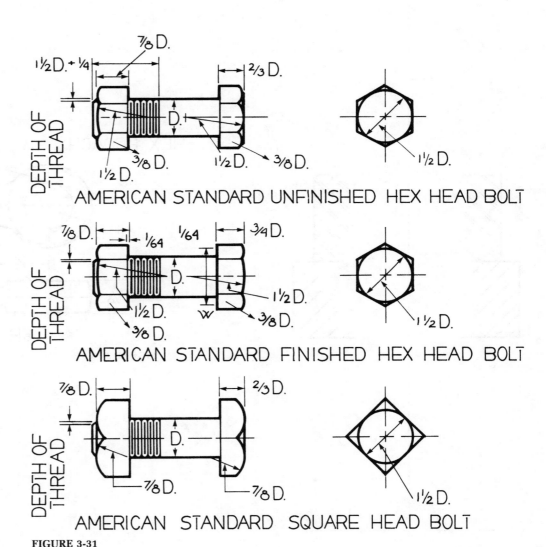

AMERICAN STANDARD UNFINISHED HEX HEAD BOLT

AMERICAN STANDARD FINISHED HEX HEAD BOLT

AMERICAN STANDARD SQUARE HEAD BOLT

FIGURE 3-31

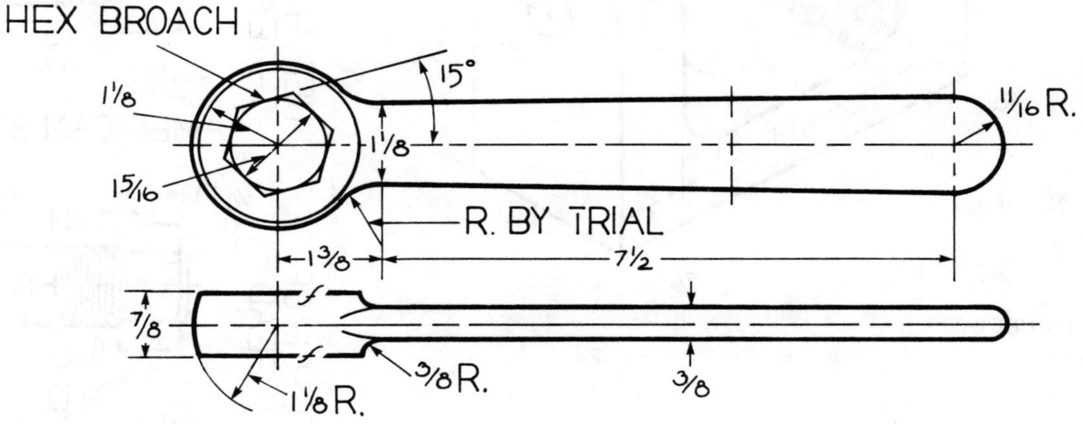

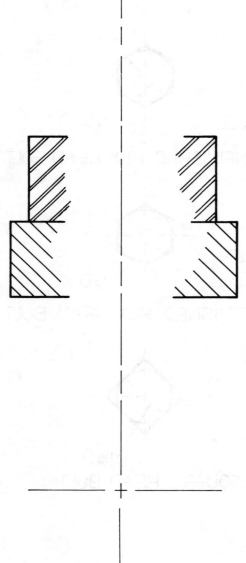

HEX BROACH

15°

$1\frac{1}{8}$

$1\frac{1}{8}$

$\frac{15}{16}$

$\frac{11}{16}$ R.

R. BY TRIAL

$1\frac{3}{8}$

$7\frac{1}{2}$

$\frac{7}{8}$

$\frac{3}{8}$ R.

$1\frac{1}{8}$ R.

$\frac{3}{8}$

FIGURE 3-33

FIGURE 3-32

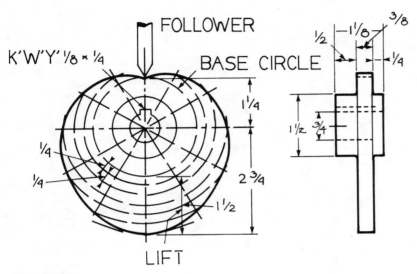

FOLLOWER

BASE CIRCLE

K'W'Y' 1/8 × 1/4

1/4

1/4

1/4

1 1/4

2 3/4

1 1/2

LIFT

1/2 1 1/8 3/8

1/4

1 1/2 3/4

FIGURE 3-34

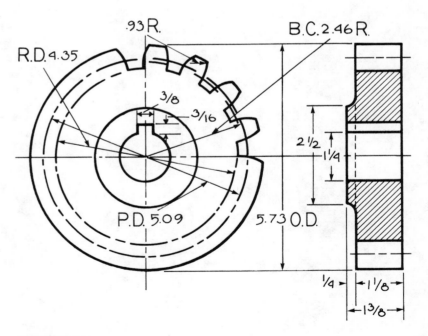

.93 R.

B.C. 2.46 R.

R.D. 4.35

3/8

3/16

2 1/2

1 1/4

P.D. 5.09

5.73 O.D.

1/4

1 1/8

1 3/8

FIGURE 3-35

4

PREPARING ENGINEERING GRAPHICS DISPLAYS

This chapter is a guide for the engineering graphics programmer for writing, compiling, loading, and executing structured graphics programs. It assumes that the user is familiar with the techniques of graphic structures (Chapter 3) but not with their implementation on a digital computer. Users unfamiliar with computer-generated displays for engineering graphics should read one of the commercially available textbooks. The current definitive standard for computer programming for graphical displays is the American National Standards Institute publication X3.9-1977.

USING FORTRAN 77

A number of factors should be taken into account in the use of FORTRAN 77 as a graphics programming language. First of all, a graphics language is used on a number of different computer systems. When the programs are converted from one machine to another, the most important areas are:

1. Language statements
2. Extensions

3. Input/output
4. Functions
5. Subroutines
6. Control flow

A particular graphics program may also have special conversion needs.

Language statements. Make certain that all statements perform the same operation. The major source of incompatibility is graphic device input/output statements (see Chapter 2). For example, FORTRAN IV used in CALCOMP-type programming does not fully describe certain statements, such as ENDFILE or REWIND; their exact performance is computer-dependent, not written program–dependent. FORTRAN 77 supports both the ANSI and IBM formats for direct-access READ and WRITE statements used throughout this book. As we saw in Chapter 1, levels of nesting in DO loops and IF statements will present no problems as there is no syntactical limit, or on the statements that follow IFs and GOTOs.

Extensions. Extensions to FORTRAN 77 used for graphic displays are:

 $INSERT for structured graphics files
 TRACE for debugging graphics blocks
 Direct file access I/O statements (see Chapter 1)
 IMPLICIT specification

Input/output. Graphic programming logical unit numbers must agree with those given in Chapter 3. In that case a job control language was unnecessary if an interactive multiuser mode gave all users direct access to disk files. The peripheral graphic devices described in Chapter 2 were assigned directly to the user.

Functions. Chapter 3 listed a great number of the normal drafting functions. The digital computer chosen to display those functions will contain mathematical functions plus a set of Boolean functions. The new graphics user should be sure all functions in the mainline graphics program are implemented on the computer chosen. These could be:

```
SINE
COSINE
ARCTANGENT
ARCTANGENT OF RATIO
HYPERBOLIC TANGENT
LOG-BASE E
LOG-BASE 2
LOG-BASE 10
EXPONENTIAL
SQUARE ROOT
ABSOLUTE VALUE
REMAINDER
TRUNCATION
POSITIVE DIFFERENCE
MAGNITUDE OF ORDER
```

Subroutines. All computer operating system calls are installation-dependent and should be replaced by structured graphics equivalents. These equivalents were described in Chapter 3 and will appear again later in the book.

Control flow. To ensure a return from the graphics program to the structured level, the last logical statement of a structured program should be:

```
CALL EXIT
```

This is analogus to the CALL PLOT(0.,0.,999) statement that is the last logical statement in a CALCOMP program or CALL FINITT, which is used in Tektronix software.

STRUCTURED PROGRAM OPERATION

Structured programs for graphical displays operate in three environments:

1. Interactive
2. Phantom user
3. Sequential job order

Interactive. The draftsperson starts the structured program operation, as outlined in Chapter 1, on a drafting workstation dedicated to the structured type program. The structured program will accept input from the video display screen keyboard and will print on the screen any output specified by either the structured program or the draftsperson, or computer-generated error messages. The interactive environment is the one most often used for:

Program development and debugging
Structured programs requiring short operation times

Data entry programs, such as graphic tablets, digitizers, and the like
Interactive graphic programs, such as system editors

Phantom user. The phantom user (draftsperson), executing programs while disconnected (logged off) from the workstation, frees the workstation for other users. The number of phantom drafting users on a graphics system is usually fixed. Phantom users accept input from a command file (list of structured steps) instead of from the video display keyboard. Output that would normally be directed back to the video screen is either ignored or directed to a *hold* file space. Drafting users may interrupt a program running as a phantom. Major drafting uses of phantoms are:

Structured files requiring long execution time (maps, large detail drawings)
Certain graphic system utilities (line printer, plotter, CRT, data tablet)
Freeing workstation for CAD or other graphics uses

Sequential job order. The sequential job procedure queues requests (fetch mode) for drafting users and then executes the jobs one at a time. The sequential job environment is especially useful when drafting usage is heavy and interactive design is at a low level.

Structured programming can contain more than a hundred different procedures, some of which use computer subsystems. However, most graphics users can do 90% of their drafting development with about a dozen procedures. This section introduces the minimum number of procedures needed by all graphics users. These procedures allow a graphics user to:

1. Use the graphics system (LOGON or LOGIN)
2. Make changes in the structured program (ATTACH or CHANGE)
3. Create new structured programs for drafting organization (ALLOC, CREATE, or PROC)
4. Save structured sequences against intrusion by others (PASSWD, SAVE, or PROFIL)
5. Remove structured sequences no longer needed (DELETE, PURGE, or SCRATCH)
6. Look at a sequence of structured statements (LIST, PDSLOOK, or LISTN)
7. Check progress of running programs (AVAIL, STATUS, or USERS)
8. Create programs at the workstations or enter them from magnetic storage (CE, FREE, ATTR, or MAGNET)
9. Rename structured programs (CNAME or RENAME)
10. Manipulate structured programs
    Determine file sizes (SIZE)
    Examine file contents (SLIST)
    Print files (SPOOL or PRINT)
11. Allow other draftspersons to use structured sequences (PROTEC or PDSLOOK)
12. Complete a work session (LOGOFF or LOGOUT)

Using a graphics system. In order to use a graphics system, the draftsperson must follow a procedure known as LOGON. Logging on identifies the user (a particular draftsperson) to the graphics system and establishes the initial contact between computer and human. Once logged on, the user has access to the structured library (drafting space), to files, and to other graphics system resources. The format of the LOGON procedure is:

```
LOGON USERID/PASSWORD
```

In other words, the user types on the keyboard LOGON, followed by the draftsperson's user identification and proper password. For example:

```
LOGON DVSTA/SEC1
DVSTA (1346) LOGGED ON AT 18'34 102882
```

The first line is typed by a draftsperson whose user idenification is DVSTA and whose password for the graphics system is SEC1. The second line, sent by the computer to the workstation display screen, indicates that the draftsperson DVSTA has been assigned the job number 1346 and is permitted to use the graphics system. In order to keep track of user time, the time is listed at LOGON 18′34, or 6:34 P.M. The time is expressed in 24-hour format, followed by the data in month-day-year format. When the user logs off the graphics system, a similar message displays the amount of time used.

A procedure like the above is used for logging on a graphics system, regardless of the manufacturer. Any typing errors, incorrect passwords, or incorrect procedures will cause error messages to appear on the workstation display screen. Most of these messages ask the user to try the log-on process again. After three or four times the system responds by logging off and asking the user to check the user's manual.

Making changes. Humans love to change their minds, so there must be a procedure whereby a draftsperson can instruct the graphics system to produce a drawing just like another one . . . with the following changes. Engineering change order (ECOs) are so common in industry that, next to LOGON, this is the most used procedure.

`ATTACH 'ACS.DVSTA.DETAIL(WALLSEC)'`

In this procedure the draftsperson is asking to attach or find a detail drawing filed under the name *wallsec*. It is located in a section of computer storage called ACS and attached to the user's space, called DVSTA because the draftsperson has logged on DVSTA working space. The draftsperson may move to another working space in the graphics system by typing:

`ATTACH NEW-SPACE`

This movement is possible because of the tree structure used in most graphics systems. If any of the working spaces within the tree structure have passwords, then the working space commands must be enclosed in single quotes, as in the example above.

Recovering from errors while attaching is a problem with most graphics systems used today. If an error message is returned following an ATTACH command, it usually indicates that a former working space was not found. Always remember that a drafting user remains attached to the previous working directory until a change has been made. A check of your users manual should clear up any problems with this procedure. (Because a number of graphics systems are available, ATTACH may be CHANGE or CALL in your application.)

Creating new programs. To automate routine drafting tasks, it is often useful to create new structured sequences. These new programs can be created within a user's space (DVSTA) or made available for the entire graphics system by:

`CREATE STRUCTURENAME`

The structurename specifies the system space that will be used to store the program. Because the system files are not available to every user, the user selects a six-letter "structurename" at random. If the user selects a structurename already in use, the graphics system will return the message:

`ALREADY EXISTS`

The user must select a structurename not in use. A shorthand method for this is:

`CE .PLOTZ`

where CE is the shorthand for CREATE and .PLOTZ represents a user program space labeled

PLOTZ. Later we will look at other more expanded uses for new program creation in which the PROC and ALLOC commands can be used to reserve structurenames.

Saving structured programs. Newly created programs can be saved and protected from unauthorized use by other draftspersons or designers by using the SAVE command and assigning a password with the PASSWD command. There are usually two levels of passwords for graphics systems: owner (author) and user (other draftsperson). If a draftsperson or designer assigns the owner password in an ATTACH string, then the author protects the program from others that may change its function. If the author of the program needs help from others, then the SAVE command is used to protect the program from being dropped from the system memory. All users of the system now have access to the program because it does not contain a password. For example:

```
LOGON DVSTA/SEC1
DVSTA (1346) LOGGED ON AT 18'34 102882
ATTACH TITLES
CE .TITLES
INPUT
00010C THIS IS A SAMPLE STRUCTURED PROGRAM
00020 PRINT 'THIS IS A SAMPLE TITLE'
00030 STOP
00040 END
00050
SAVE
END
```

In this example a draftsperson logged on the system with LOGON DVSTA/SEC1. The graphics system responded with DVSTA (1346) LOGGED ON AT 18'34 102882. Next, the draftsperson allocated some file space by ATTACH TITLES. This could have been indicated more directly:

```
ALLOC DA(TITLES) FI(FT10F001) US(AWW)
```

The ALLOC command technique is suited to IBM-type graphics systems, whereas the ATTACH command technique is used by most other manufacturers. To make sure of the allocation technique required for your system, *check your user's manual.*

Once working space has been set aside, a new program can be created. This was done on the example by CE .TITLES. The user entered the command INPUT, and the system responded with 00010, followed by 00020 each time a return was entered from the workstation keyboard. To stop the automatic generation of program line numbers, just enter a return with no message preceding it. In order to protect the program just created, the SAVE command is entered to the system after 00040 END in the example. The last command, END, is used to indicate that the file begun under CE .TITLES is now complete. The draftsperson may now go on to other tasks or leave the workstation by entering:

```
LOGOFF
```

Removing programs from the system. When structured programs are no longer needed, they may be removed from the graphics system to provide room for others. The DELETE command can also delete groups of structured programs called *drawing directories*. A directory contains similar programs that are used to display multiple drawing sheets relating to a single design (object). The format is:

```
DELETE STRUCTURENAME
```

Here the structurename refers to a single program within a directory and not to the name of the directory. When a directory name is used instead of a structurename, the graphics system responds:

```
DIRECTORY NOT EMPTY
```

To protect the contents of a directory, first each structured program must be deleted; then when the directory is empty, its name may be deleted.

Examining programs or directories. Before the deletion of a program it is often necessary to look at its contents. After LOGON and ATTACHing a directory, the user may look at the contents of that directory by:

```
LISTM
```

The graphics system responds by listing the names of the structured programs contained in that directory. If the program name cannot be found in that directory, then the user may look at all the available directory names by:

```
LISTA
```

The command LISTA is to be used to list the names of the ATTACHable directories, whereas LISTM lists the members in that directory (structurenames). For example:

```
LOGON DVSTA/SEC1
```

System responds:

```
LISTA
```

```
ACS       DVSTB     DVSTC     DVSTD     CUPID1
CUPID2    CUPID3    CALCOMP   VERSATEC  TEKPLOT
```

```
LISTM
```

```
JCLPRO    SCALER    INTRO     ARCDEF    TITLE
CRCL1     ARCS      DRAWS     MOVES     LABLS
ERASES    HDCPYS    RESIS     CAPS      TRANS
GRNDS     VLTGS     SWTCHS    PLUSS     MINUSS
RESTOR    POINTG    READIT    STORIT    QUITIT
```

In the first command, LISTA, ten directories in addition to DVSTA were listed. If the member to be deleted is attached to any of these directories, then the user must also be attached to that directory. If the member to be deleted is contained in directory DVSTA, then the LISTM command is used to print the number of members contained. If, for example, the member HDCPYS is to be deleted, it may also be listed so the user can check its contents by:

```
CE HDCPYS
```

```
LIST
```

The graphics system responds by listing the display coding for the member HDCPYS:

```
//HDCPYS  JOB (0915 - 1 - 142 - 00 - JK,:08,4),REGION = 1024K
//TEKKL    PROC  OBJECT = DUMMY,COPT = ,LOPT = ',TEST',PDS =,NAME = ,
//               REL = 10,COMP = FORTVS,SYSOUT = A,ULIB = ,'ACS.PORT801.LOAD',
//               ULIBA = "ACS.PORT801.LOAD'
//C        EXEC  PGM = &COMP,PARM = "DECK,LINECOUNT(60)&COPT'
//STEPLIB  DD    DSN = ACS.VSFORT.R&REL..LOAD,DISP = SHR
//SYSPRINT DD    SYSOUT = &SYSOUT,DCB = BLKSIZE = 120
//SYSTERM  DD    SYSOUT = A
//SYSUT1   DD    UNIT = VIO,SPACE = (CYL,(1,1)),DSN = &&UT1
//SYSUT2   DD    UNIT = VIO,SPACE = (CYL,(1,1)),DSN = &&UT2
//         DD    DSN = ACS.VSFORT.R&REL..LIB,DISP = SHR
//         DD    DSN = ACS.CALCOMP.LOAD,DISP = SHR
//         DD    DSN = ACS.TEK.TCS.UTILITY.LOAD,DISP = (SHR,PASS)
//         DD    DSN = ACS.FORTLIB.LOAD,DISP = SHR
//SYSLMOD  DD    DSN = &PDS. (&NAME),DISP = SHR
//         PEND
```

This listing indicates that the member HDCPYS is the display code for the generation of hard copies from such devices as CALCOMP plotters and direct-view storage tubes. The user, seeing that this code can be used again, decides not to delete it. If the coded listing turned out to be useless, then

```
DELETE HDCPYS
```

would remove the source from the drafting directory DVSTA.

Checking progress of running programs. Once a structured program has been entered, changed, and otherwise modified according to the diagramming shown in Chapter 3, it is ready to "run." Now an old saying comes to mind: "Anyone can write a structured program; the trick is getting it to work." During this period of converting from a diagram to a finished en-

gineering drawing, a number of STATUS checks are made. Table 4-1 represents some, but not all, of the progress checks that can be done on a graphics system.

Using the workstation for processing structured programs. Structured programs or display lists may be created directly from the keyboard or entered from an external source by the use of PROC, CE OBJECTS, FREE, or ATTR graphic systems commands. As shown earlier, some external sources involve input information from a peripheral device, such as those defined in Chapter 2:

ACOUSTIC TABLET
CIRCLE GENERATOR
CONTROL DIAL
JOYSTICKS
DISPLAY CODE GENERATOR
EVENT PRIMITIVE
AIMING SYMBOL

CONTROL BALL
FUNCTION SWITCH
FUNCTION BUTTON
DISPLAY MENU
MOUSE
CRT
CURSOR
KEYBOARD
DIGITIZER
TOUCH TABLET
THUMBWHEEL
CHARACTER GENERATOR
DATA TABLET
LIGHT PEN
DISPLAY BUFFER
DMA
ICON/PFK

The general order of input operations for a peripheral device is:

1. Obtain exclusive use of the device by FREE
2. Transfer data, display codes, and/or structured programs with ALLOC or ASSIGN
3. Relinquish exclusive use of the device by ATTR or UNASSIGN

Assigning an input device gives the draftsperson exclusive control over that device. The typical graphics system command is given from the workstation as:

ASSIGN DEVICE

where *device* is a mnemonic for the appropriate input device. Table 4-2 indicates the choices available to the user. Creating programs at the

TABLE 4-1
Useful Status Commands

Type of Status Check	Use on Graphics System
STATUS userid	Indicates system resources presently being used
STATUS (job number)	Identifies progress of drafting job by number
STATUS device	Tells user if drawing has been output to "device"
AVAIL	Tells whether there is enough room for program execution
STATUS USERS	Runs phantom job to completion
STATUS NET	Runs interactive job to completion

TABLE 4-2
Device Codes Used with ASSIGN Command

Mnemonic	Device Assigned
AS	Aiming symbol for light pen
AT	Acoustic tablet
CB	Control ball
CD	Control dial
CR	Card reader
CRT	Cathode ray tube
CU	Cursor location (thumbwheels)
DB	Display buffer (display code generators; line, and so on)
DT	Data tablet
DZ	Digitizer
EP	Event primitive (display listings from DMA)
FD	Function devices (buttons, switches, touch tablets, mouse)
IC	Programmed function key from keyboard
JS	Joystick
KB	Interactive key strokes
LP	Light pen
MT	Magnetic tape unit
PT	Paper tape unit

workstation or entering them from magnetic storage to generate an engineering display requires all the procedures described so far. Existing structured graphics diagrams can be entered into the digital computer in a variety of ways. For now let us limit the discussion to those type of diagrams that represent drawing output.

Drawings—graphic images—may represent computer input, or source coding. The draftsperson uses a hardware device called a *digitizer* or *scanner* to read the existing drawing and "code" it for storage. Depending on the age of the scanning device, storage may be on punched cards, magnetic tape, or disk. Graphic systems built after 1973 will translate from BCD (binary coded decimal) or EBCDIC (extended binary coded decimal format for IBM) representation into ASCII (American Standard code for non-IBM machines) representation, saving considerable time and effort.

An input device, such as the data tablet, is assigned by the command:

```
ASSIGN DT
```

The draftsperson may then write a short structured program to make use of the data tablet. After the ASSIGN command the draftsperson enters:

```
CE .TABLET
```

This represents a new structurename that will be saved as member TABLET in the directory DVSTA. Next, the draftsperson structures the program to capture the data sent from the data tablet. This is done by:

```
PROC O
CE OBJECT1
00010 ENDD:
SAVE
END
FREE ATTR(AWW)
FREE DA(OBJECT1)
ATTR AWW INPUT
ALLOC DA(OBJECT1)
```

The structured program TABLET can now be saved with the SAVE command. CALL EXIT, as shown earlier in this chapter, will exit the member called TABLET. The user now enters the member by the command:

```
X .TABLET
```

The member TABLET may now be used with any other member of the DVSTA directory. For example:

```
CALL 'ACS.DVSTA.TABLET(DRAW2D)'
```

can be used to input points from the data tablet, and

```
CALL 'ACS.DVSTA.TABLET(SEE2D)'
```

can be used to display the data sent from the tablet on a direct-view storage tube.

Renaming structure programs.   As in the above examples, it is often convenient or necessary to change the name of a member (structurename) or a directory. This is done with a changename command. The format is:

```
CNAME OLDNAME NEWNAME
```

Oldname is the member that exists in the directory, and *newname* is the new member name. If newname already exists in the directory, the graphics system will display the message:

ALREADY EXISTS

An incorrect oldname gives the message:

MEMBER NOT FOUND

Manipulating structured programs. Modern graphics systems are built around high-speed networks of computer equipment, the logical combination of macro-, mini-, and microcomputer components. Each of these components requires careful manipulation of items such as member size (usually stored on magnetic disk), copies of what is stored on disk, and other routine examination techniques. The SIZE command returns the number of records in the member specified by the structurename. The number of records in a member is defined as the total number of data words divided by 448. However, a zero-word-length member contains one record.

The SIZE command is used by entering:

SIZE STRUCTURENAME

The contents of a member that is stored on a graphics network can be checked by:

SLIST STRUCTURENAME

The display list of the member specified by the structurename is then printed at the draftsperson's workstation. To copy members from storage device to storage device inside the network, the command SPOOL is entered as:

SPOOL STRUCTURENAME(FORM)

The form variable is different for each workstation and route desired. *Check your graphics system user's manual.*

Controlling member access. You will remember that assigning passwords to directories allowed draftspersons working in a directory to be classified as owners or nonowners, depending on which password they used with the ATTACH. Controlled access can be established for any structured member using the PROTEC command:

PROTEC STRUCTURENAME (KEY)

The key is set so that:

0 = No access of any kind is allowed
1 = Read only
2 = Write only
3 = Read and write
4 = Delete/truncate
5 = Delete/truncate and read
6 = Delete/truncate and write
7 = All access

Completing a work session. When the draftsperson is finished with a session and wishes to leave the workstation for another user, the following command is given:

LOGOFF

It is good practice to log off after each interactive, phantom, or sequential job order. This action closes your directory and releases the graphics system to another user.

PROVIDING DISPLAY LISTS FOR STRUCTURED PROGRAMS

Now that we have a foundation in the working of structured programs, we can compare the structured diagram shown in Chapter 3 with the display list.

Display lists for JCL. The first comparison is the structured diagram for job control language (JCL) shown in Figure 4-1 and the display list below. Remember that the diagram is the program, or plan for execution, of a graphic idea or image. The display list is the result of that plan. Either an interactive or a phantom construction is used to implement the plan. In the interactive construction the draftsperson selects the structured blocks from a menu display by touching the light pen or other pointing device to the blocks required to assemble the JCL block and answering the interactive questions, such as:

INSERT STRUCTURE NAME

In this example the response is:

LICHEN1

The display list is stored for later use by the display generator.

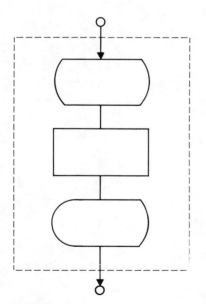

FIGURE 4-1

```
//LICHEN1 JOB (0923-2-001-00-  ,#02,1),'LIHWA BOX 22',
//     TIME=(0000,02), REGION=256K
***JOBPARM Q=T
***JOBPARM I
***ROUTE PRINT TEXT
***JOBPARM EXCP=99999999
//STEP1 EXEC FTG1CLG,PLOT=0812
XXFTG1CLG PROC   OBJECT=DUMMY,PUNCH='SYSOUT=X',COPT=,LOPT=,
XX    ULIB='ACS.PORT801.LOAD',SYSOUT=A,PLOT=0812,PLOTTER=CALCOMP
XXC        EXEC   PGM=IGIFORT,PARM='DECK,LINECNT=60&COPT'
XXSTEPLIB   DD   DSN=ACS.FORTG1.LOAD,DISP=SHR
XXSYSPRINT DD   SYSOUT=&SYSOUT,DCB=BLKSIZE=120
```

```
XXSYSUT1    DD    UNIT=VIO,SPACE=(CYL,(1,1)),DSN=&&UT1
XXSYSUT2    DD    UNIT=VIO,SPACE=(CYL,(1,1)),DSN=&&UT2
XXSYSLIN    DD    UNIT=SYSDA,SPACE=(CYL,(1,2)),DSN=&&OBJ,DISP=(MOD,PASS),
XX                DCB=(LRECL=80,RECFM=FBS,BLKSIZE=400)
XXSYSPUNCH DD     &OBJECT,DCB=BLKSIZE=80
//C.SYSIN DD *
XXL         EXEC  PGM=IEWL,COND=(5,LT,C),PARM='LIST,MAP&LOPT'
XXSYSLIB    DD    DSN=ACS.MOD2.FORTLIB,DISP=(SHR,PASS)
XX          DD    DSN=ACS.&PLOTTER..LOAD,DISP=SHR
XX          DD    DSN=ACS.CALCOMP2.LOAD,DISP=SHR
XX          DD    DSN=&ULIB,DISP=SHR
XX          DD    DSN=ACS.FORTLIB.LOAD,DISP=(SHR,PASS)
XXSYSPRINT DD     SYSOUT=&SYSOUT
XXSYSUT1    DD    UNIT=VIO,SPACE=(CYL,(1,1)),DSN=&&UT1
XXSYSLIN    DD    DSN=&&OBJ,DISP=(MOD,DELETE),UNIT=SYSDA
XX          DD    DDNAME=SYSIN
XXSYSLMOD   DD    DSN=&&PDS(MAIN),DISP=(,PASS),UNIT=SYSDA
XX                SPACE=(CYL,(1,1,1),RLSE),DCB=(RECFM=U,BLKSIZE=13030)
XXG         EXEC  PGM=MAIN,COND=((5,LT,C),(5,LT,L)),TIME=1400
XXSTEPLIB DD DSN=&&PDS,DISP=(OLD,DELETE)
XXFT01F001 DD     DDNAME=SYSIN
XXFT02F001 DD     &PUNCH,DCB=BLKSIZE=80
XXFT03F001 DD     SYSOUT=&SYSOUT,DCB=(LRECL=133,RECFM=FA,BLKSIZE=133)
XXFT06F001 DD     SYSOUT=&SYSOUT,DCB=(LRECL=133,RECFM=FA,BLKSIZE=133)
XXPLOTTAPE DD     SYSOUT=(Y,,&PLOT)
XXPLOTLOG  DD     SYSOUT=&SYSOUT
XXVECTR1    DD    DSN=&&VECTR1,UNIT=VIO,SPACE=(TRK,(1,1)),DISP=(,PASS)
XXVECTR2    DD    DSN=&&VECTR2,UNIT=VIO,SPACE=(CYL.(1,1)),DISP=(,PASS)
//G.SYSIN DD
//
```

For phantom implementation the process is similar. Instructions for preparing the display list are entered from the keyboard as:

```
//LICHEN1 JOB (0923-2-001-00-JK,:02,1)
//STEP1 EXEC FTG1CLG,PLOT = 1812
//C.SYSIN DD *
/*
//
```

The keyed (typed) instructions describe the structured diagram in words instead of graphic symbols, as was the case for interactive use. The important thing to remember is that, once a JCL structured program has been stored as a display list, it does not have to be repeated; the display list will remain until it is deleted by the draftsperson. Recall in our earlier examples of members stored under the directory DVSTA, a member JCLPRO. This member is the JCL key that unlocks the graphics system so the display generator can be used. This procedure is so common in computer programming for graphic output, it is called *turning the key*, and the start-up of a graphics system is called *turnkey*. Turnkey systems are those systems that have internal JCL. Stand-alone, turnkey systems are those that are smaller desk-top units for single users, usually design engineers.

Display lists for title blocks.   We can understand display lists further by studying the structured examples outlined in Figure 3-12 (Chapter 3), where drawing sheet sizes A, B, and C, were diagrammed. The diagram is shown in Figure 4-2 and the desired display list on page 69. This display list is saved as member TITLES. If TITLES is a new member, it is good to send it to the display generator for viewing to make sure the display list is correct. If TITLES is an old member, it will be used as a sequential job order member each time an engineering drawing is produced from the display generator. This is entered by the draftsperson at the workstation. The procedure is:

```
LOGON DVSTA/SEC1
ATTACH 'ACS.DVSTA.JCLPRO(TITLES)'
CE .DRAW1
INPUT
00010 CALL BEGIN
00020 CALL TITLE(.5)
00030 CALL DISPLA(18.,0.,999)
00040 STOP
00050 END
00060
SAVE
```

In this session the draftsperson has implemented the structured plan for a size A title block with the statement CALL TITLE(.5). If a size B title were required, then CALL TITLE (1.) would be used; if a size C, CALL TITLE (2.). The display list for TITLE has been stored in the graphics system so that a display generator can produce the graphic image for the user.

Display lists for common drafting tasks.   As you might expect, there are display lists for each

```
SUBROUTINE TITLE(SIZE)
CALL FACTOR(SIZE)
CALL RECT(0.,0.,11.25,17.,0.0,3)
CALL RECT(0.,0.,.750,1.,0.0,3)
CALL RECT(1.,0.,.750,3.5,0.0,3)
CALL RECT(4.5,0.,.375,2.5,0.0,3)
CALL RECT(4.5,.375,.375,2.5,0.0,3)
CALL RECT(7.0,0.,.375,3.5,0.0,3)
CALL RECT(7.0,.375,.375,3.5,0.0,3)
CALL RECT(10.5,.0.,.750,5.25,0.0,3)
CALL RECT(15.75,0.,.750,1.25,0.0,3)
CALL SYMBOL(.1,.1,.08,12HDRAWING  NO.,0.,12)
CALL SYMBOL(.375,.25,.25,1H1,0,1)
CALL SYMBOL(1.875,.5,.09,21HENGINEERING  GRAPHICS,0.,21)
CALL SYMBOL(1.625,.3125,.1,24HCOLLEGE  OF  ENGINEERING,0.,24)
CALL SYMBOL(4.625,.12,.1,6HSCALE:,0.,6)
CALL SYMBOL(4.625,.45,.1,5HDATE:,0.,5)
CALL SYMBOL(5.25,.45,.1,6H9-6-82,0.,6)
CALL SYMBOL(5.50,.12,.1,4HFULL,0.,4)
CALL SYMBOL(7.125,.12,.1,7HCOURSE:,0.,7)
CALL SYMBOL(8.,.12,.1,6HEG 310,0.,6)
CALL SYMBOL(7.125,.45,.1,7HDR  BY:,0.,7)
CALL SYMBOL(11.75,.1,.1,18HTITLE  OF  DRAWING,0.,18)
CALL SYMBOL(12.5,.32,0.25,11HTITLE BLOCK,0.,11)
CALL SYMBOL(16.125,.1,.1,5HGRADE,0.,5)
RETURN
END
```

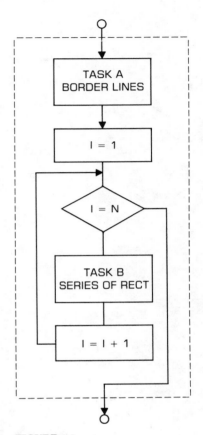

FIGURE 4-2

of the common drafting tasks. Table 4-3 indicates the display lists available and the way to call them from the workstation.

In implementation of each of the display lists, the CALL structurename followed by the proper variables must be entered to the graphics system by interactive, phantom, or sequential job order. Today's modern engineering graphics systems provide the display lists; they are not written by each user. Therefore, it is important to become familiar with the particular graphics system you will be using. Check the structurenames of all the

TABLE 4-3
Display Lists for Common Drafting Tasks

Drafting Task	Structurename	Usage
Draw a line	DISPLA	CALL DISPLA(X,Y,IPEN)
Generate a circle	CIRCLE	CALL CIRCLE(X,Y,R,SANG,N,THETA)
Blend geometric shapes	SMOOT	CALL SMOOT(X,Y,IPEN)
Create center lines	CNTRL	CALL CNTRL(X,Y)
Create dashed lines	DASH	CALL DASH(X,Y,TL,DL,THETA)
Display dimensions	DIMENS	CALL DIMENS(X,Y,HT1HT2,XLINE,THETA)
Divide line images	FACTOR	CALL FACTOR(SIZE)
Generate ellipse from CIRCLE	DFACT	CALL DFACT(XSIZE,YSIZE)
Use an irregular curve	FIT	CALL FIT(X1,Y1,X2,Y2,X3,Y3)
Erase images	ERASE	CALL ERASE
Provide drawing scales	SCALE	CALL SCALE(AR,AXL,NPT,INC)
Construct polygons	POLY	CALL POLY(X,Y,SLEN,SN,THETA)
Provide engineering lettering	SYMBOL	CALL SYMBOL(X,Y,CHT,'IBC',NCRS,THETA)
Build orthographic views	CUPID	CALL CUPID(X,Y,Z,IPEN,XTRANS,YTRANS,NDAT,ANG,SF)
Draw hidden lines	DASHL	CALL DASHL(XARRAY,YARRAY,NPTS,INC)
Display fillets and rounds	FNR	CALL FNR(X,Y,THO,PHI,R1,R2,ICODE)
Generate auxiliary views	AUXV	CALL AUXV(XDATA,YDATA,ZDATA)
Construct section views	SHADE	CALL SHADE(X,Y,Z,TLEN,THT,S)
Present axonometric objects	VANTAG	CALL VANTAG(XARRAY,YARRAY,ZARRAY)
Present oblique pictorials	VANTAC	CALL VANTAC(XARRAY,YARRAY,ZARRAY)
Use standard fasteners	FASTNR	CALL FASTNR(XPAGE,YPAGE,TYPE,THETA)
Catalog useful parts for drawings	PARTS	CALL PARTS(XPAGE,YPAGE,TYPE,SUBPIX)

display lists available for use. If a display list does not exist, then the draftsperson writes a structured diagram and implements that diagram to produce the desired display list.

The remainder of this chapter concentrates on those display lists that are formed by the draftsperson at the workstation. Readers who wish additional information on system-supplied display lists should refer to Chapter 6 and 7.

LOADING AND EXECUTING STRUCTURED PROGRAMS

In this part of the chapter we will look at display lists and the display information sent from the display generator. Consider the following example:

```
DIMENSION X(100),IPEN(100)
DATA X/2.2*7.,2*3.,2*2.,2*5.,2*6.5,2.,2*5.,2*6.5,2*7.,3*2.,3.,2.,
+3*3.,10.,2*13.5,12.5,11.,3*10.,13.5/
DATA Y/2*2.,2*3.,2*5.,2*2.,3.,2.,3.,2*6.5,2*7.5,2*6.5,2*10.,6.5,
+2*9.,2*7.5,10.,6.5,2*2.,4*5.,2.,2*3./
DATA IPEN/3,6*2,3,2,3,2,3,8*2,3,2,3,2,3,2,3,3*2,3,2*2,3,2/
CALL PLOTS
CALL TITLE(.5)
CALL DRAW2D(X,Y,IPEN,35)
CALL CIRCL(11.,5.,180.,360.,0.75,0.75,0.)
CALL PLOT(18.,0.,999)
STOP
END
```

The DIMENSION statement requests a pre-stored location in computer memory. It indicates there are 100 possible data locations available for the subprogram DRAW2D. (See Chapter 1 for more information on DIMENSION statements.) Next, the data are entered by the use of the DATA statement. And finally, a series of system-supplied and system-dependent CALLS to such items as PLOTS, CIRCL, and PLOT are given. PLOTS is commonly used if a CALCOMP plotter will generate the visual display; other calls are also common, depending on the hardware used.

The calls to CIRCL and PLOT are both contained in the CALCOMP versions, but DRAW2D is not. The draftsperson must supply the display listing for DRAW2D as:

```
      SUBROUTINE DRAW2D(X,Y,IPEN,NDATA)
      DIMENSION X(100),Y(100),IPEN(100)
      DO 100 I=1,NDATA
100   CALL PLOT(X(I),Y(I),IPEN(I))
      READ(1,4)NDASHP
4     FORMAT(I2)
      DO 5 J=1,NDASHP
      READ(1,*)X1,Y1,Z,W
      CALL PLOT(X1,Y1,3)
5     CALL DASHP(Z,W,.15)
      RETURN
      END
```

In this example 250 is too large for the use of a DATA statement, and a data error is probable at this point. The data are therefore entered and stored as a separate member under the directory DVSTA in the graphics system. This member will be ATTACHed after the //G.SYSIN DD * JCL statement in the member JCLPRO. This allows a READ statement in the program. Either input method (DATA or READ) may be used for the data. If the data base is small, it is more convenient to enter it as a DATA statement. DRAW2D is used to connect straight-line segments only. In this type of example circles and arcs required in the 2-D image display are usually entered directly in the program and are not part of the 2-D line generator.

The display lists are structured in the following manner:

```
LOGON DVSTA/SEC1
ATTACH 'ACS.DVSTA.JCLPRO(DRAW2D)
CE .PLOT1
INPUT
```

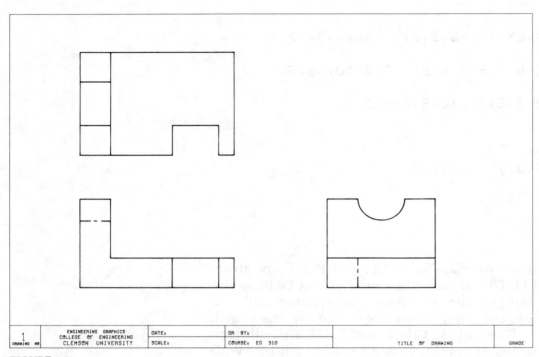

ENGINEERING GRAPHICS
COLLEGE OF ENGINEERING
CLEMSON UNIVERSITY

DATE:
SCALE:

DR BY:
COURSE: EG 310

TITLE OF DRAWING   GRADE

1
DRAWING NO

FIGURE 4-3

This listing is useful for plotting any 2-D data, such as a map or template figure. The graphics user must remember to set aside the proper amount of storage by using a dimension statement before the CALL DRAW2D. For example, if you had 250 X and Y data points (called X(I) and Y(I)), which were used to describe the graphic image, then a minimum of 250 storage locations should be provided in both the subroutine and program listing. The statement would read:

```
DIMENSION X(250),Y(250),IPEN(250)
```

The example program is then entered. There is no need to enter the DRAW2D subroutine because it already exists and has been ATTACHed from the workstation. The session is saved with the SAVE command and sent to the display generator with the result shown in Figure 4-3.

The example in Figure 4-3 is typical of most 2-D template-type image displays used for single-view drawing representations. It is not as effective for multiview applications; three-dimensional data are needed to display automatic three-view-type representations.

The existing member (PLOT1) is modified from the workstation. The DRAW2D statement is replaced with the CUPID statement. As we saw earlier, CUPID displays three-dimensional data as an engineering drawing with an optional pictorial view. In order to model or display another object, the DATA statements are changed, as:

```
DIMENSION X(100),Y(100),Z(100),IPEN(100)
DATA X/0.,3*0.5,3*1.5,2*3.5,3*2.,6*0.,2*3.5,4*2.,4*3.5,4*0.5,1.5/
DATA Y/2*0.,4*1.5,2*0.,2*0.5,4*1.5,2*0.,1.5,2*0.,2*0.5,1.5,4*0.5,
+4*0.,1.5,2*0./
DATA Z/3*-1.5,2*-0.5,6*-1.5,2*-0.,2*-1.5,7*-0.,
+-1.5,-0.,-1.5,-0.,-1.5,-0.,-1.5,4*-0.5/
DATA IPEN/3,16*2,3,4*2,3,2,3,2,3,2,3,2*2,3,2/
CALL PLOTS
CALL TITLE(.5)
CALL PLOT (3.5,2.5,-3)
CALL CUPID(X,Y,Z,IPEN,8.5,6.5,33,30.,1.)
CALL PLOT(18.0,0.0,999)
STOP
END
```

The display list CUPID is then checked by listing on the workstation monitor by:

```
CE CUPID
LIST
```

It appears as:

```
0001        SUBROUTINE CUPID(X,Y,Z,IPEN,XTRANS,YTRANS,NDAT,ANG,SF)
0002        DIMENSION X(100),Y(100),Z(100),IPEN(100),XPLOT(100),YPLOT(100)
0003        COSA=COS(ANG/57.3)
0004        SINA=SIN(ANG/57.3)
0005        DO 1 K=1,NDAT
```

```
0006              XPLOT(K)=(X(K)+Z(K)*SF*COSA)+8.2
0007              YPLOT(K)=(Y(K)+Z(K)*SF*SINA)+5.2
0008        1     CALL PLOT(XPLOT(K),YPLOT(K),IPEN(K))
0009              DO 10 J=1,NDAT
0010       10     CALL PLOT(X(J),Y(J),IPEN(J))
0011              DO 20 I=1,NDAT
0012              Z(I)=Z(I)+YTRANS
0013       20     CALL PLOT(X(I),Z(I),IPEN(I))
0014              DO 30 I=1,NDAT
0015              Z(I)=(Z(I)+XTRANS)-YTRANS
0016       30     CALL PLOT(Z(I),Y(I),IPEN(I))
0017              RETURN
0018              END
```

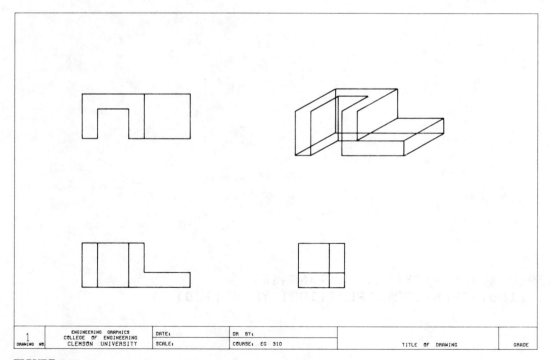

FIGURE 4-4

This listing of the member CUPID is complete and will display three-dimensional, X(I),Y(I), and Z(I) data. In addition, the pen positions (IPEN) up or down (3 or 2) must be provided. XTRANS is the distance the draftsperson wishes to display between the front and profile views. YTRANS is the physical distance between the front and horizontal views. NDAT is the number of data points required to display the object. If a pictorial is desired, the user enters a value for ANG, the angle for the display of the pictorial. SF is the scale factor used to display the pictorial. Thus, it is possible to display the working drawing at full size and reduce the pictorial of the object by any desired amount, as shown in the example display in Figure 4-4.

Modification of Display Lists

The modification of display lists depends in part on how the display list is scheduled. The SCHEDULE command is entered from the workstation each time the display list is modified in order to preview the current display image. The SCHEDULE command is given only after assignment of one of the output devices defined in Chapter 2:

ADDRESS REGISTER
BLINK
CALLIGRAPHIC DISPLAY
CRT
COM
CELL ORGANIZED RASTER DISPLAY
DARK TRACE TUBE
DIGITAL PLOTTER
DIRECT-VIEW STORAGE TUBE
DISPLAY PANEL (plasma)
DISPLAY PROCESSOR
HARD-COPY UNIT
LINE GENERATOR
OUTPUT PRIMITIVE
VIEWPORT/WINDOW

The general order of output operations is similar to that listed for input devices: the user must obtain the use of the device by FREE; the display list is sent to the display processor, which produces the correct code for the output device assigned; and, finally, the user returns the output device by the ATTR or UNASSIGN commands. An experienced user selects the output device best suited to the design situation.

Figure 4-5 is an output of the following display list.

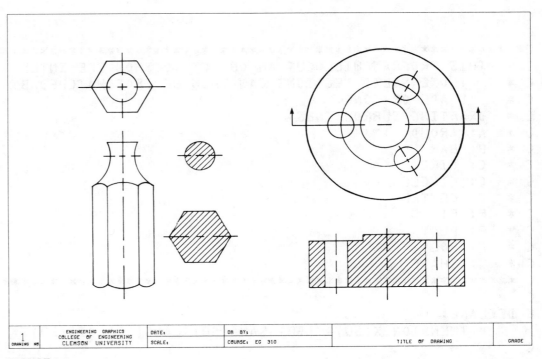

FIGURE 4-5

```
C
C
C*******************************************************************
C *    THIS PROGRAM WILL CUT AN OBJECT TO SHOW THE INTERNAL MATERIAL    *
C *       THOSE SOLID SECTIONS CAN THEN BE CROSSHATCHED BY CALLING       *
C *       SHADE OR TONE.                                                 *
C *    DRAFTING SUBROUTINES:                                            *
C *    A: AROHD                                                         *
C *    B: BAR                                                           *
C *    C: CIRCL                                                         *
C *    C: CIRCLE                                                        *
C *    C: CENTER                                                        *
C *    F: FIT                                                           *
C *    P: PLOT                                                          *
C *    P: POLY                                                          *
C *    S: SHADE                                                         *
C *******************************************************************
C
C DECLARE:
      DIMENSION X(50),Y(50),SANG(50),EANG(50),DIA(50)
C
C INPUT/OUTPUT:
      DATA X/1.5,12.,11.,10.25,8.45,2*10.69,2*2.,2*0.5,2*1.5/
      DATA Y/6.853.4*5.5,4.25,6.812,3.5,0.16,3.5,0.16,3.5,0.16/
      DATA SANG/7*0.,45.,-45.,45.,-45.,60.,-60./
      DATA EANG/7*360.,140.,-140.,140.,-140.,120.,-120./
      DATA DIA/1.,.5,.3,.1.5,3*0.90,4*0.7,2*2./
C
C DECLARE:
      DIMENSION X1(50),Y1(50),IPEN(50)
C
C INPUT/OUTPUT:
      DATA X1/0.5,1.5,2*0.,2*2.,2*0.5,2*1.5,7.,2*12.,2*10.25,2*8.75,
     +2*7.,2*8.25,2*10.75/
      DATA Y1/2*5.,3.5,0.16,3.5,0.16,3.5,0.16,3.5,0.16,2*0.,2*1.55,
     +2*1.75,2*1.55,0.,1.55,0.,1.55,0./
      DATA IPEN/3,2,3,2,3,2,3,2,3,2,3,8*2,3,2,3.2/
```

```
C
C DECLARE:
      DIMENSION XARAY(50),YARAY(50),XXARAY(50),YYARAY(50)
C
C INPUT/OUTPUT:
      DATA XARAY/2.5,3.,4.,0.,1./
      DATA YARAY/1.75,2*2.618,0.,1./
      DATA XXARAY/3.,4.,4.5,0.,1./
      DATA YYARAY/2*0.875,1.75,0.,1./
C
C DECLARE:
      DIMENSION ARAY1(50),ARAY2(50),ARAY3(50),ARAY4(50)
      DIMENSION XLOC(50),YLOC(50),XEND(50),YEND(50)
C
C INPUT/OUTPUT:
      DATA XLOC/12.5,2*10.56,11.125,9.5,7.879,4.7,4.2,1.,2.4,1.,1.6/
      DATA YLOC/5.5,3.75,7.31,1.75,1.95,2*1.75,4.5,8.,6.853,5.4,4.5/
      DATA XEND/6.5,2*9.935,11.125,9.5,7.875,2.3,2.8,1.,-0.4,1.,0.4/
      DATA YEND/5.5,4.69,6.3,3*-0.2,1.75,4.5,5.7,6.853,-0.4,4.5/
C
C DECLARE:
      DIMENSION ARAYX(50),ARAYY(50),ARAYXX(50),ARAYYY(50)
C
C INPUT/OUTPUT:
      DATA ARAYX/8.25,2*8.75,2*10.25,10.75,0.,1./
      DATA ARAYY/2*1.55,2*1.75,2*1.55,0.,1./
      DATA ARAYXX/8.25,10.75,0.,1./
      DATA ARAYYY/2*0.,0.,1./
C
C CONTROL:
      CALL PLOTS
      CALL TITLE(.5)
      CALL PLOT(2.5,2.,-3)
      CALL FIT(0.5,5.,0.5,4.,0.,3.5)
      CALL FIT(1.5,5.,1.5,4.,2.,3.5)
C
C DO LOOP STATEMENT:
```

```
      DO 10 I=1,13
C    CONTROL:
      CALL CIRCL(X(I),Y(I),SANG(I),EANG(I),DIA(I)/2.,DIA(I)/2.,0.0)
C CONTROL:
 10    CONTINUE
C
C CONTROL:
      CALL CIRCLE(3.5,4.5,0.5,0.,30,12.,ARAY1,ARAY2,ARAY3,ARAY4)
      CALL AROHD(6.5,5.5,6.5,6.,0.3,0.1,16)
      CALL AROHD(12.5,5.5,12.5,6.,0.3,0.1,16)
      CALL POLY(0.5,6.,1.,6.,0.0)
      CALL POLY(3.0,0.875,1.,6.,0.0)
C
C DO LOOP STATEMENTS:
      DO 20 I=1,23
C    CONTROL:
 20    CALL PLOT(X1(I),Y1(I),IPEN(I))
C
C DO LOOP STATEMENTS:
      DO 97 I=1,12
C
C CONTROL:
 97    CALL CENTER(XLOC(I),YLOC(I),XEND(I),YEND(I))
      CALL BAR(7.,0.,0.,1.55,0.5,1.55,2,16)
      CALL BAR(11.5,0.,0.,1.55,0.5,1.55,2,16)
      CALL SHADE(XARAY,YARAY,XXARAY,YYARAY,0.07,73.,3,1,3,1)
      CALL SHADE(ARAYX,ARAYY,ARAYXX,ARAYYY,0.07,73.,6,1,2,1)
      CALL SHADE(ARAY1,ARAY2,ARAY3,ARAY4,0.07,73.,15,1,15,1)
      CALL PLOT(18.,0.,999)
C
C CONTROL
      STOP
C
      END
```

The previous display list is complete. Notice that the program is divided into DECLARATION, INPUT/OUTPUT, CONTROL, and ARITHMETIC, as recommended in Chapter 1. The display program indicates the system-level and system-dependent drafting subroutines in a printed message. Program documentation of this type is recommended before permanent storage. The organization of this display list is ideal; you can use it to study how the structured diagram was put together by the draftsperson. Use the following display list and Figure 4-6 to trace the order in which that display was processed by the display generator.

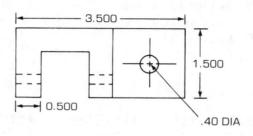

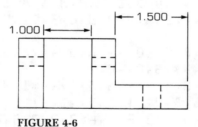

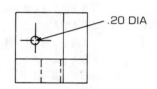

FIGURE 4-6

```
       CALL PLOTS
       CALL PLOT(.75,.75,-3)
C      ***** ADD PART FEATURES *****
       CALL ZHOLE(9.55,6.2,.2)
       CALL YHOLE(9.55,5.55,.2,.3)
       CALL YHOLE(6.1,5.55,.2,.25)
       CALL XHOLE(5.45,6.0,.2,.3)
       CALL XHOLE(4.35,6.0,.2,.3)
       CALL XHOLE(5.45,9.6,.2,.3)
       CALL XHOLE(4.35,9.6,.2,.3)
       CALL ZHOLE(6.3,10.,.2)
       CALL DIMEN(4.35,5.3,4.3,0.,.6)
       CALL DIMEN(9.15,5.3,1.8,0.,.6)
       CALL DIMEN(4.35,8.95,.5,0.,.6)
       CALL DIMEN(4.65,9.25,1.3,0.,.6)
       CALL DIMEN(5.43,10.65,.5,0.,.6)
       CALL DIMEN(9.,5.5,1.8,90.,.6)
```

```
      CALL DIMEN(4.2,9.4,1.35,90.,,.6)
      CALL DIMEN(7.15,9.4,1.,90.,,.6)
      CALL DIMEN(4.15,5.5,1.14,90.,,.6)
      CALL DIMEN(7.45,10.5,1.8,270.,,.6)
      CALL IMAGE(42,1,0,0,1,1,0,0)
      CALL PLOT(0.,0.,999)
      STOP
      END

      SUBROUTINE IMAGE(NDATA,ITOP,IBOTM,ILEFT,IRITE,IFRNT,IBACK,IPKTR)
      DIMENSION X(100),Y(100),Z(100),IPEN(100),Z1(100),XPLOT(100),
     @YPLOT(100)
      DATA X/0.,.5,.5,1.8,1.8,4.3,4.3,2.3,2.3,1.8,1.8,.5,.5,0.,0.,.5,.5,
     @.5,.5,1.8,1.8,1.8,1.8,0.,4.3,4.3,2.3,2.3,0.,0.,0.,0.,0.,0.,
     @4*2.3,4*4.3/
      DATA Y/0.,5*0.,.5,.5,6*1.8,0.,0.,1.8,0.,1.8,0.,1.8,0.,1.8,0.,0.,
     @.5,.5,1.8,1.8,3*0.,4*1.8,4*.5,0.,0./
      DATA Z/0.,0.,1.35,1.35,6*0.,2*1.35,5*0.,4*1.35,0.,0.,7*1.8,
     @0.,1.8,0.,1.8,0.,1.8,0.,1.8,0.,1.8,0.,1.8/
      DATA IPEN/3,14*2,3,2,3,2,3,2,3,2,3,6*2,3,2,3,2,3,2,3,2,3,2/
C*****SET  FRONT VIEW ORIGEN (LOWER LEFT HAND CORNER)*****
      CALL PLOT(7.25,9.2,-3)
      XTRANS=8.
      YTRANS=6.5
      IF(IPKTR.EQ.0)GOTO 200
      ANG=30.
      SF=1.
      COSA=COS(ANG/57.3)
      SINA=SIN(ANG/57.3)
      DO 1 K=1,NDATA
      XPLOT(K)=(X(K)+Z(K)*SF*COSA)+11.
      YPLOT(K)=(Y(K)+Z(K)*SF*SINA)+5.5
  1   CALL PLOT(XPLOT(K),YPLOT(K),IPEN(K))
C*****   FRONT VIEW   *****
 200  IF(IFRNT.EQ.0)GOTO 210
      DO 10 J=1,NDATA
 10   CALL PLOT(X(J),Y(J),IPEN(J))
```

```
C*****   TOP VIEW  *****
 210   IF(ITOP.EQ.0) GOTO 220
       DO 20 I=1,NDATA
       Z1(I)=Z(I)+YTRANS
 20    CALL PLOT(X(I),Z1(I),IPEN(I))
C*****   RIGHT SIDE VIEW  *****
 220   IF(IRITE.EQ.0) GOTO 230
       DO 30 I=1,NDATA
       Z1(I)=Z(I)+XTRANS
 30    CALL PLOT(Z1(I),Y(I),IPEN(I))
C*****   BOTTOM VIEW  *****
 230   IF(IBOTM.EQ.0) GOTO 240
       DO 40 I=1,NDATA
       Z1(I)=-1.*(Z(I)+YTRANS-4.5)
 40    CALL PLOT(X(I),Z1(I),IPEN(I))
C*****   LEFT SIDE VIEW  *****
 240   IF(ILEFT.EQ.0) GOTO 250
       DO 50 I=1,NDATA
       Z1(I)=-1.*(Z(I)+2.)
 50    CALL PLOT(Z1(I),Y(I),IPEN(I))
C*****   BACK VIEW  *****
 250   IF(IBACK.EQ.0) GOTO 100
       CALL PLOT(22.,0.,-3)
       DO 60 I=1,NDATA
       X1=-1.*X(I)
 60    CALL PLOT(X1,Y(I),IPEN(I))
       IF(IPKTR.EQ.1)CALL SYMBOL(13.1,5.,.2,9HPICTORIAL,0.,9)
       IF(IFRNT.EQ.1)CALL SYMBOL(2.,-.5,.2,10HFRONT VIEW,0.,10)
       IF(ITOP.EQ.1)CALL SYMBOL(2.2,6.,.2,8HTOP VIEW,0.,8)
       IF(IRITE.EQ.1)CALL SYMBOL(8.95,-.5,.2,13HRT. SIDE VIEW,0.,13)

       IF(IBOTM.EQ.1)CALL SYMBOL(1.9,-7.,.2,11HBOTTOM VIEW,0.,11)
       IF(ILEFT.EQ.1)CALL SYMBOL(-5.5,-.5,.2,13HLT. SIDE VIEW,0.,13)
       IF(IBACK.EQ.1)CALL SYMBOL(-3.9,-.5,.2,9HREAR VIEW,0.,9)
 100   RETURN
       END
```

The engineering graphics display is complete when the structured diagram has been implemented as a display list so that the display process may present a picture to the viewer. In technical terms this is *writing, compiling, loading,* and *executing* a computer program. Stop now and complete the review problems for this chapter before beginning Chapter 5.

REVIEW PROBLEMS

1. Chapter 4 introduced the graphics workstation programmable in FORTRAN 77. What important items should you check before working any of the examples at your particular workstation?

ANSWER   During this conversion the most important items are: (1) language statements, (2) extensions, (3) input/output, (4) functions available, (5) subroutines available in the system, and (6) control flow.

2.   Give three examples of graphic programs that may be run from a workstation.

ANSWER

    1.   Interactive
    2.   Phantom user
    3.   Sequential job order

3.   List several good uses for an interactive graphics program.

ANSWER   Answers will vary with users' background, but several might be: (1) program development for implementation of structured diagrams, (2) short operation of testing programs, (3) data entry from any of the input devices, and (4) network editing.

4.   What is a typical use for a phantom program executed from the workstation?

ANSWER   Large maps, highly detailed drawings, or other long operations.

5.   When are sequential jobs run from a workstation?

ANSWER   This environment is especially useful when drafting usage is heavy, and interactive design is at a low level.

6. Write the command that will allow you to log on the graphics workstation if your working directory is called GRAPH and your password is SECRET.

ANSWER

```
LOGON GRAPH/SECRET
```

7. Enter the command that will locate a display member stored under ACS and place it in your directory. The member name is PROJEK, and the drawing is named FOOTNG.

ANSWER

```
ATTACH 'ACS.GRAPH.PROJEK(FOOTNG)'
```

8. Enter the command to create a new drawing called FOOTG2.

ANSWER

```
CE .FOOTG2   or   ATTACH FOOTG2
```

9. Write the procedure for entering and saving a drawing, using the names and commands in problems 6, 7, and 8.

ANSWER

```
LOGON GRAPH/SECRET
CE .FOOTG2
INPUT
00010C PROGRAM STATEMENTS APPEAR AFTER EACH NUMBER
00020C STOP ENTERING STATEMENTS TO END INPUT NUMBERS
00030
SAVE
```

10. Delete the program saved in problem 9.

ANSWER

```
DELETE FOOTG2
```

11. List the program FOOTNG for reference checking.

ANSWER

```
CE FOOTNG
LIST
```

12. List all the programs contained in your directory by member name.

ANSWER

```
LOGON GRAPH/SECRET
LISTM
```

13. List all the other directories you have access to.

ANSWER

```
LOGON GRAPH/SECRET
LISTA
```

14. Enter the command for checking the status of FOOTNG.

ANSWER

```
STATUS(FOOTNG JOB NUMBER)*
```

15. Prepare a list of the input devices that are available to you as a draftsperson.

ANSWER   This will vary from none to all those listed in Chapter 4.

16. Enter the command for assigning the joystick as an input device.

ANSWER

```
ASSIGN JS
```

17. Change the name of FOOTNG to GRAPH1.

ANSWER

```
CNAME FOOTNG GRAPH1
```

18. Request the size of GRAPH1.

ANSWER

```
SIZE GRAPH1
```

19. Assign a password to GRAPH1 that will allow other users to read, but not write in, the member.

ANSWER

```
PROTEC GRAPH1(1)
```

20. Using squared paper and pencil, draw the graphic output that would be produced from the display list shown on the following two pages.

---

*This assumes that FOOTNG has been scheduled to run and has been assigned a job number. The number only is inserted after the STATUS command as STATUS(1346).

```
      DIMENSION X(50),Y(50),R(50),SANG(50),N(50),THETA(50)
      DATA X/3.,4.5,6.298,4.976,6.,2*4.5,3.,4.5,6./
      DATA Y/4.,6.,4.263,4.3,5.,5.5,4.1,4.,5.5,4./
      DATA R/3*.75,2.25,1.,1.5,1.09,.875,1.246,.875/
      DATA N/16,13,16,11,25,22,10,45,18,45/
      DATA SANG/263.,30.,134.,90.,145.,35.,240.,270.,225.,45.
      DATA THETA/3*8.,2*5.,5.,6.,3*5./
      CALL PLOT(0.,5.5,-3)
      DO 1 I=1,3
      X(I)=X(I)-.6
      Y(I)=Y(I)-2.
1     CALL CIRCLE (X(I),Y(I),R(I),SANG(I),N(I),THETA(I))
      CALL PLOT(1.756,2.384,3)
      CALL PLOT(3.250,4.375,2)
      CALL PLOT(4.420,4.540,3)
      CALL PLOT(6.218,2.803,2)
      CALL PLOT(5.804,1.521,3)
      CALL PLOT(2.493,1.254,2)
      CALL PLOT(8.,0.,-3)
      DO  10 I=4,5
      X(I)=X(I)-1.
      Y(I)=Y(I)-2.5
10    CALL CIRCLE (X(I),Y(I),R(I),SANG(I),N(I),THETA(I))
      CALL PLOT(5.,1.5,3)
      CALL PLOT(2.,1.5,2)
      CALL PLOT(-8.,-5.5,-3)
      DO 100 I=6,7
      X(I)=X(I)-.5
      Y(I)=Y(I)-2.
100   CALL CIRCLE (X(I),Y(I),R(I),SANG(I),N(I),THETA(I))
      CALL PLOT(3.502,1.133,3)
      CALL PLOT(1.502,2.633,2)
      CALL PLOT(2.771,4.360,2)
      CALL PLOT(5.228,4.362,3)
      CALL PLOT(6.502,2.635,2)
      CALL PLOT(4.502,1.135,2)
      CALL PLOT(8.,0.,-3)
```

```
      DO 1000 I=8,10
      X(I)=X(I)-.6
      Y(I)=Y(I)-1.2
1000  CALL CIRCLE (X(I),Y(I),R(I),SANG(I),N(I),THETA(I))
      CALL PLOT(2.402,1.925,3)
      CALL PLOT(5.402,1.925,2)
      CALL PLOT(18.,0.,999)
      STOP
      END
```

ANSWER

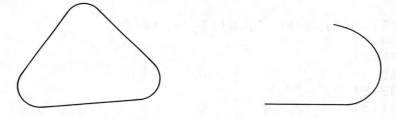

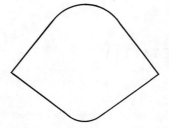

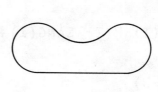

21. Complete your workstation session and sign off the system.

ANSWER

```
   LOGOFF
```

5 COMPUTER GRAPHICS HARDWARE

It has been my experience that students in academic environments receive a major exposure to software, whereas those studying in an industrial environment give greater attention to hardware. All students of engineering graphical displays should have:

A basic introduction to computer graphics *hardware*

The most fundamental treatment of *software*

An introduction to *firmware* (use of hardware and software in a single device)

Computer Programming for Graphical Displays is organized so that, after the first four general chapters, readers may branch according to their individual needs. This chapter was written for readers who are unfamiliar with the equipment defined in Chapter 2. *Hardware* refers to items that can be recognized, such as cabinets, control panels, hand-held objects, and interconnection devices such as the public telephone. If you are well-grounded in computer graphics hardware, then go on to Chapter 6, on computer graphics software. If you understand both hardware and software, you can go on to Chapter 7.

PROGRAMMING COMPUTER GRAPHICS HARDWARE

This chapter will provide basic drafting or design capability with a minimum of effort and knowledge of software. The focus is on recognition and simple uses of input and output devices. It is possible to use a graphics system language like FORTRAN 77 without the assistance of the special graphics subroutines contained in a software chapter. However, the task is greatly eased when you are familiar with the system-level commands described in Chapter 4.

The digital computer coupled with computer graphics hardware provides the capability for a wide variety of engineering graphics applications. This chapter will instruct you in selecting hardware in order to display engineering drawings in a meaningful way.

DIRECT-DISPLAY DEVICES

The devices shown in Figure 5-1 are called *direct-display devices*. In the simplest of terms a direct-display device is a hardware mechanism for moving a single graphical element (like a dot) vertically, horizontally, or both simultaneously, in order to connect or indicate a set of user-supplied points defined by X, Y, and Z coordinates. This chapter describes operation techniques to generate the commands necessary to control the direct-display device with very little effort on the part of the user. The commands are based on the following digital computers:

Digital Equipment Corp. 11/780 (VAX installation)
IBM 4341 (Graphics attachments)
Prime 750 (MEDUZA package)

No attempt has been made to check compatability to other manufacturers.

In order to use direct-display devices like those in Figure 5-1, the draftsperson must supply only the coordinates of the points to be dislayed and any labels to be printed. The user may also decide how big the finished display will be and what type of graphical element should be displayed. Direct-display devices are simple to operate once the user has spent some time with familiarization programming. A *familiarization program*—a list of instructions that begins with a command to activate the display device—is not the same as the ASSIGN command described in Chapter 4. It is designed to teach the user the various options and methods of operation.

The common direct display devices are:

1. Cathode ray tube (CRT)
2. Direct-view storage tube (DVST)
3. Pen plotter
4. Graphics tablet (data tablet)
5. Hard-copy device

Each of these devices is described in detail using a familiarization technique later in the book. The discussion here will assume that any of the pictured devices can be used.

CRT (CATHODE RAY TUBE)

At one end of the hardware spectrum is the cathode ray tube (CRT). Some CRT hardware devices

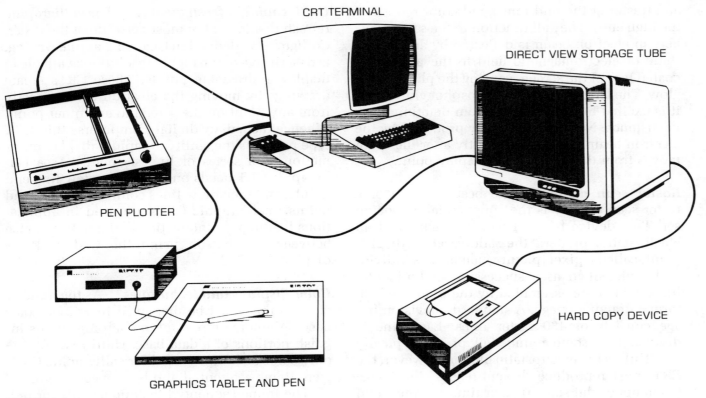

CRT TERMINAL

DIRECT VIEW STORAGE TUBE

PEN PLOTTER

HARD COPY DEVICE

GRAPHICS TABLET AND PEN

FIGURE 5-1

are termed *hard-copy* since the final display is produced on paper. Such permanent output can be a disadvantage if any interaction with the drawing information is required. Consequently, hard-copy devices have been designed to attach to either the CRT or the DVST (direct-view storage tube) to provide both permanent copies and interactive screen display.

The CRT has been used since the early devel-opment of computers to display temporary im-ages. There are three basic types of CRTs:

1. Raster scan display
2. Calligraphic refresh display
3. Color displays and techniques

These three types of CRTs fall in the perform-ance/interaction spectrum from mid-way to high end (raster at the mid range and color refresh at the high end). They all function in the same manner: an electron beam is deflected by an electrostatic or electromagnetic field to the phosphor-coated face of the screen, causing the phosphor to glow. The length of time the phosphor glows after it is excited by the electron beam determines its *persistence*. Normally, the glow produced by the electron beam fades away shortly after the beam moves from the addressable display point.

Raster scan display. The best example of a raster scan display is the commercial television set. This device functions in the manner of an electrostatic plotter: the addressable display point, called a *pixel* (picture element), is individually intensified as a succession of horizontal lines, which are assembled by the human eye to form a drawing image. A standard television image consists of 480 raster lines. Each line is divided into some number of pixels, typically 512. Unlike the electrostatic plotter, however, the CRT must reproduce the entire drawing image (contents of the screen) each time the image on the phosphor fades, so the persistence rate is important. The usual rate of 30 times a second for raster scan displays requires that the raster information be stored in digital form. The quantity of data rapidly becomes large, with 480 × 512, or 245,760, pieces of information required for a standard television image of only two intensity levels (on and off). Almost two million pieces of information are required to produce a gray-scale image with 256 intensity levels or a color image containing 256 colors. Chapter 8 of this book includes several applications for raster scan displays.

Calligraphic refresh display. The *calligraphic refresh display* is the most versatile of the CRTs. *Calligraphic*, defined in Chapter 2 as *fine writing*, is descriptive of the higher resolution available to display addressable points. These CRTs create drawings by moving the electron beam directly from any point on the screen to any other point. When attached to digital computers, this CRT type provides the ability to rapidly display information as a series of line segments. As a calligraphic CRT needs only process a few line end points, and then draw lines connecting these end points, calligraphic CRTs are used in applications that require interaction and quick response between the person using the CRT and the display.

Color displays and techniques. As the number of lines that must be displayed increases, color becomes more important in helping to distinguish portions of a data base. Until recently the only color techniques used for calligraphic CRTs were frame sequential and beam penetration.

The frame-sequential technique calls for red, green, and blue color filters to pass alternately through the operators line of sight. The motion, usually rotary, is rapid, so that each color is in front of the human eye at least once per refresh. The display list then synchronizes the rotation of the color filters with the display of lines. This is done so each line is drawn while that color's filter is between the viewer and the CRT.

Beam-penetration CRTs have two layers of phosphor, normally red and green. The electron beam's voltage is varied to cause the electrons to strike the inner layer, penetrating through the first layer or to an intermediate point. Depending on the beam's energy level, the color emitted is red, green, or other colors in the red/green spectrum. Beam penetration offers a limited number of colors and therefore limited line capacity and relatively poor line quality and brightness.

The shadow mask CRT, considered a color raster technique, has recently been used in calligraphic CRTs. Lines may be drawn at any angle, lighting up addressable display points of all three primary colors in chosen intensities to form any desired color. Colors displayed are limited only by digital considerations of the host computer.

Familiarization Program for CRTs

The CRT display requires the following program to be sent to the Digital Equipment Corporation PDP 11/780 processor for demonstration:

```
C      SDL1--SIMPLE DRAWING LANGUAGE VERSION 1
C      PROGRAM FOR DRAWING PICTURES ON THE VT 15 FROM CD INPUT
C      OF COMMANDS AND DATA
C      THIS ROUTINE CALLS THE SUBROUTINE NORM--THE CODE FOLLOWS
C
C      SUBROUTINE NORM(DRAW)
C      DOUBLE INTEGER DRAW
C      IF(DRAW.GT.0) DRAW=1
C      IF(DRAW.LE.0) DRAW=0
C      RETURN
C      END

       DOUBLE INTEGER COMND(9),COMM,DRAW
       DIMENSION MF(1000)
       DATA COMND/'ERASE','SCALE','REL  ','ABS  ','STOP ','     ',
      1          '     ','     ','     '/
       XM=1023.
       YM=1023.
       XM2=1023.
       YM2=1023.
       OCSX=1.0
       OCSY=1.0
       IX1=0
       IY1=0
```

```
         IX2=0
         IY2=0
         MFSIZ=1000
         MF(1)=0
  9      CALL DINIT(MF(1))
         CALL PLOT(2,1+2+16+128+256,0,7,0,0,0)
 10      READ(1,100) X,Y,DRAW,COMM
100      FORMAT(F10.4,F10.4,I10,A5)
 11      IF(COMND(1).EQ.COMM) GOTO 1000
         IF(COMND(2).EQ.COMM) GOTO 2000
         IF(COMND(3).EQ.COMM) GOTO 3000
         IF(COMND(4).EQ.COMM) GOTO 4000
         IF(COMND(5).EQ.COMM) GOTO 5000
         GOTO 10
C
C        ERASE COMMAND LOGIC
C
1000     MF(1) =0
         GO TO 9
C
C        SCALE COMMAND LOGIC
C
2000     READ (1,100) XM1,YM1,DRAW,COMM
C        TEST FOR BLANK COMMAND FIELD
         IF (COMND(9).NE.COMM) GOTO 11
         CALL NORM (DRAW)
C        IF DRAW EQUAL TO ONE XMAX AND YMAX SCALE
C        CHANGE WILL NOT SCALE THE ORIGIN OFFSET OF
C        THE REL COMMAND
         IF(DRAW.ED.1) GOTO 2001
         YM2=XM1
         YM2=YM1
2001     CONTINUE
         DCSX=XM2/XM1
         DCSY=YM2/YM1
         XM=XM1
         YM=YM1
         GOTO 10
```

```
C
C      REL--RELATIVE COMMAND LOGIC
C
3000   I = 1
3001   IF(MF(1).GE.(MFSIZ=2)) GOTO 9900
       READ(1,100) X,Y,DRAW,COMM
C      TEST FOR BLANK COMMAND FIELD
       IF (COMND(9).NE. COMM) GOTO 11
       CALL NORM (DRAW)
       IX = (X/XM) * 1023.
       IY = (Y/YM) * 1023.
       IF (I.EQ.1) GOTO 3002
       INT=DRAW
       CALL PLOT (1,IX,IY,INT)
       GOTO 3001
3002   CONTINUE
       IX=IFIX(FLOAT(IX)/DCSX)
       IY=IFIX(FLOAT(IY)/DCSY)
3003   CALL SETPT (IX,IY)
       I = 2
       GOTO 3001
C
C      ABS--ABSOLUTE COMMAND LOGIC
C
4000   II = 1
4001   IF(MF(1).GE.(MFSIZ=2)) GOTO 9900
       READ (1,100) X,Y,DRAW,COMM
C      TEST FOR BLANK COMMAND FIELD
       IF (COMND(9).NE. COMM) GOTO 11
       CALL NORM (DRAW)
       IX1=(X/XM)*1023.
       IY1=(Y/YM)*1023.
       IF (IT.EQ.1) GOTO 4002
       IDX = IX1 - IX2
       IDY = IY1 - IY2
       INT=DRAW
       CALL PLOT(1,IDX,IDY,INT)
       IX2 = IX1
```

```
         IY2 = IY1
         GOTO 4001
4002   CALL SETPT (IX1,IY1)
         IX2 = IX1
         IY2 = IY1
         IT = 2
         GOTO 4001
C
C        STOP COMMAND LOGIC
C
5000   STOP
C
C        DISPLAY FILE FULL ERROR
C

9900   WRITE(11,9901)
9901   FORMAT(' DISPLAY FILE IS FULL'/
     1          'TO INPUT ADDITIONAL FIGURES AN'/
     2          'ERASE COMMAND MUST BE INPUT')
         GOTO 10
         END
```

The above familiarization program allows direct and easy generation of engineering drawings. With it, anyone can learn the mechanics of CRT operation. When stored, this "canned" routine also gives a draftsperson new to CRT operation the tools to generate, and save for later use, free-form graphical sketches made up of a series of straight-line vectors. (The lines are drawn on the face of the CRT using a light pen and push button controls.) Saved sketches can be used in making more detailed drawings, thus making the familiarization program (FP) a versatile learning tool.

The graphic images generated can be as simple or as complex as desired, subject only to storage limitations of the PDP 11/780 processor. Drawings can be generated, saved, and recalled for inclusion in other drawings with a minimum use of the FP. The optimum use of the FP comes from defining a set of small meaningful drawings and using them to learn how the CRT terminal operates. The FP and CRT provide seven demonstration elements shown in Figure 5-2.

1. Display work area (1024 × 1024 matrix of addressable points)
2. Grid used for a drawing aid (may be on or off)

3. Drawing cursor (positioned by light pen)
4. Set of display vectors
5. Setpoint cross (marks origin of primitive element)
6. Blinking cross (represents next vector to be displayed)
7. Dark vector (move, not a line)

The diagram of demonstration elements in Figure 5-2 shows how the FP and CRT may be used to circumvent many software problems by interactive use of the light pen (LP) and push buttons. The demonstration process can be further aided by two basic forms of output. The first is a line printer, or hard copy, describing each primitive, called a *subpicture* (SUBPIX). The second is a copy of each SUBPIX saved as a display file. The display file, which is analogous to the main file (MF) used in Chapter 4, can be used as direct input to other direct-display devices. The FP and CRT share storage with the 11/780 but run independently when processing a display file. A SUBPIX file, analogous to a subroutine in normal digital processing, is a collection of display commands describing all or part of a graphical image. A SUBPIX file can be called by other SUBPIX files but is not displayed until they are attached to the MF.

The MF of the FP and CRT for this demonstration is set at 1000 continuous locations, as diagrammed in Figure 5-3. All or part of this file is the MF while the CRT is in operation. Display commands generated by the DRAW mode are added to the top of this file, causing it to become longer as necessary. Portions of the file are closed and used to display or recall SUBPIX files. MF(1) is the menu bar of the MF. MF(SUBPIX(N)) is the

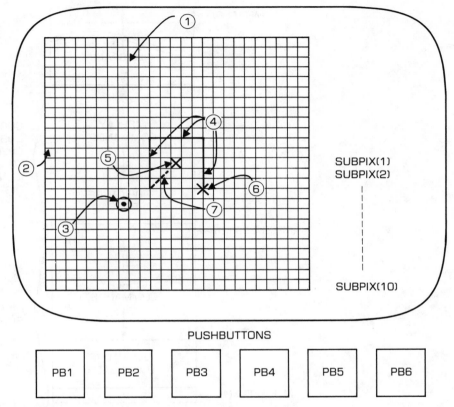

SUBPIX(1)
SUBPIX(2)

SUBPIX(10)

PUSHBUTTONS

PB1   PB2   PB3   PB4   PB5   PB6

FIGURE 5-2

current subpicture being generated by the DRAW mode. SUBPIX(N) is a primitive element in which the starting location of each FP-generated file is stored. An entry to SUBPIX(N) is made on initial use of DRAW mode. MF(XXX) is a SUBPIX containing drawing aids available in the DRAW mode, such as the grid overlay.

In addition to the MENU and DRAW, the FP has the modes of operation ERASE, SAVE,

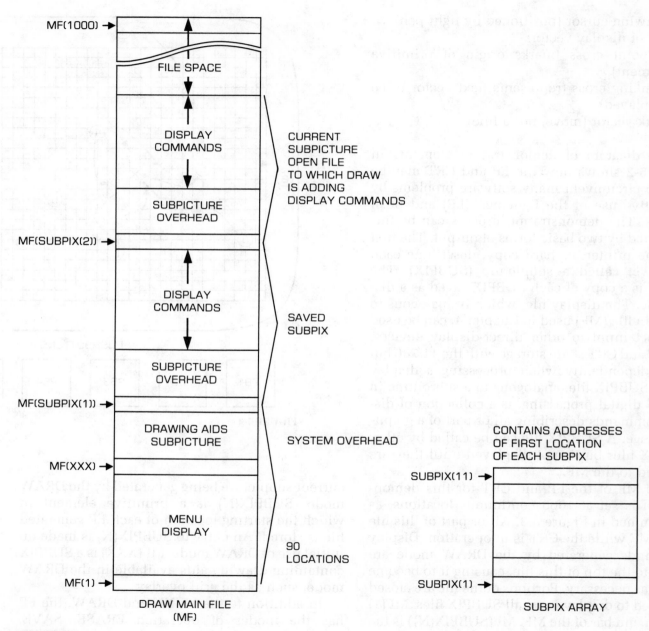

MF(1000) →

FILE SPACE

DISPLAY
COMMANDS

SUBPICTURE
OVERHEAD

MF(SUBPIX(2)) →

DISPLAY
COMMANDS

SUBPICTURE
OVERHEAD

MF(SUBPIX(1)) →

DRAWING AIDS
SUBPICTURE

MF(XXX) →

MENU
DISPLAY

MF(1) →

DRAW MAIN FILE
(MF)

CURRENT
SUBPICTURE
OPEN FILE
TO WHICH DRAW
IS ADDING
DISPLAY COMMANDS

SAVED
SUBPIX

SYSTEM OVERHEAD

90
LOCATIONS

CONTAINS ADDRESSES
OF FIRST LOCATION
OF EACH SUBPIX

SUBPIX(11) →

SUBPIX(1) →

SUBPIX ARRAY

FIGURE 5-3

REPLT, and file names. The MENU mode shown in Figure 5-4 has the menu selection at the upper right-hand corner of the CRT. The menu consists of three parts:

1. Basic listings
2. Current files
3. Saved files (SUBPIX(1), (2) . . .)

In item 1, the SUBPIX(N) origin is positioned when displayed for identification from the menu bar. Item 2 push buttons do not operate in menu mode. All interaction with the CRT is by touching the LP to the desired item on the menu and pushing the LP trigger, letting light enter.

The selection items in the basic list are INSTR (instructions), DRAW (display line), ERASE (remove line), SAVE (keep SUBPIX) and REPLT (replot). When the draftsperson touches the LP to INSTR, a list of operating instructions is printed. If LP is touched to DRAW, the screen flashes (cleared), and the CRT is returned to the DRAW mode from the MENU mode. ERASE removes a single line segment from the DRAW mode, and SAVE stores the image as a single drawing. The DRAW mode is most useful for familiarization with the CRT because a drawing cursor is always present to use with the LP. Interaction is possible with the push buttons and LP. The LP is used to move the cursor on the screen, and the drawing cursor defines and returns X and Y values for drawing purposes when any of the first three push buttons is depressed. The X and Y values define a location or are used in connection with the last X and Y value to compute a vector length for the SUBPIX. The functions of each of the push buttons are as follows:

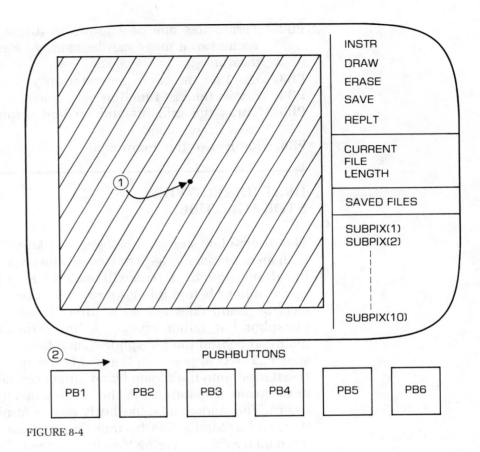

FIGURE 8-4

PB1. First, selects image origin, turning on the setpoint cross as an indicator; second selects the beginning or the first displayed vector, turning on the blinking cross as an indicator; and third, selects the length of the displayed vector, which is from the blinking cross to the present location of the drawing cursor

PB2. Terminates one or a group of displayed vectors so a move can be made to a new location

PB3. Used for the circle generator only

PB4. Erases the last function performed

PB5. Turns the grid off and on and setpoint cross drawing aids

PB6. Returns to the menu mode

DVST (DIRECT-VIEW STORAGE TUBE)

The direct-view storage tube behaves like a CRT with an extremely long-persistence phosphor—a line drawn onto the screen will remain visible for up to an hour before it fades away. However, the electron beam does not write directly onto the phosphor but rather charges a fine wire grid mounted behind the phosphor-coated face of the screen. The charge left on the grid is continually transferred onto the screen by an unfocused field of electrons (separate from the writing electron beam). The storage tube has fairly coarse resolution, and erasing a line from an image causes a momentary flash covering the entire screen. This means selective portions of the screen cannot be erased; the entire image is lost.

A recent development for storage tubes is the ability to display data in *write-thru* or *refresh* mode. The graphic cursor is displayed in this manner on all DVST terminals. Although the storage tube can thus be used in applications where refresh displays were formerly required, important differences exist between DVST- and CRT-type devices. The storage tube has no facil-

ity for intensity variation, a feature necessary to give the illusion of depth to a three-dimensional object. Furthermore, the amount of data that can be displayed in write-thru is rather limited: typically, only about 800 inches of vectors can be displayed this way.

DVSTs have been associated with digital displays for more than 20 years. Initially, the 4002 Tektronix terminal was used in place of analog scopes in military systems. Today, DVSTs are used increasingly in both research and profit-making situations, largely because DVSTs are less expensive than CRTs and can be used on large-scale networks as well as stand alone mini-processors. We will introduce the DVST and its use with the Prime 750 processor. This does not mean that DVSTs cannot be used with either DEC 11/780 or IBM 4341 processors; the DVST is independent of the processor.

The DVST is capable of displaying both alphanumeric and graphic data. Once written, the display remains visible until it is removed (erased by dropping voltage level). Therefore, it is not necessary to continually refresh the information put on the screen, as was the case for CRTs. Consequently, the DVST is as easy to use as a pencil and paper. The heavy computer programming and general I/O handling are contained within the familiarization program, making the graphics capabilities readily available to the draftsperson. It is unnecessary to retrace points or lines in a drawing over and over. Flood guns on the back of the tube flood the screen with electrons, so the picture is actually stored on the grid behind the phosphor. Another characteristic of the DVST is the fact that the cross-section of intensity of the stored image is very much like a square wave that has sharp edges and rises to a peak of intensity in the middle because the individual phosphor dots are either on or off (see Figure 5-5). The trailing edge does not exist on the DVST image as it does in the CRT refresh-type display. Note on the enlarged DVST image in Figure 5-5 that adjacent dots overlap. A display dot (addressable display point) is 10 mills in diameter. Adjacent dots are always 8 mills on center. Thus the display dots overlap in, for example, a line display. At the normal display size the display lines look continuous because the viewer's eye integrates the dots to create a crisp line display.

ENLARGED SCREEN DVST

FIGURE 5-5

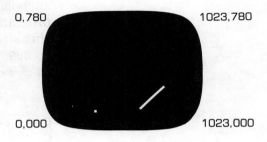

0,780   1023,780

0,000   1023,000

NORMAL-SIZE SCREEN DVST

Familiarization Program for DVSTs

The direct-view storage tube requires the following program to be sent to the Prime 750 processor for demonstration.

```
C     GRAPHIC PATTERN TO DISPLAY A GROUND SYMBOL
      SUBROUTINE GROUND
      CALL DRAWR(10.,0.)
      CALL MOVER(0.,-16.)
      CALL DRAWR(0.,32.)
      CALL MOVER(5.,-27.)
      CALL DRAWR(0.,22.)
      CALL MOVER(5.,-17.)
      CALL DRAWR(0.,12.)
      CALL MOVER(5.,-7.)
      CALL DRAWR(0.,2.)
      RETURN
      END
```

The draftsperson may use the program to develop simple electronic schematics. The user selects the desired subroutine by pressing a key from the keyboard of the workstation. The demonstration program checks which key has been depressed by checking a data file, which routes the proper response back to the DVST.

```
C        THIS PROGRAM WAS WRITTEN FOR THE GANNON PRIME TO BE USED
C        WITH THE SYSTEM COMMAND PLOT CS6...............................
C
C
C        OPENS GRAPHIC FILE FOR TEKTRONIX 4010 TERMINAL OPERATING UNDER
C        TCS SOFTWARE KNOWN AS PLOT-10...............................
         DATA IDRAW/68/,IMOVE/77/,IERASE/69/,IQUIT/81/,IHCOPY/72/
         DATA IRESIS/82/,ICAP/67/,ITRANS/84/,IGRND/71/
         CALL INITT(120)
C
C        SETS TERMINAL SCREEN WINDOW
         CALL VWINDO(0.,1000.,0.,750.)
C
C        SETS VIRTUAL SPACE DATA WINDOW
         CALL DWINDO(0.,500.,0.,375.)
         CALL MOVEA(0.,0.)
C
C        CALL FOR THE GRAPHIC CURSOR TO BE DISPLAYED
         XTO=1
         YTO=1
100      XFROM=XTO
         YFROM=YTO
105      CALL VCURSR(KEY,XTO,YTO)
         IF(KEY.NE.IDRAW)GOTO110
         CALL DRAWA(XTO,YTO)
         GOTO 100
110      IF(KEY.NE.IMOVE)GOTO120
         CALL MOVEA(XTO,YTO)
         GOTO 100
```

```
 120    IF(KEY.NE.IERASE)GOTO130
        CALL ERASE
        GOTO105
 130    IF(KEY.NE.IQUIT)GOTO140
C
C       CLOSES GRAPHICS FILE
        CALL FINITT(0,0)
 140    IF(KEY.NE.IHCOPY)GOTO150
        CALL HDCOPY
        GOTO105
C
C       DETERMINES THE ROTATION OF A SYMBOL FOR THE CIRCUIT
 150    RANGLE=ATAN2(YTO-YFROM,XTO-XFROM)*57.2957795131
        CALL RROTAT(RANGLE)
        IF(KEY.NE.IRESIS)GOTO160
        CALL RESIST
        CALL DRAWA(XTO,YTO)
        GOTO100
 160    IF(KEY.NE.ICAP)GOTO170
        CALL CAP
        CALL DRAWA(XTO,YTO)
        GOTO100
 170    IF(KEY.NE.ITRANS)GOTO180
        CALL TRANS
        CALL MOVEA(XFROM,YFROM)
C
C       BEAM IS NOW LEFT AT STARTING POINT FOR TRANSISTOR
        GOTO 105
 180    IF(KEY.NE.IGRND)GOTO100
        CALL GROUND
        CALL MOVEA(XFROM,YFROM)
C
C       BEAM IS NOW LEFT AT STARTING POINT FOR GROUND SYMBOL
        GOTO105
        END
C    THIS FILE IS A LISTING OF GRAPHIC SUBROUTINES
C    ..................IT IS NOT A PROGRAM..........
C
```

```
C
C       GRAPHIC PATTERN TO DISPLAY A RESISTOR
        SUBROUTINE RESIST
        CALL DRAWR(10.,0.)
        CALL DRAWR(3.,10.)
        CALL DRAWR(6.,-20.)
        CALL DRAWR(6.,20.)
        CALL DRAWR(6.,-20.)
        CALL DRAWR(6.,20.)
        CALL DRAWR(6.,-20.)
        CALL DRAWR(3.,10.)
        RETURN
        END
C
C
C       GRAPHIC PATTERN TO DISPLAY A CAPACITOR
        SUBROUTINE CAP
        CALL DRAWR(10.,0.)
        CALL MOVER(0.,20.)
        CALL DRAWR(0.,-40.)
        CALL MOVER(10.,40.)
        CALL DRAWR(0.,-40.)
        CALL MOVER(0.,20.)
        RETURN
        END
C
C
C       GRAPHIC PATTERN TO DISPLAY A TRANSISTOR
        SUBROUTINE TRANS
        CALL DRAWR(20.,0.)
        CALL DRAWR(0.,20.)
        CALL DRAWR(2.,0.)
        CALL DRAWR(0.,-40.)
        CALL DRAWR(-2.,0.)
        CALL DRAWR(0.,20.)
        CALL MOVER(2.,10.)
        CALL DRAWR(20.,20.)
```

```
       CALL MOVER(-20.,-40.)
       CALL DRAWR(15.,-15.)
       CALL DRAWR(2.,2.)
       CALL DRAWR(3.,-7.)
       CALL DRAWR(-7.,3.)
       CALL DRAWR(2.,2.)
       CALL MOVER(5.,-5.)
       RETURN
       END
C
C
C
```

You can understand how a DVST operates by running the familiarization program. When the DVST operator logs on a graphics system and requests this FP program, the following appears on the face of the DVST:

```
*****************************************************************************
**                                                                       **
**                        INTERACTIVE CIRCUIT BOARD                       **
**                                                                       **
**                                                                       **
**     INPUTS FROM KEY BOARD:                                            **
**                                                                       **
**          CHARACTER                    COMMAND                         **
**          =========                    =======                         **
**              M                    MOVE(NO LINE DRAWN)                  **
**              D                    DRAW FROM LAST POINT                 **
**              E                    ERASE SCREEN                         **
**              H                    COPY DRAWING                         **
**              Q                    QUIT PROGRAM                         **
**              R                    RESISTOR                            **
**              C                    CAPACITOR                           **
**              T                    TRANSISTOR                          **
**              G                    GROUND                              **
```

```
**              V                       BATTERY                                     **
**              S                       SWITCH                                      **
**              L                       TITLE OF DRAWING( 0 THRU 40)                **
**              +                       PLUS SIGN                                   **
**              -                       MINUS SIGN                                  **
**                                                                                  **
************************************************************************************

HIT RETURN
```

This page, listing what the FP is capable of, is an interactive circuit design program that accepts inputs from the keyboard. The characters that may be used are listed with a description of the commands. The last message at the bottom of the screen is HIT RETURN. When the return key is depressed, the screen erases, and a crosshairs appears on the screen. This screen represents the write-thru portion of the DVST. It can be moved by thumbwheels on the side of the keyboard or by a joystick, allowing a DVST operator to locate points (digitize) or communicate the X and Y location information back to the FP. The FP stores the information in a way that will enable the operator to use it for drawing images and creating figures on the face of the DVST. In other words, this process is really a way to create data base for the computer FP.

To illustrate, let's move the crosshairs down into the lower left-hand portion of the screen and do some simple drawing. At this point the user may communicate to the FP stored in the computer by pressing a key on the keyboard. For example, let's tell the FP that we just moved into the lower left-hand portion of the DVST screen.

We do this by depressing the M key. Remember that this means MOVE (no line drawn). If you are actually following this procedure on a DVST, you noticed that the screen flashed bright green, and the crosshairs reappeared. This indicated that the display point was stored as data base.

Now let's draw a line. First move the crosshairs to the right, as shown in Figure 5-6. Type a D from the keyboard. A dark line replaces the crosshairs between the M location and the D location. Notice that this line is much brighter than crosshairs that now appear. The line is permanently placed on the screen until it is erased.

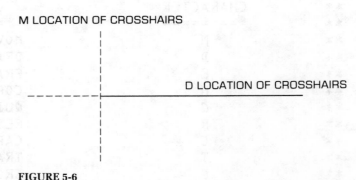

FIGURE 5-6

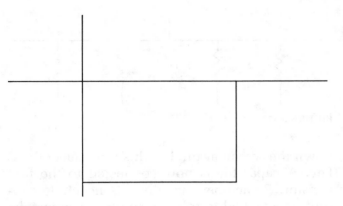

FIGURE 5-7

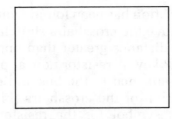

FIGURE 5-8

Follow the example in Figure 5-7 by moving the crosshairs upward on the screen and pressing the D key. This displays a line 90 degrees to the first line. Now move the crosshairs to the left and depress the D key again. Complete the box shape by again moving the crosshairs and pressing D (Figure 5-8).

This procedure can be used to create any straight-line images, but it is not appropriate for circular features. If you want to draw a circle, a key from the keyboard must represent that image stored in the computer FP as part of the subroutine list. (It does not exist in this example, but it is in Chapter 10.) Suppose the C key represented this circle function. If you press C, the FP will assume that the present location of the crosshairs is the center of a circle. You move the crosshairs to represent the radius of the circle and depress the C again. The circle will appear at the desired location on the DVST screen.

We can demonstrate another capability with this FP. We will begin by pressing the E key to clear the screen, deleting the data base created by

the last figure (box). Depress the M key and position the crosshairs by use of the thumbwheels. Stop the crosshairs at the top middle of the DVST. Depress the M key again and move straight down the screen about a half-inch. Depress the D key and notice that a line appears. Move to the left side of the DVST and press the M key; then move to the right side of the DVST and press the D key. Notice that a line now appears connected at 90 degrees to the shorter line image. Let's say this represents a bus line for an electronic circuit. From this bus we will be able to display more of the inputs from the keyboard. So far we have demonstrated M for MOVE (dark vector—unseen), D for DRAW (bright vector—seen), E for ERASE and delete the subpicture file.

Select a position on the bus toward the left side of the screen by turning the thumbwheels until the crosshairs are directly over the top of the longer of the two visible lines. Now indicate that this is a move by depressing the M key (Figure 5-9).

FIGURE 5-9

Once this location has been found, you may place a symbol. Move the crosshairs straight down the screen for a distance greater than one inch, and depress the R key. A resistor now appears on the screen. It is attached to the bus and ends at the current location of the crosshairs (Figure 5-10). The graphic symbol for the resistor has been drawn by the subroutine attached to the FP. In this manner symbols like the resistor may be located at any position between any two points. The location of the resistor was determined when the crosshairs were moved straight down the screen.

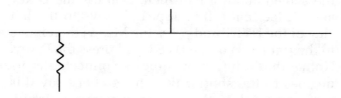

FIGURE 5-10

Suppose that the diagram required a series of parallel resistors. They would be displayed by moving the crosshairs back up to the bus and selecting the proper distance to the right of the last resistor. This is done by pressing M and moving the crosshairs down the screen until they align at the bottom of the existing resistor. Press the R key again, and a resistor appears in parallel with the first. You repeat the procedure until all the resistors are displayed as shown in Figure 5-11.

You can continue the circuit by placing the crosshairs over the end of the first resistor and pressing M. Now move the crosshairs straight

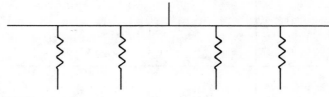

FIGURE 5-11

down the screen again, but this time select the C key. A capacitor is now connected to the first resistor. Remember that there is no circle subroutine attached to this FP, so the C key may be used for the capacitor subpicture. Moving straight down the screen again, press the G key to attach a ground symbol to the capacitor. No moves were required in this series of symbols because the symbols are connected in series; they are not parallel, as the resistors were. Next, move the crosshairs between the first resistor and the capacitor and press the M key. Move left on the screen and press the T key. A transistor now appears attached between the first resistor and capacitor, as shown in Figure 5-12. This demon-

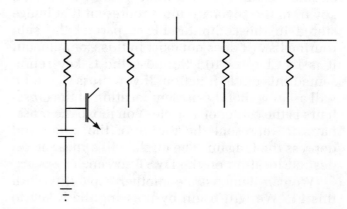

FIGURE 5-12

strates horizontal placement of symbols. A second row of symbols (capacitor, ground and transistor) may be added parallel to the first, as shown in Figure 5-13.

The diagram is completed when the user selects the placement of the last inputs from the keyboard—namely, V, S, and L. The V input places the battery within the circuit, and S displays an off–on switch. The L key is used to create the lettering shown in Figure 5-13. The L subroutine may be structured to return the DVST to alpha, mode, allowing the draftsperson to type the labels directly from the keyboard, or to read in an alpha array, which contains the labels to be plotted.

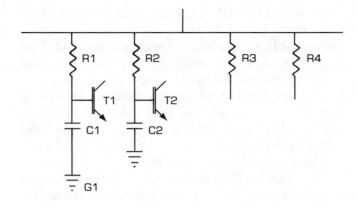

EXAMPLE EXERCISE FOR
THE 4010 DVST TERMINAL—CIRCUIT LOGIC

FIGURE 5-13

PEN PLOTTERS

The devices above, and many others, may be grouped, by performance and interaction ability, along a spectrum. At the lower end of this spectrum lie pen and ink plotters, in which a computer-driven pen creates a stroke-by-stroke drawing. Plotters are unmatched for resolution (a measure of the density of addressable display points) but are extremely slow compared to more sophisticated graphic direct-display devices.

Next on the spectrum lies the electrostatic dot matrix printer/plotter. This device operates by placing elements of a dot matrix into a pattern of filled and empty areas, which the human eye sees from a reasonable distance as a drawing. A plotter of this type is known as a *raster* device. A raster device produces a display image as a succession of horizontal lines. Raster-type plotters are typically of coarse resolution but are capable of producing several hundred raster lines per minute. Most engineering drawings consist of a series of horizontal and nonhorizontal line segments. The nonhorizontal line segments must be converted to raster information—a sorting process that may require up to several minutes to complete.

Pen plotters or electrostatic plotters are devices that provide graphic capability for a wide variety of engineering and scientific applications. The program and subroutines listed in the familiarization program are designed to provide that capability with a minimum of effort and graphic programming. There are a number of manufacturers for both pen plotters and electrostatic plotters. The programming illustrated here is for the pen plotter CALCOMP 936 or the VERSATEC 8236 electrostatic.

The CALCOMP plotter is available in a large number of industrial sites and educational institutions. It is a mechanism for moving a pen either vertically or horizontally, or in both directions simultaneously, to connect or indicate a set of programmer-supplied points defined by the X and Y coordinates. The graphics user supplies the coordinates of the points to be plotted, any labels to be printed, the size of the finished plot, and the type of lines to be drawn.

The VERSATEC plotter draws an entire raster of data across the paper width simultaneously instead of mechanically moving a pen back and forth. Nothing on the VERSATEC moves except the paper, fan, and tone pump. The graphics is electronic, not mechanical. Programmed voltage is applied to an array of densely spaced (220/inch) writing nibs embedded in a stationary writing head. Upon digital command the nibs selectively create minute electrostatic dots on the paper passing over the writing head. The paper is then exposed to liquid toner, producing a permanent graphic image. Because of this raster-type output electrostatic plotters allow much more choice of size and line image type than wet-ink plotters. Electrostatic plotters also produce tonal shading of areas. However, the resolution of the plotter line is not as good as that of the wet-ink plotter.

Familiarization Program for Plotters

The familiarization program listed below contains five options, or drawings, that may be recalled from the storage section of the FP. It is able to produce any of the subjects discussed so far. It will provide the necessary operational experiences for either the CALCOMP or VERSATEC plotter.

```
//CVBRM1   JOB (0923-1-311-00- ,:10,3)
//STEP1 EXEC FTG1CLG,PLOT=0812
//C.SYSIN DD  *
C*************************************************************************
C
C
C
C*************************************************************************
C
C  THIS PROGRAM ALLOWS THE USER TO SUBMIT A SINGLE CARD WHICH DRAWS
C  ANY DRAWING BETWEEN 1 AND 5.   THE PLOTD CARD SHOLD READ AS FOLLOWS
C      PLOTD=N
C  WHERE THE LETTER  P  IS IN THE SEVENTH COLUMN OF THE CARD AND N IS
C  THE NUMBER OF THE DRAWING BETWEEN 1 AND 5.
```

```
C=====================================================================
C=                C A T A L O G   O F   D R A W I N G S          =
C=-------------------=-=-=-=-=-=-=-=-=-=-=-=-=-----------------------=
C=      PLOTD#              DRAWING DESCRIPTION                    =
C=                                                                =
C=        1                TITLE BLOCK AND SIMPLE PART            =
C=        2                THREE VIEW                             =
C=        3                THREE VIEW AND PART FEATURE            =
C=        4                DIMENSIONING                           =
C=        5                SECTIONING                             =
C=                                                                =
C=====================================================================
C
C
C
C>>>>>>>>>>>>>>>>>>>>>>>>>>>>>>>>>>>><<<<<<<<<<<<<<<<<<<<<<<<<<<<<<<<<<<
C
      IF (PLOTD.EQ.1) CALL DRAW1
      IF (PLOTD.EQ.2) CALL DRAW2
      IF (PLOTD.EQ.3) CALL DRAW3
      IF (PLOTD.EQ.4) CALL DRAW4
      IF (PLOTD.EQ.5) CALL DRAW5
      IF ((PLOTD.LT.1).OR.(PLOTD.GT.5)) CALL DUMP
      STOP
      END
      SUBROUTINE DRAW1
C
C******************     D R A W I N G   1     **********************
C
C  THIS SUBROUTINE DRAWS A TITLE BLOCK AND A SIMPLE PART.
C
      CALL PLOTS
      CALL FACTOR(.647)
      CALL TITLE
      CALL SYMBOL(.1875,.25,.375,'01',0.,2)
      CALL SYMBOL(10.125,.375,.2,'PART PIECE A',0.,12)
```

```
C      THIS IS A UNIVERSAL DIGITIZING PROGRAM.
       READ(31,1)NPTS
     1 FORMAT(I4)
       DO 10 I=1,NPTS
       READ(31,2)X,Y,IPEN
     2 FORMAT(2F6.3,I2)
    10 CALLPLOT(X,Y,IPEN)
       CALL PLOT(0.,0.,999)
       RETURN
       END
       SUBROUTINE DRAW2
C
C****************      D R A W I N G   2      **********************
C
C  THIS PROGRAM IS A THREE VIEW DIGITIZING PROGRAM.
       DIMENSION XP(50),YP(50),ZP(50),IPEN(50)
C
C      THE FOLLOWING 11 LINES CONTAIN THE DATA BASE FOR THE DRAWING.
       DATA XP/5.0,5.0,2.5,2.5,2.5,0.0,0.0,3.8,3.8,2.5,2.5,3.8,3.8,0.0,0.
      +0,2.5,2.5,2.5,5.0,5.0,5.0,2.5,2.5,2.5,0.0,0.0,2.5,2.5,2.5,3.8,3.8,
      +2.5,5.0,0.0/
       DATA YP/0.0,2.0,2.0,0.0,0.0,0.0,3.8,3.8,2.0,2.0,2.0,2.0,3.8,3.8,0.
      +0,0.0,0.0,2.0,2.0,0.0,0.0,0.0,2.0,2.0,0.0,3.8,3.8,0.0,2.0,2.0,0.0,0.0,
      +0.0,0.0,0.0/
       DATA ZP/0.0,0.0,0.0,0.0,1.8,2.6,2.6,1.4,1.4,1.8,5.9,6.3,6.3,5.1,5.
      +1,5.9,7.7,7.7,7.7,7.7,0.0,0.0,1.8,1.8,2.6,5.1,5.9,5.9,7.7,1.4,6.3,
      +0.0,0.0,0.0/
       DATA IPEN/3,3,2,2,2,2,2,2,2,2,3,2,2,2,2,2,2,2,2,2,2,2,2,3,2,2,3,2,3,2,
      +2,3,2,3,2,3/
C
C      THE NEXT STATEMENT INITIALIZES THE PLOTTER.
       CALL PLOTS
C
C      THE FOLLOWING COMMAND SCALES DOWN THE DRAWING.
       CALL FACTOR(.647)
C
C      THE NEXT STATEMENT DRAWS THE TITLE BLOCK.
       CALL TITLE
```

```
C
C       THE FOLLOWING 2 LINES CONTAIN INFO. FOR DRAWING#, AND TITLE.
        CALL SYMBOL(.1875,.25,.375,'02',0.,2)
        CALL SYMBOL(10.125,.375,.2,'3-VIEW DRAWING      ',0.,20)
C
C       MAIN 3-VIEW PROGRAM
        CALL PLOT(1.433,1.233,-3)
C
C       THIS DO LOOP DRAWS THE FRONT VIEW.
        DO 10 I=1,34
   10 CALL PLOT(ZP(I),YP(I),IPEN(I))
C
C       THE FOLLOWING 2 COMMANDS DRAW THE HIDDEN LINE IN THE FRONT VIEW.
        CALL PLOT(1.8,2.0,3)
        CALL DASHP(5.9,2.0,.2)
        CALL PLOT(0.,4.283,-3)
C
C       THIS DO LOOP DRAWS THE TOP VIEW.
        DO 11 J=1,34
   11 CALL PLOT(ZP(J),XP(J),IPEN(J))
        CALL PLOT(9.133,-4.283,-3)
C
C       THIS DO LOOP DRAWS THE RIGHT SIDE VIEW.
        DO 12 K=1,34
   12 CALL PLOT(XP(K),YP(K),IPEN(K))
        CALL PLOT(0.,0.,999)
        RETURN
        END
        SUBROUTINE DRAW3
C
C******************   D R A W I N G   3   ***********************
C
C       THIS PROGRAM IS A THREE VIEW DIGITIZING PROGRAM.
        DIMENSION XP(50),YP(50),ZP(50),IPEN(50)
C
C       THE FOLLOWING 11 LINES CONTAIN THE DATA BASE FOR THE DRAWING.
        DATA XP/5.0,5.0,2.5,2.5,2.5,0.0,0.0,3.8,3.8,2.5,2.5,3.8,3.8,0.0,0.
       +0,2.5,2.5,2.5,5.0,5.0,5.0,2.5,2.5,2.5,0.0,0.0,2.5,2.5,2.5,3.8,3.8,
```

```
      +2.5,5.0,0.0/
       DATA YP/0.0,2.0,2.0,0.0,0.0,0.0,3.8,3.8,2.0,2.0,2.0,2.0,3.8,3.8,0.
      +0,0.0,0.0,2.0,2.0,0.0,0.0,2.0,2.0,0.0,3.8,3.8,0.0,2.0,2.0,0.0,0.0,
      +0.0,0.0,0.0/
       DATA ZP/0.0,0.0,0.0,0.0,1.8,2.6,2.6,1.4,1.4,1.8,5.9,6.3,6.3,5.1,5.
      +1,5.9,7.7,7.7,7.7,7.7,0.0,0.0,1.8,1.8,2.6,5.1,5.9,5.9,7.7,1.4,6.3,
      +0.0,0.0,0.0/
       DATA IPEN/3,3,2,2,2,2,2,2,2,2,3,2,2,2,2,2,2,2,2,2,2,2,3,2,2,2,3,2,3,2,
      +2,3,2,3,2,3/
C
C       THE NEXT STATEMENT INITIALIZES THE PLOTTER.
        CALL PLOTS
C
C       THE FOLLOWING COMMAND SCALES DOWN THE DRAWING.
        CALL FACTOR(.647)
C
C       THE NEXT STATEMENT DRAWS THE TITLE BLOCK.
        CALL TITLE
C
C       THE FOLLOWING 3 LINES CONTAIN INFO. FOR DRAWING#, AND TITLE.
        CALL SYMBOL(.1875,.25,.375,'03',0.,2)
        CALL SYMBOL(10.125,.375,.2,'3-VIEW DRAWING      ',0.,20)
C
C       MAIN 3-VIEW PROGRAM
        CALL PLOT(1.433,1.233,-3)
C
C       THIS DO LOOP DRAWS THE FRONT VIEW.
        DO 10 I=1,34
   10 CALL PLOT(ZP(I),YP(I),IPEN(I))
C
C       THE FOLLOWING 2 COMMANDS DRAW THE HIDDEN LINE IN THE FRONT VIEW.
        CALL PLOT(1.8,2.0,3)
        CALL DASHP(5.9,2.0,.2)
C
C       THE FOLLOWING COMMAND DRAWS THE CIRCLE IN THE FRONT VIEW.
        CALL CIRCL(4.35,2.,0.,360.,.5,.5,0.)
        CALL PLOT(0.,4.283,-3)
```

```
C
C      THIS DO LOOP DRAWS THE TOP VIEW.
       DO 11 J=1,34
   11 CALL PLOT(ZP(J),XP(J),IPEN(J))
C
C      THE FOLLOWING 6 COMMANDS DRAW THE HIDDEN LINES AND THE TROUGH IN
C      THE TOP VIEW.
       CALL PLOT(3.35,5.,3)
       CALL PLOT(3.35,3.8,2)
       CALL DASHP(3.35,0.,.2)
       CALL PLOT(4.35,5.,3)
       CALL PLOT(4.35,3.8,2)
       CALL DASHP(4.35,0.,.2)
       CALL PLOT(9.133,-4.283,-3)
C
C      THIS DO LOOP DRAWS THE RIGHT SIDE VIEW.
       DO 12 K=1,34
   12 CALL PLOT(XP(K),YP(K),IPEN(K))
C
C      THE FOLLOWING 4 COMMANDS DRAW THE HIDDEN LINES IN THE SIDE VIEW.
       CALL PLOT(5.,1.5,3)
       CALL DASHP(0.,1.5,.2)
       CALL PLOT(0.,2.5,3)
       CALL DASHP(3.8,2.5,.2)
       CALL PLOT(0.,0.,999)
       RETURN
       END


       SUBROUTINE DRAW4
C
C******************     D R A W I N G   4     **********************
C
C      THIS PROGRAM IS A THREE VIEW DIGITIZING PROGRAM.
C
C      THE FIRST DIMENSION STATEMENT IS FOR THE DRAWING.
       DIMENSION XP(50),YP(50),ZP(50),IPEN(50)
```

```
C
C       THE NEXT DIMENSION STATEMENT IS FOR THE CENTERLINES.
        DIMENSION XC(25),YC(25),TLEN(25),THETA(25),DASH(25),SPACE(25),ALIN
       +E(25)
C
C       THE FOLLOWING 11 LINES CONTAIN THE DATA BASE FOR THE DRAWING.
        DATA XP/5.0,5.0,2.5,2.5,2.5,0.0,0.0,3.8,3.8,2.5,2.5,3.8,3.8,0.0,0.
       +0,2.5,2.5,2.5,5.0,5.0,5.0,2.5,2.5,2.5,0.0,0.0,2.5,2.5,2.5,3.8,3.8,
       +2.5,5.0,0.0/
        DATA YP/0.0,2.0,2.0,0.0,0.0,0.0,3.8,3.8,2.0,2.0,2.0,2.0,3.8,3.8,0.
       +0,0.0,0.0,2.0,2.0,0.0,0.0,2.0,2.0,0.0,3.8,3.8,0.0,2.0,2.0,0.0,0.0,
       +0.0,0.0,0.0/
        DATA ZP/0.0,0.0,0.0,0.0,1.8,2.6,2.6,1.4,1.4,1.8,5.9,6.3,6.3,5.1,5.
       +1,5.9,7.7,7.7,7.7,7.7,0.0,0.0,1.8,1.8,2.6,5.1,5.9,5.9,7.7,1.4,6.3,
       +0.0,0.0,0.0/
        DATA IPEN/3,3,2,2,2,2,2,2,2,2,3,2,2,2,2,2,2,2,2,2,2,2,3,2,2,3,2,3,2,
       +2,3,2,3,2,3/
C
C       THE NEXT 7 LINES CONTAIN THE DATA BASE FOR THE CENTERLINES.
        DATA XC/5.475,5.475,5.475,12.200/
        DATA YC/3.700,3.700,7.800,3.700/
        DATA TLEN/1.0,1.0,3.0,3.0/
        DATA THETA/90.,0.,90.,0./
        DATA DASH/.125,.125,.125,.125/
        DATA SPACE/.062,.062,.062,.062/
        DATA ALINE/.25,.25,.25,.25/
C
C       THE NEXT STATEMENT INITIALIZES THE PLOTTER.
        CALL PLOTS
C
C       THE NEXT COMMAND SCALES DOWN THE ENTIRE DRAWING AND THE TITLE
C       BLOCK.
        CALL FACTOR(.647)
        CALL SYMBOL(5.0,.12,.1,'1" = 3.091"',0.,11)
C
C       THE NEXT STATEMENT DRAWS THE TITLE BLOCK.
        CALL TITLE
```

```
C
C       THE NEXT SUBROUTINE PUTS IN THE DIMENSIONS.
        CALL DIME
C
C       THE NEXT SUBROUTINE DRAWS THE LEADER FOR THE HOLE.
        CALL LEADER(7.352,2.4,6.852,2.4,5.652,3.523)
        CALL SYMBOL(7.402,2.338,.125,'1 INCH DIA. HOLE',0.,16)
C
C       THE FOLLOWING 2 LINES CONTAIN INFO. FOR DRAWING#, AND TITLE.
        CALL SYMBOL(.1875,.25,.375,'04',0.,2)
        CALL SYMBOL(10.125,.375,.2,'DIMENSIONING          ',0.,20)
C
C       THE FOLLOWING DO LOOP DRAWS THE CENTER LINES.
        DO 30 M=1,4
     30 CALL CENTER(XC(M),YC(M),TLEN(M),THETA(M),DASH(M),SPACE(M),ALINE(M)
       +)
C       MAIN 3-VIEW PROGRAM
        CALL PLOT(3.550,2.700,-3)
C
C       THE NEXT COMMAND SCALES DOWN ONLY THE FRONT VIEW.
        CALL FACTOR(.324)
C
C       THIS DO LOOP DRAWS THE FRONT VIEW.
        DO 10 I=1,34
     10 CALL PLOT(ZP(I),YP(I),IPEN(I))
C
C       THE FOLLOWING 4 COMMANDS DRAW THE HIDDEN LINE IN THE FRONT VIEW.
        CALL PLOT(1.8,2.0,3)
        CALL DASHP(2.8,2.0,.1)
        CALL PLOT(4.9,2.0,3)
        CALL DASHP(5.9,2.0,.1)
C
C       THE FOLLOWING COMMAND DRAWS THE CIRCLE IN THE FRONT VIEW.
        CALL CIRCL(4.35,2.,0.,360.,.5,.5,0.)
C
C       THE NEXT COMMAND SCALES THE DRAWING BACK UP.
        CALL FACTOR(.647)
        CALL PLOT(0.,3.850,-3)
```

```
C
C      THE NEXT COMMAND SCALES DOWN THE TOP VIEW.
       CALL FACTOR(.324)
C
C      THIS DO LOOP DRAWS THE TOP VIEW.
       DO 11 J=1,34
   11 CALL PLOT(ZP(J),XP(J),IPEN(J))
C
C      THE FOLLOWING 6 COMMANDS DRAW THE HIDDEN LINES AND THE TROUGH IN
C      THE TOP VIEW.
       CALL PLOT(3.35,5.,3)
       CALL PLOT(3.35,3.8,2)
       CALL DASHP(3.35,0.,.1)
       CALL PLOT(4.35,5.,3)
       CALL PLOT(4.35,3.8,2)
       CALL DASHP(4.35,0.,.1)
C
C      THE NEXT COMMAND RESETS SCALE.
       CALL FACTOR(.647)
       CALL PLOT(7.400,-3.850,-3)
C
C      THE NEXT COMMAND SCALES DOWN THE SIDE VIEW.
       CALL FACTOR(.324)
C
C      THIS DO LOOP DRAWS THE RIGHT SIDE VIEW.
       DO 12 K=1,34
   12 CALL PLOT(XP(K),YP(K),IPEN(K))
C
C      THE FOLLOWING 4 COMMANDS DRAW THE HIDDEN LINES IN THE SIDE VIEW.
       CALL PLOT(5.,1.5,3)
       CALL DASHP(0.,1.5,.1)
       CALL PLOT(0.,2.5,3)
       CALL DASHP(3.8,2.5,.1)
       CALL PLOT(0.,0.,999)
       RETURN
       END
```

```
      SUBROUTINE DRAW5
C
C********************       D R A W I N G  5       ********************
C
C     THIS PROGRAM IS A THREE VIEW DIGITIZING PROGRAM.
C
C     THE FIRST DIMENSION STATEMENT IS FOR THE DRAWING.
      DIMENSION XP(50),YP(50),ZP(50),IPEN(50)
C     THE NEXT DIMENSION STATEMENT IS FOR THE CENTERLINES.
      DIMENSION XC(25),YC(25),TLEN(25),THETA(25),DASH(25),SPACES(25),ALIN
     +E(25)
C
C     THE FOLLOWING 11 LINES CONTAIN THE DATA BASE FOR THE DRAWING.
      DATA XP/5.0,5.0,2.5,2.5,2.5,0.0,0.0,3.8,3.8,2.5,2.5,3.8,3.8,0.0,0.
     +0,2.5,2.5,2.5,5.0,5.0,5.0,2.5,2.5,2.5,0.0,0.0,2.5,2.5,2.5,3.8,3.8,
     +2.5,5.0,0.0/
      DATA YP/0.0,2.0,2.0,0.0,0.0,0.0,0.0,3.8,3.8,2.0,2.0,2.0,2.0,3.8,3.8,0.
     +0,0.0,0.0,2.0,2.0,0.0,0.0,0.0,2.0,2.0,0.0,0.0,3.8,3.8,0.0,2.0,2.0,0.0,0.0,0.0,
     +0.0,0.0,0.0/
      DATA ZP/0.0,0.0,0.0,0.0,1.8,2.6,2.6,1.4,1.4,1.8,5.9,6.3,6.3,5.1,5.
     +1,5.9,7.7,7.7,7.7,7.7,0.0,0.0,0.0,1.8,1.8,2.6,5.1,5.9,5.9,7.7,1.4,6.3,
     +0.0,0.0,0.0/
      DATA IPEN/3,3,2,2,2,2,2,2,2,3,2,2,2,2,2,2,2,2,2,2,2,3,2,2,3,2,3,2,
     +2,3,2,3,2,3/
C
C     THE NEXT 7 LINES CONTAIN THE DATA BASE FOR THE CENTERLINES.
      DATA XC/5.475,5.475,5.475,12.200/
      DATA YC/3.700,3.700,7.800,3.700/
      DATA TLEN/1.0,1.0,3.0,3.0/
      DATA THETA/90.,0.,90.,0./
      DATA DASH/.125,.125,.125,.125/
      DATA SPACE/.062,.062,.062,.062/
      DATA ALINE/.25,.25,.25,.25/
C
C     THE NEXT STATEMENT INITIALIZES THE PLOTTER.
      CALL PLOTS
```

```
C
C          THE NEXT COMMAND SCALES DOWN THE ENTIRE DRAWING AND THE TITLE
           BLOCK.
           CALL FACTOR(.647)
           CALL SYMBOL(5.0,.12,.1,'1" = 3.091"',0.,11)
C
C          THE NEXT STATEMENT DRAWS THE TITLE BLOCK.
           CALL TITLE
C
C          THE NEXT SUBROUTINE PUTS IN THE DIMENSIONS.
           CALL DIME
C
C          THE NEXT SUBROUTINE DRAWS THE LEADER FOR THE HOLE.
           CALL LEADER(7.352,2.4,6.852,2.4,5.652,3.523)
           CALL SYMBOL(7.402,2.338,.125,'1 INCH DIA. HOLE',0.,16)
C
C          THE FOLLOWING 2 LINES CONTAIN INFO. FOR DRAWING#, AND TITLE.
           CALL SYMBOL(.1875,.25,.375,'05',0.,2)
           CALL SYMBOL(10.125,.375,.2,'SECTIONING          ',0.,20)
C
C          THE FOLLOWING DO LOOP DRAWS THE CENTER LINES.
           DO 30 M=1,4
       30  CALL CENTER(XC(M),YC(M),TLEN(M),THETA(M),DASH(M),SPACE(M),ALINE(M)
          +)
C
C          MAIN 3-VIEW PROGRAM
           CALL PLOT(3.550,2.700,-3)
C
C          THE NEXT COMMAND SCALES DOWN ONLY THE FRONT VIEW.
           CALL FACTOR(.324)
C
C          THIS DO LOOP DRAWS THE FRONT VIEW.
           DO 10 I=1,34
       10  CALL PLOT(ZP(I),YP(I),IPEN(I))
C
C          THE FOLLOWING 4 COMMANDS DRAW THE HIDDEN LINE IN THE FRONT VIEW.
           CALL PLOT(1.8,2.0,3)
```

```
      CALL DASHP(2.8,2.0,.1)
      CALL PLOT(4.9,2.0,3)
      CALL DASHP(5.9,2.0,.1)
C
C     THE FOLLOWING COMMAND DRAWS THE CIRCLE IN THE FRONT VIEW.
      CALL CIRCL(4.35,2.,0.,360.,.5,.5,0.)
C
C     THE NEXT COMMAND SCALES THE DRAWING BACK UP.
      CALL FACTOR(.647)
      CALL PLOT(0.,3.850,-3)
C
C     THE NEXT COMMAND SCALES DOWN THE TOP VIEW.
      CALL FACTOR(.324)
C
C     THIS DO LOOP DRAWS THE TOP VIEW.
      DO 11 J=1,34
   11 CALL PLOT(ZP(J),XP(J),IPEN(J))
C
C     THE FOLLOWING 6 COMMANDS DRAW THE HIDDEN LINES AND THE TROUGH IN
C     THE TOP VIEW.
      CALL PLOT(3.35,5.,3)
      CALL PLOT(3.35,3.8,2)
      CALL DASHP(3.35,0.,.1)
      CALL PLOT(4.35,5.,3)
      CALL PLOT(4.35,3.8,2)
      CALL DASHP(4.35,0.,.1)
C
C     THE NEXT COMMAND RESETS SCALE.
      CALL FACTOR(.647)
      CALL PLOT(7.400,-3.850,-3)
C
C     THE NEXT COMMAND SCALES DOWN THE SIDE VIEW.
      CALL FACTOR(.324)
C
C     THE NEXT 8 COMMANDS DRAW THE SIDE VIEW.
      CALL BAR(0.,0.,0.,1.5,5.0,1.5,2,10)
      CALL BAR(0.,2.5,0.,1.3,3.8,1.3,2,10)
```

```
CALL PLOT(0.,1.5,3)
CALL PLOT(0.,2.5,2)
CALL PLOT(3.8,2.5,3)
CALL PLOT(3.8,2.0,2)
CALL PLOT(5.0,2.0,2)
CALL PLOT(5.0,1.5,2)
CALL PLOT(0.,0.,999)
RETURN
END
```

GRAPHICS TABLETS

Graphics or data tablets serve as the standard, general-purpose graphic input device in the direct-display devices shown in Figure 5-1. A stylus, or pen, whose X, Y coordinates are read by the familiarization program, positions or points to the drawing elements on the tablet. Immediately after the tablet position is read, a cursor may be generated by the refresh and device processor (IBM graphics attachment) to indicate the position of the pen on the tablet. In conjunction with the rest of the direct-display devices, the tablet and pen can perform the interactive functions usually reserved for such graphic input devices as light pens, joysticks, and function switches.

Familiarization Program for Graphics Tablets

The graphics tablet must be connected to a computer terminal such as the DVST, which in turn is connected to the CRT. The CRT contains a keyboard and is the input to the FP. The DVST display screen is the output from the FP. The draftsperson begins the operation from the keyboard by entering:

```
LOGON
USER ID/PASSWD
```

The FP responds:

```
***********************************************************************************
**                                                                             **
**    GRAPHICS TABLET ROUTINES CAN BE RUN FROM THIS ID BY EXECUTING            **
**       TWO PROCS.                                                            **
**                                                                             **
**    _____        **
**                                                                             **
**    FOR MORE INFORMATION HIT PAGE KEY AND TYPE  X .INFO                      **
**                                                                             **
***********************************************************************************
```

The user types:

`X .INFO`

The FP responds:

```
*********************************************************************
**                                                                 **
**        PROCEDURE:                                               **
**                        TO INITIALIZE — ENTER X .PROTAB          **
**                        CALLING A TABLET PROGRAM — X .DRAW  NAME  **
**            WHERE NAME DEFINES WHICH TABLET FUNCTION IS DESIRED   **
**                                                                 **
*********************************************************************
```

The user enters:

`X . PROTAB`

The FP responds:

```
PROC 0
CE VIEWCMD
00010 ENDD;
SAVE
END
```

The user enters:

`X .DRAW DRAW2D`

The FP responds:

```
@@@@@@@@@@@@@@@@@@@@@@@@@@@@

        START OF CREATE 2-D

@@@@@@@@@@@@@@@@@@@@@@@@@@@@
```

DO YOU WISH PRINT-OUT AS A DEBUGGING AID?

ENTER 0, 1, 2, OR 3 FOR LEVEL OF DEBUGGING

The user selects and types the number, followed
by RETURN.

0

The FP responds:

ENTER THE TERMINAL BAUD RATE

The user selects from 110 to 2400 and enters the
selection:

2400

The FP responds:

ENTER DATABASE NAME OR IDENTIFYER

The user selects a storage identifier that can be
remembered later.

DVST1

The FP responds:

ENTER THE LENGTH OF THE SCALE INDICATOR

The user types in a number that will represent the
scale length of the data tablet used.

The FP responds:

INPUT THE BEGINNING POINT OF THE SCALE INDICATOR

The user checks to make sure that the data tablet control box has been turned on and that the electric pencil has been plugged in. If these are in order, the user may touch the pencil to the tablet surface. The data light on the control box will blink, and the FP responds:

INPUT THE ENDING POINT OF THE SCALE INDICATOR

The user now moves to a new location on the data tablet and touches the surface again. The CRT terminal now reads:

INPUT THE ORIGIN LOCATION FOR THE INPUT DATA

The user touches the pencil over the origin of the drawing. The FP responds:

INPUT THE UPPER LEFT-HAND CORNER OF THE DISPLAY WINDOW

The user sends the opposite corner of the drawing to the FP.

INPUT THE LOWER RIGHT-HAND CORNER OF THE DISPLAY WINDOW

The user touches the tablet one last time to complete the tablet setup.

PROCEED WITH TABLET INPUT—WHEN CURSOR APPEARS ON THE DVST, ENTER

S   TO START 2-D INPUT SESSION

E   TO ERASE THE DVST

C   TO CONTINUE CREATION OF DATABASE

Q   TO QUIT FP

T   TO TERMINATE INPUT SESSION, STAY IN FP

A crosshairs called a cursor now appears on the DVST. The tablet operator types S from the keyboard, and the DVST screen is erased. Now data from the tablet surface may be entered and stored as an engineering drawing by any of the following:

1. The pen-type device used on most data tablets allows the user to draw directly on a piece of paper. The paper is taped onto the tablet, and the draftsperson draws in the normal manner. The pen touches are recorded directly through the paper. The tablet sends the X, Y locations to the control box connected to the DVST.

2. A mouse-type device is used when a paper drawing is not needed. If a plastic overlay were used on the tablet surface, the mouse could be positioned over a preprinted symbol on a menu list and traced for input to a data file. The mouse is quicker than a pen.

3. A joystick, which resembles a tiny pilot's control stick, is used to move the cursor on the DVST screen. By locating points with the cursor, the user may describe a freehand sketch directly on the face of the DVST. The joystick is faster than the thumbwheels, the pen, or the mouse. In this case the tablet houses a menu of symbols. In the case of the DVST, keys from the keyboard were assigned symbols. When joysticks are used in connection with data tablets, the data tablet acts like a temporary page for queueing. The cursor is moved on the face of the DVST until it matches the menu item desired. The location of the cursor is sent to the FP, and a graphic display is returned to the DVST.

HARD-COPY DEVICES

A device like that shown in Figure 5-1 is connected to the output side of the DVST. The data tablet provides input to the DVST, and the contents of the screen are copied by the hard-copy unit. There are no familiarization programs written for hard-copy units. They are simple to operate, as follows:

1. Turn unit on and allow a short "warmup period."
2. Turn on DVST and post an engineering drawing.
3. Press "make copy" button on either the keyboard or the control panel of the hard-copy unit.
4. Wait for the "sweep" across the DVST.
5. Remove the finished copy from the hard-copy unit.
6. Check to see if "darkness" setting needs to be adjusted on the control panel of the hard-copy unit.
7. Make any adjustment in darkness.

REVIEW PROBLEMS

1. The direct-display devices discussed in this chapter were demonstrated by the use of three familiarization programs. What were these programs, and what computers were they written for?

ANSWER

CRTs................Digital equipment 11/780
DVSTs ....PRIME 750
Pen plotter ....IBM 4341

2. List the common direct-display devices introduced in this chapter.

ANSWER

Raster scan CRT
Calligraphic refresh CRT
Color CRT
DVST
CALCOMP plotter
VERSATEC plotter
Graphics or data tablet
Hard-copy unit

3. Describe, in your own words, how a raster scan CRT might be used in a drafting and design environment.

ANSWER Variable with each reader

4. Prepare a check list or table of attributes that compare the operational characteristics of raster scan, calligraphic, and color displays.

ANSWER (See Table 5-1.)

5. Enter the FP for CRTs and practice building several subpictures.

6. Enter the FP for DVSTs and practice building sample circuits.

TABLE 5-1
Table of CRT Characteristics

Attribute	Continuous Line Images	Tone Images	Shade Capability	Other Possible Attributes
Raster scan	NO	YES	YES	—
Calligraphic	YES	NO	YES	—
Color CRT	YES	YES		

7. Enter the FP for pen plotters and output one of the sample drawings available.

8. Enter the FP for data tablets and practice building a graphical image from the graphics tablet surface.

9. Save the input from the data tablet exercise in problem 8 in the main memory file of the digital computer you used. List this for verification purposes.

ANSWER (example)

POINT COORDINATES

X	Y	
0.0	0.0	0
4.500	0.0	0
4.500	3.000	0
0.0	3.000	0
0.0	0.0	-3
4.500	0.0	-3

4.500	0.500	-3
4.500	1.000	-3
4.500	1.000	-2
4.500	1.000	-1
4.500	1.000	-1
4.500	1.500	-1
4.500	3.000	-1
0.0	3.000	-1
0.0	1.500	-1

10. Send the data file from problem 9 to the DVST screen for a graphic verification.

11. Before erasing the DVST screen from problem 10, press the hard-copy key on the keyboard.

12. Prepare a simple familiarization program for each of the devices located at your workstation that have not been shown in Chapter 5.
SUGGESTIONS:
    Light pen
    Joystick
    Mouse
    Tracking ball
    Digitizer
    Acoustic tablet
    Menu overlay for graphics tablet
    Touch tablet

13. Prepare a one-page outline for each of the devices in problem 12. This outline should include which of the direct-display devices is used for each item, what the item does, what its benefits are, and how to ATTACH the FP for demonstration.

14. Expand the FP for CRTs to include more SUBPIX file space.
ANSWER Change the dimension statements in the present listing.

15. Expand the FP for direct-view storage tube terminals so that additional electronic symbols can be displayed.
ANSWER Enlarge DATA blocks at beginning of the FP by providing storage locations for each desired symbol. ILAMP may be used to store a symbol, for

instance. An unused key may be assigned by its ASCII number as /94/.

Now prepare to test for 94 with an IF statement. If KEY is 94, then branch to SUBROUTINE LAMP, which describes the graphical elements contained in the symbol.

16. Expand the FP for pen plotters by providing "drawing no. 6" as an additional option.

ANSWER Write the coding for a CALCOMP or VERSATEC plotter drawing, as shown on page 108.

17. Develop a FP program that will respond to the prompts shown on page 121.

ANSWER Depends on host computer and graphics tablet manufacturer guidelines.

18. Expand the FP for pen plotters and the FP for data tablets so that a sketch entered by the data tablet can be routed and plotted by the pen plotter.

ANSWER Depends on host computer and type of storage device used.

19. Expand the FP for pen plotters and CRT so that a CRT image can be routed to the pen plotter.

ANSWER Depends on hardware used.

20. Prepare a single FP that will demonstrate a CRT, DVST, pen plotter, data tablet, and hard-copy unit.

ANSWER Depends on hardware used.

6

PROGRAMMING

GRAPHICAL

ROUTINES

In this chapter we will study the most interesting part of computer programming for graphical displays: the programming techniques needed for describing three-dimensional objects in a two-dimensional space. We begin by describing template drawing using basic or simple graphic entities, such as the display point, line, plane, and wireform. With these simple display entities the draftsperson can construct for display, objects called *primitive elements*—rectangles, circles, ellipses, polygons, and splines. Additional items are listed in Figure 6-1 along with the character generation for lettering.

The second and third parts of this chapter contain information on programming transformations for three-dimensional picture graphics.

Complete programs will be presented for orthographic representation of simple and complex production objects.

2-D GEOMETRIC CONSTRUCTIONS

Computer-generated two-dimensional constructions result from a properly written computer program for a graphics output (and input) device, as described in Chapter 5. Together, the program and the device are the medium by which a graphics programmer manipulates visual information. The end result may be the design of an automobile; the teaching of a lesson in engineering

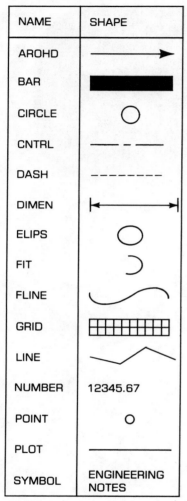

NAME	SHAPE
AROHD	
BAR	
CIRCLE	
CNTRL	
DASH	
DIMEN	
ELIPS	
FIT	
FLINE	
GRID	
LINE	
NUMBER	12345.67
POINT	
PLOT	
SYMBOL	ENGINEERING NOTES

FIGURE 6-1

mechanics; the training of an airplane pilot; entertainment such as animated cartoons; or the manipulation of colors, mass, or forms.

One authority (Machover, 1977) breaks down two-dimensional geometric constructions into the following six general application areas:

1. Management information
2. Scientific graphics
3. Command and control
4. Image processing
5. Real-time image generation
6. Electrical and mechanical diagrams

Each of these application areas can require markedly different programming, as we will see in Chapter 7.

Another way to look at the programming necessary for two-dimensional geometric constructions is in terms of the visualization functions or engineering services provided by computer graphic devices:

1. Template drawing
2. Graphic entities
3. Primitive elements
4. Character generation

Most two-dimensional applications implemented by graphics programmers use one or more of the above functions or services. We will review each of them, with examples.

Template Drawing

Perhaps one of the greatest advantages of a properly programmed graphics system is the fact that it replaces the plastic template and drawing

paper as a drafting medium. A software system that presents at the screen the proper tools for image creation and manipulation can make a user much more productive than a draftsperson working at a drawing table with templates. Among the many documented studies of increased productivity, Feder (1975) cites productivity time ratios ranging from 1.9 to 17 times improvement where engineering drawings and/or machine parts are the end products.

In an earlier book *Computer-Aided Graphics and Design*, I described a system of template drawing that normally would be done with paper and pencil and showed why the computer programmed technique is faster in an engineering drawing environment. Repetitive template symbols do not have to be redrawn, but are instantaneously called from computer storage. Any symbol occurring in the electrical or mechanical diagram is immediately displayed on the DVST rather than having to be reprogrammed, and analytic geometry constructions are performed by the main program and do not have to be calculated and sent to a plotter. In addition, circuit design accuracy is often better than can be achieved manually.

All laborious processes involving templates are trivial to the user with a graphics system of programming. Given the proper data-base design, a new orientation of the symbol, such as rotation or mirror image, requires only that the user state the request in precise form.

Graphic Entities

The results of the computations for template drawing can be displayed as graphic entities as they occur and before all chain analytic geometry constructions are complete. This process is very important because it provides real-time feedback to the diagram designer or to an engineer who may be doing a parameter study for a new design. The engineer can terminate a particular computation if the partial results show that different parameters are required. Such a dynamic technique is common with DVST-type terminals, but much more immediately useful information can be provided with a CRT-type device. Users report significant savings in main computer time when computations can be aborted early and when several options can be explored in the time normally required to make one hand drawing.

With graphic entities large amounts of information can be presented in a short time. Many computer programs for graphical display are based on the fact that a graphics console can display a large quantity of information at once and, for a regenerated CRT, the console can display changes every display cycle. Recall from Chapter 5 that CRT displays usually cycle at 40 to 60 times per second to avoid flicker.

Chapter 5 also described the resolution of various display devices. The smallest graphical entity that is clearly related to the display is POINT. The example on page 134 is typical of programming necessary to display a single point. The type of display device determines the size of the point. For example, a color system of 512 × 512 picture elements (pixels) will be quite different from a DVST, which contains 1024 display units (dots).

Figure 6-2 shows how the concept of a point can be displayed as a LINE, and the example program presents typical graphical programming required to display a line segment. In the case of the

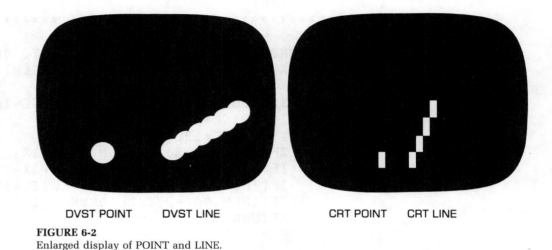

DVST POINT   DVST LINE   CRT POINT   CRT LINE

FIGURE 6-2
Enlarged display of POINT and LINE.

DVST the dots are overlapped to create a very sharp output for the human eye. Highest resolution CRTs tend to be monochromatic, but 1000 lines are available in color. Described plasma panels of 512 × 512 addressable point resolution with the PLATO system from Control Data Corporation are the most popular devices of this type. The CDC system offers the advantage of rear-projected color photographs. Monochromatic displays may be programmed with up to 4096 × 4096 addressable points.

Many applications use the POINT and LINE software to create plane surface displays. Figure 6-3 is an example of PLANE used in the construction of simple views for the user to display and manipulate. A software system called ECOSITE, developed by Mallary and Ferraro (1977), made use of the PLANE concept to describe complex views of land sites. McCleary (1977) has used the PLANE concept in his study of ocean bottom

```
C********************** POINT **********************
C
C   SUBROUTINE POINT MAY BE USED TO OUTPUT AN ENTITY
C   ON A DVST TYPE TERMINAL BY EXECUTING THE FOLLOWING:
C
      SUBROUTINE POINT(XPAGE,YPAGE,IPEN)
      IX=XPAGE*130.
      IY=YPAGE*130.
      IF(IPEN.EQ.3) CALL MOVABS(IX,IY)
      IF(IPEN.EQ.2) CALL DRWABS(IX,IY)
      IF(IPEN.EQ.-3)CALL MOVREL(IX,IY)
      IF(IPEN.EQ.-2)CALL DRWREL(IX,IY)
      RETURN
      END

C********************** LINE **********************
C
C SUBROUTINE LINE MAY BE USED TO OUTPUT AN ENTITY
C ON A DVST TYPE TERMINAL BY EXECUTING:
C
      SUBROUTINE LINE(SX,SY,EX,EY)
      IX=SX*130.
      IY=SY*130.
      CALL MOVABS(IX,IY)
      KX=EX*130.
      KY=EY*130.
      CALL DRWABS(KX,KY)
      RETURN
      END

C****************************************************
```

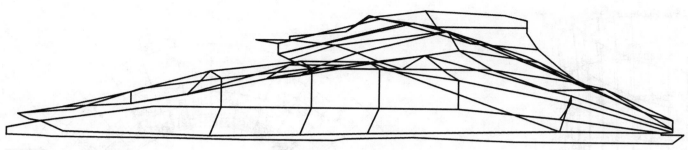

FIGURE 6-3
Use of graphic entity PLANE to construct an object.

data. In this case color aids in the differentiation of data, such as depth and shipping density.

A graphics programmer can create change or the illusion of change at a graphics console by using the POINT, LINE, and PLANE software to build objects called *wireforms*. Later we will describe a system that employs multiple planes of information, where each plane can contain a portion of action. An automatic interpolation technique provides for the illusion of continuous motion. A portion of *Computer-Aided Graphics and Design* points out the problems of automatic interpolation due to the insufficiency of information available to translate a 2-D view of a plane into another view without a 3-D data base.

WIREFORM graphics presentation for changing information includes the status of oil refineries, power distribution systems, and rocket launchings. Some air-traffic control systems combine both radar inputs and digitized information about specific flights on the same screen.

Representation of an unbuilt object can sometimes provide insight into potential problems before construction. For example, consider a

WIREFORM program for designing a cooling tower. In Figure 6-4 the engineer may study how the tower will look in elevation; Figure 6-5 represents the horizontal view of the same cooling tower. Another example might be viewing an unbuilt building from various viewing points, under changing lighting conditions and architectural modifications.

Primitive Elements

Many techniques have been created to support the use of the common primitive elements. Mallary and Ferraro (1977) discuss 35 primitive elements used in producing engineering drawings. We will discuss only the following elements:

Rectangle....................CALL RECT
Circle.......................CALL CIRCLE
Ellipse......................CALL ELPSE
Polygon......................CALL POLY
Spline.......................CALL FIT

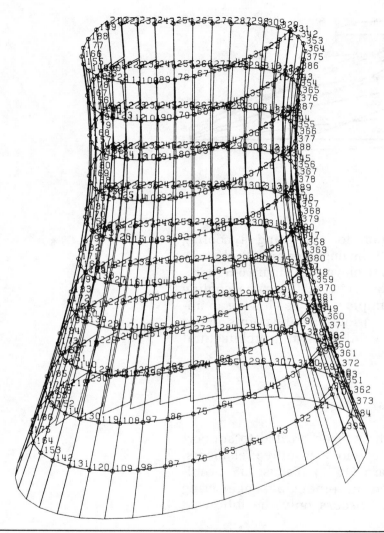

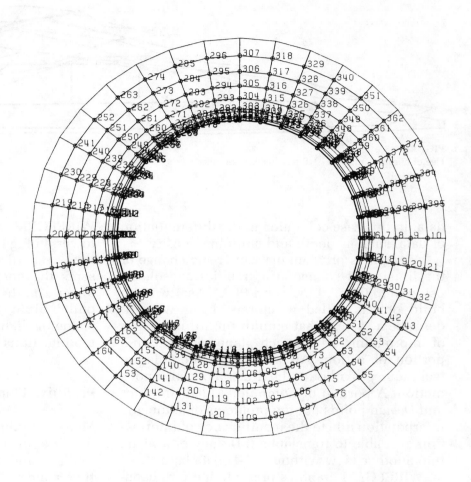

GEOMETRY

SCALE REDUCTION TITLE
  X   1.0000
  Y   1.0000   COOLING TOWER
  Z   0.8000

DATE
 3/22/79
TIME
22:51:28.70
ICES STRUDL-II
  IUG VERSION

FIGURE 6-4

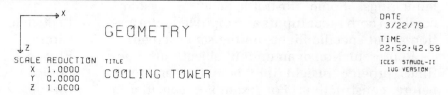

GEOMETRY

SCALE REDUCTION TITLE
  X   1.0000
  Y   0.0000   COOLING TOWER
  Z   1.0000

DATE
 3/22/79
TIME
22:52:42.59
ICES STRUDL-II
  IUG VERSION

FIGURE 6-5

These five primitve elements will allow the graphics programmer to describe histograms, empirical density functions, pie charts, contour plots, discriminant analysis diagrams, cluster analysis diagrams, Chernoff "faces" (which will be used for shades and shadows) and Andrews' sine curves. A number of other cartographic techniques are possible by the combination of graphic elements and primitive elements. The description of the graphics programming for RECT, shown below and on page 138, is useful in vari-

ous forms for maps and engineering drawings. The listing shown is typical of rectangle descriptions. It has not been tested on all types of display consoles, but it works well on DVST and plotter-type output devices.

With the listing for the primitive element CIRCLE the graphics programmer works with a two-dimensional representation of the primitive (instead of a linear line string). Primitives like CIRCLE and ELPSE replace alphanumeric human—machine communication. Many uses of

```
C************** RECT ****************************
      SUBROUTINE RECT(X,Y,WD,HT,THETA)
      THETA=(3.14159/180.)*THETA
      A=X+COS(THETA)*WD
      B=Y+SIN(THETA)*WD
      C=A-SIN(THETA)*HT
      D=B+COS(THETA)*HT
      E=C-COS(THETA)*WD
      F=D-SIN(THETA)*WD
      CALL PLOT(X,Y,3)
      CALL PLOT(A,B,2)
      CALL PLOT(C,D,2)
      CALL PLOT(E,F,2)
      CALL PLOT(X,Y,2)
      RETURN
      END

C****************** CIRCLE *************************
      SUBROUTINE CIRCLE(X,Y,R,SANG,N,THETA)
      X=X-R
      SANG=(3.14/180.)*SANG
      XX=R*(.-COS(SANG))
      YY=R+(SIN(SANG))
```

```
      DX=X+XX
      EY=Y+YY
      CALL PLOT(DX,EY,3)
      THETA=(3.14/180.)*THETA
      THETA1=THETA
      DO 260 I=1,N
      FEE=SANG+THETA
      PX=R*(1-COS(FEE))
      SY=R*(SIN(FEE))
      DX=X+PX
      EY=Y+SY
      CALL PLOT(DX,EY,2)
  260 THETA=THETA+THETA1
      Y=0.
      X=0.
      R=0.
      SANG=0.
      N=0
      THETA=0.
      RETURN
      END


C ******************** ELIPS ******************
      SUBROUTINE ELIPS(XO,YO,A,B,ALPHA,THETO,THETF,IV)
C
C     ELIPS DRAWS AN ELLIPTICAL ARC
C
C     XO,YO ARE THE COORDINATES OF THE STARTING POINT OF THE ARC
C     A IS HALF THE LENGTH OF THE ELLIPSE ALONG THE HORIZONTAL AXIS
C     B IS HALF THE LENGTH OF THE ELLIPSE ALONG THE VERTICAL AXIS
C     ALPHA IS THE ANGLE OF INCLINATION
C     THETO IS THE ANGLE OF THE STARTING POINT FROM THE CENTER
C     THETF IS THE ANGLE OF THE FINAL POINT
C     IV IS A CODE:
C          IV=2, DRAW A LINE FROM CURRENT PEN POSITION TO THE STARTING POINT
C          IV=3, DON'T DRAW A LINE
C
```

```
C          IF THE DIMENSIONS ARE ZERO, RETURN

4


C
C

C


C


C


C
```

SOURCE CODE FROM COMMERCIAL VENDORS IS PROTECTED BY COPYRIGHT LAWS USERS SHOULD CONTACT THE VENDOR OF THEIR CHOICE FOR COMPLETE SOFTWARE LISTING

computers before the advent of interactive graphics programming employed alphanumeric input and batched plotted output. In this older graphics technology, the output for numerically controlled drawing machines and machine tools, for example, would be directed by input statements created by parts programmers. The statements would describe the geometry of parts to be produced using special languages. Today, primitive elements displayed on graphics consoles allow the designer to construct the parts pictorially, thus eliminating the need for geometric languages.

Shown on page 140 is the listing for the graphics program that describes POLY. Using RECT, CIRCLE or ELPSE, and POLY, the user works entirely with geometric, primitive elements as construction tools at the screen in a manner similar to working at a drafting table. The FIT listing enables the draftsperson to simulate and observe processes for verification before committing real sources. Directions given to a numerically controlled machine tool can be graphically and visually verified at the screen of a graphics console before driving the real machine, as shown in the software listing for N/C verification. In this type

```
C **************** POLY **********************
      SUBROUTINE POLY(X,Y,SL,RN,TH)
```

```
C ********************  FIT  ***********************
      SUBROUTINE FIT(XA,YA,XB,YB,XC,YC)
```

```
C
C       THIS PROGRAM WAS WRITTEN FOR THE PRIME TO BE USED WITH THE SYSTEM
C       COMMAND PLOT CS7..............................................
C
C

        CALL PLOTS(0,0,0)
        CALL FACTOR(.5)
        CALL PLOT(14.,10.,-3)
        CALL AXIS(-12.,-8.,'INCHES',6,28.,0.,-12.,1.)
        CALL AXIS(-12.,-8.,'INCHES',6,20.,90.,-8.,1.)
        CALL CENTRL(0.,0.,0.,1.,16.,12.,12.,8.)
        X=-10.
        Y=10./7.*X+10.
        CALL PLOT(X,Y,3)
        DO 2 I=1,30
        X=X+0.1
        Y=70./49.*X+10.
        CALL PLOT(X,Y,2)
        IF (I.NE.I/2*2) GO TO 2
        CALL CCIRCL(X,Y,0.,360.,.25,.25,0.)
        CALL PLOT(X,Y,3)
2       CONTINUE
C
C       DATA IS NOW SENT TO A POST PROCESSOR
C       FOR NUMERICAL CONTROL MACHINE TOOLING
C
        X1=-7
        DO 4 I=1,100
        X1=X1+.07
        Y1=-5./49.*X1**2+5.
        CALL PLOT(X1,Y1,2)
        IF (I.NE.I/2*2) GO TO 4
        CALL CCIRCL(X1,Y1,0.,360.,.25,.25,0.)
        CALL PLOT(X1,Y1,3)
4       CONTINUE
C
C       DATA IS NOW PROCESSED FOR AN N/C VERTICAL MILLING MACHINE
```

```
C       UNDER APT CONTROL
C
        X2=0
        DO 6 I=1,100
        X2=X2+.086
        Y2=-5.+(100.-X2**2)**.5
        CALL PLOT(X2,Y2,2)
        IF (I.NE.I/2*2) GO TO 6
        CALL CCIRCL(X2,Y2,0.,360.,.25,.25,0.)
        CALL PLOT(X2,Y2,3)
6       CONTINUE
C
C       DATA IS NOW IN DIRECT NUMERICAL CONTROL FORMAT
C
        X3=X2
        DO 8 I=1,20
        X3=X3+0.1
        Y3=-1.*3.**.5*X3+15.
        CALL PLOT(X3,Y3,2)
        IF (I.NE.I/2*2) GO TO 8
        CALL CCIRCL(X3,Y3,0.,360.,.25,.25,0.)
        CALL PLOT(X3,Y3,3)
8       CONTINUE
        CALL PLOT(0.,0.,999)
        CALL STOP
        END
        SUBROUTINE CCIRCL(XC,YC,ANGO,ANGF,RADO,RADF,DX)
        THO=ANGO*3.14159/180.
        X=XC+RADO*COS(THO)
        Y=YC+RADO*SIN(THO)
        CALL CIRCL(X,Y,ANGO,ANGF,RADO,RADF,DX)
        RETURN
        END
        SUBROUTINE CENTRL(X,Y,ANG,DL,XPLEN,YPLEN,XMLEN,YMLEN)
C
C       CENTRL DRAWS A PAIR OF ORTHOGANAL DASHED LINES
C       INTERSECTING AT THE POINT (X,Y) AND ROTATED BY THE ANGLE ANG.
```

```
C     XPLEN IS THE LENGTH OF THE LINE IN THE POSITIVE X DIRECTION,
C     XMLEN IS THE LENGTH OF THE LINE IN THE NEGATIVE X DIRECTION, ETC.
      CALL DASH(X,Y,XPLEN,DL,ANG)
      CALL DASH(X,Y,YPLEN,DL,ANG+90.)
      CALL DASH(X,Y,XMLEN,DL,ANG+180.)
      CALL DASH(X,Y,YMLEN,DL,ANG+270.)
      RETURN
      END
```

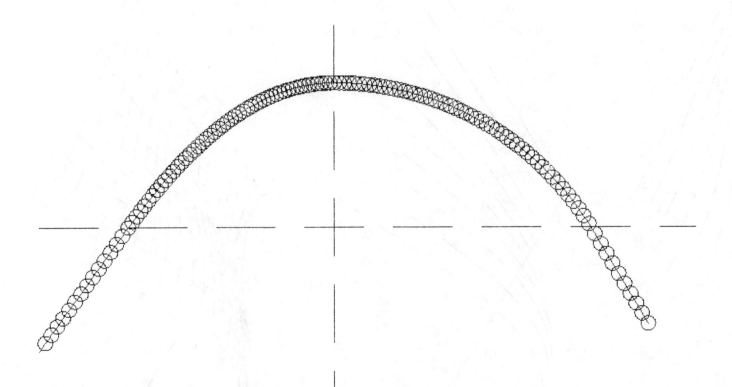

of example the system can picture a "tool" traveling its programmed path with continuous motion, providing verification that can avoid costly errors on the machine floor.

Theoretical models constructed from splines is perhaps the area of greatest challenge. Figure 6-6 is an output of such computational and storage capacity of the subroutine FIT, FIT4, SMOOT, and others described in this text.

Character Generation

Computer programs for graphical displays frequently contain text and graphics in line drawings, graphs, images, and the like. In fact, some engineering documents consist of 30% character generation. Text generation is most often done on line printers such as the IBM 1403 by using appropriate character sets. Though the text print-

FIGURE 6-6

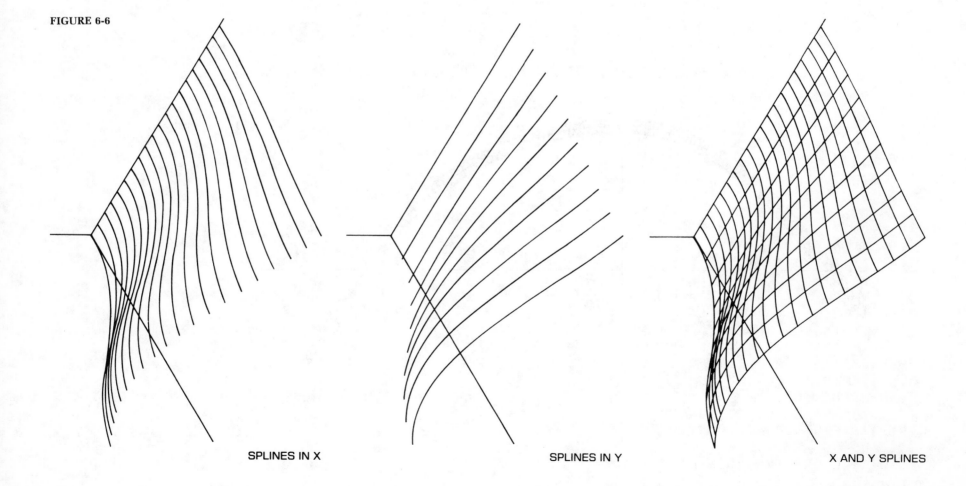

SPLINES IN X   SPLINES IN Y   X AND Y SPLINES

ing is outstanding, the line images are not as good as other types of display hardware. A good blend is the IBM 3800 raster printer, one of many printer-plotters on the market. The next choice is to develop a text capability for digital plotters. A subroutine for text material for output on a digital plotter is listed beginning below and running to page 148. The obvious drawback of this approach is the lack of turn-around time from the command string to the display. In other words, a plotter is an extremely slow way of producing text materials.

This section will describe a means of producing high-speed text with adequate line quality. The advantage is that text and line images are treated together in order to store the entire document digitally and eliminate expense and potential errors.

```
      SUBROUTINE NOTE(X,Y,ITEXT,NC)
      DIMENSION X(1),Y(1)
      DIMENSION NBUF(6),ITG(2),IBUF(13)
      DIMENSION ITEXT(1)
      DIMENSION IT1(2)
      COMMON /PLTCOM/
     &SAME,PREF(2),LDC(2),C(2),RORG(2),CMAT(10,3),LMT(2),
     &XYDOTS(2),SPX,SPY,MIX,NSKP,NBAD,
     &NPLOT,MINX,MAXX,NDX,NDY,LTYPE,LWDTH,DEGRAD,
     &NBITS,NBTM1,NBYTE,NBYM1,NCHAR,NCHM1,MSK(7),IBT(16)
      EQUIVALENCE (C(1),ITG(1))
      EQUIVALENCE (T1,IT1(1))
      DATA IBUF(1)/:40/
      DATA IDASH/:55/
      DATA IDOTT/:56/,NTXT/:60/
      DATA IOV1/'##'/,IOV2/'# '/
      X0=X(1)
      Y0=Y(1)
      IF (X0.EQ.SAME) X0=PREF(1)
      IF (Y0.EQ.SAME) Y0=PREF(2)
C-----EXAMINE 'NC' FOR PROCESSING SPECIFICATIONS
      IF (NC) 200,300,50
   50 ND=NC-1000
      IF (ND.GE.0) GO TO 400
C-----**ALPHANUMERIC TEXT**
      ND=NC
  110 CALL DRAW(X0,Y0,1,0)
```

```
C-----INSERT 'ALPHA TEXT FOLLOWS' CODE INTO DATA STREAM
      I=IBT(9)+ND
      CALL POUT(1,I)
C-----COMPUTE WORD COUNT AND INSERT ALPHA TEXT
      I=(ND+NBYM1)/NBYTE
      IF (ND.NE.NC) GO TO 130
      CALL POUT(I,ITEXT)
      GO TO 150
  130 CALL POUT(I,NBUF)
C-----UPDATE PEN POSITION TO END OF TEXT LINE
  150 X0=X0+FLOAT(ND)*SPX
      WHILE=Y0+FLOAT(ND)*SPY
      CALL DRAW(X0,Y0,1,0)
      RETURN
C-----**SYMBOL PLOTTING**
  200 IDS=CMAT(5,3)
      CALL DRAW(X,Y,1,IDS)
      I=MOD(IDS,10)
      IF (I.NE.0) IDS=IDS-I+9
      J=AND(SHFT(ITEXT(1),8),NCHM1)
      IF (J.EQ.0) J=AND(ITEXT(1),NCHMI)
      I=IBT(8)+J
      ND=-NC
      K=NSKP
      L=1
      DO 250 J=1,ND
      CALL DRAW(X(L),Y(L),1,IDS)
      K=K+1
      IF (K.LT.NSKP) GO TO 250
      CALL POUT(1,I)
      K=0
  250 L=L+MIX
      RETURN
C-----**INTEGER NUMBER VALUE TEXT GENERATION**
  300 T1=ITEXT(1)
      ND=0
      GO TO 500
C-----**REAL NUMBER VALUE TEXT GENERATION**
```

```
C-----(ITEXT IS ACTUALLY FL. PT. NUMBER)
  400 CONTINUE
      IT1(1)=ITEXT(1)
      IT1(2)=ITEXT(2)
C-----*NUMERIC VALUE TO ALPHANUMERIC TEXT*
C-----NRQD IS THE MINIMUM NUMBER OF CHARACTERS REQUIRED
C-----TO GUARANTEE AT LEAST ONE DIGIT TO THE LEFT OF THE REAL OR
C-----IMPLIED DECIMAL POINT.
  500 NRQD=ND+2
C-----K IS THE VALUE I WILL HAVE JUST BEFORE THE FIRST DIGIT TO THE
C-----LEFT OF THE DECIMAL WOULD BE PROCESSED IF IT WERE NOT FOR THE
C-----DECIMAL POINT ITSELF, OR ZERO IF NO DECIMAL POINT IS NEEDED.
      K=0
      IF (ND.NE.0) K=ND+2
      T2=AINT(ABS(T1)*10.0**ND+0.5)
C-----T2 IS NOW A POSITIVE, FLOATING POINT INTEGER, THE DIGITS
C-----OF WHICH REPRESENT THE ORIGINAL NUMBER.
C
C-----IF ALL DIGITS ARE ZERO, PREVENT MINUS SIGN
      IF (T2.EQ.0.0) T1=0.0
C-----ALLOW FOR TEN DIGITS.  NOTE THAT THE LOOP STARTS WITH I .EQ. 2
C-----TO ALLOW FOR THE PAID IN IBUF.
      L=11
C-----ALSO FOR A DECIMAL, IF REQUIRED.
      IF (ND.GT.0) L=L+1
      DO 520 I=2,L
      IF (I.NE.K) GO TO 510
C-----AT THIS POINT, A DECIMAL POINT IS REQUIRED.  FURTHERMORE,
C-----I-2 .EQ. K-2 .EQ. ND DIGITS TO THE RIGHT OF THE DECIMAL HAVE
C-----BEEN PROCESSED, SO THIS IS THE PLACE FOR THE DECIMAL.
      IBUF(I)=IDOTT
      GO TO 520
C-----GENERATE THE NEXT DIGIT (FROM RIGHT TO LEFT).
  510 T3=T2
      T2=AINT(T2/10.0)
      IBUF(I)=IFIX(T3-10.0*T2)+NTXT
  520 IF (T2.EQ.0.0.AND.I.GE.NRQD) GO TO 530
C-----AT THIS POINT, TEN DIGITS HAVE BEEN PROCESSED AND
```

```
C-----MORE ARE YET REQUIRED.  PLOT ### IN PLACE OF THE NUMBER.
      ND=3
      NBUF(1)=IOV1
      NBUF(2)=IOV2
      GO TO 110
C-----THE DIGITS AND DECIMAL POINT ARE NOW IN IBUF
C-----PUT A MINUS SIGN IN IBUF IF REQUIRED.
  530 IF (T1.GE.0.0) GO TO 540
      I=I+1
      IBUF(I)=IDASH
  540 CONTINUE
C-----THE NUMBER IS NOW COMPLETELY ASSEMBLED IN IBUF IN REVERSE
C-----ORDER.  IT IS NOW REVERSED AND PACKED INTO NBUF, TWO CHARACTERS
C-----PER WORD.
      J=1
      DO 550 III=2,I,2
      II=I+2-III
      NBUF(J)=OR(SHFT(IBUF(II),-8),IBUF(II-1))
  550 J=J+1
C-----THERE ARE NOW I-1 DESCRIBABLE CHARACTERS IN NBUF TO BE PLOTTED
      ND=I-1
      GOTO 110
      END
```

Font style.   One of the important aspects of the 3800 is its ability to load new type fonts (character descriptions) into the writable character generator memory. Characters are defined as a series of dots or print points. Output can be printed at 6, 8, or 12 lines per inch, and 10, 12, or 15 characters per inch. The resolution is not symmetric, however; at 8 lines per inch and 12 characters per inch, the character space or box is 15 print points wide and 18 print points high. The character boxes are contiguous, so both the interline spacing (leading) and intercharacter spacing must be included within the 15 × 18 point box. The output page on a printer-plotter is treated as a mapped entity. For a given character box, only characters placed within the uniform array of rows and columns are available.

The upper limit of character codes available on a single page is 255. One font requires 64 positions of character generator memory (12 pitch Gothic). If lowercase and italics or boldface are added, additional character generator storage is required.

Vector-stroked characters.   If the character generation subprogram were modified in order to produce text material on a CRT, a vector-by-vector character could be built at the higher speeds associated with CRTs. A graphics system that incorporates vector-stroked characters is, in effect, an all-points-addressable printer. This system will produce camera-ready copy of high-quality printed text and graphics. The high-resolution printer uses a computer-controlled CRT that is capable of projecting an image of 800 dots per inch. On a CRT these dots are called *pixels* and not printer points.

The printer projects text characters onto film by referencing appropriate fonts, as described earlier. Enhancements to the software allow engineers to send their own raster data to the printer as either fonts or vector-stroked special characters.

TRANSFORMATIONS

A core system for transformations has been proposed by the graphics standards planning committee of the Association for Computing Machinery Special Interest Group for Graphics (SIGGRAPH). The transformation concepts of the core system, described in the documentation containing the standard, are:

1. The separation of input (software) and output (hardware) transformation techniques
2. The standardization, or at least the minimization, of the programming differences for producing transformations on plotters, DVSTs, and CRTs
3. The concept of two coordinate systems—the WORLD coordinate system, in which the display axis is transformed, and the DEVICE coordinate system, in which the picture data is transformed
4. The concept of display file transformation, which contains device coordinate information for shifting, rotation, and revolution
5. The notion of display file–transformed segments, each of which can be independently transformed as a subpicture
6. The special combination of functions used to transform WORLD coordinate data into DEVICE coordinates by invoking a viewing transformation

Because specific transformations vary greatly in their capabilities, and because engineering application requirements can vary so much, the transformations described in this book will be presented in four levels, corresponding to the multilevels proposed in the core standard.

Translation (Shifting)

At the first level the core system recommends that graphic output needs of *translation*, or shifting, (ability to move a picture sideways or up and down) be established with no incremental picture modification, only total picture replacement. Certain types of plotter output and DVST presentations fall into this level. Capabilities provided at this first level include all 2-D and 3-D output primitives and their attributes, viewing transformations, and control functions. Only nonretained picture segments can be used. Neither retained segment nor interactive capabilities are provided. A display program and typical output for this first-level transformation are shown on pages 150–157.

```
USER: RYAN

ENG

******************************************************************************
******************************************************************************


MMMM   M    M   MMM   M    M
M    M M   M  M   M   M    MM   M M
M    M M MM M   M    M MMM M
MMMM      M   MMMMM M M M
M  M     M    M    M M M M
M   M    M    M    MM MM
M    M   M    M    MM   M


MMMMM M   M   MMM
M      MM  M M   M
M      M M M M
MMMM   M M M M
M      M M M M  MM
M      M  MM M   M
MMMMM M    M  MMMM


******************************************************************************
******************************************************************************

LABEL:    PRT001  -FORM       -COPIES   1

SPOOLED:    06/17/82 08:55
STARTED:    06/17/82 08:55, ON: CENP   BY: CEN


     CALL INITT(120)
7685  TEST=0
```

```
      PRINT 8856
8856  FORMAT('BORE ? APPROXIMATELY 1.')
      READ(1,*)BORE
      PRINT 8857
8857  FORMAT('STROKE ? APPROXIMATELY 1.')
      READ(1,*)STROKE
      PRINT 8855
8855  FORMAT('CONNECTING ROD LENGTH ? APPROXIMATELY 1.5 X STROKE.')
      READ(1,*)CRL
      IF(CRL.LT.STROKE)CALL WRONG(TEST)
      IF(TEST.EQ.1)GOTO7685
      PRINT 8858
8858  FORMAT('TEMP OF INCOMING AIR ? IN FAHRENHEIT.')
      READ(1,*)TEMP
      PRINT 8859
8859  FORMAT('PRESSURE OF INCOMING AIR ? AMBIENT IS 14.7 LBS/SQ IN.')
      READ(1,*)PRESS
      PRINT 8860
8860  FORMAT('DECK HEIGHT ? APPROXIMATELY .15 IN.')
      READ(1,*)DECK
      STR=STROKE
      CALL ERASE
      CALL ENG(4.,1.+STR/2.,STR/2.,90.,36,30.,TEMP,PRESS,BORE,DECK,CRL)
C  IT'S A 2-STROKE
      CALL FINITT(0,0)
      CALL EXIT
      END
C************** ENGINE ****************************************************
      SUBROUTINE ENG(X,Y,R,SANG,N,THETA,TEMP,PRESS,BORE,DECK,CRL)
      STROKE=R*2
      X1=X+R
      COMP=(STROKE+DECK)/(DECK)
      SANG=(3.1415927/180.)*SANG
      XX=R*(1.-COS(SANG))
      YY=R*(SIN(SANG))
      IF(YY.EQ.R)CALL FIRE(X1,Y,BORE,R,CRL,DECK)
      DX=X+XX
```

```
      DY=Y+YY
      FY=SQRT((CRL**2)-(XX**2))+DY
      PRESS2=((STROKE+DECK)/((STROKE+DECK)-(YY+R)))*PRESS
C   CALCULATION FOR TEMPERATURE IS WRONG. SHOULD BE USING PERFECT GAS
C   EQUATION. (P*V)/(M*R)=T, WHERE P IS PRESS*144 FOR LBS/SQ FT,
C   V IS ((STROKE-DECK)-(YY+R))*144 FOR SQ FT, R IS 53.3, AND M IS
C   NOT KNOWN.
      TEMP2=((STROKE+DECK)/((STROKE+DECK)-(YY+R)))*TEMP
      CALL TPLOT(X1,Y,3)
      CALL TPLOT(DX,DY,2)
      CALL TPLOT(X1,FY,2)
      CALL PISTON(X1,FY,BORE)
      CALL CASE(X1,Y,BORE,R,CRL,DECK)
      CALL COMPP(COMP)
      CALL PRESSS(PRESS2)
      CALL TEMPP(TEMP2)
      THETA=(3.1415927/180.)*THETA
      CALL HALT
      CALL ERASE
      DO 200 I=1,N
      FEE=SANG+THETA*I
      XX=R*(1.-COS(FEE))
      YY=R*(SIN(FEE))
      IF(YY.EQ.R)CALL FIRE(X1,Y,BORE,R,CRL,DECK)
      DX=X+XX
      DY=Y+YY
      FY=SQRT((CRL**2)-(XX**2))+DY
      PRESS2=((STROKE+DECK)/((STROKE+DECK)-(YY+R)))*PRESS
      TEMP2=((STROKE+DECK)/((STROKE+DECK)-(YY+R)))*TEMP
      CALL TPLOT(X1,Y,3)
      CALL TPLOT(DX,DY,2)
      CALL TPLOT(X1,FY,2)
      CALL PISTON(X1,FY,BORE)
      CALL CASE(X1,Y,BORE,R,CRL,DECK)
      CALL COMPP(COMP)
      CALL PRESSS(PRESS2)
      CALL TEMPP(TEMP2)
```

```
      CALL HALT
200   CALL ERASE
      RETURN
      END
C************ PISTON ***********************************************************
      SUBROUTINE PISTON(A,B,BORE)
      CALL TCIR(A-.1*BORE,B,.1*BORE,0.,36,10.)
      CALL TPLOT(A-.5*BORE,B-.5*BORE,3)
      CALL TPLOT(A-.5*BORE,B+.5*BORE,2)
      CALL TPLOT(A+.5*BORE,B+.5*BORE,2)
      CALL TPLOT(A+.5*BORE,B-.5*BORE,2)
      CALL TPLOT(A-.5*BORE,B-.5*BORE,2)
      CALL TPLOT(A-.5*BORE,B+.25*BORE,3)
      CALL TPLOT(A+.5*BORE,B+.25*BORE,2)
      CALL TPLOT(A-.5*BORE,B+.35*BORE,3)
      CALL TPLOT(A+.5*BORE,B+.35*BORE,2)
      CALL TPLOT(A-.5*BORE,B+.45*BORE,3)
      CALL TPLOT(A+.5*BORE,B+.45*BORE,2)
      RETURN
      END
C************ CASE ************************************************************
      SUBROUTINE CASE(X1,Y,BORE,R,CRL,DECK)
      CALL TPLOT(X1-.5*BORE,Y-R+CRL-.6*BORE,3)
      CALL TPLOT(X1-.5*BORE,Y+R+CRL+.5*BORE+DECK,2)
      CALL TPLOT(X1+.5*BORE,Y+R+CRL+.5*BORE+DECK,2)
      CALL TPLOT(X1+.5*BORE,Y-R+CRL-.6*BORE,2)
      RC=SQRT(((-R+CRL-.6*BORE)**2)+((.5*BORE)**2))
      X=.5*BORE/RC
      ANG=(180./3.1415927)*ATAN2(1-X*X,X)
      ANG1=180.-ANG
      CALL TCIR(X1-RC,Y,RC,ANG1,22,(180.+2.*ANG)/20.)
      RETURN
      END
C************ COMPRESSION RATIO ***********************************************
      SUBROUTINE COMPP(COMP)
      CALL MOVABS(20,10)
      CALL ANMODE
```

```
       PRINT 2011,COMP
2011   FORMAT('THE COMPRESSION RATIO IS ',F5.2)
       RETURN
       END
C************ TEMP ***********************************************************
       SUBROUTINE TEMPP(TEMP2)
       CALL MOVABS(20,54)
       CALL ANMODE
       PRINT 1301,TEMP2
1301   FORMAT('TEMPERATURE IS NOW  ',F7.2,  '  DEGREES F.')
       RETURN
       END
C************ PRESSURE *******************************************************
       SUBROUTINE PRESSS(PRESS2)
       CALL MOVABS(20,98)
       CALL ANMODE
       PRINT 1401,PRESS2
1401   FORMAT('PRESSURE IS NOW    ',F6.2,'  LBS/SQ IN.')
       RETURN
       END
C************ FIRE ***********************************************************
       SUBROUTINE FIRE(X1,Y,BORE,R,CRL,DECK)
       CALL TPLOT(X1,Y+R+CRL+.5*BORE+DECK,3)
       CALL TPLOT(X1-DECK,Y+R+CRL+.5*BORE,2)
       CALL TPLOT(X1,Y+R+CRL+.5*BORE+DECK,3)
       CALL TPLOT(X1,Y+R+CRL+.5*BORE,2)
       CALL TPLOT(X1,Y+R+CRL+.5*BORE+DECK,3)
       CALL TPLOT(X1+DECK,Y+R+CRL+.5*BORE,2)
       CALL MOVABS(20,142)
       CALL ANMODE
       PRINT 1104
1104   FORMAT('SPARK PLUG FIRES AT TDC.')
       RETURN
       END
C************ HALT ***********************************************************
       SUBROUTINE HALT
       CALL MOVABS(20,230)
```

```
        CALL ANMODE
        PRINT 1332
1332    FORMAT('ENTER ANY INTEGER'/' TO CONTINUE.')
        READ(1,*)NOTHIN
        RETURN
        END
C************** TPLOT ***********************************************************
        SUBROUTINE TPLOT(XPAGE,YPAGE,IPEN)
        IX=XPAGE*128
        IY=YPAGE*128
        IF(IPEN.EQ.3)CALL MOVABS(IX,IY)
        IF(IPEN.EQ.2)CALL DRWABS(IX,IY)
        IF(IPEN.EQ.-3)CALL MOVREL(IX,IY)
        IF(IPEN.EQ.-2)CALL DRWREL(IX,IY)
        RETURN
        END
C*********** TCIR **************************************************************
        SUBROUTINE TCIR(Q,W,RR,S,N,T)
C   SEE HOW THE VARIABLES AT THE END ARE *NOT* REINITIALIZED TO ZERO.
        SANG=(3.1415927/180.)*S
        XXX=RR*(1.-COS(SANG-T*3.1415927/180.))
        YYY=RR*(SIN(SANG-T*3.1415927/180.))
        DXX=Q+XXX
        DYY=W+YYY
        CALL TPLOT(DXX,DYY,3)
        THETA=(3.1415927/180.)*T
        DO 260 I=1,N
        FEE=SANG+THETA*(I-1)
        XXX=RR*(1.-COS(FEE))
        YYY=RR*(SIN(FEE))
        DXX=Q+XXX
        DYY=W+YYY
        CALL TPLOT(DXX,DYY,2)
260     CONTINUE
        RETURN
        END
```

```
C************** WRONG *********************************************************
      SUBROUTINE WRONG(TEST)
      TEST=1
      PRINT 2134
2134 FORMAT('THE CONNECTING ROD LENGTH IS SHORTER THAN THE STROKE'.)
      RETURN
      END
```

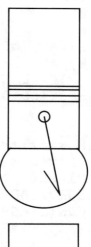

ENTER ANY INTEGER
TO CONTINUE.

PRESSURE IS NOW   15.93 LBS/SQ IN.
TEMPERATURE IS NOW   74.33 DEGREES F.
THE COMPRESSION RATIO IS 7.67

ENTER ANY INTEGER
TO CONTINUE.

PRESSURE IS NOW   26.54 LBS/SQ IN.
TEMPERATURE IS NOW   123.85 DEGREES F.
THE COMPRESSION RATIO IS 7.67

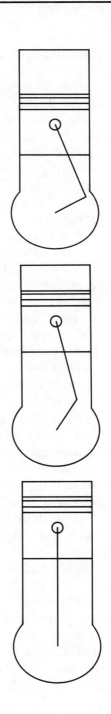

ENTER ANY INTEGER
TO CONTINUE.

PRESSURE IS NOW   43.13 LBS/SQ IN.
TEMPERATURE IS NOW   201.25 DEGREES F.
THE COMPRESSION RATIO IS 7.67

ENTER ANY INTEGER
TO CONTINUE.

PRESSURE IS NOW   79.50 LBS/SQ IN.
TEMPERATURE IS NOW   370.99 DEGREES F.
THE COMPRESSION RATIO IS 7.67

ENTER ANY INTEGER
TO CONTINUE.

SPARK PLUG FIRES AT TDC.
PRESSURE IS NOW   115.00 LBS/SQ IN.
TEMPERATURE IS NOW   536.67 DEGREES F.
THE COMPRESSION RATIO IS 7.67

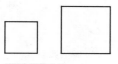

FIGURE 6-7

FIGURE 6-8

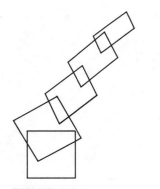

FIGURE 6-9

Scaling

Level 2 provides additional capabilities over level 1 that allow incremental picture sizing called *scaling*. In addition, retained segments can be created, deleted, or renamed. The visibility/invisibility (IPEN) are supported. Interactive capabilities and advanced level transformation are not supported.

To help understand both level 1 and 2 transformation, let's consider the data-base listing in Table 6-1.

The data-base listing on the preceding pages displays a square image two units by two units on a plotter or DVST. The image represents a plane surface located at 3.750 units along the Z axis. In order to translate (move) this image along the X axis of the display device, the entire list under the X column must have an amount added (+) or subtracted (−). This amount must be a constant. If + is used, the image will be replotted to the right of the last image displayed; if a − constant is used, then a replotted image will appear to the left of the last displayed image. The two-unit square can also be moved up or down the plotter surface or DVST screen by adding or subtracting from the Y column of the data-base listing. Adding or subtracting constants from both the X and Y data listing gives combinations of translation, with the following results:

1. Up and to the right
2. Up and to the left
3. Down and to the left
4. Down and to the right

Translation along the Z axis with a plane surface causes no movement as far as the display ability.

TABLE 6-1
Data-Base Listing

X	Y	Z	IPEN
10.250	4.375	3.750	3
10.250	6.375	3.750	2
12.250	6.375	3.750	2
12.250	4.375	3.750	2
10.250	4.375	3.750	2

If scaling is desired, then columns are multiplied or divided by constants to change their display sizes. If both X and Y are transformed, then the data base is FACTORED, as shown in Figure 6-7. If only X and Y is scaled, then the aspect ratio is changed as shown in Figure 6-8.

Rotation

At level 3 the core system provides the detectability of the Z axis and interactive capabilities in addition to the capabilities provided by levels 1 and 2. Again using the data-base listing as an example, a *rotation* of the two-unit square can be made by using the X and Y columns and application of the sine and cosine computer functions. In this case the square can be made to rotate about any desired axis. Figure 6-9 is a display where all three levels have been employed. Here rotation is used with scaling and shifting (translation) to produce the sense of motion.

Revolution

At level 4 the core system supports rotation of display axis as well as images with respect to the axis. This concept is called *revolution*. In order to display this concept, a refresh, dual graphics processor is required. Plotter output is not possible, nor is a DVST or CRT screen where the Z axis is assumed to be a point in the center of the screen with the axis running in and out of the screen. Stereo plotting is often used to demonstrate revolution on the lower-order CRTs. Figure 6-10 is a stereo plot. In order to see revolution, the viewer wears a special pair of viewing glasses that place the objects together. When the CRT moves the stereo pairs in animation, the viewer senses the concept of revolution.

Combination

Machover (1977) gives an up-to-date description of the various graphics devices and their capabilities when they are used in combination. The author points out that the majority of output equipment used in computer programming for graphical displays is CRTs, but with great diversity among them. Imaging techniques may be raster scan or random beam drive (calligraphic). The random beam may be a regenerative type or a storage device. The resolution of graphics hardware types varies greatly from one to another. A device may be capable of drawing only alphanumeric and special characters, or it may have an addressability and resolution capability to create images of photographic quality.

Devices that have the ability to produce combination transformations have function generators built in as part of the hardware rather than having software produce the functions. The aim of this book is to have the software do as much as possible to keep the cost of the hardware to a minimum, but it is good to understand how function generators work. A simple example is a circle generator. We have already studied how the subroutine CIRCLE can display this function. A hardware function for a circle requires only X and Y coordinate data and a radius for a wired-in circle generator to position and move the beam of electrons on the face of the CRT. Without the generator, CALL CIRCLE will calculate the coordinates of many straight-line segments to display the circle.

FIGURE 6-10

3-D PICTURE GRAPHICS

This section describes a picture-building method that consists of high-level applications, building tools, and a relational data base. The method is designed for a graphics programmer to interactively create and modify graphics applications that are device-independent. Data within the data base are self-describing (as shown in the case of the square earlier); therefore, if the programmer wishes only to display pictures, no application engineering programs need to be written. This method is significant because of its general usefulness and its high level of user interface.

The main elements of a 3-D picture system are:

1. Data base for world picture graphics (wireframe)
2. Session supervision (surface identification)
3. Special graphics effects (solid surface reflection)

TABLE 6-2
Data-Base Listing

PTS	X	Y	Z
1	0.0	0.0	0.0
2	1.0	0.0	0.0
3	1.0	1.0	0.0
4	0.0	1.0	0.0
5	0.0	0.0	1.0
6	1.0	0.0	1.0
7	1.0	1.0	1.0
8	0.0	1.0	1.0

IPEN = 1,2,3,4,1,5,6,7,8,5,−2,6,−3,7,−4,8

TABLE 6-3
Data-Base Listing

PTS	X	Y	Z	IFLAG
1	0.0	0.0	0.0	3
2	1.0	0.0	0.0	2
3	1.0	1.0	0.0	2
4	0.0	1.0	0.0	2
5	0.0	0.0	1.0	3
6	1.0	0.0	1.0	2
7	1.0	1.0	1.0	2
8	0.0	1.0	1.0	2

Wireframe

Table 6-2 illustrates the wireframe method of describing and storing line (wires) information about a mechanical part in a data base. Assuming an engineering requirement to design a part that can be represented by three orthogonal projections, the system might allow construction of three unrelated views that contain a single line. The programming result is a data structure that is relatively simple to design and manage, one that is used in many 2-D/3-D engineering drawing systems.

If plotted, the data base listing would result in a one-unit cube pictured in Figure 6-11. Each of the wireframe 3-D points is listed under PTS. The IPEN list gives the order of connection with a − sign for pen up. If −1,2,3,4,1,5,6,7,8,5 were displayed as shown above, only a portion of the wireframe would be reproduced.

The disadvantage here is that a later change in a line in one view does not automatically change the other representations of that line. The designer has to change the other views as well. A way to overcome this apparent disadvantage is to add a fourth column to the PTS array. Now each surface of the object above is a 4 × 4 array containing a visibility flag shown in Table 6-3.

The IFLAG coding means that display points labeled 2 have a visible line or wire attaching them, and a code of 3 means that an invisible wire should be displayed when making a three-view orthographic drawing, as shown in Figure 6-12. Now the data base contains only one interpretation of any line in 3-D space. To make an engineering drawing, the user requests multiple views of the wireframe model to be projected on a single viewing surface.

The IFLAG concept also introduces another level of programming for the data-base construction. A line in the 2-D representation can logically be connected to other lines that are part of the same view. In addition, it provides an opportunity where a line in the 3-D model can be

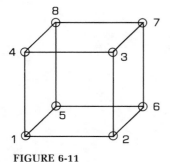

FIGURE 6-11

connected to other lines in the same surface, and therefore a way to sort surfaces that can be logically connected if they belong to the same part.

The degree of connectivity the graphics programmer chooses affects the complexity of the final data-base design and determines the kinds of operator or tool that can be created for the engineering drawing on the screen. The key consideration in the design of a data base is the degree of data change to be allowed or required at the screen. If an engineering application calls only for viewing a complex object in different views—perhaps even transformations in real time—the data-base design probably does not have to be complex and have many relationships. If, on the other hand, the graphics programmer expects to be able to change the design of the object on the screen and requires sophisticated transformations for making changes, the data base will have to be expanded with IFLAG type columns.

(line, for example), the IFLAG is changed from a 2 to a 3 or from a 3 to a 2. This technique allows the graphics programmer to identify each plane surface.

As with all graphics terminal environments, a session supervisor also handles other functions called *graphics support*. A supervisor is responsible for collecting from the graphics programmer names of the applications to be run, with the named data files to be used, and for aiding in application transition. The subsystem can also be used for debugging a program. Writing graphics support software routines is one of the richest and most varied areas of modern engineering graphics because it embraces subsystems, languages, and algorithms (outlined in Chapter 2). It is the progress in surface identification that has allowed the completion of the ACM-SIGGRAPH Standard on Computer Graphics. There are now hardware-oriented software systems commercially available for handling simple surface displays and advanced graphic displays.

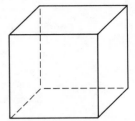

FIGURE 6-12

Surface Identification

A general computer program or graphics subsystem keeps track of the current contents of the screen so the data-base design can be updated. An example of updating is indicating which sections of data base represent plane surfaces. In our example data-base listing, a quad element, or four-sided surface, has been used. Storing each surface under a storage name containing that section of data base is usually handled by a pointing device, such as a light pen and CRT. When the light pen is placed over the element in question

Solid Identification

Engineering applications that require solid identification use additional techniques to create the illusion of reality. The graphics programmer is concerned about creating the illusion of solid objects, not wireframes. Several techniques pioneered by the Evans and Sutherland Company have given the graphics programmer a method of shading each of the wireframe surfaces. The shading can be enhanced for shadows, use of multiple light sources, colors of many hues, and tones and texture. Many Evans and Sutherland papers have been written on these subjects, all designed to be used on the E&S Picture System II. Examples of these are hidden-line and hidden-surface elimination, illusion of solids, and texture, tone, and shadows.

The hidden-line problem has been addressed by every writer interested in computer graphics. In theory, each solution is written algorithmically so that a software routine can determine the data to be displayed, since some data points, lines, or surfaces lie behind another. For example, Newman and Sproull's (1973) classic text on the principles of computer graphics presents ten different techniques of hidden-line or hidden-surface elimination. The authors concluded that sorting is at the heart of the hidden-feature problem. In engineering-oriented computer graphics hidden lines are not eliminated. The data base contains an IFLAG column for the display of dashed lines, or the shading of plane surfaces covers up the unwanted hidden lines. Solid identification is more important in computer-aided design and manufacturing than graphics for most engineers.

When the graphics programmer fills in or shades the various plane surfaces of a wireframe object with color or shades of gray, the result is the illusion of solidity, as shown in Figure 6-13.

These types of output follow the plane surface boundaries that define the solid's shape and attempt to fill in the plane with shades of gray, while keeping separate shapes or areas distinct.

Most real objects have some texture. To create a sense of reality on the computer graphics display screen, subprograms have been written to add texture to displays.

Using the simple pixel shading system shown in Figure 6-13, the graphics programmer can assign texture to any part of the plane surface that represents the solid object. Data bases can be assigned a column where 0 through 4 for texture can be displayed with each pixel. Of course, the time to display each solid will be increased from three to seven times with this technique.

Reflection of Light from a Solid

Subprograms have also been written using the simple concept shown above to represent light reflections off objects or to create shading. For these types of application the pixel symbol is expanded so that less background is visible, as shown in Figure 6-14.

This kind of work, based on experimental measurement of light reflecting from real objects, is used to differentiate between light reflections from smooth or textured surfaces. In all cases objects are broken into patches (pixels), and light intensity is calculated rather than assigned for each datum in the data base. The patterns can be mathematically defined, or they may come from scanned (digitized) black-and-white photos.

Whenever light is present, a shadow is cast. Shadows for graphical displays are also calcu-

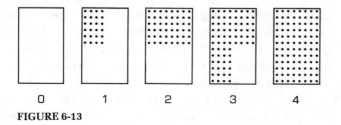

0   1   2   3   4

FIGURE 6-13

FIGURE 6-14

lated by use of simple descriptive geometry procedures. Shadow creation, which aids in depth perception, is used to model realistic images. It may also be important to an understanding of spatial relationships or whether objects are invisible because of shadows.

REVIEW PROBLEMS

1. List the basic graphic entities used in all programming software routines.

ANSWER

1. Display point (visible dot image)
2. Display line (draw visible line image)
3. Display space (move invisible line image)
4. Plane (three or more visible lines)
5. Wireform (3-D object of three or more planes)

2. List the primitive elements and sketch their shapes.

ANSWER

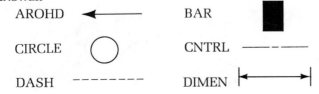

AROHD   BAR

CIRCLE   CNTRL

DASH   DIMEN

ELIPS   FIT

FLINE   GRID

LINE   NUMBER 0987654321

POINT   POLY

PLOT   RECT

SYMBOL NOTES   SPLINE

3. Prepare a list of uses for 2-D geometric constructions.

ANSWER

1. Management information
2. Scientific graphics
3. Command and control
4. Image processing
5. Real-time image generation
6. Electrical and mechanical diagrams

4. Prepare a template drawing using the FP program (Chapter 5) as shown in Figure 6-15.

5. Use the graphic entities POINT and LINE to create a simple wireform cube as shown in Figure 6-11.

6. Use the graphic entities LINE and PLANE to create the modified cube shown in Figure 6-16.

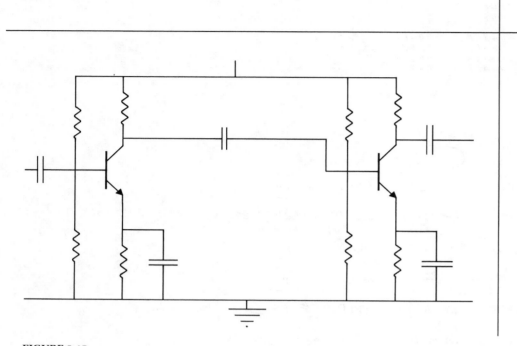

FIGURE 6-15

7. Use the primitive element RECT to create the simple diagram shown in Figure 6-17.

8. Use the primitive element CIRCLE to create the simple picture shown in Figure 6-18.

9. Use the primitive element ELPSE to create the object shown in Figure 6-19.

10. Use the primitive element POLY to create the subpicture shown in Figure 6-20.

11. Use the primitive element FIT to display the surface shown in Figure 6-21.

12. Use the character generator NOTE to enter the following labels:

DETAIL DRAWING
EQUIPMENT ARRANGEMENT
PROFILE MILLING
WIRING DIAGRAM
MATERIALS LIST
PARTS LIST
POCKET FLOOR ROUGHING
SLANT FLOOR KELLERING
NC EXAMPLE

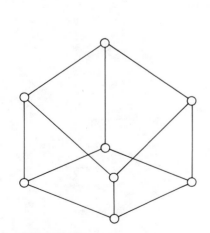

FIGURE 6-16

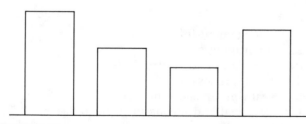

FIGURE 6-17

FIGURE 6-19

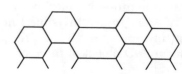

FIGURE 6-20

FIGURE 6-21

13. Use the primitive CIRCLE and the transformation known as "shifting" as shown in Figure 6-22.

14. Use the primitive ELIPS and the transformation known as "scaling and Shifting" as shown in Figure 6-23.

15. Use the primitive RECT and the transformation known as "rotation" as shown in Figure 6-24.

16. List the main ingredients in a 3-D picture system.

ANSWER

1. Data base for world and picture graphics (wire-frame)
2. Session supervision (surface identification)
3. Special graphics effects (solid surface reflection.

17. Enter the data base necessary to display the objects shown in Figure 6-25.

18. Write the list of pen connections called IPEN's for object A in Figure 6-25.

19. Write the list of pen connections called IFLAG's for object B in Figure 6-25.

20. Indicate a shaded surface for object C in Figure 6-25 to illustrate an illusion of solidarity.

ANSWER

FIGURE 6-22

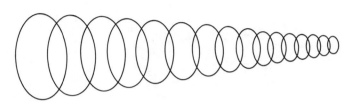

FIGURE 6-23

FIGURE 6-24

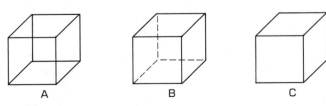

FIGURE 6-25

7

USING HARDWARE AND SOFTWARE SUCCESSFULLY

This chapter was written for graphics programmers. A graphics programmer must have knowledge of both software (commands to a graphics system) and hardware (equipment that makes up the graphics system). As we saw in Chapter 1, most architectural and engineering techniques lack an effective coupling between the human-generated commands and the machine responses. In Chapters 1–6 we looked at a graphics system approach to such a coupling. We can now look in more detail at the network concept on which the system is based.

Figure 7-1a shows the *star network* discussed in earlier chapters. It follows the hierachical system of graphical workstation satellites, which control peripherals such as digital plotters (Fig-ure 7-16). This type of hardware/software system does not force the draftsperson or other user to change thinking, language, or time-response habits. Engineers can use the network as a single workstation (Figure 7-2a) to test design ideas, or a drafting department can use the workstation in mass (Figure 7-2b).

HARDWARE ARCHITECTURE

The term *hardware architecture* refers to both the way individual pieces of equipment are assembled and the way these pieces are connected to form a graphics network.

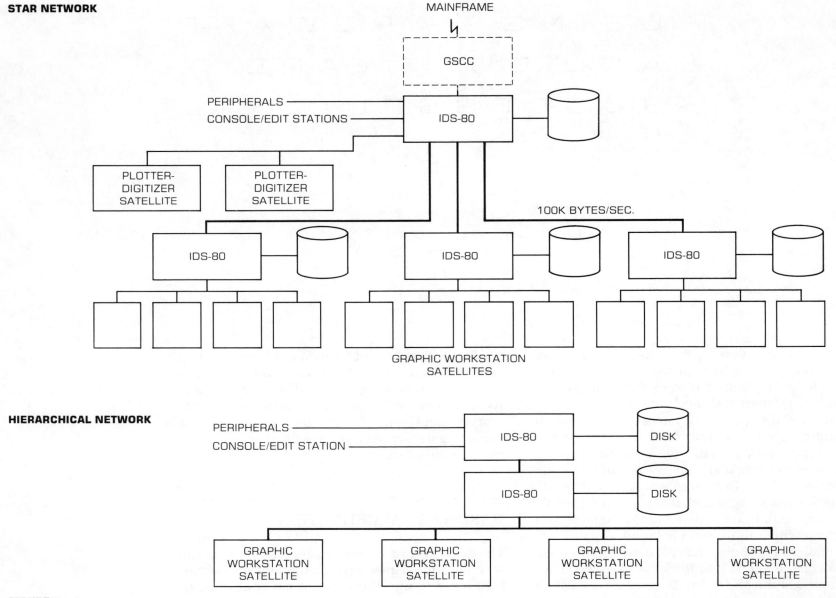

FIGURE 7-1
Graphics system network (courtesy of Gerber Instrument Co.).

(a)

(b)

FIGURE 7-2
Hardware available for a graphics network (courtesy of Gerber Instrument Co.).

Network Architecture

An example of individual workstation architecture is diagrammed in Figure 7-3. It consists of:

1. Connection line to processor (main computer)
2. The local workstation processor, which holds the display file
3. A second (dual) processor, which contains the character generator
4. The vector generator and display screen

Connection to main processor. In Chapter 5 we discussed connection to one of three mainline computers and pointed out that many other types of processor exist. The first three figures for this

GRAPHIC WORKSTATION SATELLITE
Display Output Architecture

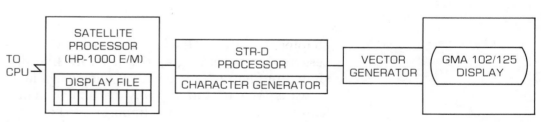

FIGURE 7-3
Graphic workstation architecture

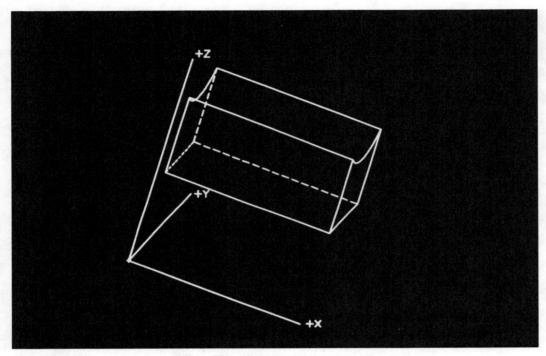

FIGURE 7-4
Display of basic entities.

chapter illustrate Hewlett Packard (HP) processors. Moreover, a graphics network like that shown in Figure 7-1 is only one choice available to users. When studying any particular manufacturer's architecture, it is important to be aware of the original equipment manufacturer (OEM). The examples used so far in this chapter are typical of all manufacturers of graphics system in that OEM hardware is common. In Figure 7-2a, for example, the users are operating a keyboard manufactured by the supplier (Gerber), and the display screen is OEM Tektronix. In Figure 7-2b the local processor is OEM HP, and the hard-copy

unit is OEM Tektronix. Regardless of the main processor at the user's location, graphic systems of several more manufacturers may be attached. Study the operations manuals for your particular system for hardware architecture diagrams and data.

Local processors.   Processors that appear at the workstation, such as those shown in Figure 7-2b, are designed to handle the display file, character and vector generators, and display screen. Keep in mind, however, that this is a general discussion of *all local processors*, not just the one pictured in Figure 7-2b.

Data ultimately placed in a local processor must originate in the memory of the main processor or computer controlling the network. In earlier chapters we called the computer-based description of the data to be displayed a *data base*. As this data base may be vastly different in form from the display file that is generated, a local processor is required. As we learned in Chapter 4, data bases may be highly structured, requiring a complex program to weave through them, or they may be very straightforward. The data base contains the coordinates of points in the structure to be displayed, along with instructions for interpreting those points. There may also be pointers, substructure names, and other nongraphic information.

As explained in Chapter 6, points are the basic geometric entities in the data base, as shown in Figure 7-4. There are three ways to specify the position of a point. The most common is simply to state its absolute coordinates. A second way, called *relative coordinates*, states the displacement required to get to a point from the previous point. The position of a point may also be indicated in relation to a previously set origin. This variation of relative coordinates is called *origin offset*. In a table of points different codes are used to distinguish among absolute, relative, and origin offset. Graphics (local processor) systems are often designed to understand codes for several common sequences of basic instructions—for example, "move, draw, move, draw . . ."—so that large tables of points can be processed based on a single prespecified code. Such sequences handled by local processors can be very useful in eliminating overhead costs that would otherwise be required for each new type of command code.

If a structured program is to be displayed by a local process, it is most efficiently defined by two-dimensional data. In this case, called *CUPID1* in other chapters, it is common to supply the cartesian X–Y coordinates for each point in the structured program, and then perhaps a single Z coordinate that applies to all the points. If, however, the structured program is nonplanar, it must be defined as three-dimensional data, where a coordinate triple of the form is given for each point that is displayed (see Figure 7-5). CUPID (commonly used programming for image displays) uses a full computer word for each coordinate of each point. In a 16-bit word processor the largest expressable positive number is 32767. This is sufficient for most applications. If the need ever arises for larger numbers, the local processor uses an alternative means of expressing data called *homogeneous coordinates*.

The second processor.

The data base is seldom identical to the display file that is used in the local processor. The data base represents a scene, or collection of structured steps, whereas the display file represents some view of that scene. To

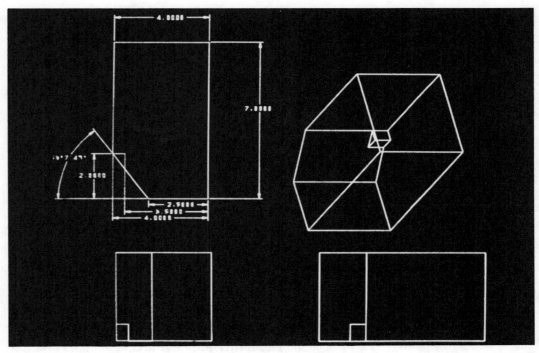

FIGURE 7-5
Display of non-planar CIPID 1 data base from local processing.

create a display file, the data base usually must undergo some transformation; it may need to be changed in size, position, or orientation; it may have to be put in perspective as seen from a given viewpoint; or parts of it may need to be removed to keep the scene within a given display area. In Chapter 6 all of these steps were expressed mathematically and implemented in software. Such techniques are relatively slow. With a second processor they can be done in hardware. Though a second processor is less flexible, it is much faster. As many of the steps involved in structured programming are invariant from application to application, implementing them in special-purpose hardware can be very worthwhile. Any calculations unique to a given application can still be performed in software.

The second processor has three main functions:

1. Character generation
2. Vector generation
3. Display screen conversions

Character generation. Almost all graphics applications call for the presentation of alphanumerics on the screen at various times. It is possible to define character shapes in the data base like other picture elements. Later we will explain how text can be rotated, clipped, and otherwise manipulated. Another method for handling text properties is by generating the actual strokes of the characters just prior to drawing them on the screen. The hardware device that accepts character codes and produces the strokes is called a *character generator*. Character generators generally provide flexibility in the size, shape, and orientation of the characters they produce. To display a string of characters using the hardware approach, a display program must first stipulate character size, shape, and orientation. The program then positions the beam where the string is to begin and inserts a set of packed character codes, called a *text string*. The character generator then interprets the string, looks up the set of strokes associated with each code, sizes and orients the strokes properly, and displays the characters on the screen.

The vector generator and display screen. The vector generator is used to read the data base pro-

vided from the local processor and move the electron beam between the two points. Vector generators can be made to display lines in a choice of modes and textures, such as blinking, solid, dashed, or dotted. Vector generators can also service more than one type of display screen at a time, such as the CRT and DVST.

In some graphic applications the data base is to be displayed in its entirety by the vector generator. Often, however, only a portion of the data base is to be sent to the screen. The region containing the portion of the data base to be seen is called a *window* (see Chapter 2). Determining what parts of the data are within the window and what parts are not is a hardware function. In fact, in software this determination is so time consuming that it jeopardizes the formation of the display screen.

Graphics systems like those pictured in this chapter address the windowing problem by performing a visibility check in hardware after the transformation stage and then displaying only these lines on the screen. One type of windowing, called *clipping*, compares all lines with the boundaries of a program-specified window. Lines or portions of lines outside the window are eliminated, and only visible lines are passed to the screen.

Another approach to windowing, called *scissoring*, makes available a screen coordinate drawing space somewhat larger than the screen itself and then intensifies only those lines actually on the screen. Scissoring is easier and less time consuming to use than clipping. However, scissoring permits an effective drawing area only slightly larger than the screen, as opposed to the much larger drawing area permitted by clipping.

Coordinate data remaining after the clipping

or scissoring processes, which may be of any size and at any position in the data-base definition space, should be properly scaled (mapped) so that they fill some prespecified area on the screen, known as the *viewport*. How is the viewport different from a window? A window exists as a frame around the data; a viewport exists as part or all of the screen area. An advantage of program-specified viewports is that several may be assigned in the same program, each receiving different data. This technique proves convenient for many purposes in graphics, such as simultaneously showing different views of an object, as depicted in Figure 7-5.

User Workstation Architecture

So far we have looked at network architecture, including the hardware located at each satellite workstation. A user's workstation is slightly different from a network workstation. Up to four individual display screen output and input work areas may be attached to each satellite workstation, as shown in Figure 7-1. Figure 7-6 illustrates a single-user workstation terminal. Though this particular workstation is unique to its manufacturer, it does contain many of the universal hardware items:

1. DVST display screen
2. ASCII keyboard
3. Function buttons
4. Menu bar
5. Mechanical crosshairs control

DVST display screen. The display screen pictured in Figure 7-6 is a direct-view storage tube

FIGURE 7-6
Individual workstation terminal (courtesy of Gerber Instrument Co.).

with write-thru capability. A refresh buffer provides write-thru portions from the vector generator, which allows the write-thru and DVST update rates to differ. Although a refresh rate of at least 30 frames per second is required for CRTs to avoid flicker, an update rate of 10–20 frames per second is adequate to provide write-thru. In a screen equipped with a refresh buffer, each frame can be shown two, three, or more times while the next frame is being computed by the second processor. Data elements in a refresh buffer are referred to as elements of a *transferred display file*. Frames stored in this buffer may be read out and used to refresh the write-thru any number of times before a DVST frame is created. For example, new frames may be created 20 times each second while the static (DVST) picture is presented. Thus, the presence of a refresh buffer allows both static and refresh update to proceed at their respective rates, limiting the amount of data that can be displayed and the complexity of the engineering drawing parts that can be processed.

The advantage of this type of display screen is that it can display smoothly changing drawing parts. Lines drawn on the write-thru portion of a DVST do not move, of course, but the illusion of motion is imparted by continual redrawing of the engineering drawing part with lines at slightly different positions each time, or each frame. The eye blends this sequence of frames together into a dynamic part because the individual frames are not left on the storage portion of the DVST. The rate at which the write-thru frames can be displayed is known as the *update rate*, in contrast to the *refresh rate* for a CRT screen.

In many engineering graphics applications, only a portion of a drawing changes dynamically; therefore, it should be possible to update (place in write-thru mode) that portion of the drawing. To enable this, the display file must be created as a series of segments. Then, when only a part of a drawing is to be changed, its segment is "opened" in a free area of the buffer, and the new data are output. When the creation of the write-thru segment is completed, the segment is "closed" and added to the data, which are being

updated as the "old" segment is deleted. This allows use of the buffer in a *double-buffered* mode without requiring the buffer to be divided in half. The segmentation method must also preserve the order of segments, or else the amount of time between updates of a given segment will vary, producing noticeable variations in the intensity of write-thru lines as compared with storage lines. A common complaint of users is the intensity difference between storage and write-thru line images.

ASCII keyboard. Sophisticated graphics applications often require that the user be able to change the form or content of the engineering drawing. As we have seen, input devices for engineering graphics interaction include light pens, function switches, control dials, joysticks, trackballs, and data tablets. The key to using each of these input devices is the ASCII keyboard, illustrated in Figure 7-7. In Figure 7-7a the operator is keying in short message strings to the graphics system. Notice that the keyboard has two additional sets of keys both right and left of the keyboard. These are programmable function buttons, described in the next section. Directly above the keyboard is a menu area. The large white strip contains printed help commands necessary for operating the graphics system (see Chapter 4). Directly above the white strip is a darker, black-faced menu bar where messages are returned to the user. A low-intensity red-light character form is used to reduce eyestrain.

Function buttons. Two types of function button are available. *Function switches,* whose polarity

FIGURE 7-7
ASCII Keyboard.

can be read, are located to the left of the ASCII keyboard (Figure 7-7b). Each button can be assigned a meaning unique to the program. Often associated with each button is a light that may be programmably turned off and on to provide operator feedback as to the polarity of the button or switch. More common types of function buttons are shown to the right of the keyboard and in Figure 7-8. When the operator presses the button marked *line parallel to line*, a hardware function aligns the input parallel to another displayed line on the screen. The buttons to the left are software-dependent; the buttons to the right are hardware-dependent.

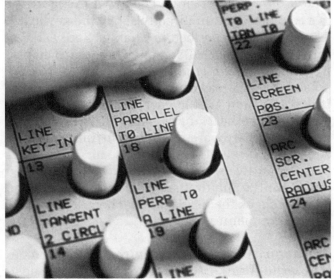

FIGURE 7-8
Function buttons.

FIGURE 7-9
Menu area.

FIGURE 7-10
Use of the mechanical cursor.

Menu bar.   The menu area shown in Figure 7-9 is a two-part section directly above the keyboard. The menu bar described in Chapter 1 appeared at the bottom of the CRT screen, whereas in Chapter 5 it appeared in the right-hand portion of the CRT screen. Menu areas can appear almost anywhere it is convenient for the user. In the hardware example shown here, there is no CRT, so the menu must be a hardware-related item rather than a software presentation like those in Chapters 1 and 5. Hardware menu areas are more detailed and useful to the draftsperson using the system. Always check the user's manual before taking advantage of menu items.

Mechanical crosshairs control.   DVSTs contain write-thru cursors (crosshairs) for the positioning of input or output instructions, data, or drawing parts. The cursor must be movable on the screen. Typical devices are thumbwheels, a joystick, or the hardware innovation shown in Figure 7-10. The mechanical cursor is extremely useful and faster than either the thumbwheels or the joystick for positioning the graphics cursor.

SOFTWARE ARCHITECTURE

The term *software architecture* refers to the way the software is assembled in terms of both individual lines of coding and the placement of these lines in a structured program. This section presents software assembly hints for improving the performance of graphical routines. Some of these hints are merely reminders of good coding practice; others take advantage of implementation techniques shown in Chapter 4. All offer some speed-up in graphics program execution. The areas of concern are:

1. DO loops
2. statement numbers
3. Multidimensioned arrays
4. Processor sequences
5. Function calls and subroutines
6. IF statements
7. I/O and statement sequence

DO statements. DO loops or statements were introduced in Chapter 1 and have been used in almost every chapter of this book. Correct architecture removes the invariant expressions from DO loops. For example:

```
DO 10 I = 1,20
A = 2.79
    .
    .
    .
10 CONTINUE
```

should be changed to:

```
A = 2.79
DO 10 I = 1,20
    .
    .
    .
10 ........... (WHERE ............ IS ANY EXECUTABLE STATEMENT)
```

If no executable statements appears at the end of the DO loop, then a CONTINUE may be used to close the loop. *Never leave a loop unclosed.* Correct architecture also optimizes unnecessary subscript calculations. Study the two choices below.

```
        SUM = 0
        DO 11 I = 1,50
11      SUM = SUM + ARRAY(I)
        ARRAY(N) = ARRAY(N) + SUM
```
Correct Architecture

The source code on the left is more efficient than the one on the right.

```
      DO 11 I = 1,50
11      ARRAY(N) = ARRAY(N) + ARRAY(I)
```
Incorrect Architecture

Remember to minimize DO loop set-up time for software architecture. When nesting DO loops (such as the hand-coded graphics structures shown in Chapter 3), order the loops so that the fewer iteration count loops are on the outside, and the higher iteration count loops are on the inside.

```
EXAMPLE 1
    DO 12 J = 1,5
      DO 22 K 1,100
            .
            .
            .
22    CONTINUE
12 CONTINUE
```
Correct Architecture

```
EXAMPLE 2
    DO 12 J = 1,100
      DO 22 K = 1,5
            .
            .
            .
22    CONTINUE
12 CONTINUE
```
Incorrect Architecture

Example 1 is the correct architecture for the following reasons. The execution time for a DO loop consists of three major items:

1. Set-up time (ST)—the time required to initialize the index
2. Increment test time (IT)—the time to reach the bottom of the loop
3. Time to execute the statements inside the loop (T)

For the two examples shown the real time required to execute the DO 12 loops is:

```
EXAMPLE 1: TIME = 5   * (ST + 100IT + 100T)
EXAMPLE 2: TIME = 100 * (ST + 5IT + 5T)
```

which will result in:

```
EXAMPLE 1: TIME = 5ST = 500IT + 500T
EXAMPLE 2: TIME = 100ST + 500IT + 500T
```

Example 1 is smaller, making it the correct architecture.

Statement numbers.   Correct architecture eliminates unnecessary statement numbers—that is, those that structured program control will never access. Most of these types of optimizations are performed between statement numbers; therefore, the fewer statement numbers, the better.

```
EXAMPLE 1
IF (J.EQ.0) K = L
```
Correct Architecture

```
EXAMPLE 2
    IF (J.EQ.0) GOTO 44
       K = L
44 STATEMENTS CONT'D...
```
Incorrect Architecture

Multidimensioned arrays.   Good software architecture makes reference memory as sequential as possible. For multidimensioned arrays, the leftmost subscript varies the fastest in structured programming, so when large portions of an array are addressed, paging and working the set can be significantly reduced by indexing the leftmost subscript the fastest. Use the example of the nested DO loop and place the leftmost in the inner loop. For example:

```
    DO 13 J = 1,100
      DO 23 K = 1,100
23      ARRAY(K,J) = 3.25
13 CONTINUE
```

is far more efficient than accessing the structured program by:

```
ARRAY(J,K) = 3.25
```

If correct software architecture can be maintained without multidimensioned arrays, memory addressing can be even more efficient. For each dimension over one, this saves one looping per effective address calculation. For example, the number of loopings = number of dimensions − 1. To illustrate, the example above could have been written as:

```
    DIMENSION JKARRAY (1)
    EQUIVALENCE (ARRAY(1,1),JKARRAY (1))
      DO 14 J = 1,10000
14 JKARRAY(1) = 3.25
```

using correct architecture and saving considerable processor time.

Processor sequences.   Paging time can be significantly reduced by ordering routines by frequency of use, rather than alphabetically. In correct architecture the main routine must always be placed in the processor first. Good architecture requires that processor memory allocation be:

```
MAIN
END
MOST USED SUBROUTINES
LEAST USED SUBROUTINES
```

For graphic processors divided into "local" and "secondary" functions, V-mode code executes faster than R-mode code. If a V-mode program plus data is less than 64K words, and the sub-routines are not shared with other processors, use the local processor to compact the graphic image. The structured programming introduced in Chapter 3 allows V-mode program statements faster access to variables in COMMON. If a COMMON block is loaded into the same processor as the procedure area or link area that accesses it, the structured program will address the common variables directly, rather than through a two-word pointer, which is indirect. Therefore, correct architectural processor loading of routines with frequently accessed COMMON areas in V-mode will increase execution speeds.

Function calls and subroutines. Correct architecture eliminates redundant function calls with equal arguments. For example, study these two cases:

```
EXAMPLE 1
TEMP = SIN(X)
A = TEMP * TEMP
```
Correct Architecture

```
EXAMPLE 2
A = SIN(X) * SIN(X)
```
Incorrect Architecture

Example 1 is much faster than example 2. When it is practical, always use statement functions instead of formal FUNCTION subprograms. In processor V-mode this eliminates a lengthy coding and storing process. Try to minimize the number of arguments passed to and from a function or subroutine regardless of whether it is a statement function or a separate function subprogram.

Some of the library functions are not optimized for time-critical operations. The graphic character routines (symbol, label, and number) are convenient, but very slow. Remember the

80/20 rule of software architecture: 80% of a graphics program's time is spent on 20% of the code (Experts will debate this rule, but it is true.) Therefore, standard library functions are adequate in the nontime, critical 80% of the architecture.

If statements.   Correct architecture minimizes compound logical connectives within an IF statement whenever possible. To illustrate:

```
EXAMPLE 1
IF (A.EQ.B) GOTO 44
IF (C.EQ.D) GOTO 44
```
Correct Architecture

```
EXAMPLE 2
IF (A.EQ.B.OR.C.EQ.D) GOTO 44
```
Incorrect Architecture

Both examples have the same effect, but example 1 is much faster than example 2.

Logical IFs are always preferred to arithmetic IF statements in software architecture. Many graphics programs have sections that look like this:

```
  IF (I-J) 1,2,3
1 STATEMENT CONT'D IF MINUS RESULT
         .
         .
2 STATEMENT CONT'D IF ZERO RESULT
         .
         .
3 STATEMENT CONT'T IF PLUS RESULT
```

A correct architecture would be:

```
  IF (I.EQ.J) GOTO 2
  STATEMENTS FOR PLUS AND MINUS CASES
2 STATEMENT FOR ZERO TEST
```

which is preferred.

I/O and statement sequences. Correct graphics architecture for read and write statement structure can significantly speed up data transfers. Study these examples:

EXAMPLE 1

```
      INTEGER TEXT (40)
      CALL LABEL(5,'TEXT',40,$99)
```

Correct Architecture

EXAMPLE 2

```
      INTEGER TEXT (40)
      READ (5,20,END=99) TEXT
   20 FORMAT(40A2)
```

Incorrect Architecture

Example 1 is faster than example 2.

Statements in software are sequenced or grouped much like an outline, starting on the left-hand side of the page and indenting for each portion of software that performs a like function. For example, the software listing used through the first six chapters would appear as the subroutines below.

```
C
C*****************************************************************************
C      BEGIN OF GRAPHIC LISTING........PROGRAM LISTING TO FOLLOW
C*****************************************************************************
C
C   BBBBBB  EEEEE  GGGGGG  II  NN  NN      LL      II  SSSSSS  TTTTTT
C   BB  BB  EE     GG      II  NNN NN      LL      II  SS          TT
C   BBBBBB  EEEEE  GG GGG  II  NNNNNN      LL      II  SSSSSS      TT
C   BB  BB  EE     GG  GG  II  NN NNN      LL      II      SS      TT
C   BBBBBB  EEEEE  GGGGGG  II  NN  NN      LLLLLL  II  SSSSSS      TT
C
C
C*****************************************************************************
C      BEGIN OF GRAPHIC LISTING........PROGRAM LISTING TO FOLLOW
C*****************************************************************************
C
```

```
C**********************************************************************
C**********************************************************************
C
C
C     GRAPHIC IS A SOFTWARE PACKAGE TESTED UNDER WATFIVE & FORTRAN IV G1
C     ALL USER INPUT AND OUTPUT TO GRAPHIC IS OF THE FORMATS:
C          REAL-F10.4
C          INTEGER-I5
C          STRING-ANY LENGTH IS ACCEPTABLE UP TO 72 CHARACTERS. IN THE
C                 CASE OF A KEY WORD WHERE ONLY THE FIRST 4 CHARACTERS
C                 ARE REQUIRED.
C
C**********************************************************************
C**********************************************************************
C
C** INDEX OF GRAPHIC CONTENTS ** GRAPHIC INDEX ** GRAPHIC INDEX **
C
C**********************************************************************
C**********************************************************************
C
C
C  1) INDEX
C  2) HEADING SUBS
C        A. BEGIN
C        B. TITLE
C            I.  FILLT
C            II. RDMESS
C            III.CMESS
C        C. ENDD
C  3) PICTORIAL SUBS
C        A. CUPID1
C            I.    ISO
C            II.   FVIEW
C            III.  TVIEW
C            IV.   PVIEW
C            V.    PSECTN
C        B. CUPID2
```

```
C          C. CUPID3
C             I.    ROTATE
C   4) DRAFTING SUBS
C          A. ANGSP
C          B. CENTER
C          C. CIRCLE
C          D. DASH
C          E. DASHCR
C          F. DIMLIN
C          G. LEADER
C   5) MATH SUBS
C          A. AXDIST
C          B. ARTAN
C          C. CCOORD
C          D. DSCRT
C          E. PCOORD
C          F. SIMON
C   6) DATA PROCESSING SUBS
C          A. RDC1
C          B. RDC2
C          C. RDC3
C          D. DAC12
C          E. DAC21
C          F. RDSMN


C*********************************************************************************
C*********************************************************************************
C
C** HEADING SUBROUTINES **HEADING SUBS *** HEADING SUBS **
C
C*********************************************************************************
C*********************************************************************************
C
C
      SUBROUTINE BEGIN
C*********************************************************************************
C          THIS SUB INITIATES CALL PLOTS FOR CALCOMP PACKAGE. USED
C          IN PLACE OF CALCOMP COMMAND FOR GRAPHIC ROUTINES. PRINTS
```

```
C           THE "NON-GRAPHIC" "BEGIN" AT THE BEGINNING OF EACH BLOCK
C           OF "GRAPHIC" PRINTOUT.
C           WRITTEN BY DANIEL L. RYAN
C
      CALL PLOTS
      RETURN
      END
C
C

      SUBROUTINE TITLE
C*******************************************************************************
C           STANDARD EG 310 TITLE BLOCK. MOVES THE PLOTTER ORIGIN TO THE
C           LOWER LEFT HAND CORNER OF THE TITLE BLOCK.
C           WRITTEN BY DANIEL L. RYAN
C
      COMMON /TIT/ TX,TY
      CALL PLOT(0.5,0.5,-3)
      WRITE(3,99998)
99998 FORMAT('1** GRAPHIC EXEC READ UNDER SUB TITLE **')
      WRITE(3,1)
    1 FORMAT(' THE DRAWING WIDTH & HEIGHT')
      READ(1,2) TX,TY
    2 FORMAT(2F10.4)
      WRITE(3,3) TX,TY
    3 FORMAT(' DRAWING WIDTH=',F10.4,/,' DRAWING HEIGHT=',F10.4)
      CALL RECT ( 0.000, 0.000, TY-1.0, TX-1.0, 0.0, 3)
C
          XFACT=(TX-1.0)/17.0
          IF ((TX-1.0) .LT. 17.0( CALL DFACT(XFACT,1.0)
          CALL RECT ( 0.000, 0.000,  0.750,  1.000, 0.0, 3)
          CALL RECT ( 1.000, 0.000,  0.750,  3.500, 0.0, 3)
          CALL RECT ( 4.500, 0.000,  0.375,  2.500, 0.0, 3)
          CALL RECT ( 4.500, 0.375,  0.375,  2.500, 0.0, 3)
          CALL RECT ( 7.000, 0.000,  0.375,  3.500, 0.0, 3)
          CALL RECT ( 7.000, 0.375,  0.375,  3.500, 0.0, 3)
          CALL RECT (10.500, 0.000,  0.750,  5.500, 0.0, 3)
          CALL RECT (16.000, 0.000,  0.750,  1.000, 0.0, 3)
```

```
      CALL SYMBOL ( 0.100,0.120,0.080,11HDRAWING NO.,0.0,11)
      CALL SYMBOL ( 2.000,0.500,0.090,20HENGINEERING GRAPHICS,0.0,20)
      CALL SYMBOL ( 1.750,0.312,0.100,22HCOLLEGE OF ENGINEERING,0.0,22)
      CALL SYMBOL ( 4.625,0.170,0.100,5HDATE:,0.0,5)
      CALL SYMBOL ( 4.625,0.500,0.100,6HSCALE:,0.0,6)
      CALL SYMBOL ( 7.125,0.170,
     +0.100,32HCOURSE:  E.G. 310 COMP. GRAPHICS,0.0,32)
      CALL SYMBOL (7.125,0.500,0.100,8HDWG. BY:,0.0,8)
      CALL SYMBOL (12.500,0.120,0.100,18HTITLE  OF  DRAWING,0.0,18)
      CALL SYMBOL (16.250,0.120,0.100,5HGRADE,0.0,5)
      CALL FILLT(TX,TY)
    CALL DFACT(1.0,1.0)
C******************************************************************
    RETURN
    END
C
C

    SUBROUTINE FILLT(TX,TY)
C******************************************************************
C        THIS SUB FILLS THE TITLE BLOCK WITH THE DWG NUMBER, DATE,
C        SCALE AND TITLE. "FILLT" CALLS SUB "RDMESS" WHICH READS THE
C        RESPONSE TO A PROMPT AND CALLS SUB "CHMESS" WHICH CENTERS THE
C        MESSAGE WITHIN A RECTANGLE.
C        WRITTEN BY DANIEL L. RYAN
C

    DIMENSION MESS(74)
C

    WRITE(3,99998)
99998 FORMAT(///,' ** GRAPHIC EXEC READ UNDER SUB FILLT **')
    WRITE(3,1)
  1 FORMAT(' DRAWING BY')
    CALL RDMESS(MESS,ICT)
    CALL CHMESS(8.000,0.500,2.500,0.10,0.10,MESS,0.0,ICT)
    WRITE(3,2)
  2 FORMAT(' THE DRAWING NUMBER')
    CALL RDMESS(MESS,ICT)
    CALL CHMESS(0.125,0.200,0.750,0.500,0.250,MESS,0.0,ICT)
```

```
      WRITE(3,3)
    3 FORMAT(' THE DRAWING DATE')
      CALL RDMESS(MESS,ICT)
      CALL CHMESS(5.250,0.170,1.500,0.100,0.100,MESS,0.0,ICT)
      WRITE(3,4)
    4 FORMAT(' THE DRAWING SCALE')
      CALL RDMESS(MESS,ICT)
      CALL CHMESS(5.250,0.500,1.500,0.100,0.100,MESS,0.0,ICT)
      WRITE(3,5)
    5 FORMAT(' THE DRAWING TITLE')
      CALL RDMESS(MESS,ICT)
      CALL CHMESS(10.750,0.250,5.000,0.500,0.250,MESS,0.0,ICT)
C********************************************************************************
      RETURN
      END
C
C

      SUBROUTINE RDMESS(MESS,ICT)
C********************************************************************************
C         THIS INPUT READS THE RESPONSE TO THE PROMPTS ISSUED BY A
C         SUB (SEE FILLT). WILL ONLY READONE CARD INTO "MESS".  ECHOS
C         A RESPONSE.  READS ONE BLANK AHEAD.  USES TWO
C         CONSECUTIVE BLANKS TO DELIMIT RECORD OF INPUT.
C         WRITTEN BY DANIEL L. RYAN
C

      DIMENSION MESS(74)
      DATA IBLANK/4H    /
C
      MESS(73)=IBLANK
      MESS(74)=IBLANK
      READ(1,1)(MESS(I),I=1,72)
    1 FORMAT(72A1)
      ICT=0
      DC 100 I=1,71
          IF ((MESS(I) .EQ. IBLANK) .AND. (MESS(I+1) .EQ. IBLANK,)
     +    GO TO 100
          ICT=ICT+1
```

```
 100      CONTINUE
       IF(MESS(72) .NE. IBLANK) ICT=72
       WRITE(3,3)(MESS(I),I=1,ICT)
     3 FORMAT(' ',72A1)
C***********************************************************************
       RETURN
       END
C
       SUBROUTINE CHMESS(BOXOX,BOXOY,BOXX,BOXY,CH,MESS,ANG,ICT)
C***********************************************************************
C         THIS SUB TAKES A MESSAGE(STRING "MESS" OF LENGTH ICT, EACH
C         CHARACTER HAS THE DIMENSIONS OF CH BY CH) AND PLACES IT INTO
C         A PRESCRIBED BOX(BOXX BY BOXY). THE BOX HEIGHT MUST BE LARGER
C         THAN OR EQUAL TO THE CHARACTER HEIGHT(I.E. BOXY>=CH) OR THE
C         SUB WILL BE RETURNED AFTER IT PRINTS AN ERROR MESSAGE.
C         WRITTEN BY DANIEL L. RYAN
C
       DIMENSION MESS(74)
       COMMON /TIT/ TX,TY
C
       XFACT=(TX-1.0)/17.0
       IF((TX-1.0) .LT. 17.0) CALL DFACT(XFACT,1.0)
       CH1=CH
       IF (BOXY .LT. CH1) WRITE(3,99998)
99998 FORMAT(' ** GRAPHIC ERROR ** BOX HEIGHT LESS THAN CH ** BOXY < CH
      +** EXEC SYMBOL WRITE UNDER SUB "CHMESS" **')
       IF (BOXY .LT. CH1) GO TO 99999
       IF (ICT*CH1 .LT. BOXX*0.95) GO TO 200
  100 CH1=CH1*0.95
       IF (ICT*CH1 .GE. BOXX*0.95) GO TO 100
  200 RMOY=BOXOY+((BOXY-CH1)/2.0)
       RMOX=BOXOX+((BOXX-(CH1*ICT))/2.0)
       DO 300 I=1,ICT
          CALL SYMBOL(RMOX,RMOY,CH1,MESS(I),ANG,1)
  300     RMOX=RMOX+CH1
C***********************************************************************
99999 RETURN
       END
```

```
C
      SUBROUTINE ENDD
C***********************************************************************
C         THIS SUB CALLS THE TERMINATION OF THE CALCOMP PACKAGE.
C         IT IS USED BY "GRAPHIC" IN PLACE OF CALCOMP CALL. PRINTS
C         THE  "END" AT THE END OF EACH BLOCK OF "GRAPHIC" PRINTOUT.
C         MOVES THE PLOTTER ORIGIN BACK TO THE ORIGINAL Y-ORIGIN AND
C         ADVANCES THE PLOTTER X-ORIGIN PAST THE TITLE BLOCK, IN A
C         READY POSITION FOR NEXT BLOCK OF GRAPHIC DRAWING.
C         WRITTEN BY DANIEL L. RYAN
C
      COMMON /TIT/ TX,TY
C
      CALL PLOT(TX+6.0,-0.5,999)
      RETURN
      END
C
C
C
C
C***********************************************************************
C***********************************************************************
C
C** PICTORIAL SUBROUTINES ** PIC SUBS ** PIC SUBS ** PIC SUBS**
C
C***********************************************************************
C***********************************************************************
C
C
      SUBROUTINE CUPID1
C***********************************************************************
C         CUPID V-1 (CLEMSON UNIVERSITY PICTORIAL IMAGE VERSION ONE)
C         DRAWS THE 3  STANDARD ORTHOGRAPHIC PROJECTIONS AND AN
C         OPTION TO DRAW A CABINET DRAWING. IF ANG OF CABINET
C         PROJECTION IS EQUAL TO ZERO (0.0) THEN THE CAB. DWG. WILL
C         BE SKIPPED.
C         WRITTEN BY DANIEL L. RYAN
```

```
      COMMON /CUPD1/ X(100),Y(100),Z(100),IP(100),NDATA
C
      CALL RDC1(NDATA,XSET,YSET,X0,Y0,ANG,SF,SF1,X,Y,Z,IP)
      CALL FACTOR(SF)
      CALL PLOT(X0,Y0,-3)
          IF (ANG .NE. 0.0) CALL ISO(ANG,SF1)
          CALL FVIEW
          CALL TVIEW (YSET)
          CALL PVIEW (XSET)
          CALL FACTOR(1.0)
      RETURN
      END
C
      SUBROUTINE ISO (ANG,SF)
C**********************************************************************
C         THIS SUB DRAWS THE ISOMETRIC VIEW FOR CUPID1
C
      COMMON /CUPD1/ X(100),Y(100),Z(100),IP(100),NDATA
      DIMENSION XPLOT(100),YPLOT(100)
C
      CALL FACTOR(SF)
      COSA=COS(ANG/57.3)
      SINA=SIN(ANG/57.3)
      DO 10 I=1,NDATA
          XPLOT(I)=(X(I)+Z(I)*COSA)+12.5
          YPLOT(I)=(Y(I)+Z(I)*SINA)+6.67
   10     CALL PLOT(XPLOT(I),YPLOT(I),IP(I))
      CALL FACTOR(1.0)
C**********************************************************************
      RETURN
      END
C
C
      SUBROUTINE FVIEW
C**********************************************************************
C     THIS DRAWS THE FRONT VIEW (X,Y AXIS)
      COMMON /CUPD1/ X(100),Y(100),Z(100),IP(100),NDATA
```

```fortran
C
      DC 10 I=1,NDATA
   10     CALL PLOT(X(I),Y(I),IP(I))
C*********************************************************************
      RETURN
      END
      SUBROUTINE TVIEW (YSET)
C*********************************************************************
C     THIS DRAWS THE TOP VIEW (X,Z AXIS)
C
      COMMON /CUPD1/ X(100),Y(100),Z(100),IP(100),NDATA
      DIMENSION Z1(100)
C
      DO 10 I=1,NDATA
          Z1(I)=Z(I)+YSET
   10     CALL PLOT(X(I),Z1(I),IP(I))
C*********************************************************************
      RETURN
      END
C
C
      SUBROUTINE PVIEW (XSET)
C*********************************************************************
C     THIS DRAWS THE PROFILE VIEW (Y,Z AXIS)
C
      COMMON /CUPD1/ X(100),Y(100),Z(100),IP(100),NDATA
      DIMENSION Z1(100)
C
      DO 10 I=1,NDATA
          Z1(I)=Z(I)+XSET
   10     CALL PLOT(Z1(I),Y(I),IP(I))
C*********************************************************************
      RETURN
      END
C
C
```

```
      SUBROUTINE PSECTN
C*********************************************************************
C         THIS SUB DRAWS A SECTION FROM A CUPID V-1 DATA BASE. THE
C         SECTION IS DRAWN IN THE PLACE OF THE ISOMETRIC, THEREFORE
C         ANG IN THE REGULAR DATA BASE MUST BE 0.0. REQUIRES A SEPARATE
C         DATA BASE CONSTRUCTED FOR THE CUT OBJECT.

      COMMON /CUPD1/ X(100),Y(100),Z(100),IP(100),NDATA
C
      CALL RDC1(NDATA,XSET,YSET,X0,Y0,ANG,SF,SF1,X,Y,Z,IP)
      CALL FACTOR(SF)
      DO 10 I=1,NDATA
   10    Y(I)=Y(I)+YSET
      CALL PVIEW(XSET)
C
      RMAXX=X(1)
      DO 20 I=2,NDATA
   20    IF(X(I) .GT. RMAXX)RMAXX=X(I)
      RMAXY=Y(1)
      DO 30 I=2,NDATA
   30    IF(Y(I) .GT. RMAXY)RMAXY=Y(I)
      CALL SLINE(RMAXX,-0.75,RMAXX,RMAXY+0.75,2,-1)
      CALL FACTOR(1.0)
C*********************************************************************
      RETURN
      END
C
C
      SUBROUTINE CUPID2(SF)
C*********************************************************************
C    TAKES A THREE DIMENSIONAL DATABASE AND CONVERTS IT TO A TWO
C    DIMENSIONAL DATA BASE USING AN AXIOMETRIC MATRIX TRANSFORMATION.
C         NP=NUMBER OF POINTS TO BE PLOTTED
C         NC=NUMBER OF COMMANDS NECESSARY TO DRAW PICTORIAL
C         NV=NUMBER OF VIEWS TO BE DRAWN
C         SPACE=SPACE ALLOWED FOR EACH VIEW
```

```
C          P(I,J)=ARRAY CONTAINING 3-D DATA BASE(X,Y,Z)
C          IC(NC)=ARRAY CONTAINING POINT CONNECTIONS
C          VP(NV,3)=ARRAY CONTAINING AMOUNTS OF ROTATION IN (X,Y,Z)
C          DIRECTIONS
C          MODIFIED BY DANIEL L. RYAN
C
      DIMENSION P(100,3),IC(200),VP(100,3),PP(100,3)
      CALL FACTOR (SF)
      CALL RDC2 (P,NP,VP,NV,IC,NC,SPACE)
C   FOR EACH VIEW DO THE FOLLOWING TRANSFORMATIONS AND PLOTTING.
      DC 5 I=1,NV
C  CONVERT 3-D X,Z ROTATIONS FOR TRANSFORMATION TO THE X OF THE
C  PLOTTER.
      A=ARTAN(VP(I,1),VP(I,3))
      SA=SIN(A)
      CA=COS(A)
C  CONVERT 3-D X-POINTS FOR PLOTTER X-COORDINATES. PREPARE 3-D
C  Z-POINTS FOR FINAL ROTATION TRANSFORMATION TO PLOTTER Y.
      DO 6 J=1,NP
      PP(J,3)=P(J,3)*CA+P(J,1)*SA
      PP(J,1)=P(J,1)*CA-P(J,3)*SA
  6       CONTINUE
C  CONVERT Y ROTATION FOR Y TRANSFORMATION TO PLOTTER.
      VPP=VP(I,3)*CA+VP(I,1)*SA
      A=ARTAN(VP(I,2),VPP)
      SA=SIN(A)
      CA=COS(A)
C  CONVERT 3-D Y,Z COORDINATES TO PLOTTER Y.
      DO 7  J=1,NP
      PP(J,2)=P(J,2)*CA-PP(J,3)*SA
  7       CONTINUE
C  ADD X,Y TRANSFORMATIONS TO THE POINTS FOR PLOTTING (Y=6.0,
C  X=SPACE*I).
      DO 11 K=1,NP
      PP(K,2)=PP(K,2)+6.0
      PP(K,1)=PP(K,1)+SPACE*I
  11      CONTINUE
```

```
C  FOR EACH VIEW PLOT EACH TRANSFORMED DRAW COMMAND.
C  IF POINT COMMAND IS NEGATIVE THEN PEN IS UP AND STMT. #9 IS
C  EXECUTED ELSE PLOT W/ PEN DOWN.
       DO 8 J=1,NC
       IF (IC(J) .LT. 0) GO TO 9
       CALL PLOT(PP(IC(J),1),PP(IC(J),2),2)
       GO TO 8
  9    K=-IC(J)
       CALL PLOT(PP(K,1),PP(K,2),3)
  8    CONTINUE
  5    CONTINUE
C  MOVE PLOTTER ORIGIN TO END OF DRAWING FOR OPERATE
       XSET=(SPACE*NV)+8.0
       CALL PLOT(XSET,0.0,-3)
       CALL FACTOR(1.0)
C*********************************************************************
       RETURN
       END
C
C

       SUBROUTINE CUPID3
C*********************************************************************
C         CUPID V-3
C         VERSION THREE   PLOTS SCULPTURED SURFACES FOR THE X,Y,Z AXIS.
C              AXLIN=THE LENGTH OF THE AXIS
C              NAX=IF NAX IS EQUAL TO 1 THEN AXIS LINES ARE PROVIDED FOR
C                      THE VIEWER.
C              SF=THE SCALE FACTOR FOR WINDOWING THE AXIS LENGTH.
C              N=THE NUMBER OF DATA POINTS.
C              A,B,C=THE ARRAYS CONTAINING THE POINT COORDINATES IN THREE
C                      SPACE.
C         WRITTEN BY DANIEL L. RYAN
       DIMENSION A(500),B(500),C(500),BUFR(500),P(20,20)
C
       CALL RDC3(AXRD,NAX,SF,AXLN,A,B,C,N)
       CALL FACTOR(SF)
       AXLN1=AXLN+0.001
```

```
C   SET THE VALUES FOR A MIN-MAX SEARCH.
        XH=0.0
        YH=0.0
        ZH=0.0
        XL=100.0
        YL=100.0
        ZL=100.0
        NN=10
 C   FIND THE MIN & MAX FOR A,B &C.
        DO 1 I=1,N
        IF (XH .LE. A(I))XH=A(I)
        IF (YH .LE. B(I))YH=B(I)
        IF (ZH .LE. C(I))ZH=C(I)
        IF (XL .GE. A(I))XL=A(I)
        IF (YL .GE. B(I))YL=B(I)
        IF (ZL .GE. C(I))ZL=C(I)
  1     CONTINUE
C   DECRETIZE THE DATA IN A,B &C.
        DO 2 I=1,N
        A(I)=(A(I)-XL)/(XH-XL)*AXLN
        B(I)=(B(I)-YL)/(YH-YL)*AXLN
        C(I)=(C(I)-ZL)/(ZH-ZL)*AXLN
  2     CONTINUE
C   FILL THE ARRAY "P" WITH THE VALUE ZERO.
        DO 3 I=1,NN
        DO 4 J=1,NN
        P(I,J)=0.0
  4     CONTINUE
  3     CONTINUE
C    LOCATE THE C DATA IN ARRAY P ACCORDING TO THE A&B DATA.
        DO 5 I=1,N
        IX=A(I)/AXLN1*NN+1.0
        IY=B(I)/AXLN1*NN+1.0
        IF (C(I) .GT. P(IX,IY))P(IX,IY)=C(I)
  5     CONTINUE
C   IF NAX IS EQUAL TO 1 THEN AXIS LINES ARE PRODUCED FOR THE VIEWER.
        IF (NAX.NE.1) GO TO 10
```

```
      X=AXLN
      Y=-YL/(YH-YL)*AXLN
      Z=-ZL/(ZH-ZL)*AXLN
      CALL ROTATE(X,Y,Z)
          CALL PLOT(X,Y,3)
          X=-XL/(XH-XL)*AXLN
          Y=-YL/(YH-YL)*AXLN
          CALL ROTATE(X,Y,Z)
          CALL PLOT(X,Y,2)
          Z=AXLN
          X=-XL/(XH-XL)*AXLN
          Y=-YL/(YH-YL)*AXLN
          CALL ROTATE(X,Y,Z)
          CALL PLOT(X,Y,1)
          X=-XL/(XH-XL)*AXLN
          Z=-ZL/(ZH-ZL)*AXLN
          Y=-YL/(YH-YL)*AXLN
          CALL ROTATE(X,Y,Z)
          CALL PLOT(X,Y,3)
          Y=AXLN
          X=-XL/(XH-XL)*AXLN
          Z=-ZL/(ZH-ZL)*AXLN
          CALL ROTATE(X,Y,Z)
          CALL PLOT(X,Y,2)
C  DRAWS THE SURFACE GRID LINES FOR VALUES ON THE X-AXIS.
   10 DO 6 I=1,NN
      X=I*AXLN/NN
      SX=X
      IP=3
      DO 7 J=1,NN
      X=SX
      Y=J*AXLN/NN
      Z=P(I,J)
      CALL ROTATE(X,Y,Z)
      CALL PLOT(X,Y,IP)
    7     CONTINUE
    6     CONTINUE
```

```
C   DRAWS THE SURFACE GRID LINES FOR VALUES ON THE Y-AXIS.
      DO 8 I=1,NN
      Y=I*AXLN/NN
      SY=Y
      IP=3
      DO 9 J=1,NN
      Y=SY
      X=J*AXLN/NN
      Z=P(J,I)
      CALL ROTATE(X,Y,Z)
      CALL PLOT(X,Y,IP)
      IP=2
    9    CONTINUE
    8    CONTINUE
      CALL FACTOR(1.0)
C*************************************************************************
      RETURN
      END
C
C

      SUBROUTINE ROTATE(X,Y,Z)
C*************************************************************************
C        ROTATES THE Z,X,Y AXIS FOR SUB CUPID3 TO A STANDARD ISOMETRIC
C        VIEW.
C        WRITTEN BY DANIEL L. RYAN
      DATA C1/0.707/,C2/0.808/,S1/0.707/,S2/-.587/
C
      SY=Y
C
      Y=Z*C2+X*C1*S2+Y*S1*S2+5.0
      X=SY*C1-X*S1+10.0
C*************************************************************************
      RETURN
      END
C
C
C
```

```
C
C*********************************************************************
C*********************************************************************
C
C** DRAFTING SUBROUTINES ** DRAFT SUBS ** DRAFT SUBS **
C
C*********************************************************************
C*********************************************************************
C
C
      SUBROUTINE ANGSP(XP,YP,RC,SP,EP,RL,ILEAD)
C*********************************************************************
C             THIS SUB DRAWS AN ANGLE SPECIFICATION DIMENSION.
         SP=SP/57.3
         EP=EP/57.3
         SIZE=0.0625
C      THIS DRAWS THE DIM. LINE.
         SX=XP+R
         CALL CIRCL (SX,YP,SP,EP,R,R,0.0)
C      THIS DRAWS THE ARROW @ THE STARTING POINT.
         XLOC=XP+R*COS(SP)
         XLOC=YP+R*SIN(SP)
         CALL AROHD (XLOC-0.005,YLOC-0.005,XLOC,YLOC,0.124,0.0,17)
C      THIS DRAWS THE ARROW @ THE ENDING POINT.
         XLOC=XP+R*COS(EP)
         YLOC=YP+R*SIN(EP)
         CALL AROHD (XLOC-0.005,YLOC-0.005,XLOC,YLOC,0.124,0.0,17)
C      CHECK TO SEE IF LEADER LINES ARE REQD.
         IF (ILEAD .EQ. 0) GO TO 30
C      THIS DRAWS A LONG LEADER @ EP & SHORT ONE @ SP.
         IF (ILEAD .NE. 1) GO TO 10
         XLOC=(XP+RC+0.125)*COS(EP)
         YLOC=(YP+RC+0.125)*SIN(EP)
         XPLOC=(XP+0.0625)*COS(EP)
         YPLOC=(YP+0.0625)*SIN(EP)
         CALL PLOT(XLOC,YLOC,3)
         CALL PLOT(XPLOC,YPLOC,2)
```

```fortran
        XLOC=(XP+RC+0.125)*COS(SP)
        YLOC=(YP+RC+0.125)*SIN(SP)
        XPLOC=(XP+RL+0.0625)*COS(SP)
        YPLOC=(YP+RL+0.0625)*SIN(SP)
        CALL PLOT(XLOC,YLOC,3)
        CALL PLOT(XPLOC,YPLOC,2)
C       THIS DRAWS LONG LEADERS @ EP & SP.
   10   IF (ILEAD .NE. 2) GO TO 20
        XLOC=(XP+RC+0.125)*COS(EP)
        YLOC=(YP+RC+0.125)*SIN(EP)
        XPLOC=(XP+0.0625)*COS(EP)
        YPLOC=(YP+0.0625)*SIN(EP)
        CALL PLOT(XLOC,YLOC,3)
        CALL PLOT(XPLOC,YPLOC,2)
        XLOC=(XP+RC+0.125)*COS(SP)
        YLOC=(YP+RC+0.125)*SIN(SP)
        XPLOC=(XP+0.0625)*COS(SP)
        YPLOC=(YP+0.0625)*SIN(SP)
        CALL PLOT(XLOC,YLOC,3)
        CALL PLOT(XPLOC,YPLOC,2)
C       THIS DRAWS SHORT LEADERS @ EP & SP.
   20   IF (ILEAD .NE. 3) GO TO 30
        XLOC=(XP+RC+0.125)*COS(SP)
        YLOC=(YP+RC+0.125)*SIN(SP)
        XPLOC=(XP+RL+0.0625)*COS(SP)
        YPLOC=(YP+RL+0.0625)*SIN(SP)
        CALL PLOT(XLOC,YLOC,3)
        CALL PLOT(XPLOC,YPLOC,2)
        XLOC=(XP+RC+0.125)*COS(EP)
        YLOC=(YP+RC+0.125)*SIN(EP)
        XPLOC=(XP+RL+0.0625)*COS(EP)
        YPLOC=(YP+RL+0.0625)*SIN(EP)
        CALL PLOT(XLOC,YLOC,3)
        CALL PLOT(XPLOC,YPLOC,2)
C       THIS LETTERS THE ANGLE DIMENSION.
   30   ANG=((EP-SP)/2.0)+SP
        FACT=ATAN(0.15625/(RC+0.0625))
```

```
      ANG=ANG+FACT
      XLOC=(XP+RC+0.0625)*COS(ANG)
      YLOC=(YP+RC+0.0625)*SIN(ANG)
      CALL NUMBER(XLOC,YLOC,SIZE,DEG,ANG,-5)
C********************************************************************
      RETURN
      END
      SUBROUTINE CENTER (X1,Y1,X2,Y2,INC)
C********************************************************************
C         THIS SUB DRAWS A SINGLE CENTER LINE GIVEN THE STARTING POINT
C         (X1,Y1), THE ENDING POINT (X2,Y2) AND THE INTEGER LENGTH OF
C         THE BASIC CENTER LINE PATTERN IN INCHES (INC).
C         WRITTEN BY DANIEL L. RYAN
C
      DIMENSION XA(4), YA(4)
C
      XA(1)=X1
      XA(2)=X2
      XA(3)=0.0
      XA(4)=1.0
      YA(1)=Y1
      YA(2)=Y2
      YA(3)=0.0
      YA(4)=1.0
      NPT=2
      CALL CNTRL(XA,YA,NPT,INC)
C********************************************************************
      RETURN
      END
C
C
      SUBROUTINE CIRCLE(X,Y,R,SANG,N,THETA)
C********************************************************************
C         THIS SUB DRAWS A CIRCLE GIVEN THE CENTER POINT OF THE CIRCLE
C         (X,Y), THE RADIUS OF THE CIRCLE (R), THE STARTING POINT OF
C         THE CIRCLE IN DEGREES (SANG), THE INCREMENT OF EACH FACET
C         IN DEGREES (THETA), AND THE NUMBER OF TIMES THE INCREMENT IS
```

```
C          TO BE ADVANCED. IF AN ARC IS REQUIRED THEN THE NUMBER OF
C          DEGREES OF ARC=N*THETA.
C          WRITTEN BY DANIEL L. RYAN
C
      X=X-R
      SANG=(3.14/180.)*SANG
      XX=R*(1-COS(SANG))
      YY=R*(SIN(SANG))
      DX=X+XX
      DY=Y+YY
      CALL PLOT(DX,DY,3)
      THETA=(3.14/180.)*THETA
      THETA1=THETA
      DO 2 I=1,N
          FEE=SANG+THETA
          PX=R*(1-COS(FEE))
          SY=R*(SIN(FEE))
          DX=X+PX
          EY=Y+SY
          CALL PLOT(DX,EY,2)
    2     THETA=THETA+THETA1
C*****************************************************************************
      RETURN
      END
C
C
      SUBROUTINE DASH (X,Y,EX,EY,DASH1)
C*****************************************************************************
C          THIS SUB DRAWS A SINGLE DASHED LINE GIVEN THE STARTING POINT
C          (X,Y), THE ENDING POINT (EX,EY) AND THE LENGTH OF THE DASH
C          SEGMENT (DASH1).
C          WRITTEN BY DANIEL L. RYAN
C
      CALL PLOT (X,Y,3)
      CALL DASHP (EX,EY,DASH1)
C*****************************************************************************
      RETURN
      END
```

```
C
C
      SUBROUTINE DASHCR(X,Y,R)
C*********************************************************************
C         THIS SUB DRAWS A DASHED CIRCLE GIVEN THE CENTER POINT OF THE
C         CIRCLE (X,Y) AND THE RADIUS (R).
C         WRITTEN BY DANIEL L. RYAN
C
      X=X-R
      SANG=.1047
      DO 4 I=1,20
          XX=R*(1-COS(SANG))
          YY=R*SIN(SANG)
          DX=X+XX
          EY=Y+YY
          CALL PLOT(DX,EY,3)
          THETA=.1047
          THETA1=THETA
          DO 2 J=1,2
              FEE=SANG+THETA
              PX=R*(1-COS(FEE))
              SY=R*(SIN(FEE))
              DX=X+PX
              EY=Y+SY
              CALL PLOT(DX,EY,2)
    2         THETA=THETA+THETA1
          SANG=SANG+THETA
    4     CONTINUE
C*********************************************************************
      RETURN
      END
C
C
      SUBROUTINE DIML(X,Y,HT1,HT2,XLINE,THETA)
C*********************************************************************
C         THIS SUB DRAWS A SINGLE DIMENSION LINE GIVEN THE STARTING
C         POINT (X,Y), THE DISTANCE FROM THE STARTING POINT TO THE
C         DIMENSION LINE (HT1), THE DISTANCE FROM THE STARTING POINT TO
```

```
C          THE END OF THE LEADER LINE (HT2), THE LENGTH OF THE DIMENSION
C          (XLINE) AND THE ANGLE OF ROTATION (THETA).
C          WRITTEN BY DANIEL L. RYAN
C
      CALL PLOT(X,Y,3)
      THETA=3.14/180.*THETA
      A=X+COS(THETA)*XLINE
      B=Y+SIN(THETA)*XLINE
      CALL PLOT(A,B,2)
      C=A-SIN(THETA)*HT2
      D=B+COS(THETA)*HT2
      CALL PLOT(C,D,3)
      C1=A+SIN(THETA)*.125
      D1=B-COS(THETA)*.125
      CALL PLOT(C1,D1,2)
      E=X-SIN(THETA)*HT1
      F=Y+COS(THETA)*HT1
      CALL PLOT(E,F,3)
      E1=X+SIN(THETA)*.125
      F1=Y-COS(THETA)*.125
      CALL PLOT(E1,F1,2)
      CALL PLOT(A,B,3)
      AR1=A-SIN(1.8326-THETA)*.125
      AR2=B-COS(1.8326-THETA)*.125
      CALL PLOT(AR1,AR2,3)
      CALL PLOT(A,B,3)
      AR3=A-COS(.2618+THETA)*.125
      AR4=B-SIN(.2618+THETA)*.125
      CALL PLOT(AR3,AR4,2)
      CALL PLOT(X,Y,3)
      AR5=X+COS(.2618+THETA)*.125
      AR6=Y+SIN(.2618+THETA)*.125
      CALL PLOT(AR5,AR6,2)
      AR7=X+SIN(1.8326-THETA)*.125
      CALL PLOT(X,Y,2)
C*************************************************************************
      RETURN
      END
```

```
C
C

      SUBROUTINE LEADER(X, Y, BAR, X2, Y2)
C***************************************************************************
C          THIS SUB DRAWS A LEADER LINE GIVEN THE STARTING POINT (X,Y),
C          THE LENGTH FROM THE STARTING POINT TO THE BEND IN THE LEADER
C          (BAR), AND THE LOCATION OF THE ARROW HEAD (X2,Y2).
C           WRITTEN BY DANIEL L. RYAN
C
      CALL PLOT (X,Y,3)
      CALL PLOT (X+BAR,Y,2)
      CALL AROHD (X+BAR,Y,X2,Y2,0.125,0.0,17)
C***************************************************************************
      RETURN
      END
C
C***************************************************************************
C***************************************************************************
C
C** MATHMATICAL SUBROUTINES ** MATH SUBS ** MATH SUBS ** MATH SUBS **
C
C***************************************************************************
C***************************************************************************
C
C

      SUBROUTINE AXDIST(A,B,DIST)
C***************************************************************************
C          THIS SUB CALCULATES THE DIFFERENCE BETWEEN TWO POINTS ON A
C          GIVEN AXIS LINE. USEFUL WHEN USED IN CONJUNCTION W/ SUB
C          "PCOORD" IN FINDING THE DISTANCE BETWEEN TWO POINTS IN
C          CARTESIAN SPACE.
C          WRITTEN BY DANIEL L. RYAN
C
      EPS=0.001
      IF((A .GT. EPS) .AND. (B .GT. EPS))XDIST=ABS(A-B)
      IF((A .GT. EPS) .AND. (B .LT. EPS)) DIST=A+ABS(B)
      IF((A .LT. EPS) .AND. (B .GT. EPS))DIST=ABS(A)+B
      IF((A .LT. EPS) .AND. (B .LT. EPS))DIST=ABS(A-B)
```

```
C********************************************************************
      RETURN
      END
C
C
      FUNCTION ARTAN(Y,X)
C********************************************************************
C          THIS SUB LOCATES THE VALUE ON THE TANGENT GRAPH FOR TWO POINTS
C          GIVEN A POINT ON THE X-AXIS AND THE POINT ON THE Y-AXIS.
      DATA EPS/0.001/
      AX=ABS(X)
      AY=ABS(Y)
      IF (AX .GT. EPS.AND.AY .GT. EPS) GO TO 1
      IF (AX .LT. EPS.AND.AY .LT. EPS) GO TO 3
      IF (AX .LT. EPS) GO TO 2
   3  ARTAN=0.0
      RETURN
   2  ARTAN=(3.14159*AY)/(Y*2.0)
      RETURN
   1  ARTAN=ATAN2(Y,X)
C********************************************************************
      RETURN
      END
C
C
      SUBROUTINE SIMON(A,U,NM,EPS)
C********************************************************************
C          THIS SUB RETURNS THE SOLUTION OF SYSTEMS OF SIMULTANEOUS
C          EQUATIONS.
C              NOB - NUMBER OF PROBLEMS TO BE SOLVED.
C                N - NUMBER OF EQUATIONS FOR EACH PROBLEM.
C              EPS -A SMALL NUMBER FOR TESTING FOR A ZERO DIAGONAL.
C          A(I,J) - COEFFICIENTS OF THE UNKNOWNS IN THE EQUATIONS.
C              C(I) - CONSTANTS OF THE EQUATIONS.
      DIMENSION A(50,50),U(50)
C
      DO 9015 I=1,NM
```

```
      K=I
      IF (I-NM) 9021,9007,9021
C    TEST TO SEE WHETHER DIAGONAL ELEMENT IS ZERO OR NOT
 9021 IF (ABS (A(I,I))-EPS) 9006,9006,9007
C  ADD SUBSEQUENT EQUATIONS TO THE CURRENT ONE
 9006 K=K+1
      U(I)=U(I)+U(K)
      DO 9023 J=1,NM
 9023 A(I,J)=A(I,J)+A(K,J)
      GO TO 9021
 9007 DIV=A(I,I)
      U(I)=U(I)/DIV
C    DIVIDE ALL THE ELEMENTS OF I-TH EQUATION BY A(I,I)
      DO 9009 J=1,NM
 9009 A(I,J)=A(I,J)/DIV
C    REDUCE THE I-TH ELEMENT OF THE OTHER EQUATIONS TO ZERO
      DO 9015 MM=1,NM
      DELT=A(MM,I)
      IF (ABS (DELT)-EPS) 9015,9015,9016
 9016 IF (MM-I) 9010,9015,9010
 9010 U(MM)=U(MM)-U(I)*DELT
      DO 9011 J=1,NM
 9011 A(MM,J)=A(MM,J)-A(I,J)*DELT
 9015 CONTINUE
C************************************************************************
      RETURN
      END
      SUBROUTINE PCOORD (X,Y,RAY,ANG)
C************************************************************************
C          THIS SUB CONVERTS CARTESIAN COORDINATES(X,Y,) TO POLAR
C          COORDINATE SYSTEM(RAY,ANGLE). RAY IS OF THE SAME CONVENTION
C          AS X&Y BUT THE ANGLE IS RETURNED IN DEGREES.
C
C              POINT ON Y-AXIS?
C              POINT ON X-AXIS?
      IF (X .EQ. 0.0) GO TO 170
      IF (Y .EQ. 0.0) GO TO 260
```

```
C               COMPUTE POLAR COORDINATES.
      RAY=SQRT(X**2.0+Y**2.0)
      ANG=(ATAN(Y/X)*180.0/3.1415927)
      GO TO 99999
  170 IF (Y .EQ. 0.0) GO TO 240
      RAY=ABS(Y)
C               IS POINT ABOVE OR BELOW ORIGIN?
      IF (Y .LT. 0.0) GO TO 220
      ANG=90.0
      GO TO 99999
  220 ANG=270.0
      GO TO 99999
C               POINT IS AT ORIGIN
  240 RAY=0.0
      ANG=0.0
      GO TO 99999
C               POINT IS ON X-AXIS
  260 RAY=ABS(X)
C               IS POINT TO LEFT OR RIGHT OF ORIGIN?
      IF(X .LT. 0.0) GO TO 300
      ANG=0.0
      GO TO 99999
  300 ANG=180.0
C***********************************************************************
99999 RETURN
      END

      SUBROUTINE CCOORD(RAY,ANG,X,Y)
C***********************************************************************
C         THIS SUB CONVERTS POLAR COORDINATES (RAY,ANG) TO CARTESIAN
C         COORDINATES (X,Y).X&Y ARE RETURNED IN THE SAME CONVENTION
C         AS RAY BUT THE ANGLE MUST BE GIVEN IN DEGREES.
C         WRITTEN BY TOM MACKNIGHT & DANIEL L. RYAN
C---------------------------------------------------------------------
C
C               CONVERT FROM DEGREES TO RADIANS.
      RADANG=(ANG-INT(ANG/360.0)*360.0)*3.1415927/180.0
```

```
C               CALCULATE CARTESIAN COORDINATES
      X=RAY*COS(RADANG)
      Y=RAY*SIN(RADANG)
C********************************************************************
      RETURN
      END
C
C

      SUBROUTINE DSCRT(A,K,LGTH,NEWA)
C********************************************************************

C         THIS SUB WILL RETURN THE DECRETIZED VALUES(RNEWA) FOR AN ARRAY
C         (A) GIVEN THE ARRAY'S LENGTH(K) AND THE LENGTH OF THE LINE
C         OVER WHICH THE DATA IS TO BE DECRETIZED(AXLGHT).
C
      DIMENSION A(500),RNEWA(500)
      DATA AH/1000.0/,AL/-1000.0/
      DO 100 I=1,K
      IF(A(I) .GT. AH)AH=A(I)
      IF(A(I) .LT. AL)AL=A(I)
  100 CONTINUE
      DO 200 I=1,K
  200 RNEWA(I)=((A(I)-AL)/(AH-AL))*AXLGHT
C********************************************************************
      RETURN
      END
C********************************************************************
C********************************************************************
C
C** DATA PROCESSING SUBROUTINES ** DAT PRO SUBS ** DAT PRO SUBS**
C
C********************************************************************
C********************************************************************
C
C

      SUBROUTINE RDC1(NDATA,XSET,YSET,XO,YO,ANG,SF,SF1,X,Y,Z,IP)
C********************************************************************
```

```
C          READS THE DATA FROM INPUT FOR CUPID V-1 TYPE STRUCTURE.
      DIMENSION X(100),Y(100),Z(100),IP(100)
C
      WRITE(3,7000)
 7000 FORMAT('1** GRAPHIC EXEC READ UNDER SUB "RDC1" **'/)
      READ(1,8005) X0,Y0
 8005 FORMAT(2F10.4)
      WRITE(3,7005) X0,Y0
 7005 FORMAT(' X ORIGIN=',F10.4,/,' Y ORIGIN=',F10.4)
      READ(1,8001) XSET,YSET
 8001 FORMAT(2F10.4)
      WRITE(3,7001) XSET,YSET
 7001 FORMAT(' XSET=',F10.4,/,' YSET=',F10.4)
      READ(1,8002) SF,SF1
 8002 FORMAT(2F10.4)
      WRITE(3,7002) SF,SF1
 7002 FORMAT(' SF=',2X,F10.4,/,' SF1=',1X,F10.4)
      READ(1,8003) ANG
 8003 FORMAT(F10.4)
      WRITE(3,7003) ANG
 7003 FORMAT(' ANG=',1X,F10.4)
      WRITE(3,2)
    2 FORMAT(//,' ** VALUES FOR CUPID V-1 DRAW COMMANDS **')
      WRITE(3,9001)
 9001 FORMAT('0',13X,'X POINT',9X,'Y POINT',9X,'Z POINT',8X,'PEN')
      WRITE(3,9000)
 9000 FORMAT(' ',11X,'**********',6X,'**********',6X,'**********',6X,
     +'*****')
      I=0
   10 I=I+1
      IF(I .GT. 100) GO TO 20
      READ(1,8004) X(I),Y(I),Z(I),IP(I)
 8004 FORMAT(3F10.4,I5)
      IF(IP(I) .EQ. -999) GO TO 30
      WRITE(3,7004) I,X(I),Y(I),Z(I),IP(I)
 7004 FORMAT(' ',I5,3(6X,F10.4),6X,I5)
      GO TO 10
```

```
   20 WRITE(3,99998)
99998 FORMAT(' ** GRAPHIC ENDING INPUT ** NEXT POINT OUT OF BOUNDS ** EX
     +EC UNDER "RDC1" **')
   30 NDATA=I-1
C****************************************************************************
      RETURN
      END
C
C
      SUBROUTINE RDC2(P1,NP1,VP1,NV1,IC1,NC1,SPACE1)
C****************************************************************************
C          READS THE DATA STRUCTURED FOR CUPID V-2.
      DIMENSION P1(100,3),IC1(200),VP1(100,3)
C
      NP1=0
      NV1=0
      NC1=0
      WRITE(3,7000)
 7000 FORMAT('1** GRAPHIC EXEC READ UNDER SUB "RDC2" **'/)
      READ(1,8001) SPACE1
 8001 FORMAT(F10.4)
      WRITE(3,7001) SPACE1
 7001 FORMAT(' SPACE=',F10.4)
C
      WRITE(3,7005)
 7005 FORMAT(//,' ** THE COORDINATE VALUES FOR THE POINTS. **',//,' ',
     +13X,'XPOINT',9X,'Y POINT',9X,'Z POINT',/,' ',11X,'*********',6X,
     +'*********',6X,'*********')
   10 NP1=NP1+1
      IF(NP1 .GT. 100) GO TO 99993
      READ(1,8002) (P1(NP1,I),I=1,3)
 8002 FORMAT(3F10.4)
      IF(P1(NP1,1) .EQ. -999.0) GO TO 19
  100 WRITE(3,7002) NP1,P1(NP1,1),P1(NP1,2),P1(NP1,3)
 7002 FORMAT(' ',I5,3(6X,F10.4))
      GO TO 10
   19 NP1=NP1-1
```

```
C
      WRITE(3,7007)
 7007 FORMAT(//,' ** THE AXIS ROTATIONS FOR EACH VIEW. **',//,' ',11X,
     +'X ROTATION',6X,'Y ROTATION',6X,'Z ROTATION',/,' ',11X,'*********
     +',6X,'**********',6X,'**********')
   20 NV1=NV1+1
      IF(NV1 .GT. 100) GO TO 99995
      READ(1,8003) (VP1(NV1,I),I=1,3)
 8003 FORMAT(3F10.4)
      IF(VP1(NV1,1) .EQ. -999.0) GO TO 29
  200 WRITE(3,7003) NV1,VP1(NV1,1),VP1(NV1,2),VP1(NV1,3)
 7003 FORMAT(' ',I5,3(6X,F10.4))
      GO TO 20
   29 NV1=NV1-1
C
      WRITE(3,7006)
 7006 FORMAT(//,' ** THE POINT COMMANDS. **',//,' ',11X,'POINT',/,' ',
     +12X,'CMD',/,' ',11X,'*****')
   30 NC1=NC1+1
      IF(NC1 .GT. 200) GO TO 99997
      READ(1,8004) IC1(NC1)
 8004 FORMAT(I5)
      IF(IC1(NC1) .EQ. -999) GO TO 39
      WRITE(3,7004) NC1,IC1(NC1)
 7004 FORMAT(' ',I5,6X,I5)
      GO TO 30
   39 NC1=NC1-1
      GO TO 99999
C
99993 WRITE(3,99994)
99994 FORMAT(' ** GRAPHIC1 ENDING ** NEXT POINT OUT OF BOUNDS ** EXEC UND
     +ER SUB "RDC2" **')
      GO TO 99999
99995 WRITE(3,99996)
99996 FORMAT(' ** GRAPHIC ENDING INP1UT ** NEXT VIEW ROTATION OUT OF BOUND
     +S ** EXEC UNDER SUB "RDC2" **')
      GO TO 99999
```

```
99997 WRITE(3,99998)
99998 FORMAT(' ** GRAPHIC ENDING INPUT ** NEXT POINT COMMAND OUT OF BOUND
     +DS ** EXEC UNDER SUB "RDC2" **')
C**********************************************************************
99999 RETURN
      END
C
C

      SUBROUTINE RDC3(AXRD,NAX,SF,AXLN,X,Y,Z,ICNT)
C**********************************************************************
C        THIS SUB READS THE DATA FOR CUPID V-3 TYPE STRUCTURES. WILL
C        READ DATA FOR ONE, TWO OR THREE AXIS ACCORDING TO THE VALUE
C        SUPPLIED THROUGH ARGUMENT "AXRD" AND MUST HAVE 1, 2, OR 3
C        AS A VALUE ACCORDING TO THE NUMBER OF AXIS TO BE READ.
C
      DIMENSION X(500),Y(500),Z(500)
      DATA IXGRID/10/,IYGRID/10/
C
      WRITE(3,7000)
 7000 FORMAT('1** GRAPHIC EXEC READ UNDER "RDC3" **'/)
      READ(1,8001)NAX
 8001 FORMAT(I5)
      ISCRT=INT(NAX*10.0)
      GP TO (10,20),NAX
   10 WRITE(3,7001)
 7001 FORMAT(/,' AXIS LINES WILL BE PRODUCED FOR THE VIEWER')
      GO TO 70
   20 WRITE(3,7002)
 7002 FORMAT(/,' AXIS LINES ARE TO BE OMITTED FROM DRAWING')
   70 READ(1,8003)SF
 8003 FORMAT(F10.4)
      WRITE(3,7003)SF
 7003 FORMAT(/,' SF=',F10.4)
      READ(1,8004)AXLN
 8004 FORMAT(F10.4)
      WRITE(3,7004)AXLN
 7004 FORMAT(/,' AXLN=',F10.4)
```

```
      READ(1,8005) AXRD
 8005 FORMAT(I5)
      ISORT=INT(AXRD*10.0)+20
      GO TO (30,40,50,60),ISORT
C
C     THIS SUB PROG SEGMENT READS THE DATA FOR THE Z AXIS ONLY.
C     TESTS TO SEE IF THIS SEGMENT SHOULD BE IMPLEMENTED.
      30 WRITE(3,7005)
 7005 FORMAT(/,' ** GRAPHIC READING THE Z-AXIS **',/)
      WRITE(3,7011)
 7011 FORMAT(//.' ** THE COORDINATE VALUES FOR THE POINTS. **',//,' ',
     +13X,'XPOINT',9X,'Y POINT',9X,'Z POINT',/,' ',11X,'**********',6X,
     +'**********',6X,'**********')
      ICNT1=IXGRID*IYGRID
      IF (ICNT1 .GT. 500) GO TO 99997
      ICNT=0
      DO 200 J=1,IXGRID
      DO 100 K=1,IYGRID
      ICNT=ICNT+1
      X(ICNT)=FLOAT(J)
      Y(ICNT)=FLOAT(K)
      READ(1,8006)Z(ICNT)
 8006 FORMAT(F10.2)
      WRITE(3,7006) ICNT,X(ICNT),Y(ICNT),Z(ICNT)
 7006 FORMAT(' ',I5,3(6X,F10.4))
  100 CONTINUE
  200 CONTINUE
      GO TO 80
C
C     THIS SUB PROG SEGMENT READS THE DATA FOR Y & Z AXIS.  TESTS
C     TO SEE IF THIS SEGMENT SHOULD BE IMPLEMENTED.
C     THIS SUB PROG SEGMENT READS THE DATA FOR X, Y & Z AXIS.
C     TESTS TO SEE IF THIS PROG SEGMENT SHOULD BE USED.
   50 WRITE(3,7009)
   40 WRITE(3,7007)
 7007 FORMAT(/,' ** GRAPHIC READING Y,Z-AXIS **',/)
      WRITE(3,7012)
```

```
7012 FORMAT(//,' ** THE COORDINATE VALUES FOR THE POINTS. **',//,' ',
    +13X,'XPOINT',9X,'Y POINT',9X,'Z POINT',/,' ',11X,'**********',6X,
    +'**********',6X,'**********')
     ICNT=0
 300 INCT=INCT+1
     IF (ICNT .GT. 500) GO TO 99997
     READ(1,8008)Y(ICNT),Z(INCT)
8008 FORMAT(2F10.4)
     IF(Y(ICNT) .EQ. -999.0) GO TO 80
     X(ICNT)=FLOAT(ICNT)
     WRITE(3,7008) ICNT,X(ICNT),Y(ICNT),Z(ICNT)
7008 FORMAT(' ',I5,3(6X,F10.4))
     GO TO 300
C
7009 FORMAT(/,' ** GRAPHIC READING X,Y,Z-AXIS **',/)
     WRITE(3,7013)
7013 FORMAT(//,' ** THE COORDINATE VALUES FOR THE POINTS. **',//,' ',
    +13X,'XPOINT',9X,'Y POINT',9X,'Z POINT',/,' ',11X,'**********',6X,
    +'**********',6X,'**********')
     ICNT=0
 500 ICNT=ICNT+1
     IF(ICNT .GT. 500) GO TO 99997
     READ(1,8010)X(ICNT),Y(ICNT),Z(ICNT)
8010 FORMAT(3F10.4)
     IF(X(ICNT) .EQ. -999.0) GO TO 80
     WRITE(3,7010) ICNT,X(ICNT),Y(ICNT),Z(ICNT)
7010 FORMAT(' ',I5,3(6X,F10.4))
     GO TO 500
  80 ICNT=ICNT-1
     GO TO 99999
C
C   THIS SUB PROG SEGMENT FILLS THE X,Y,Z-AXIS WITH TEST DATA. IF
C   "NAX" IS 4 THEN THE CALL TO SUB "CUPID3" WAS FOR TESTING "CUPID3".
  60 DEG=0.0
     DO 700 I=1,10
     DO 600 J=1,10
     ICNT=ICNT+1
     X(ICNT)=FLOAT(I)
```

```
      Y(ICNT)=FLOAT(J)
      DEG=DEG+0.0157
      Z(ICNT)=2*SIN(DEG)
  600 CONTINUE
  700 CONTINUE
      GO TO 99999
C
99995 WRITE(3,99996)
99996 FORMAT(' ** GRAPHIC ERROR ** AXRD OF SUB RDC3 NOT EQUAL TO 1,2,3 O
     +R 4 **')
      GO TO 99999
99997 WRITE(3,99998)
99998 FORMAT(' ** GRAPHIC ENDING INPUT ** NEXT POINT OUT OF BOUNDS ** EX
     +EC UNDER SUB "RDC3" **')
C*******************************************************************************
99999 RETURN
      END
C
C
      SUBROUTINE DAC12(NDATA,X,Y,Z,IP,P,NP,IC,NC)
C*******************************************************************************
C          THIS SUB CREATES A CUPID V-2 DATA STRUCTURE FROM A CUPID
C          V-1 DATA BASE.
C          WRITTEN BY TOM MACKNIGHT & DANIEL L. RYAN
C
      DIMENSION X(100),Y(100),Z(100),IP(100),P(100,3),IC(200)
C
      WRITE(2,1)
      WRITE(3,1)
    1 FORMAT('1** GRAPHIC EXEC DATA CONVERSION FROM CUPID1 TO CUPID2 TYP
     +E DATA STRUCTURE **')
C
C          SET THE FIRST P1, P2, & P3 POINT EQUAL TO THE FIRST X, Y, & Z
C          POINT FOR FIRST CHECK THROUGH LOOP.
      P(1,1)=X(1)
      P(1,2)=Y(1)
      P(1,3)=Z(1)
```

```
      NP=1
      NC=0
      I=0
C         FOR EACH CUPID V-1 X,Y & Z POINT, CHECK TO SEE IF IT HAS BEEN
C         ESTABLISHED AS A CUPID V-2 P1,P2 & P3 POINT.
  100 I=I+1
      ITEST=0
      DO 200 J=1,NP
  200     IF((X(I) .EQ. P(J,1)) .AND.
     +        (Y(I) .EQ. P(J,2)) .AND.
     +        (Z(I) .EQ. P(J,3)) ) ITEST=1
C         IF POINT HAS NOT BEEN CREATED ESTABLISH IT.
      IF(ITEST .EQ. 1) GO TO 300
      NP=NP+1
      P(NP,1)=X(I)
      P(NP,2)=Y(I)
      P(NP,3)=Z(I)
  300 NC=NC+1
C         IF ALL THE CUPID V-1 POINTS HAVE BEEN SEARCHED AND POINTS
C         ESTABLISHED AS CUPID V-2 POINTS THEN END THIS SEGMENT.
      IF(NC .EQ. NDATA) GO TO 400
      GO TO 100
C
C         FOR EACH CUPID V-1 POINT SET THE CORRESPONDING CUPID V-2 DRAW
C         COMMAND. THE POINT IS LOCATED BY A SEARCH THROUGH THE
C         ESTABLISHED CUPID V-2 POINT LIST.  IC(I) IS GIVEN THE
C         POINT ARRAY VALUE AND MADE NEG IF IP(I)=3.
  400 DO 600 I=1,NC
          DO 500 J=1,NP
              IF ((X(I) .EQ. P(J,1)) .AND.
     +            (Y(I) .EQ. P(J,2)) .AND.
     +            (Z(I) .EQ. P(J,3)) ) IC(I)=J
              IF ((X(I) .EQ. P(J,1)) .AND.
     +            (Y(I) .EQ. P(J,2)) .AND.
     +            (Z(I) .EQ. P(J,3)) .AND.
     +            (IP(I) .EQ. 3)) IC(I)=-1*J
  500     CONTINUE
```

```
600       CONTINUE
      WRITE(2,2)
      WRITE(3,2)
   2 FORMAT(//,' ** VALUES FOR CUPID V-2 POINTS **')
      WRITE(3,3)
   3 FORMAT('0',13X,'X POINT',9X,'Y POINT',9X,'Z POINT')
      WRITE(3,4)
   4 FORMAT(' ',11X,'*********',6X,'*********',6X,'*********')
      DO 10 I=1,NP
  10      WRITE(3,5) I,P(I,1),P(I,2),P(I,3)
   5      FORMAT(' ',I5,3(6X,F10.4))
      WRITE(2,11)(P(I,1),P(I,2),P(I,3),I=1,NP)
  11 FORMAT(3F10.4)
      WRITE(2,6)
      WRITE(3,6)
   6 FORMAT(//,' ** VALUES FOR CUPID V-2 DRAW COMMANDS **')
      WRITE(3,7)
   7 FORMAT('0',60X,'DRAW',/,' ',13X,'X POINT',9X,'Y POINT',
     +          9X,'Z POINT',9X,'CMD')
      WRITE(3,8)
   8 FORMAT(' ',11X,'*********',6X,'*********',6X,'*********',
     +          6X,'*****')
      DO 20 I=1,NC
  20      WRITE(3,9) I,X(I),Y(I),Z(I),IC(I)
   9      FORMAT(' ',I5,3(6X,F10.4),6X,I5)
      WRITE(2,12)(IC(I),I=1,NC)
  12 FORMAT(I5)
C*******************************************************************

99999 RETURN
      END
      SUBROUTINE DAC21(P,NP,IC,NC,NDATA,X,Y,Z,IP)
C*******************************************************************
C         THIS SUB CREATES A CUPID V-1 TYPE STRUCTURE FROM CUPID V-2
C         DATA.
      DIMENSION X(100),Y(100),Z(100),IP(100),P(100,3),IC(200)
```

```
C
      WRITE(2,1)
      WRITE(3,1)
    1 FORMAT('1** GRAPHIC EXEC DATA CONVERSION FROM CUPID2 TO CUPID1 DAT
     +A STRUCTURE **'/)
      NDATA=NC
      WRITE(3,7)
    7 FORMAT(//,' ** VALUES FOR CUPID V-2 POINTS **')
      WRITE(3,8)
    8 FORMAT('0',13X,'X POINT',9X,'Y POINT',9X,'Z POINT')
      WRITE(3,9)
    9 FORMAT(' ',11X,'**********',6X,'**********',6X,'**********')
      DO 50 I=1,NP
   50 WRITE(3,11)I,(P(I,J),J=1,3)
   11 FORMAT(' ',I5,3(6X,F10.4))
C         FOR EACH CUPID V-2 DRAW COMMAND SET PEN IN DOWN POSITION.
C         IF COMMAND IS NEG(PEN UP) THEN MAKE PEN COMMAND FOR CUPID
C         V-1 PEN UP.  EACH X,Y & Z POINT OF CUPID V-1 THE CORRESPONDING
C         P1,P2 & P3 POINT IS ASSIGNED.
      DO 100 I=1,NC
         IP(I)=2
C        CONVERT IC(I) TO THE ABS VALUE ONLY IF IC(I) IS NEG.
         IF(IC(I) .LT. 0) IP(I)=3
         K=IC(I)
         IF(IC(I) .LT. 0) K=-1*IC(I)
         X(I)=P(K,1)
         Y(I)=P(K,2)
         Z(I)=P(K,3)
  100    CONTINUE
      WRITE(2,2)
      WRITE(3,2)
    2 FORMAT(//,' ** VALUES FOR CUPID V-1 DRAW COMMANDS **')
      WRITE(3,3)
    3 FORMAT('0',13X,'DRAW',/,' ',13X,'CMD',9X,'X POINT',9X,'Y POINT,'
     +          9X,'Z POINT',9X,'PEN')
      WRITE(3,4)
```

```
   4 FORMAT(' ',11X,'****',6X,'**********',6X,'**********',6X,
    +          '**********',6X,'****')
     DO 200 I=1,NC
          WRITE(3,5)I,IC(I),X(I),Y(I),Z(I),IP(I)
   5      FORMAT(' ',I5,6X,I5,3(6X,F10.5),6X,I5)
     WRITE(2,6)X(I),Y(I),Z(I),IP(I)
   6 FORMAT(3F10.4,I5)
 200 CONTINUE
C***********************************************************************
     RETURN
     END
C
C

     SUBROUTINE RDSMN
C***********************************************************************
C
C

     DIMENSION A(50,50),C(50)
  11 FORMAT('1** GRAPHIC EXEC READ UNDER "RDSMN" **',/)
   7 FORMAT (I5)
   1 FORMAT (F10.4)
   2 FORMAT (I5,F10.4)
   3 FORMAT (' ',I5)
   4 FORMAT (' ',F10.4)
     WRITE(3,11)
     READ (1,7) NOB
     DO 8 II=1,NOB
C    WRITE OUT PROBLEM NUMBER
     WRITE (3,3) II
C    READ SIZE OF MATRIX AND A SMALL NUMBER TO DETECT WHETHER DIAGONAL
C    ELEMENT IS ZERO OR NOT
     READ(1,2) N,EPS
     READ (1,1) ((A(I,J),J=1,N),I=1,N)
     READ (1,1) (C(I),I=1,N)
     CALL SIMON(A,C,N,EPS)
C    WRITE OUT RESULTS
     WRITE (3,4) (C(I),I=1,N)
```

```
      8 CONTINUE
C*******************************************************************
        RETURN
        END
        SUBROUTINE XFLIP(Z)
C*******************************************************************
C          THIS SUB RE-SORTS THE DATA FOR FLIPPING THE X-AXIS OF CUPID V-3
C
        DIMENSION Z(500)
C
        DO 300 I=1,10
            DO 100 J=1,10
  100          Z(100+J)=Z(J)
                DO 200 K=1,10
  200              Z((J-1)*10+K)=Z(J*10+K)
  300 CONTINUE
C*******************************************************************
        RETURN
        END
C
C
        SUBROUTINE YFLIP(Z)
C*******************************************************************
C          THIS SUB RE-SORTS THE DATA TO FLIP THE Y-AXIS OF CUPID V-3.
C
        DIMENSION Z(500)
C
        DO 200 I=1,10
            TEMP=Z((I-1)*10+1)
            DO 100 J=1,9
                Z((I-1)*10+J)=Z((I-1)*10+J+1)
  100          CONTINUE
            Z(I*10)=TEMP
  200      CONTINUE
C*******************************************************************
        RETURN
        END
```

```
C
C
C
C
C*********************************************************************
C*********************************************************************
C
C*********************************************************************
C      END OF GRAPHIC LISTING........DRIVER SUBS TO FOLLOW
C*********************************************************************
C
C
C      EEEEEE  NN   NN  DDDDD      LL      II  SSSSSS  TTTTT
C      EE      NNN  NN  DD DDD     LL      II  SS         TT
C      EEEEE   NNNNNN   DD  DD     LL      II  SSSSSS     TT
C      EE      NN NNN   DD DDD     LL      II     SS      TT
C      EEEEEE  NN   NN  DDDDD      LLLLLL  II  SSSSSS     TT
C
C
C*********************************************************************
```

REVIEW PROBLEMS

1. List the hardware components of a star network.

ANSWER

    Graphic workstation satellites (four per local processor)

    Three local processors tied to one control processor

    Two plotter-digitizer satellites

    Direct-display devices and console/edit station

    Linkage to mainframe computer

2. List the hardware components of a hierarchical network.

ANSWER   First three items of star network

3. List the hardware components of an individual graphic workstation.

ANSWER

    Connection line to processor

    Local processor that contains the display file

    Secondary processor/character generator

    Vector generator and display screen monitor

4. Describe in your own words how each of these hardware items works.

ASCII keyboard
Buffered processor
Character generator
Crosshair control
Display screen monitor
DVST
Function buttons
Local processor
Main computer
Main processor
Menu bar
Secondary processor
Vector generator
Viewport
Window

5. Describe in your own words how each of these software items works.

DO loops
Function calls
IF statements
I/O statements
Main programs
Multidimensioned arrays
Processor sequences
Statement numbers
Subroutines

8
PROGRAMMING
ANIMATION

This chapter discusses the graphics programming necessary for three-dimensional coordinate systems and the display of wireforms. We will introduce the following concepts of display technology:

1. Transparency
2. Diffusion of multisurfaces
3. Polygonal surfaces
4. Intensity interpolation
5. Normal interpolation

In order to do these types of motion display (animation) a three-dimensional transformation package must be written to include the following:

1. Roll, pitch, and yaw

2. Translation and scaling
3. Rotation of the display axis

The subroutines on pages 226–227 illustrate such a software approach. The graphics programmer must input the data structure necessary to describe the object to be animated, such as that in Table 8-1. Next, the programmer inputs the order in which the data points are to be connected. This is normally referred to as the IPEN string; for example:

```
IPEN = -1,2,3,4,1,5,6,7,8,5,-4,8,-3,7,-2,6
```

Before the display of motion, several other inputs are also necessary, including the number of frames to be repeated during the animation and the spacing between views. When repeated on a

```
SUBROUTINE CUPID2
DIMENSION P(100,3),IC(200),VP(100,3),PP(100,3)
READ(1,1)NP,NC,NV
WRITE(3,10)NP,NC,NV
READ(1,2)SPACE
WRITE(3,101)SPACE
READ(1,3)((P(I,J),J=1,3),I=1,NP)
WRITE(3,102)
WRITE(3,103)
WRITE(3,104)((P(I,J),J=1,3),I=1,NP)
READ(1,3)((VP(I,J),J=1,3),I=1,NV)
WRITE(3,105)
WRITE(3,103)
WRITE(3,104)((VP(I,J),J=1,3),I=1,NV)
READ(1,4)(IC(I),I=1,NC)
WRITE(3,106)
WRITE(3,107)(IC(I),I=1,NC)
CALL PLOTS
CALL FACTOR(1.5)
CALL PLOT(2.0,2.0,-3)
DO 5 I=1,NV
A=ARTAN(VP(I,1),VP(I,3))
SA=SIN(A)
CA=COS(A)
DO 6 J=1,NP
PP(J,3)=P(J,3)*CA+P(J,1)*SA
PP(J,1)=P(J,1)*CA-P(J,3)*SA
6     CONTINUE
VPP=VP(I,3)*CA+VP(I,1)*SA
A=ARTAN(VP(I,2),VPP)
SA=SIN(A)
CA=COS(A)
DO 7 J=1,NP
```

```
        PP(J,2)=P(J,2)*CA-PP(J,3)*SA
7       CONTINUE
        DO 11 K=1,NP
        PP(K,2)=PP(K,2)+6.0
        PP(K,1)=PP(K,1)+SPACE*I
11      CONTINUE
        DO 8 J=1,NC
        IF (IC(J).LT.0) GO TO 9
        CALL PLOT(PP(IC(J),1),PP(IC(J),2),2)
        GO TO 8
9       K=-IC(J)
        CALL PLOT(PP(K,1),PP(K,2),3)
8       CONTINUE
5       CONTINUE
        XSET=(SPACE*NV)+8.
        CALL PLOT(XSET,0.,999)
1       FORMAT(3I5)
2       FORMAT(F10.3)
3       FORMAT(3F10.2)
4       FORMAT(10I5)
10      FORMAT('1',20X,'NUMBER OF POINTS TO BE PLOTTED=',I5,/,21X,'NUMBER
       105 PEN MOVEMENTS REQD  =',I5,/,21X,'NUMBER OF VIEWS TO BE DRAWN
       1=',I5)
101     FORMAT('0',20X,'SPACE PROVIDED FOR EACH VIEW  =',F6.2)
102     FORMAT(///,30X,'POINT COORDINATES')
103     FORMAT(/,20X,'X',20X,'Y',20X,'Z')
104     FORMAT(/,F25.3,2F20.3)
105     FORMAT(///,30X,'VANTAGE POINTS')
106     FORMAT(/,30X,'PLOT COMMANDS')
107     FORMAT(10X,10I5)
        RETURN
        END
```

TABLE 8-1
Data Structure

X	Y	Z
0.	0.	0.
.5	0.	0.
.5	1.	0.
0.	1.	0.
0.	0.	.5
.5	0.	.5
.5	1.	.5
0.	1.	.5

CRT, the spacing is usually zero, with a call to ERASE entered between each frame. If the desired output is to appear on a digital plotter, a space of 5 to 10 inches is usually specified, allowing filming onto 16mm or 35mm format, respectively.

3-D COORDINATE SYSTEMS AND WIREFORMS

For animation to be properly programmed and displayed on an output device, the data describing the object must be in X, Y, and Z columns as shown in Table 8-1. Here, the data represent a simple rectangular box. If this box, described by the data structure and connected by the IPEN array shown above was displayed on a raster scan CRT and animated, it might look like Figure 8-1. Here, the animation is about the Z axis. The X axis is located in the usual horizontal direction, with the Y axis in the vertical direction on the face of the CRT. Each frame of the animation has been left on the screen in Figure 8-1. There are a total of 36 frames for each complete rotation around the Z axis. It is clear that a raster scan CRT is the display device because of the "jagged line problem" in frames other than 0, 90, 180, 270, and 360. Because of the data structure used, the box appears as a 2-D rectangle. In order for the box to appear as a wireform, as in Figure 8-2, an additional axis must be animated.

The term *transparency* comes from the fact that all lines of an object are visible. The animation around the Z axis (Figure 8-1) did not show this transparency. Figure 8-2 is the same rotation about the Z axis viewed or rotated 90 degrees. This concept is known as *revolution of axis*. The software listing under CUPID1 is common for revolution-type animation; the subroutine CUPID1 shown earlier was used to represent three separate working views of an object. Orthographic-type presentations of frontal, horizontal, and profile are really single frames of animation during revolution. Pure rotation about three axes is programmed as listed in subroutine CUPID2. Pure animation of a wireform object can best be described as a rolling or tumbling action in free space. The object will rotate or turn about three reference axes—X, Y, Z. If the origin is fixed (placed at common values), full animation will take place inside of a perfect sphere. To illustrate, one row of data from the data structure in Table 8-1 together with one element (column) of the IPEN array represent a single wire of the object shown in Figures 8-1 and 8-2. If only this much information is given to subroutine CUPID2 and full animation with fixed origin (SPACE = 0.), then the output will appear as Figure 8-3.

Transparency

The raster scan CRT terminal has been associated with simple animation of transparent wireform objects for the past decade or so. Initially, wireforms were used in animation because of the direct data structure and ease of display. If the graphics programmer liked the animation sequence and approved the transformations (smoothness of frame changes), then a surface

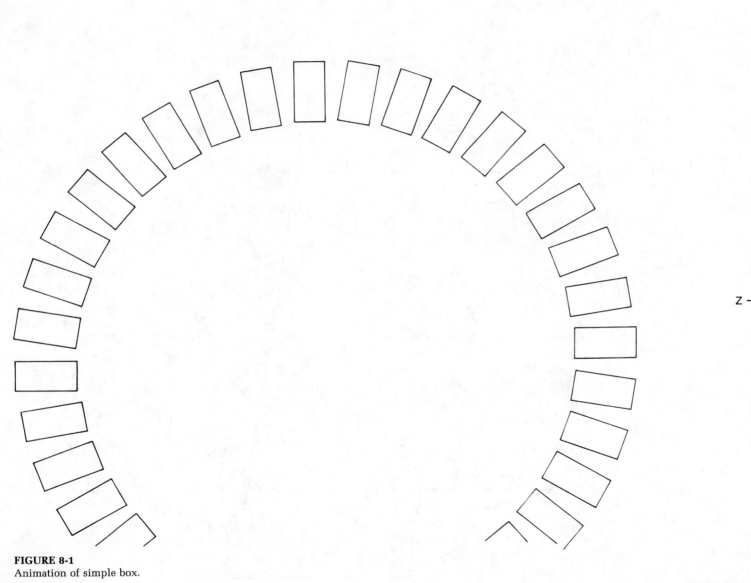

FIGURE 8-1
Animation of simple box.

FIGURE 8-2

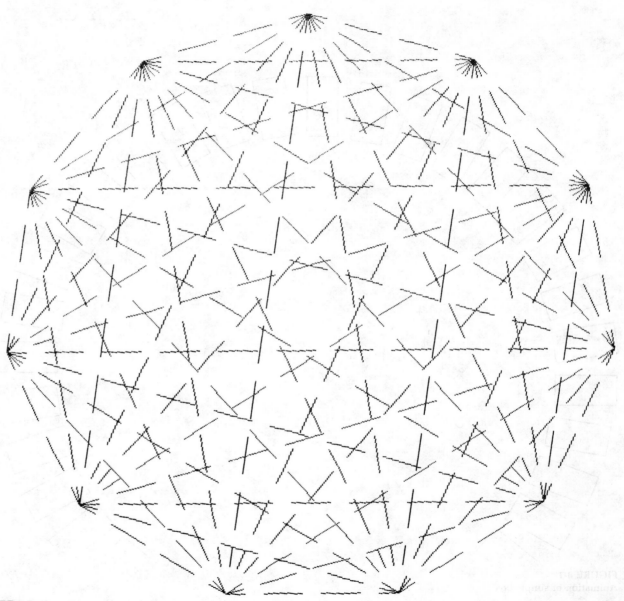

FIGURE 8-3
Full animation.

shading was added, as described in Chapter 6. If the animation was not correct, then the data structure was modified and viewed again.

With this transparency approach many objects were animated so their motion could be studied during the design sequence. This analysis coupled with the animation became known as *simulation*. The use of raster scan CRTs for simulation is relatively new.

The use of transparent wireforms for animation dates from the pioneering work done by Dr. Ivan Sutherland on Sketch Pad in the late 1950s and early 1960s. Today, transparent wireforms are commonly used as the first step in CAD in both research and profit-making situations such as computer-aided machine design. The inclusion of this concept in many freshman engineering programs across the country is an indication of the present and anticipated importance of this fundamental tool for the graphics programmer.

Diffusion of Multisurfaces

Often the graphics programmer is required to shift the origin during animation. SPACE is set equal to a constant or a variable, depending on the design application. Now the visual concept of a sphere is replaced by a donut-like viewing space (Figure 8-4). Regardless of the viewing space defined, a diffusion of multisurfaces always results. In order to properly display these types of animation, a CRT must be used. As we have seen, within the CRT a stream of electrons impinges on the phosphor screen, emitting light. Because of the nature of the CRT and the multi-

surfaces to be displayed on the screen, at least three parameters can be controlled to produce multisurface animation.

Polygonal surfaces. Here, the electron beam is deflected by both magnetic and electrostatic fields. A primary advantage of the CRT for polygonal surfaces is that the beam has negligible inertia and therefore can be moved at very high speeds (compared to a plotter). Two basic deflection schemes are used in polygonal construction. The first process, called the *rasterscan*, is the same as in a home television set. The beam is moved in the X direction and then is rapidly reset to the starting horizontal point and moved again horizontally. At the same time the beam is moving slowly in the vertical direction. A typical polygon consists of 525 (maximum) horizontal lines repeated 30 times a second.

A second method for beam deflection is known as *random positioning*. In this case the beam can be moved simultaneously in an X and a Y direction, along a straight or a curved path, to produce the diffusion of multisurfaces. This is the same way an artist uses a pencil and paper to produce a picture.

Intensity interpolation. By properly modulating either the cathode or the control grid of the CRT, the graphics programmer can turn off the beam while it is being moved to a location on the screen and then turn it on at the desired spot. In addition, the programmer can vary the intensification in order to achieve a number of light output levels.

Intensity interpolation can be used with either raster scan or random position. With the raster

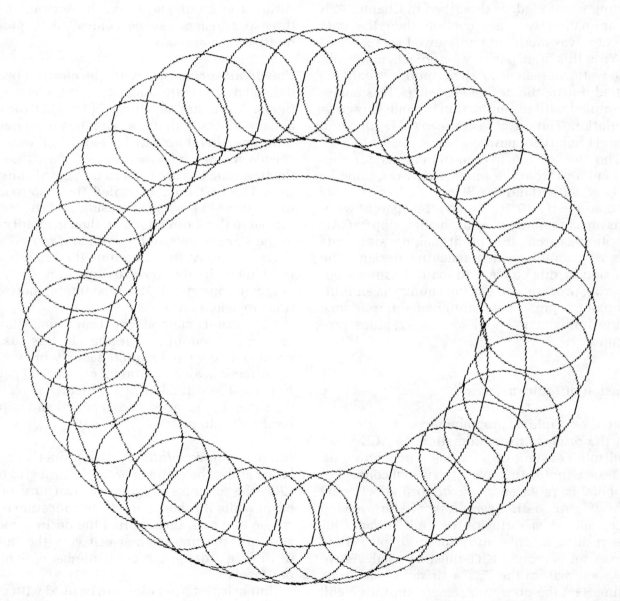

FIGURE 8-4

scan, as in digital TV, the beam is turned off and on in response to control signals from the animation program. Areas of dark and light combine to form the desired picture during the animation sequence. With random positioning the beam is generally turned off until the desired position is reached and then turned on while the beam is deflected along the programmed path for animation.

Normal interpolation. Normally, the CRT beam is focused with an electrical lens system. The graphics programmer usually wants to create as round and as small a beam cross-section as possible for animation. However, it is possible to intentionally distort the beam and change its cross-section. During normal interpolation, the beam is extruded through a stencil so that its cross-section is formed into a display symbol (element). When the beam strikes the phospher, light is emitted across the entire cross-section, and the element appears in animation.

All three systems for the diffusion of multisurfaces depend on the observer's visual memory or on the phosphor persistence to present an animated image that does not flicker. Phosphors are categorized by the length of time required for the image to decay to 10% of its initial value (Table 8-2). The light from some phosphors dies out within microseconds (usec) after the beam moves to another location, whereas other phosphors will continue to emit light for milliseconds. On special storage tubes like the DVST, the image stays until it is intentionally erased.

Except in the special storage tubes, where animation is not possible, image persistence is a

TABLE 8-2

Time Required for 90% Decay	Phosphor Class	
Less than 1 usec	Very Short	VS
1 usec to 10 usec	Short	S
10 usec to 1 msec	Medium short	MS
1 msec to .1 sec	Medium	M
1 sec to 1 sec	Long	L
Longer than 1 sec	Very long	VL

hardware function of the CRT chosen. Animation is often made easier by the use of color. A broad range of colors is available to the graphics programmer. Phosphors emit a white, green, blue, yellow, red, or orange light glow. Several phosphors can be combined in one tube to achieve multicolor animations. In single-coated phosphor CRTs color is a function of the hardware, but in multicoated phosphor CRTs the animation frame color can be under program control.

The type of animation shown in Figures 8-1 and 8-2 is known as *single-plane motion*, even though the object that is under animation control is a wireform containing 3-D data structure.

3-D TRANSFORMATION PACKAGES

The software listed at the beginning of this chapter provides for single, double-, or triple-plane motion. In the recent past several such software systems have been written for aiding in the conventional two-dimensional animation process. It is rare to find software for 3-D animation. The main purpose of earlier 2-D systems was to let the computer produce missing wireforms based on extreme drawings by animators. Though these processes had some success and have a great deal of potential, the need for higher level output and engineering quality prompted the CUPID software shown in this chapter. The transition from simple 2-D wireforms on direct-display devices to the more complicated and detailed finite element models is now possible.

Comparing former animation techniques with the CUPID approach makes it clear that using the former models was quite tedious. The computer can be used to greatly speed up the vantage point problem as well as to make animation cheaper. Vantage points are based on the older conventional animation techniques; they are the fundamental concepts used in situations ranging from the limited Saturday morning cartoons to the full animation necessary for finite element modeling. With the vantage point system there are roughly three categories for computer animation: art and graphic animation (movies), 3-D animation (engineering analysis), and key-frame animation used for simulation.

Animation can also be characterized by the kinds of transformations that can be performed with vantage points. An important concept is *inbetweening*, where a graphics programmer uses a graphical structures approach to construct wireforms based on two extreme poses of a wireframe, usually vantage points 0., 0., 0. and 1., 1., 1.. The CUPID subprogram uses linear transformations

TABLE 8-3

Ascending X	Descending Y	Merging Z
0.	1.	0.
.1	.9	.1
.2	.8	.2
.3	.7	.3
.4	.6	.4
.5	.5	.5
.6	.4	.4
.7	.3	.3
.8	.2	.2
.9	.1	.1
1.	0.	0.

(SPACE) and simple linear interpolation to create the wireforms needed between 0. and 1. Table 8-3 shows the range of vantage points for each plane motion.

Roll, Pitch, and Yaw

Vantage points can best be explained by studying basic revolution concepts in free space. In Figures 8-5, 8-6, 8-7, and 8-8, a single side has been shaded for better visibility. Moreover, during animation the graphics programmer views a single object moving in space; the four objects shown are for illustration only. Figure 8-5a displays a single wireform of a cube having a vantage point of 0., 0., 0. Figure 8-5b represents 0., 0., .25, or 90 degrees of plane motion around the Z axis. Mo-

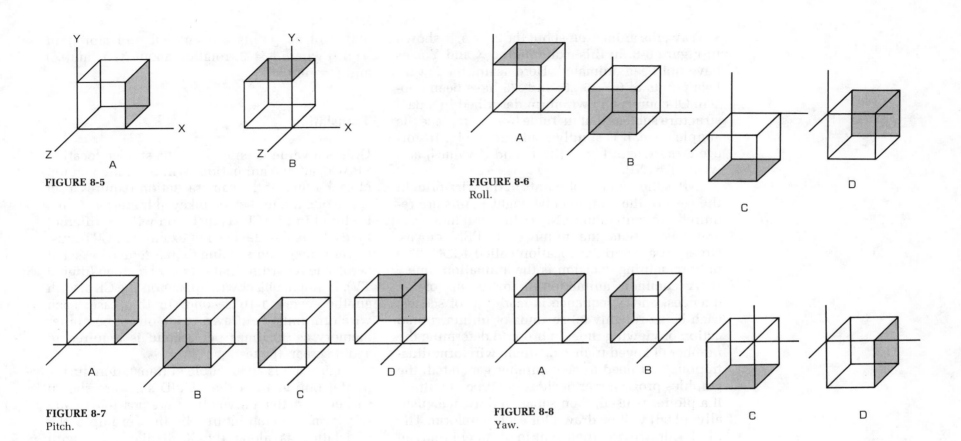

FIGURE 8-5

FIGURE 8-6
Roll.

FIGURE 8-7
Pitch.

FIGURE 8-8
Yaw.

tion around each of the axes is shown in Figure 8-6 as Roll, or animation around the X axis. In this example vantage points of 0., 0., 0. were chosen for part a; .25, 0., 0. for part b; .5, 0., 0. for part c; and .75 for part d. Multiple rotations could have been input into the software listing; however, the concept of ROLL could not have been modeled.

Pitch—the animation about the Y axis—is shown in Figure 8-7. In this example the X and Z axes have not been animated. The four vantage points illustrated are: 0., 0., 0.; − 0., .25, 0.; − 0., .5, 0.; − and 0., .75, 0.. The total range of vantage points shown in Table 8-3 would result in a smooth animation sequence during the demonstration of pitch shown in Figure 8-7.

Yaw, the animation about the Z axis, is shown in Figure 8-8. In this example the X and Y axes have not been animated. Here again, the Z vantage points of 0., .25, .5, and .75 have been chosen. Of course, any wireform described in a data structure such as that in Table 8-1 can replace the simple cube. It is simply read into the P(I,J) storage array where I = 3 (X, Y, and Z values) and where J = NP.

NP is the number of points in the wireform. In the case of the simple cube, eight points are required for animation. Next, the graphics programmer inputs the number of IPEN moves, stored in a computer location called ICON. The only remaining decision is the animation time.

A common animation is made up of sequences, and a sequence is made up of scenes, each being roughly 30 seconds of uninterrupted action or viewing time. In order to determine the number of keyed frames or single wireform illustrations that need to be computer generated, the graphics programmer decides the type of output. If a plotter is used, then separate drawings (usually inked) will be drawn for each wireform. The plotter drawing is then sent to a camera (movie) station, where 16 or 24 frames per second are selected. To produce 30 seconds of animation, 30 × 16, or 480, separate drawings are needed. This is entered in the storage location NV, or number of view-frames. Next, the graphics programmer selects 480 vantage points, either in graphical structure mode or data structure mode. Graphics mode means that a random selection is decided on by the programmer; data mode means that a regular combination of roll, pitch, and yaw is automatically calculated for the wireform. The 480 vantage points are entered and stored in VP(I,J) where I = 3 (rotation about X, Y, and Z) and J = 480.

Translation

Unless a value is entered in the storage location SPACE, all 480 animations will be plotted on top of each other. If the camera station requires a set space of 6 inches between keyed frames, then 6.0 is stored in SPACE. Translation will be different for each display device. For example, a CRT must be refreshed, and spacing therefore may be set at zero. The recording station may be video (digital TV). A single object will appear on the CRT, with another every 1/16 second. In this case, each wireform must be drawn twice out of computer memory as 30 times per second is required to avoid screen flicker.

Figure 8-9 is an example of translation during plotter output from the CUPID software shown earlier. Note that curved lines are possible in any wireform data structure. In this example the translation is along the X display axis, with SPACE set equal to 6 inches. The wireform contains line segments, portions of CALL CIRCLE (arcs), and circles. Each of the circles represents 60 data points for linear interpolation. Combinations of roll, pitch, and yaw were input as vantage points. None of the frames shows single-plane rotation. None of the frames uses single-surface shading for ease of translation viewing. Figure 8-9 represents 30 seconds, or one scene. This scene will be part of a sequence used in simulation.

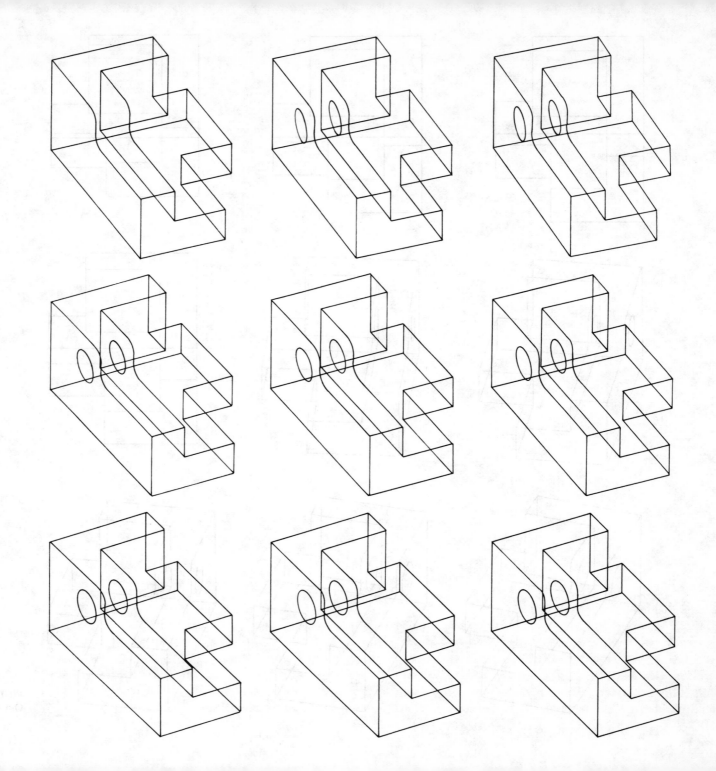

FIGURE 8-9
(Continued)

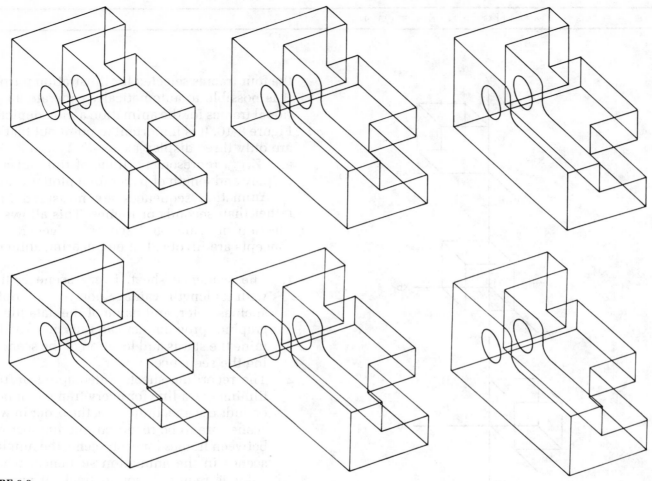

FIGURE 8-9
(Continued)

Scale

During a scene the scale entered in the storage location SF is usually left constant. This is particularly true for translation along the X axis or the Y axis. But because the Z axis of most CRT displays is considered to be into the face of the tube, scaling is often done. Figure 8-10 is an example of

translation along the Y axis with SF set at .75 of the data structure. The same data points (values) are used in Figures 8-5, 8-6, 8-7, 8-8, and 8-10. SF was input as .75 and left constant for each of the frames shown. Note that only four key frames are shown in Figure 8-10. This does not mean that only 4/16 of a second of animation is present; several in-between frames exist between each of

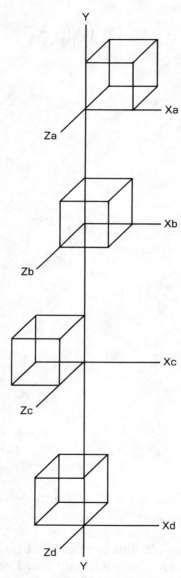

FIGURE 8-10

the four frames selected for illustration purposes. It is possible to automatically generate 99 additional frames for the animation action depicted in Figure 8-10. It is important to point out that there are only three display axes—X, Y, and Z. $X_{a,b,c,d}$ and $Z_{a,b,c,d}$ represent portions of time for a CRT display and length of paper for a plotter drawing.

Animation sequences are measured in feet rather than seconds or frames. This allows for a selection of scales and scenes. In general, two concepts are involved in engineering animation:

1. The sequence sheet. Every scene is listed, with its length, vantage points, vital options such as color, and name of the data file. The graphics programmer can thus quickly determine the status and location of the scene during the sequence.
2. The recording sheet. Videotaping or 16mm filming has a line for every frame that begins or ends a scene, indicating the order in which scenes are to be recorded, the number of in-between frames for each scene, the number of scenes in the animation sequence, whether color is required, sound track (if any), and composition of photography or videotaping.

Rotation

The most important transformation during animation is the *rotation* of the display axes. In Figure 8-11 notice the changing scale factor and the rotation of the object with respect to the display axes. What if the display axes were free to move also? This is true for the CUPID3 listings that appear in Chapter 9. Several concepts hold true when axes are transformed:

1. Parallel lines remain parallel under any axis rotation due to the orthogonal relationships of the axes.
2. The display-device origin remains invarient during the animation sequence or scene.
3. 2-D figures like parallelograms and rectangles retain their shape during all rotations.
4. Rotation by a variable storage location (THETA) yields

$$\begin{bmatrix} COS\ (THETA) & SIN\ (THETA) \\ -SIN\ (THETA) & COS\ (THETA) \end{bmatrix} = \begin{bmatrix} 0 & 1 \\ -1 & 0 \end{bmatrix} FOR\ 90°$$

whereas reflection about the Y axis is

$$\begin{bmatrix} 1 & 0 \\ 0 & -1 \end{bmatrix}$$

and reflection about the X axis is

$$\begin{bmatrix} -1 & 0 \\ 0 & 1 \end{bmatrix}$$

If scaling is required, then

$$\begin{bmatrix} SF_1 & 0 \\ 0 & SF_2 \end{bmatrix}$$

where SF_1 scales X and SF_2 scales Y.

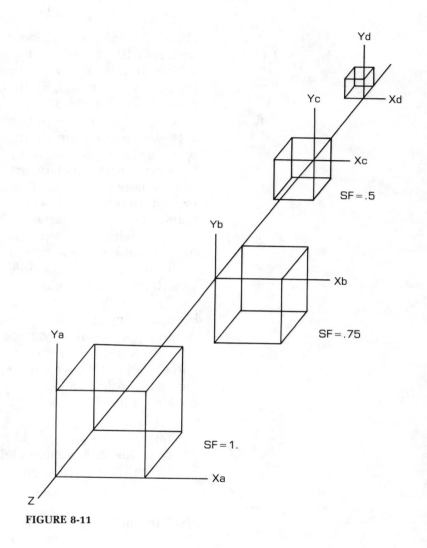

FIGURE 8-11

SURFACE DESCRIPTION AND SHADING

Filling in the areas created by the polygonal surfaces of the wireform with color or shades of gray gives the illusion of solidity. Automatic algorithms for doing this are described by Pavlidis

(1978). These types of algorithm are based on the concepts illustrated in Figures 6-13 and 6-14, which follow known boundaries that define shapes and attempt to fill in the display area with color or shades of gray, yet keep separate shapes or areas distinct. The previous examples (Figure 6-13 and 6-14) were limited to quad elements, or four-sided polygonal surfaces. A procedure for storing each shaded surface under a separate storage name was also discussed. Although this procedure was ideally suited for the level of programming in chapter 6, a manual method of pointing with a light pen is not suitable during the animation scene or sequence. Hundreds of thousands of surfaces would have to be hand selected using this process.

To avoid this hand selection, techniques have been developed to shade wireform objects containing polygonal or curved surfaces. Authors such as Atherton, Weiler, and Greenberg (1978) and Crow (1977) have addressed problems of surface description and shading with the following considerations:

1. Single or multiple light sources are present.
2. Does the light source yield divergent rays?
3. Is the light source from a single point with parallel rays?

Pixel Intensity

Figures 6-13 and 6-14 make reference to pixel (raster scan) intensity for surface shading. Surface shading can also be done by random positioning CRTs; in that case it is refered to as *linear intensity*. For purposes of our discussion, the factors usually controlled in surface description

and shading algorithms for CRT output are deflection and intensity. Because of the nature of a CRT, these are controlled with analog voltages. The complex digital-to-analog conversion is done in two main sections—interface and display generation.

Interface portions of the display contain the CRT, the deflection circuits that position the beam, and the video circuits that modulate the beam. The type of deflection circuit depends on whether the display is a raster scanning or a random positioning display device.

Display generation consists of a dot generator (example of display shown in Figure 6-13), a character generator (example of display shown in Figure 6-14), and a set of traditional digital-to-analog converters, which change the digital X and Y designations into corresponding analog signals to position the beam on the screen. In this elementary pixel positioning system, each pixel needs a separate instruction as to its value 0 through 4. The screen has 512 or 1024 addressable locations in the X and Y directions.

To display the shading character **##**, a series of 18-bit digital words would be sent from the computer. Consequently, one of the early decisions (pixel intensity or linear intensity) concerns the amount of computer software to make a shading symbol compared with the amount of display hardware needed to accomplish the same thing. To help reduce the computer software requirements, the typical pixel intensity CRT contains several other elements that modify the outputs of the various dot generators. The shading generator usually has a digital size control, allowing several shading pixels to be programmed with one or two digital bits. The digital size control is generally a digitally controlled attenuator operating on the analog output voltages of the pixel generator.

At the output of the dot generator, it is possible to connect a line shading control function. Instead of being displayed solid (as in linear intensity), the line will appear to be dotted, dashed, or dot-dashed. This effect could be created by the graphics programmer's written instructions, but pixel intensity hardware allows the control to be done with one or two digital bits. Also in the pixel intensity system, the line structure can be modified without affecting the time in which the pixel is displayed. The display from the dot, shading, and function generators can be routed through the digitally controlled intensity modifier so that the intensity of any of the pixels can be varied by a one- or two-bit digital word. The intensity can be further modified under graphics programmer control so that any of the pixels can be made to blink. Blink control is now available as a hardware element on most graphic CRT displays.

With all the pixel generation and function modifiers, it is often necessary to provide terminal logic that decodes the computer word sent and returns the information to the appropriate generator or modifier function (intensity). This process has been properly named the *display processing function* (DPF). In the very simplest use, the DPF acts as a decoder. In more complex usage, several other hardware functions are assigned to the DPF:

Pixel intensity
Vector function (for linear intensity CRTs)
Dither generation

For example, the stringing of pixels across the line in a printer-plotter can be done by logic in the DPF. Only the initial position of the first pixel in the line must be programmed. Subsequent pixels are then streamed out, and the hardware takes care of advancing the pixel to the next location. Spacing between pixels can be made equal to the pixel size. Provision can be made so that, when the pixels reach the end of the line, the line automatically resets to the left-hand margin and advance by the appropriate space to begin the next line of pixels. Circuits can be included in the DPF so that pixels can be rotated by 90 degrees and displayed horizontally instead of vertically, or the pixels can be superimposed.

Linear Intensity

Earlier we saw an example of linear intensity where the typical phosphor in a CRT emitted a light for only the time that the beam impinges on the phosphor. There may be some persistence or afterglow, but not exceeding several milliseconds. In this way linear intensity can be used to create the impression of a continuous image. This is done with a display generator that contains storage; in other words, the dot generator for pixel intensity becomes a vector generator for linear intensity. Random access memory, delay line, or memory drum types of processor have been named *display processor units* (DPU). If the DPU is available in the CRT, the computer only has to load the DPU with a frame of data for the vector to be displayed. The DPU would recycle the data internally as frequently as necessary to refresh the picture. The computer would be required only to change a line. Then the computer program would address the DPU as necessary, and the new vector would appear on the display screen.

Dither

The combination of pixel and linear intensity is known as *dither*. The analog signals from the various pixel generators and vector (linear) generators are combined into appropriate deflection and video line drivers, which feed the CRT display analog inputs. Frequently, the animation character deflection voltages are separated from the other deflection voltages. Therefore, the output of the display generator would consist of major deflection analog signals, with minor deflection analog signals (dither) and a video signal. Several line drivers are required for the dither display. Examples of some additional drivers for plotter outputs are listed below.

Pixel Plotter	Linear Plotter	Dither Plotter
Versatec	Calcomp	Varian
Various printer/plotters	Auto-trol	Gould

The presentation of images on each of the plotters may be identical, but the line quality is quite different.

REVIEW PROBLEMS

1. List the fundamental concepts in the CUPID programming for animation.

ANSWER

a. Transparency
b. Diffusion of multisurfaces
c. Polygonal surfaces
d. Intensity interpolation
e. Normal interpolation

2. List the attributes of the subroutine CUPID2.

ANSWER

a. Roll, pitch, and yaw
b. Translation and scaling
c. Rotation of the display axis

3. Using the data structure in Table 8-1 as a guide, prepare the data structure for the object shown in Figure 8-12

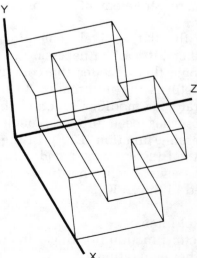

FIGURE 8-12

ANSWER

Data Structure

X	Y	Z
0.0	0.0	0.0
2.0	0.0	0.0
2.0	1.0	0.0
1.0	1.0	0.0
1.0	1.5	0.0
0.0	1.5	0.0
2.0	0.0	1.5
2.0	0.0	1.5
2.0	0.5	1.5
2.0	0.5	0.5
2.0	1.0	0.5
1.0	1.0	0.5
1.0	1.5	0.5
0.25	1.5	0.5
0.25	0.5	0.5
0.25	0.5	2.0
0.0	0.5	2.0
0.0	1.5	2.0
0.25	1.5	2.0
0.0	0.5	2.3
0.0	0.0	2.3
1.0	0.0	2.3
1.0	0.5	2.3
1.0	0.5	1.5
1.0	0.0	1.5

4. On the basis of the data structure in problem 3, label the points (X, Y, Z) on the object in Figure 8-13.

5. On the basis of the point labels from problem 4, and with the IPEN array on page 223 as a guide, list the IPEN connections for Figure 8-13.

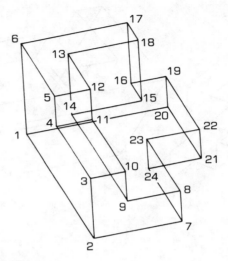

FIGURE 8-13

ANSWER

$-1,2,3,4,5,6,1,-2,7,8$
$9,10,3,-10,11,4,-11,12,5,-12$
$13,14,15,16,17,18,-16,19,20$
$1,-20,21,22,19,-21,24,23,22,-24,7$
$-8,23,-9,14,-13,18,15,-6,17$

6. Submit the data from the above problem solutions to the CUPID2 subroutine for processing and display the results.

ANSWER See Figure 8-14.

7. Using Figure 8-2 as a guide, supply the vantage points necessary to move the object defined in problems 3–5 into a single orthographic view. Display the results.

ANSWER See Figure 8-15.

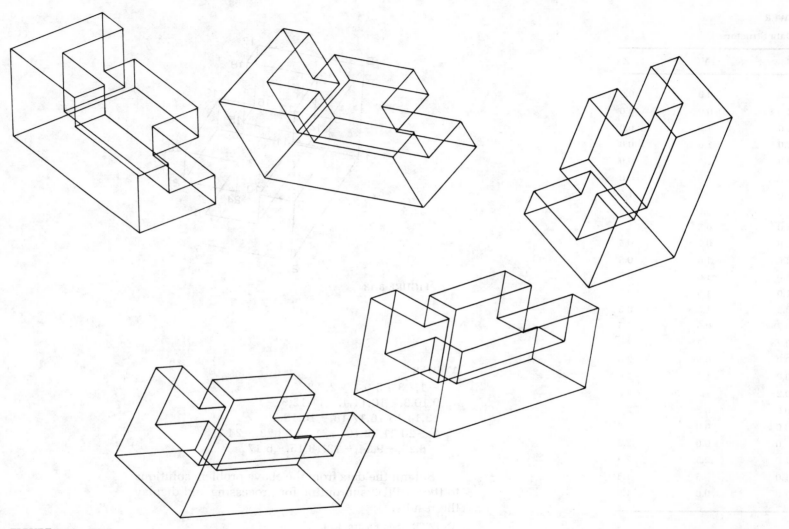

FIGURE 8-14

FIGURE 8-15

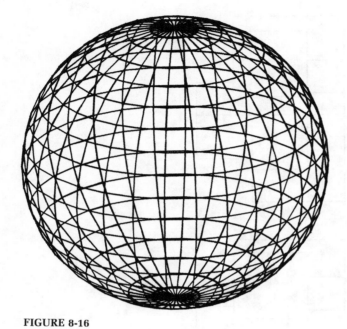

FIGURE 8-16

8. Using Figure 8-3 as a guide, output a single row of data from problem 3 and a column of data from problem 5. This represents a single wire from the display object. Display this element in full animation.

ANSWER   See Figure 8-16.

9. Advanced display techniques called *polygonal surfaces* can be used in place of a single line in full animation. Input a rectangle to form a simple three-dimensional prism shape. Inside this prism display another smaller prism.

ANSWER   See Figure 8-17.

10. Using simple translation of data, move the smaller prism displayed in Figure 8-17 outside the larger prism. Keep two surfaces coplanar.

ANSWER   See Figure 8-18.

11. Move the smaller prism so that the top surfaces are not mutually parallel (in-line) but appear to be joined at a common surface.

ANSWER   See Figure 8-19.

12. Move the smaller prism so that the back sides are mutually parallel.

ANSWER   See Figure 8-20.

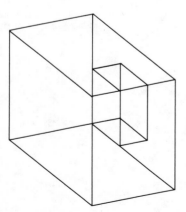

FIGURE 8-17

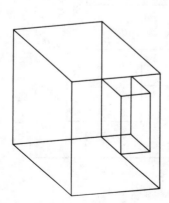

FIGURE 8-18

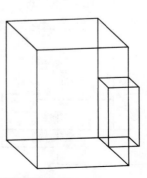

FIGURE 8-19

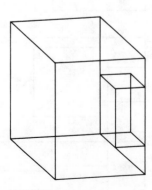

FIGURE 8-20

13. Repeat problems 8, 9, 10, 11, and 12 using an intensity interpolation technique.

ANSWER   See Figure 8-21.

14. Repeat problem 13 using normal interpolation techniques.

ANSWER   See Figure 8-22.

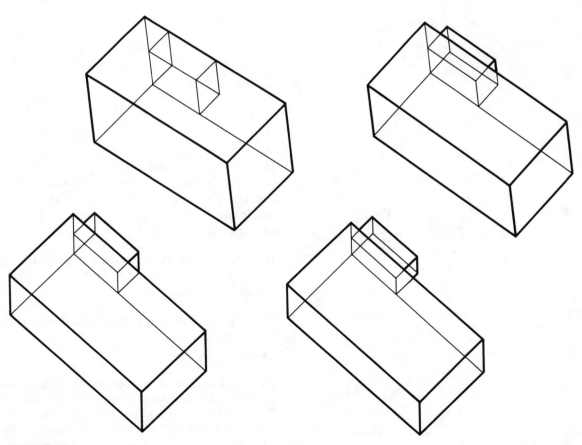

FIGURE 8-21

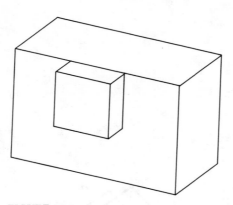

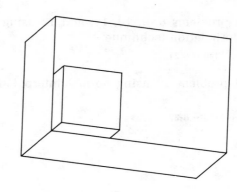

FIGURE 8-22

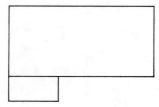

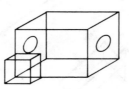

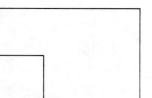

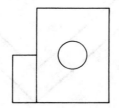

FIGURE 8-23

15. Add a location for a cylinder to be placed through the larger prism, as shown in Figure 8-23. Display a cylinder with a ruled surface through the location.

ANSWER   See Figure 8-24.

16. Display the object shown in problem 14 to illustrate roll, pitch, and yaw.

ANSWER   See Figure 8-25.

17. Display the objects shown in problem 15 to illustrate roll, pitch, and yaw.

ANSWER   See Figure 8-26.

18. To illustrate the importance of translation, display the animation from problem 13 with SPACE = 0.0. *OPTIONAL:* Now enter the data base from problem 3. Set SPACE = 0.0 also and display the result.

ANSWER   See Figure 8-27.

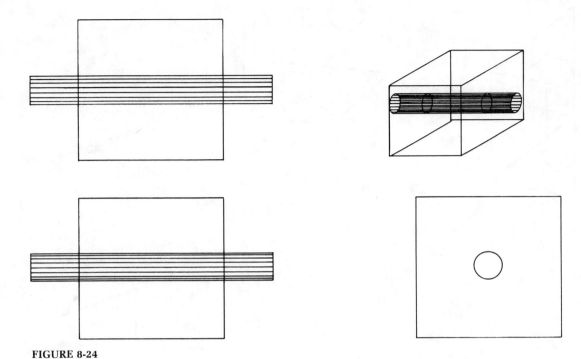

FIGURE 8-24

19. To demonstrate surface description and shading, input a shaded surface on the smaller prism shown in Figure 8-23.

ANSWER   See Figure 8-28.

20. Submit the data from problem 19 to full animation, including rotation and scaling.

ANSWER   See Figure 8-29.

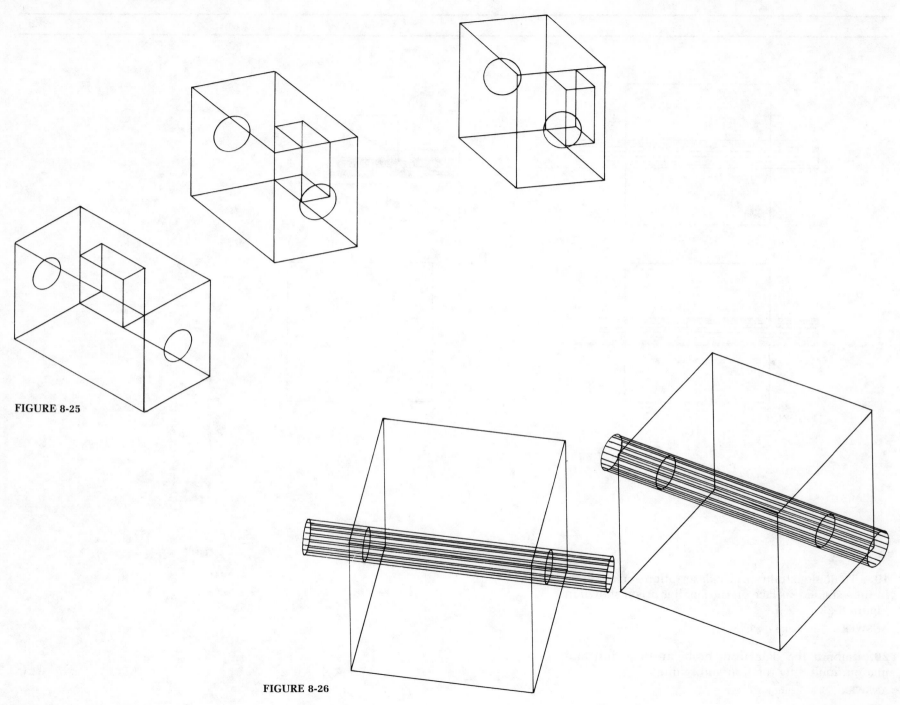

FIGURE 8-25

FIGURE 8-26

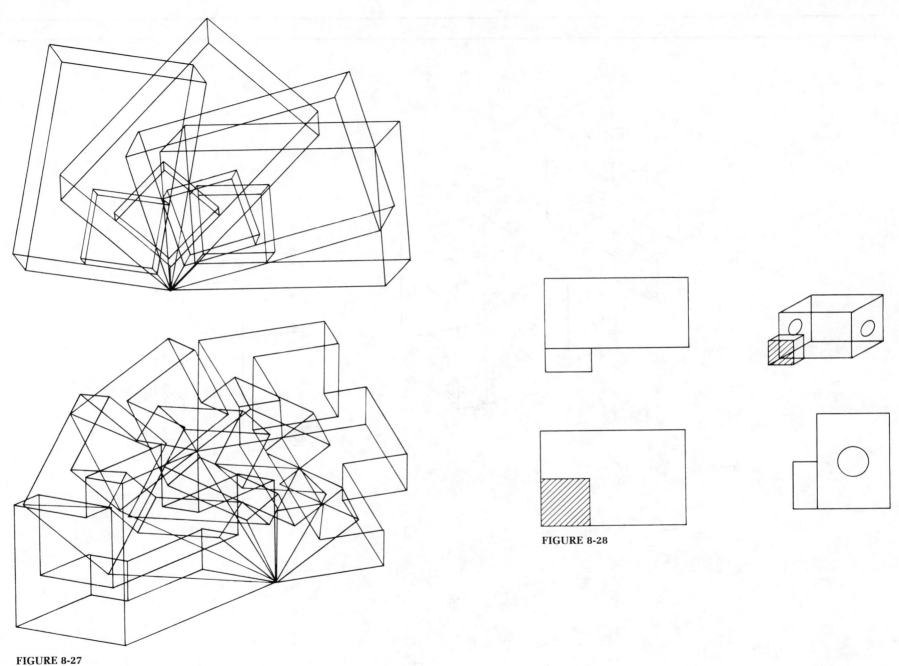

FIGURE 8-27

FIGURE 8-28

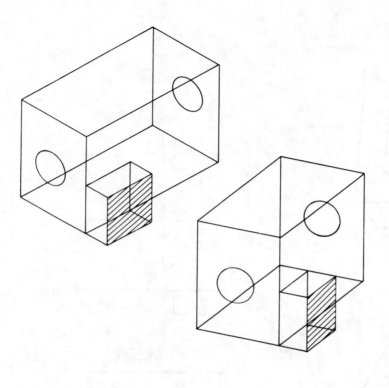
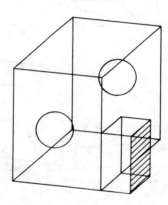

FIGURE 8-29

9 PROGRAMMING SIMULATION TECHNIQUES

Simulation is a combination of animation and engineering analysis. Simulation techniques apply to nearly all areas of engineering education.

Simulation is initially somewhat hard to comprehend, but with further demonstration and examples, supported by study of the figures in this chapter, it should be one of the most enjoyable parts of computer programming for graphical displays.

Computer graphics used to simulate a real-time operation requires a number of display techniques:

Hidden-line removal during rotation
Surface shading during rotation
Data structures for simulation displays

In the case of hidden-line removal, the object being simulated appears solid to the observer. Surface shading causes the simulated object not only to appear three-dimensional but to vary with time. For instance, a building may be displayed as it would appear in early morning or late afternoon. Or a machine part may appear to be machined during the simulation, with chip removal programmed in real time.

Using the example of a machine part, the basic steps involved in simulation can be programmed. First a wireform model is constructed using the CUPID data structure described in chapters 6 and 8 for single-view displays and animation, respectively. The program on pages 256–258 was written for the computer-aided manufacture of finite

```
C       PROGRAM TO TEST SURF SHOWN AS CUPID3 IN CHAPTER 7.
        CALL PLOTS
        DIMENSION X(500),Y(500),Z(500)
        ICNT=0
        DO 200 J=1,10
        DO 300 K=1,10
        ICNT=ICNT+1
        X(ICNT)=J
        Y(ICNT)=K
        READ(1,100)Z(ICNT)
100     FORMAT(F10.2)
300     CONTINUE
200     CONTINUE
        NAX=2
        CALL SURF(X,Y,Z,ICNT,NAX)
        CALL PLOT(0.,0.,999)
        STOP
        END

        SUBROUTINE SURF(A,B,C,N,NAX)
        DIMENSION A(500),B(500),C(500),BUFR(500),P(20,20)
        DATA AXLN/3.0/
        AXLN=5.
        AXLN1=AXLN+0.001
        XH=0.0
        YH=0.
        ZH=0.
        XL=100.
        YL=100.
        ZL=100.
        NN=10
        DO 1 I=1,N
        IF(XH.LE.A(I))XH=A(I)
        IF(YH.LE.B(I))YH=B(I)
        IF(ZH.LE.C(I))ZH=C(I)
        IF(XL.GE.A(I))XL=A(I)
        IF(YL.GE.B(I))YL=B(I)
```

```
        IF(ZL.GE.C(I))ZL=C(I)
1       CONTINUE
        DO 2 I=1,N
        A(I)=(A(I)-XL)/(XH-XL)*AXLN
        B(I)=(B(I)-YL)/(YH-YL)*AXLN
        C(I)=(C(I)-ZL)/(ZH-ZL)*AXLN
2       CONTINUE
        DO 3 I=1,NN
        DO 4 J=1,NN
        P(I,J)=0.
4       CONTINUE
3       CONTINUE
        DO 5 I=1,N
        IX=A(I)/AXLN1*NN+1.
        IY=B(I)/AXLN1*NN+1.
        IF (C(I).GT.P(IX,IY))P(IX,IY)=C(I)
5       CONTINUE
        IF(NAX.NE.1) GO TO 10
        X=AXLN
        Y=-YL/(YH-YL)*AXLN
        Z=-ZL/(ZH-ZL)*AXLN
        CALL ROTATE(X,Y,Z)
        CALL PLOT(X,Y,3)
        X=-XL/(XH-XL)*AXLN
        Y=-YL/(YH-YL)*AXLN
        CALL ROTATE(X,Y,Z)
        CALL PLOT(X,Y,2)
        Z=AXLN
        X=-XL/(XH-XL)*AXLN
        Y=-YL/(YH-YL)*AXLN
        CALL ROTATE(X,Y,Z)
        CALL PLOT(X,Y,1)
        X=-XL/(XH-XL)*AXLN
        Z=-ZL/(ZH-ZL)*AXLN
        Y=-YL/(YH-YL)*AXLN
        CALL ROTATE(X,Y,Z)
        CALL PLOT(X,Y,3)
```

```
          Y=AXLN
          X=-XL/(XH-XL)*AXLN
          Z=-ZL/(ZH-ZL)*AXLN
          CALL ROTATE(X,Y,Z)
          CALL PLOT(X,Y,2)
10        CONTINUE
          DO 6 I=1,NN
          X=I*AXLN/NN
          SX=X
          IP=3
          DO 7 J=1,NN
          X=SX
          Y=J*AXLN/NN
          Z=P(I,J)
          CALL ROTATE(X,Y,Z)
          CALL PLOT(X,Y,IP)
          IP=2
7         CONTINUE
6         CONTINUE
          DO 8 I=1,NN
          Y=I*AXLN/NN
          SY=Y
          IP=3
          DO 9 J=1,NN
          Y=SY
          X=J*AXLN/NN
          Z=P(J,I)
          CALL ROTATE(X,Y,Z)
          CALL PLOT(X,Y,IP)
          IP=2
9         CONTINUE
8         CONTINUE
          RETURN
          END
```

faces. In other words, computer-aided design techniques are used to provide input for machine-part production.

Simulation software is ideally suited for the engineering computer laboratory because it is a real-time computing system made up of two different types of computer device. *The analog computer* allows the graphics programmer to compute by wiring together on a patch panel mathematical building blocks that will allow an engineer to model electronically differential equations that represent by voltages the manufacturing analyses to be done. The results are then graphically displayed on devices such as the X, Y plotter, strip chart recorder, or CRT, which plot the variable voltages versus time. These types of display unit and electronic display are ideally suited for modeling problems when the solutions are being solved in repetitive operation mode—that is, over and over again, very rapidly, so that refresh graphics in an animated mode is quite easy. This, of course, is not simulation but animation.

In a simulation laboratory the analog computer is tied to a *digital computer* (which houses the program) through an interface system that takes the voltage from the analog computer and turns them into digital words to be transmitted on to the digital computer. Conversely, it turns digital words back into analog voltages. This process allows the two dissimilar computers to talk to each other and to address certain problems that would be extremely difficult for either computer to solve independently. One of these problem areas is hidden-line removal during rotation.

HIDDEN-LINE REMOVAL DURING ROTATION

If the hidden-line problem is approached with the aid of only the digital computer, an algorithmic situation must determine the data to display. Since those data points, lines, or surfaces lie behind those of another object in a line of sight for the display device, automatic algorithms have been introduced. These are usually CPU-intensive and very costly in display time. The noted computer graphics programmers Sutherland, Sproull, and Schumaker (1974) have developed ten different techniques for hidden-line or hidden-surface elimination.

Hidden-line or Hidden-surface Elimination

For digital computing hidden-line or hidden-surface elimination is a sorting problem—that is, sorting objects (subpictures) into those to be displayed and those not to be displayed. A medium-sized digital computer (IBM 4341, DEC 11/780, or Prime 750) with storage capability both on magnetic discs and in core memory is required. This allows for the refresh graphic system to model machine parts (or other objects) dynamically so that an analog computer may make modifications under CPU control. A graphics programmer can thereby obtain moving (rotation or revolution) displays with hidden lines removed. This method of hidden-line or hidden-surface removal requires a fair amount of computer hardware to support the simulation, and thus this type of system is rather expensive.

In order to better understand the process of simulation, a technique used in Chapter 5 may prove helpful. Assuming that the reader is seated in front of a DVST terminal, if a refresh CRT and digital computer housing the CUPID programs from Chapters 5, 6, and 8 is in place, the reader can actually follow the procedure to be explained.

Let's begin the demonstration by reading the CUPID programs off a magnetic disc into core memory. For this example, we will use a simple machine part, shown in Figure 9-1. By reading the data structure for this part, we can move to the CRT to see the results of the program execution.

The CUPID2 program is now executing. From this point our interaction with the program will be from the keyboard of the CRT. We can see the animation on the face of the tube, as shown in Figure 9-2. CUPID2 provides a dynamic display of the machine part in three dimensions directly on the face of the CRT, rotating the part in real time so that we can see the object moving in space. Naturally, the figure does not move in this book, but it would if a programmer were following at a CRT.

The hidden-line or hidden-surface control is going to be done with push buttons. As we saw in Chapter 5, six push buttons can be programmed from the keyboard. We can control around which axis the animation will occur (roll, pitch, yaw), leaving three buttons for such things as start, stop, and menu selection. The first three buttons have been programmed for X, Y and Z axes ani-

mation, as shown in Chapter 8. Assuming that Figure 9-2 is stationary on the CRT, let's begin by pressing button 1. When we push the fourth button, programmed for "start roll," the machine part begins to rotate around the X axis. This animation will continue until we press the fifth button, which stops it. If we press the second and fourth buttons the machine part will rotate around the Y axis. By selecting various combinations, we can view rotation around all three display axes. Notice that the Z axis is straight into the face of the CRT.

Another noticeable characteristic is that we see both the front and the back of the machine part. All points that are connected are shown connected because of the program characteristic of the data structure used in Chapter 6. We need to test the surfaces to be hidden. When we push the sixth button, the software listing at the beginning of this chapter reads all the data for the machine part and displays it, as shown in Figure 9-3. This figure is called a *primitive presentation* because the object appears to be solid without the aid of shading. So far, the demonstration has included graphics programming, prestored and selected by the push of a button.

The main point here is that the computer is doing computions on the basis of which buttons are pushed. The programs selected perform all the calculations necessary to do all geometry simulations to change each vector between displays. The refresh capability of the system (digital) is now being used to its fullest because the digital computer end of the system is computing in between every presentation of the picture on the screen—at least 30 times a second. New information is being placed in the display list and being

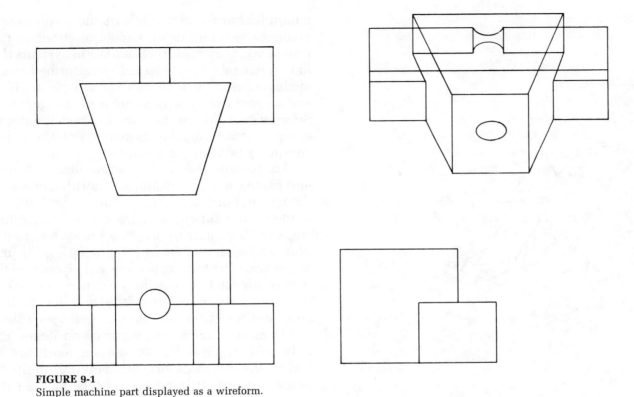

FIGURE 9-1
Simple machine part displayed as a wireform.

displayed between each updated presentation. This type of simple simulation fools us into thinking that it is continuous, just as we are fooled into thinking a series of still pictures moving at 24 frames a second on a movie screen are continuous.

Example Algorithm

The procedure thus far has enhanced the animation capability of the simulation process by introducing a testing routine as an algorithm. As a graphics programmer begins the analysis portion of the simulation, more complex displays are required. The amount of data structure increases, and consequently the amount of information that must be computed between each presentation of the picture grows tremendously. Figure 9-1 is a very simple picture (wireform) that can be animated easily, as shown in Figure 9-2. When the sixth push button was pushed, the rate of display became slightly slower, as shown in Figure 9-3, because a primitive is a slightly more compli-

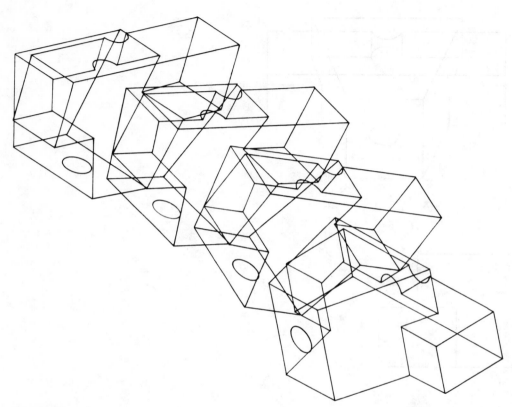

FIGURE 9-2
Animation of the simple part.

computer hardware that allows the graphics programmer to do all of these computations in real time, very, very rapidly. Simulation systems that have a laboratory test capability performed on the analog computer will be expensive. Graphical systems for this type of simulation are generally referred to as *hybrid* systems because the digital computer performs the animation and the analog computer performs the analysis.

To continue the simulation demonstration and make use of the example algorithm stored in the hybrid portion of the system, we shall use the light pen attachment. The first example algorithm stored will demonstrate use of the system to display and generate tooling for shaping the machine part. The tooling profiles will appear on the face of the CRT. Using the light pen, a graphics programmer can position the tool for various cuts, and select options such as tool speed (both RPM and feed rates) and other menu items. The light pen expands the simulation hardware by giving the graphics programmer the ability to point at words printed on the face of the CRT, representing tool commands. We can also use the push buttons, as we have done earlier.

The light pen (Figure 9-4) looks like a wand with a push button on the side. The push button is a very simple mechanism, which does nothing but open an aperture, allowing light to enter through the small opening in the end of the wand. The light that enters and gets by the shutter or aperture goes down through a cord that appears to be an electrical connection. Actually the cord is optical, containing a fiber optics bundle. The fibers carry the light as it comes in through the front of the wand down inside the display device

cated picture and requires much more computation for the hidden-line removal.

During the analysis portion of the simulation, it will be necessary to assign tooling properties to the analog computer portion of the system. Stress, strain, temperature, and other tool conditions such as wear can be modeled on the analog more easily than digital analysis programs. So at this point the simulation requires specialized

and trigger a photomultiplier tube, causing an electrical switch action inside the algorithm. The logic of the algorithm then can be switch-selected: simulation portions can be displayed by virtue of the fact that the light pen has seen light at the right time. Because the light that is seen must be the light from the face of the CRT, the light pen is impervious to the local room light, which does not have the sharp wave-front properties necessary to trigger the photo-multiplier tube.

Only certain portions of the display screen will be programmed to be sensitive to the light pen during the process of building a scene-by-scene, sequence-by-sequence animation display. This is consistent with the animation process discussed in Chapter 8, which indicated that the tool is actually being displayed 30 times or more a second. Portions of the CRT are made sensitive to the light pen for selecting tool direction, speed, contact force, and material removal (rate of tool feed into the part) as production of the part is simulated on the screen.

The caption page for the tool displays (shown in Figure 9-5) that appear on the CRT screen is a simple description of the tools available. We will begin the display process by looking at the menu items that we can select with the light pen. These menu items enable us to exercise a great deal of control over the animation scene creation and the analysis process. We will be able to create animation sequences and then use the sequences to create other real-time simulations. In this process the algorithm is comparable to the computer programmed subroutine, and the creation of a scene is comparable to the formation of a subpicture in

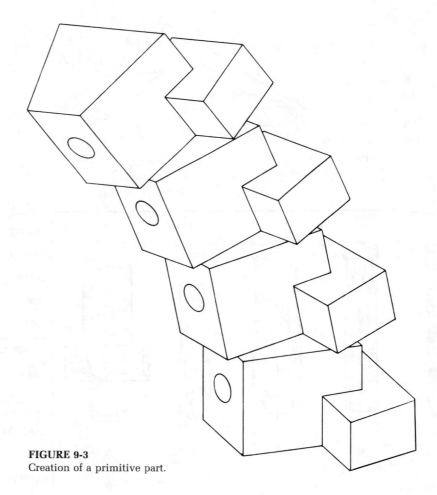

FIGURE 9-3
Creation of a primitive part.

animation. These subpictures will be used to create other scenes and finally the simulation sequence for laboratory testing purposes. All the information that we have stored about the tool (SUBPIX) and will create during the simulation is stored in the computer in such a way that we can

actually use it later for input in another laboratory simulation program session.

In addition to what we see on the screen, still
frames can be directed, replicated, and brought
out on hard copy on a device like a pen plotter.
The illustrations in this chapter have been generated in such a manner, which is called *data-base
structuring*.

Data-base Structuring

Let's start the data-base structuring so that, during the demonstration discussed in Chapter 8, a
graphics programmer could follow along. The
light pen is pointed at one of the operations
in the menu list in Figure 9-5. If the light
pen is pointed at the first menu item, called
INSTRUCTIONS, and the aperture is opened,
then a list of operating instructions would be
printed on the line printer (see Chapter 5).

If the light pen is pointed at the menu command DRAW, notice that the menu disappears,
the screen clears, and a background grid appears.
Though this grid is too light to appear in any of
the figures used in this book, it is there for the
graphics programmer to place data structures that
have been previously stored as subpictures or
subroutines. Figure 9-1 is a data structure drawn
by a subroutine. Figure 9-5 is a subpicture of the
available tools plus alphanumeric information.
With the grid as a locator, subpictures and subroutine images can be placed to start a simulation
sequence.

If the light pen is pointed at the menu command DRAW, an octagon-shaped small figure is
displayed. As we point at the octagon, the light

FIGURE 9-4
Hand-held light pen.

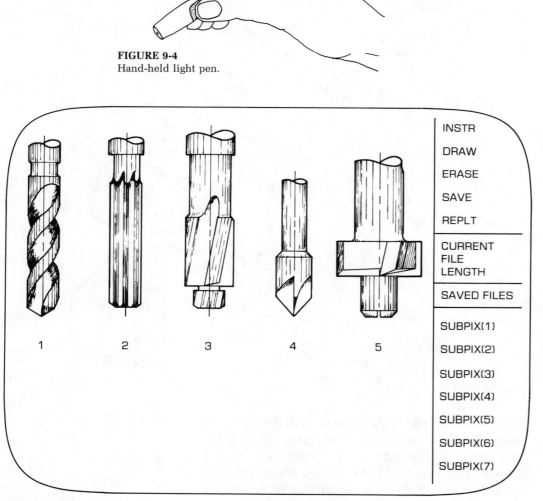

FIGURE 9-5
Caption page for the tool display.

INSTR

DRAW

ERASE

SAVE

REPLT

CURRENT
FILE
LENGTH

SAVED FILES

SUBPIX(1)

SUBPIX(2)

SUBPIX(3)

SUBPIX(4)

SUBPIX(5)

SUBPIX(6)

SUBPIX(7)

1   2   3   4   5

pen captures it, and we are able to move it around on the screen. This process aids in locating a sub-picture or subroutine image and is, in itself, animation. The light pen is sensitive to the borders of the octagon. The octagon is actually running under the light pen to the center of the octagon figure. As the light pen is moved, the octagon is recentered and follows the light pen anywhere on the face of the CRT. It will move only when the light pen aperture is open; when the wand switch is closed, the cursor can be left at any location. This is a good example of animation under direct programmer control because the data structuring is being done by updating of the display list that is stored in memory.

SURFACE SHADING DURING ROTATION

To start the simulation process, we will recall the machine part shown in Figure 9-1, the tool in Figure 9-5, and the DRAW command. The light pen will be used to define a surface of the part to be machined. A program is entered from magnetic disk to assist in this interactive process. We will press push button one of the buttons programmed to respond to vector strokes, and place the light pen on the edge of the surface to be shaded, causing a MOVE or dark vector to be placed in the data base. The surface shading will consist of bright vectors and dark vectors displayed across the face of the machine part. Each time a vector is placed in the data base, we press push button one for MOVE and then push button two for DRAW or the bright vector, thereby

completing the data-base structuring as shown in Figure 9-6.

We have discussed data-base structuring as it relates to animation and presentation. It may also be used to represent simulated tool movements. For example, after the vector strokes are placed on the surface to be shaded, we can press push button six to return to the menu selection. The menu list is now longer than it was before as an expanded list of commands are available for our use. The DRAW command allows us to switch back to where we were and continue the shading process; pushing push button six lets us come back to the menu selection again. If we point the light pen to the ERASE command, we will erase (from memory) all the shading we just did. Let's point the light pen to the SAVE command, however, saving the shading in the data-base structuring file called $SUBPIX_6$. If we then place the light pen over the REPLOT command in the menu list and open the aperture, the line printer just copies the X, Y, and Z data structure.

We have also discussed example algorithms. In this application an example algorithms tells how much of the display file resource we have used so far. The current file length is 129 locations out of 1000 locations in our display file. That is adjustable in the program, as we saw in Chapter 2; for this machine part simulation the file was set at 1000 locations. The algorithm for save files is the description or programming that is activated when the graphics programmer places the light pen over the SAVE command. Similar algorithms support the ERASE, REPLOT, and DRAW menu selections as part of the collection of algorithms called *SDL* (simulation design language) in the working software.

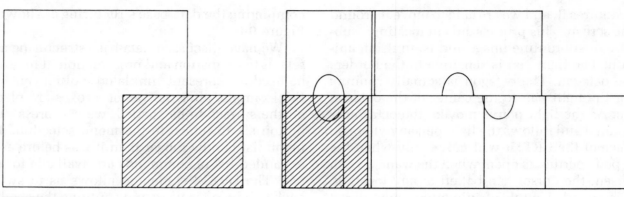

FIGURE 9-6
Surface shading on the simple part.

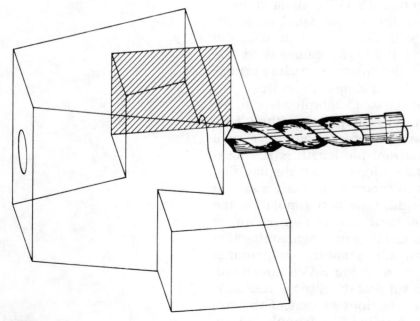

FIGURE 9-7
Tool and part interaction.

Intensity Shading

SDL-type software displays the machine part and the cutting tool, supports the light pen activities, and starts and stops the animation required (tool rotates, part moves, surface travel shading). Figure 9-7 includes all of these concepts plus intensity shading for the chip removal. During animation, the tool moves to the machine part, the machine part is turned by numerical control during the tool contact, and the manufacturing operation is tested in real-time in the design laboratory. In Figure 9-7 the tool has contacted the part. As the tool enters the part, a hole is created. This hole can be shaded for ease of study. At the same time, a counter contained in a box in the upper left-hand corner of the display screen is keeping track of the weight of the part in grams. The temperature of the tool is recorded and displayed for reference. Notice that, as the tool enters the part, the part weight decreases as the tool temperature increases. If a color CRT were used for Figure 9-7, the tool point would change color from a light green (normal room temperature) to a dull gray (normal operating temperature) to a dull red—indicating that cooling fluid is needed or the tool will fail. Intensity shading, then, can be a color in the case of tooling. It can also represent weight analysis during the manufacturing cycle. Intensity shading is keyed mathematically to known material of the part, rate of tool path into the part, and type of coolant selected. These are all variables that can be selected by the graphics programmer and simulated in the laboratory before the manufacture planning sheets are released to the plant for production.

One of the main advantages of a hybrid simulation system is the ability to vary the intensity displayed by the varying voltage of the analog signal. As temperature, pressure, or rate increases, so does the voltage in the simulated circuit. As the analog is converted to a digital signal for input as data base, the intensity diagrams (see Chapter 4) are applied. So the graphics programmer really has three ways to display information during the simulation:

1. Data from a subroutine or subpicture created from memory
2. Interactive data structuring
3. Analog models

DATA STRUCTURES FOR SIMULATION DISPLAYS

Data structures for simulation displays may be developed directly at the time of the real-time simulation, as we have done, or they may be pre-programmed and stored offline in software files such as CUPID2, which was used for animation in Chapter 8. If offline software is used, then the graphics programmer must develop the input data before the test is made.

For example, point the light pen over the menu command ERASE and open the aperture to clear Figure 9-7 from the display. Next point the light pen at $SUBPIX_6$ and press the aperture switch. The Figure 9-6 now appears on the screen because the data for that picture is stored in that computer file—we listed that file by using the REPLOT command earlier. How did the data get into $SUBPIX_6$? It could have been saved from a working session, or it could have been manipulated and stored from a software package like CUPID2. In this case both are true. Figure 9-1 was used to begin a working session, and the data base for 9-1 came from CUPID2. It was displayed from a preprogrammed subroutine, and the shaded surface was added at the CRT by the graphics programmer.

Animation (CUPID2)

We would begin a working session to develop input data for this type of simulation by clearing the screen and redrawing another picture much as the previous surface was shaded. Though nothing requires a graphics programmer to draw on grid lines, in this example we will use the grid to modify the profile of the part slightly. The part could be displayed from memory and certain lines selectively removed, or it could be built from scratch. The necessary modifications, shown in Figure 9-8, were done by using the push buttons for bright and dark vector strokes.

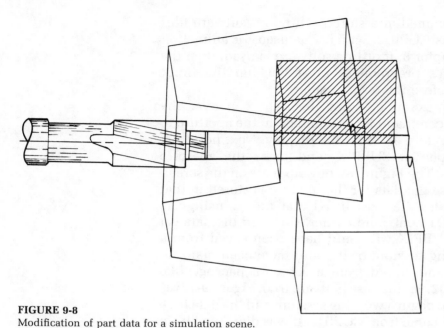

FIGURE 9-8
Modification of part data for a simulation scene.

Figure 9-8 is what is needed for a simulation scene to be used in a surface test later. A solid cross in the lower left-hand corner of the part in Figure 9-6 indicates the origin of this subpicture. This is a tracking symbol similar to the octagon used earlier. The cross appeared as the first dark vector was defined in the data base; the tracking symbol can be located anywhere on the part that is convenient. The origin for objects constructed from the subroutine CUPID2 is located here, so the common location will prove helpful later. When we use this subpicture later in the simulation scene, we will actually position the part relative to the origin point.

Next, we press push button six to return to the menu selection. We position the light pen over the SAVE command, and the modified part is stored under SUBPIX$_7$. SUBPIX$_6$ still looks like Figure 9-6, and SUBPIX$_7$ is a modified version of this same part. SUBPIXs can be an entire new part or combinations of SUBPIX$_5$ and SUBPIX$_6$. In other words, SUBPIXs can be used in the creation of other SUBPIXs. The system now has two versions of the same part; either SUBPIX can be used during the animation portion of the simulation. There is only one copy of the SUBPIX during animation, but the hybrid system will use it over and over again, much as we use subroutines in digital-only programs.

A standard procedure in simulation processes is displaying the direction of light used for shadows during the animation sequence. In the CUPID2 data structure the light is assumed to be from the sun or from some other source of parallel rays. The direction is the diagonal of the data-structure model from the top, left, front corner to the lower, right, rear corner, as shown in Figure 9-9. In a CUPID1 data structure the direction of light will appear to be the diagonal of a square, as shown in Figure 9-10. Simulation of light to create shaded construction for CUPID1 views is of minor importance here because single views are not used in animation or simulation processes.

The advantages of including a light source during the animation portion of the simulation are simplicity of shadow construction to add illusion of solidarity, and precise digital information from the shadows for simulation enhancement. If the wireform is the major output of most animation software listings like CUPID2, then the addition of light source and shadow is a valid

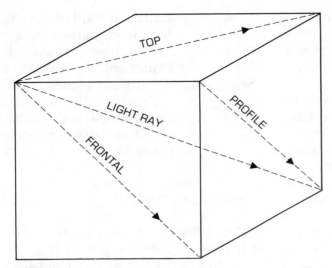

FIGURE 9-9
Direction of light for simulation in 3-D.

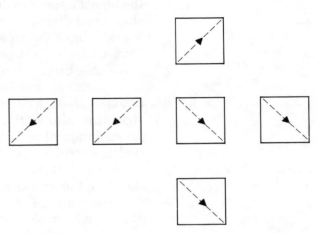

FIGURE 9-10
Direction of light for simulation in 2-D.

technique for representing the transparent wireform as a solid object.

First, the visibility of the wireform shown in Figure 9-11 must be tested. Second, the wireform must be displayed as a primitive with hidden lines and surfaces deleted, as shown in Figure 9-12. Third, an algorithm must be developed to determine the direction of light on different animated views. There are at least three mathematical solutions for this algorithm.

1. The direction is input for the object as a constant (integer), and each frame (view) is made to conform to that direction. This method is particularly logical if the animated object will be displayed on a direct-view output device such as a plotter or DVST (with write-thru). However, this algorithm is limited on

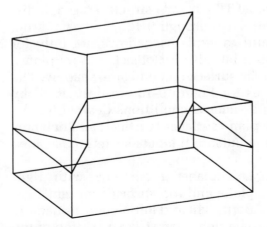

FIGURE 9-11
Wireform model.

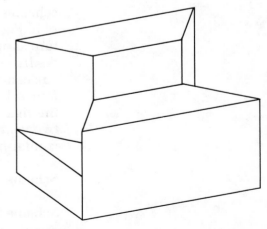

FIGURE 9-12
Primitive model by selective erase.

refreshed CRT displays because two faces of the object appear in complete shadow. These shadowed displays will not simulate the animated object as clearly as techniques that have variable light or shadow areas.

2. A variable direction of light can be chosen for each frame as a separate input at the same time the vantage point is chosen. This type of algorithm allows the most effective display presentation of each individual frame. If carried to extremes (such as a random number generation), it will cause confusion in understanding the animated object.

3. A compromise of the first two techniques was developed for the remaining figures in this unit. The same direction of light was used (each frame assumed to be turned the same way and in the same plane), but the light was programmed to come from either left or right to secure the best shadow effect.

Figure 9-13 illustrates the basic shadow schemes for a CUPID2 data structure used to display Figures 9-10 through 9-12. This data structure is useful to explain shadows not only for boxlike cubes but also for objects cut by planes adjacent to the surface receiving the shadow. The four schemes for Figure 9-13 are designated by the light-and-shadow conditions desired for the two visible plane surfaces (vertical) and one horizontal plane outside the data structure.

Scheme 1. Left plane in shadow with right plane and top surfaces in light.

Scheme 2. Both right and left planes in shadow. The light may strike a portion of the top and extend onto the floor (horizontal) in front of the object and is a prominent part of the animation.

Scheme 3. Right planes in shadow with left planes and top in light.

Scheme 4. All surface planes in light. The direction of light may cause a small shadow to appear to the rear of the object and be a minor part of the animation.

Simulation (CUPID3)

CUPID3 is a major extension of the animation and single-view displays discussed so far. The main objective of the simulation data-base system is to provide the graphics programmer with a descriptive technique for surface generation. This software approach is very basic in its geometry and useful for the presentation of finite element models. It is also highly useful and extendable through the computer-aided design of machine parts and elements of computer-aided manufacturing planning systems.

CUPID software presented throughout this book is evolutionary in at least four ways.

1. The nominal descriptive powers (points, lines, planes, solids, and wireforms) are improved or vendor-supplied software. This can be done by expanding the set of primitive solids to include spheres, cones, and shaded surfaces.

2. CUPID's transformation packages included rotation, shifting, scaling, revolution, and windowing.

3. The ability to display more than a single view

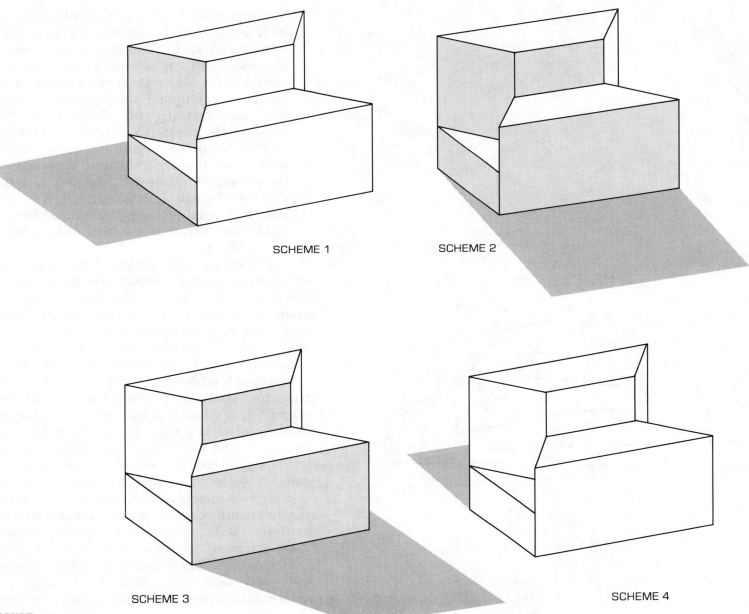

SCHEME 1

SCHEME 2

SCHEME 3

SCHEME 4

FIGURE 9-13

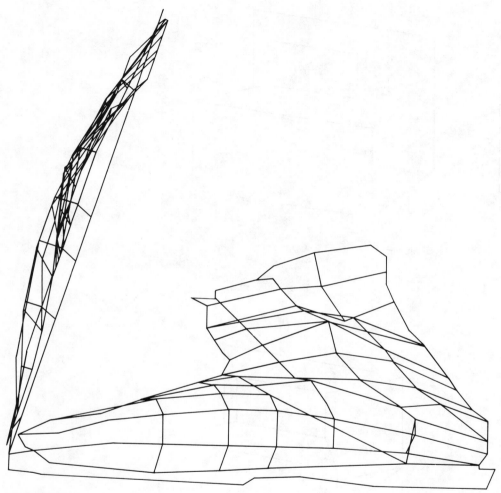

FIGURE 9-14
Analysis of sculptured surface.

of a pictorial in chain fashion provides animation scenes and sequences for the application of analysis to simulation techniques.

4. Because CUPID is intended to be the data structure for a host of applications that are common to computer-aided design, graphics, and manufacturing, the ability to analyze sculptured surfaces makes numerical-control machined surface definition easier. Figure 9-14 is the output of a surface displayed from the computer program at the beginning of this chapter. The data describing the surface were then submitted to the program listed for animation in Chapter 8, resulting in the surface in animation.

The graphics programming we have been describing is an improvement over the display of only straight lines and circular arcs. These single geometric forms limited the graphics programmer trying to display any objects having free-flowing or "sculptured" surfaces. Sculptured surfaces are difficult to analyze for machining by N/C. Because sculptured surfaces are normally transferred as contours from drafting layouts to a 3-D model, and finally produced as a production die, the process is tedious, costly, and potentially inaccurate. The blending of the CUPID software during simulation has helped the graphics programmer solve this problem. Automotive and aerospace companies have computer-aided design and manufacturing programs that deal with the design and display of a sculptured surface. These programs are very costly and are often closely guarded. The blending of CUPID software deals only with the display of a sculptured surface; it occupies the middle ground between tedious manual processes and super sophisticated computer modeling. It is at the command of the graphics programmer, not the mathematican or systems computer programmer. All that is required is a working knowledge of the concepts in Chapters 2, 3, 8, and 9 of this book.

The graphics programmer develops simulated surfaces as a blend of second-order curves such as circles, parabolas, and hyperbolas, and defines these curves by specifying only ten coordinate points. The programmer defines the curves forming the network of the surface. The computer then blends in the connecting surface patches and prints out coordinate points from which plotter drawings, CRT displays, DVST prints, or an N/C tape can be made. CUPID software does have limitations: because each curve is a segment of a single-order curve, no curve can have inflection points. But second-order curves are completely adequate for the typical part that is to be molded or die cast. In a nutshell, the graphics programmer can display complex three-dimensional surfaces while dealing with only two and one-half axes at a time.

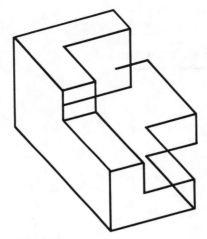

FIGURE 9-15

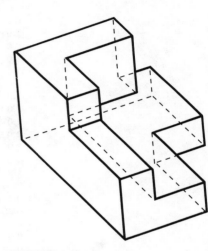

FIGURE 9-16

REVIEW PROBLEMS

1. Simulation requires animation, analysis of data, and special presentation techniques. List those graphical techniques that are most useful for simulation.

ANSWER
1. Hidden-line removal during rotation
2. Surface shading during rotation
3. Data structures for simulation displays

2. One method of hidden-line removal is the modification of the IPEN list shown in problem 5, Chapter 8. Change the IPEN list to display the object shown in Figure 9-15.

ANSWER
$-1,2,3,4,5,6,1-2,7,8$
$9,10,3,-10,11,4,-11,12,5,-12$
$13,-14,15,-16,-17,18,-16,19,-20$
$-1,-20,-21,22,19,-21,24,-23,22,-24,-7$
$-8,23,-9,-14,-13,18,15,-6,17$

3. An improved method of hidden-line removal is the addition of an IFLAG column to the data structure. Change the display of the object to match the example shown in Figure 9-16.

ANSWER

DATA STRUCTURE

X	Y	Z	IFLAG
0.0	0.0	0.0	3
2.0	0.0	0.0	2
2.0	1.0	0.0	2
1.0	1.0	0.0	2
1.0	1.5	0.0	2
0.0	1.5	0.0	2
2.0	0.0	1.5	2
2.0	0.0	1.5	2
2.0	0.5	1.5	2
2.0	0.5	0.5	2
2.0	1.0	0.5	2
1.0	1.0	0.5	2
1.0	1.5	0.5	2
0.25	1.5	0.5	3
0.25	0.5	0.5	2
0.25	0.5	2.0	3
0.0	0.5	2.0	3
0.0	1.5	2.0	2
0.25	1.5	2.0	2
0.0	0.5	2.3	3
0.0	0.0	2.3	3
1.0	0.0	2.3	2
1.0	0.5	2.3	2
1.0	0.5	1.5	3
1.0	0.0	1.5	3

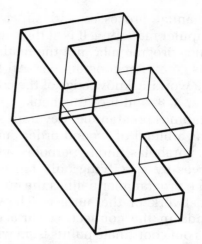

FIGURE 9-17

4. Another method of hidden-line removal is the variable line intensity technique described in Chapter 8, which may be done on a CRT with light pen input. Create a display to match the example shown in Figure 9-17.

5. Various combinations of hidden-line removal exist, one of which is called *haloed line effect*. Create a display to match the example shown in Figure 9-18.

6. Surface shading during rotation can be seen by studying the output from problem 20 in Chapter 8. Use

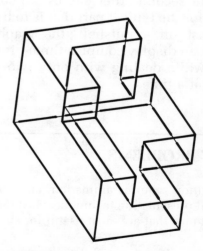

FIGURE 9-18

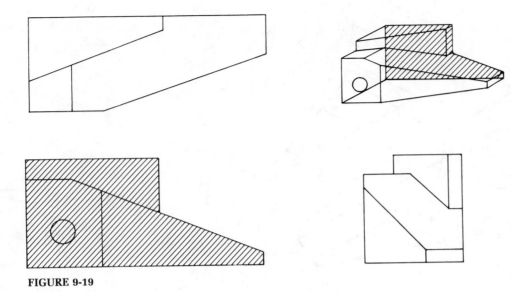

FIGURE 9-19

this type of shading and display an output as shown in the example in Figure 9-19.

ANSWER   See Figure 9-20.

7.   Another type of shading, known as *parallel ruling*, was used in problem 15 of Chapter 8 to represent a cylinder. Now use this type of shading during rotation as shown in the example in Figure 9-21.

ANSWER   See Figure 9-22.

8.   Data structures for simulation displays may be quite simple, as in the case of the data for problem 8 of Chapter 8. Use this set of data, make a copy, and scale the copy several times. Now model the two sets of data together as a large and a small sphere. Simulate the earth and moon orbits through space.

ANSWER   See Figure 9-23.

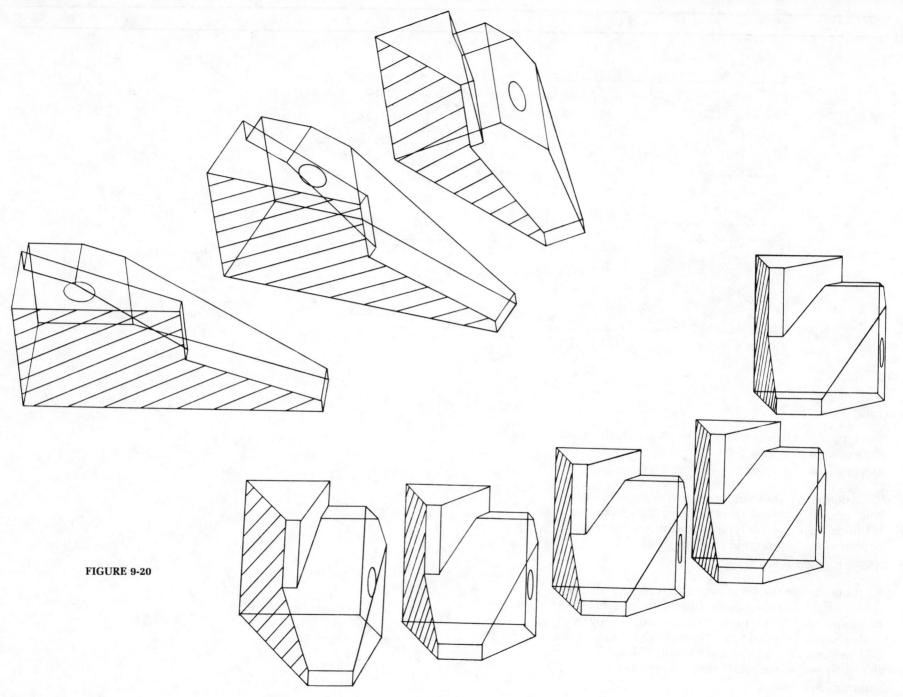

FIGURE 9-20

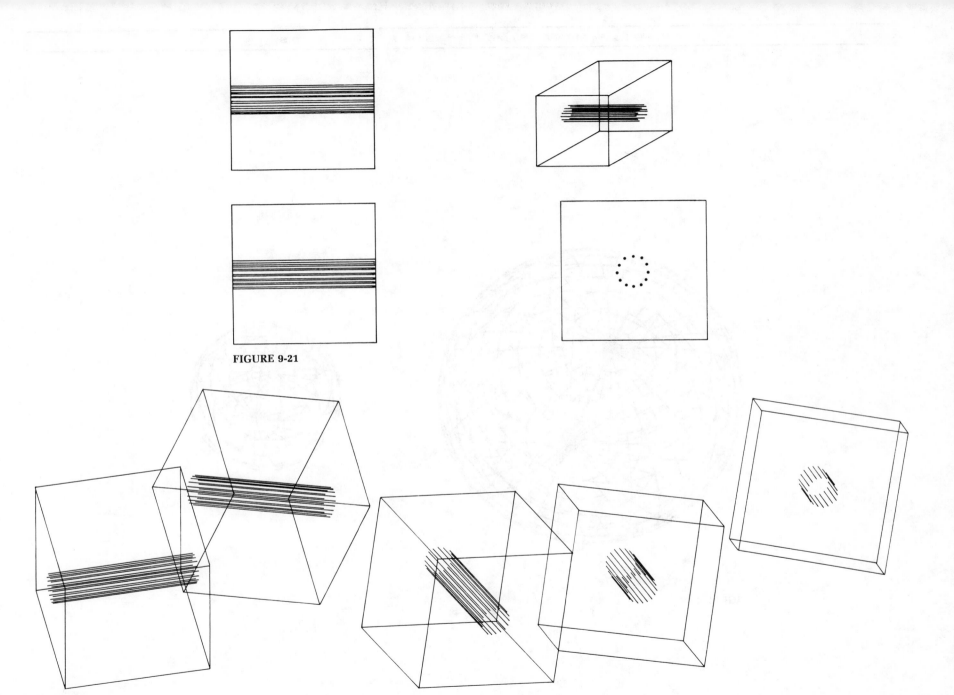

FIGURE 9-21

FIGURE 9-22

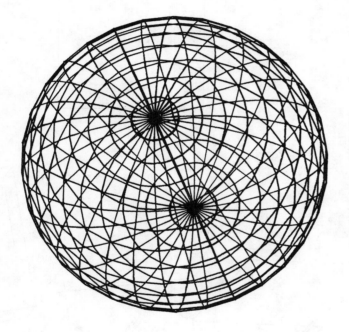
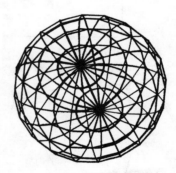

FIGURE 9-23

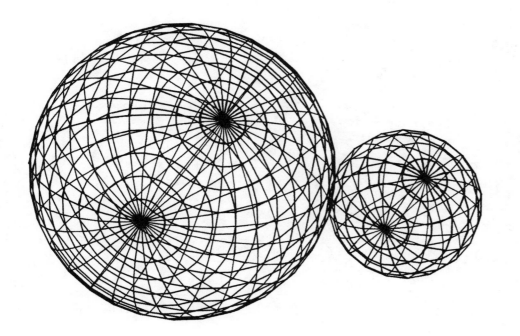

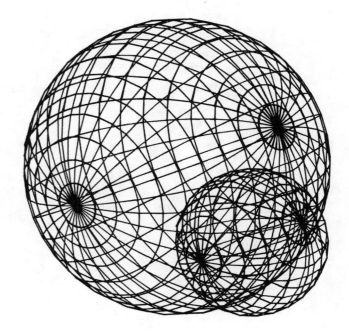

10 PROGRAMMING SURVEY

If you have progressed through the first nine chapters of *Computer Programming for Graphical Displays,* you have noticed a definite programming relationship, which is diagrammed in Figure 10-1. The main support base for the user's program is the software, firmware, and hardware available for the display of engineering drawings. The final chapter of the book provides a general survey of computer programming for graphical displays.

The benefits of having a computer produce routine graphical images are:

1. The designer or draftsperson is freed to perform other, nonroutine, tasks. How much time is taken up with routine tasks that are better done by a machine? The answer varies from office to office, but a number of studies point out savings of 20 to 30% of an average work day with computer graphics.

2. The output devices that display the image are more accurate and of much higher quality (ink on mylar is as easy as pencil on paper in a manual mode) than hand drawing images. If you have 20 draftspersons working in a single office space, there will be 20 different styles of lettering, line weights, and production speeds. The computer produces uniform lettering and line weights and constant production.

3. Once the program has been written, it is available for use in a variety of ways. It may be presented as a CRT image, an image on microfilm, an inked drawing on paper or

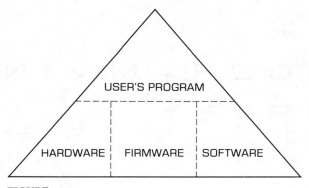

FIGURE 10-1

film, a photographic negative or positive, a scribbed map, a cut-and-peel mask, or all of these at the same time. The electronic image is available at the push of a button. It can be scaled into another sized drawing by the push of a button. Details or parts of drawings can be erased, removed, and stored separately, making cut-and-paste drafting a thing of the past. A properly programmed computer can change rough sketches into finished drawings or scan a detailed drawing and produce a pictorial sketch that looks freehand.

4. The graphical image is used for computer-aided design analysis or computer-aided process control and production. Engineering drawings are two-dimensional representations of three-dimensional objects. These representations can include complex information used to define manufacturing processes. The production, interpretation, and maintenance of these drawings are skilled and time-consuming tasks.

FREEING DRAFTING TASKS AND TIME

Adopting the comprehensive programming system described throughout this book can free designers or draftspersons for other tasks. If engineering drawing and design are done on a general-purpose computer, engineering becomes one of several users rather than a single user, and costs can be shared. Moreover, as the system can run on any general-purpose machine, it is transportable in a matter of days when new computers are purchased. The attributes of this type of system are:

1. A complete 2-D and 3-D drafting/design functionality with a cost-effective workstation system
2. System modularity
3. A common data base
4. The 32-bit architecture of the hardware
5. Networking for distributed processing

The correct application of these attributes in programming will result in considerable time-versus-task savings in all areas. The system is flexible, highly desirable for users, and cost-effective at any level of operation.

2-D and 3-D functionality. The programming system described in the first nine chapters can best be illustrated by Figure 10-2. Notice the system has two portions. The lower portion is the 2-D graphics programming system described in Chapter 1. The 2-D data are passed to the lower portion from the 3-D model (data base) or from the designer's notes. The rough notes go through analysis and then into the 3-D modeler. From this, the 2-D drawings are produced. A benefit of the programming system is that associated items such as wiring or parts lists can be produced from the 2-D module. At the same time, the plot spooler can send drawings or data listings to a printer or prepare numerical-control machine tool output instructions.

System modularity.   The 2-D module just described is one of two modules that can be used with this system. The 3-D module can be used for animation and simulation properties. A benefit of the 3-D module is the mesh interface that is used to produce finite element models. The commonly used programs for image displays (CUPID) described earlier illustrate the relationship of the 2-D design module and the 3-D module with respect to engineering drawings. Because this programming is part of a general-computer system, features such as interface to nondesign functions, compatibility with other software, an extensive library, and the full support of ACM-SIGGRAPH are possible. We will look at each of these features in turn.

1. The 2-D module is a schematic and drafting programming system that uses geometric construction techniques familiar to designers and draftspersons. It has powerful ANSI, ISO, and BS dimensioning capabilities, and annotation features such as macro definition of objects.

2. The software compatibility can be seen in Table 10-1. Locate the present host computer at your location and read across to the prod-

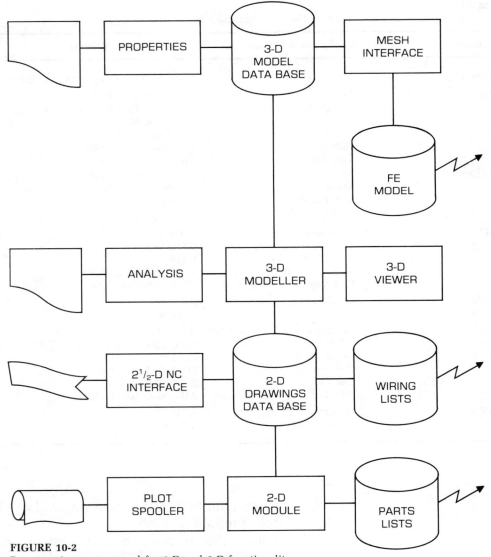

FIGURE 10-2
Programming system used for 2-D and 3-D functionality.

TABLE 10-1
Software Compatability Chart for Major Computer Manufacturers

Computer	Vendors of Software	Product
Control Data	MCAUTO	CADE (2-D, Surface), AD200 (2-D, 3-D, NC)
Digital Equipment	Dr. Hanratty	AD2000 (2-D, 3-D, NC)
	MCAUTO	UNIAPT (NC), UNIGRAPH (2-D, 3-D)
		GDS (2-D), BDS (architectural)
	MDSI	COMPACT II (NC)
	Shape Data Ltd.	ROMULUS (3-D, FEM)
	Compeda	DRAGON (2-D), PDMS (piping)
Data General	MCAUTO	UNIAPT, UNIGRAPH
	MDSI	COMPACT II
	CDC Cybernet	AD200
Hewlett-Packard	Dr. Hosdorff	ITS 10 (2-D, 3-D)
IBM	Dr. Hanratty	AD2000
	CADAM (Lockheed)	CADAM
	MCAUTO	CADE,
	MAG I	Synthavision (3-D)
	Cali Assoc.	SPADES (shipbuilding)
Interdata	Dr. Hanratty	AD2000
	Lockheed	CADAM
Prime	Dr. Hanratty	AD2000
	MCAUTO	GDS, BDS
	Dr. Hosdorff	ITS 10
	CAD Systems	EUCLID (2-D, 3-D)
	Cali Assoc.	SPADES
	SRS, Inc.	AUTOKON (shipbuilding)
UNIVAC	SRS, Inc.	AUTOKON
	Shape Data Ltd.	ROMULUS

uct column to find the software available for that computer system.

3. State-of-the-art programming systems provide library symbols. These libraries can be used as schematic systems using both standard and customized symbol libraries for such applications as electrical wiring diagrams, process flow sheets, and piping and instrumentation diagrams. Through the 2-D module the user of a library constructs schematics, annotates and dimensions drawings, and views the 3-D models. Features incuded in the library are:

Automatic cross-hatching	Macro language
Multiple type fonts	Mirroring
Any number of views	Eight line types

4. ACM support is available for the following:

3-D modeling accessed via 2-D drawing convention
No geometric language to learn
Generation of auxiliary, orthogonal, oblique axonometric, or perspective projections
Automatic calculation of intersection lines
Visible, invisible, or dashed hidden lines
Automatic construction of 3-D objects by the 3-D modeler scanning 2-D drawings
A 3-D viewer that will section any solid

Common data base.   A common data base between the 2-D and 3-D portions of the system makes possible certain modeling operations, which include:

Sweeps. The primitive elements shown earlier—for example, general polygons with straight or curved sides—may be swept to produce slabs with holes.
Revolutions. Primitive elements may be revolved around a center line to give a volume.
Shifting. Primitive elements may be shifted along lines to generate volumes.

Ruled surfaces. Any surface may be ruled, as illustrated in Chapter 9.

Piping. As shown in Chapters 7 and 9, piping in 3-D can be used effectively.

Subpictures. Any previously defined object may be called up at any position and orientation, and made part of the current model.

Hardware.   The hardware described in Chapters 5 and 7 defines objects in a way familiar to designers and draftspersons. For example, using two related 2-D views to define profiles, depths, and connection points closely resembles manual design techniques and also makes the programming easy to learn and apply to CAD 3-D programming systems. Fairly complex machine parts can be constructed with this approach. The programming system introduced in this book was designed to be modified for integration into a company's drafting and design standards. Because the graphic information is contained in separate CUPID modules, the menu, line-type definitions, dimension formats, and drawing formats are easily modified. As shown in Chapter 7, all commands issued via the menu or keyboard can be echoed back to the terminal for immediate verification and checking. The menu design shown in Chapter 4 allows extensive user-defined symbol libraries. In other words, it allows designers and draftspersons to use conventional engineering graphics to communicate ideas. *Remember*, detailed modifications can be written in FORTRAN, PL/I, PASCAL, or BASIC.

Networks for distributed processing.   Distributed processing allows the ease-of-use features described above. All input is accepted from either menus or alpha CRT or both. Commands between network points are English-like, and the default menu features symbolic and printed network commands. There are no "mystery" error messages in network communications; because the programming system developed throughout is part of a multi-indexed data-access system (see Figure 10-1), error messages are concise and point to the drawing location that caused them. The programming system used here is part of a much larger system containing software products, a library of engineering firmware techniques, and advanced computer graphics hardware. The user's program interacts readily with other software systems, thus extending the total system capability. For example, a user's program may interact directly with a software package called ROMULUS written by Shape Data Limited in England and distributed in the United States by Evans and Sutherland of Utah. ROMULUS is used via the network menu.

IMPROVING DRAFTING PRODUCTIVITY

Carefully considering where computer programming for graphical displays can best be used can improve drafting productivity. Table 10-2 indicates some drafting/design functions and how the programming best fits with that activity.

Usually three key personnel will indicate where programming is needed: the drafting room manager, the engineering design manager, and the product manufacturing manager.

TABLE 10-2
How Drafting/Design Functions Fit Computer Programming Efforts

Activities	Mechanical Parts	Assembly	Surfaces	Buildings	Piping	Mapping	Structures
Diagrams	X	X	X	X	X	0	X
Schematics	X	X	X	X	X	0	0
Layouts	X	X	X	X	X	0	X
2-D Drawing	X	X	X	X	X	X	X
3-D Drawing	X	X	X	X	X	0	X
FE Models	X	0	X	0	0	0	X
Interference checks	X	X	X	X	X	0	X
Tolerancing	X	X	0	0	0	0	0
Parts Lists	X	X	0	X	X	0	0
Bill of Mat'l	X	X	0	X	X	0	X

X   Programming well suited

0   Programming not suited

Drafting manager.   The drafting room manager is familiar with and may use turnkey products described in this text. The programming for these products must:

> Adhere to applicable standards (ANSI, ISO, BS, or ACM-SIGGRAPH)
> Be easy to teach
> Have standard menus with some company customization built in
> Be efficient when completing 2-D drafting assignments
> Have 3-D visualization capability
> Interface to other tasks, such as FEM
> Interface to other software systems

> Provide efficiency in checking completed drawings
> Have the ability to implement engineering change orders

Engineering manager.   The engineering manager has all of the above needs plus additional specific needs, including:

> Quality control of design through standard file names, ECO level tracking, drawing archival/retrieval, and drawing security
> Accurate communication of ECOs
> System cost-effectiveness for analysis and management of documents

Manufacturing manager. The manufacturing manager's programming needs are:

Access to the design process output drawings

Ability to receive parts schedules, bill of materials, and related lists

Use of information on NC machine operations (CAM)

A programming system designed to assist the manufacturing engineer accepts graphic data directly. The user enters commands directed toward one of three subsets of manufacturing CAM functions: NC machining, CNC (computerized NC), or direct NC (DNC).

Only those items that were common to all three CAM functions were discussed in this text. Every CAM operation can be controlled by the user so that a tool can be plunged straight into the start point on a surface as shown in Figure 10-3a, or enter on a ramp as shown in Figure 10-3c. The same common flexibility is shown in Figure 10-3b and d. CAM procedures such as these are derived from an extensive programming background of successfully generating numerical-control systems to provide the most efficient but least expensive NC, CNC, or DNC system.

CAM allows several forms of tool path display. Display of the tool and part tangent points provides an exact view of the part when completed, as shown in Figure 10-4, since that portion of the part the tool actually sweeps out is displayed. This method reduces any lengthy cycle for debugging such a program before design criteria can be interfaced with the NC machine. However, CNC or DNC could accomplish the same end in a fraction of the time and with greater precision. Interactive procedures allow the operator to define both rough and finish cuts. Dynamic display capability ensures that the manufactured product will be machined by CAM exactly as it was seen on the CRT screen. The manufacturing engineer is able to view the path of the tool by displaying the center line of the tool.

The ability to view both the tool path and the outline of the tool in motion from a 3-D perspective (shown in Figure 10-3d) provides collision checking and reduces time and cost of program debugging and test machining. The most common alternative is the display of the tool center as it moves through space. Both of these types of display, as well as the rough cut for tangent and tool offset, can be generated simultaneously. This capability assures congruence of part display and part machining before output generation. CAM uses the display screen as the depth at which a portion of a part is defined. This depth may be changed to correspond to any machining depth.

CAM provides two types of tool display containment—Z-level and curve, which may be used singularly or in combination. Under display containment an unlimited number of curves may be used. The containment defined by a curve may limit the tangent points on the surface or the edge of the tool, however.

The following parameters are user-controlled in display of a tool:

Tool diameter or radius

Tool flats or corner radius

Tool length, gage stops

Tool number

FIGURE 10-3
Examples of CAM operations:
(a) NC Example; (b) Profile Milling;
(c) Pocket Floor Roughing; and (d)
Slant Floor Kellering.

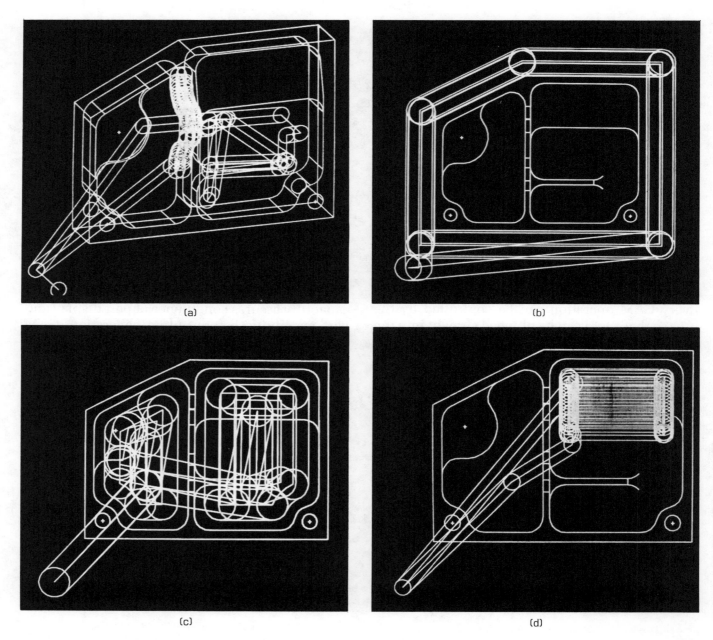

(a)

(b)

(c)

(d)

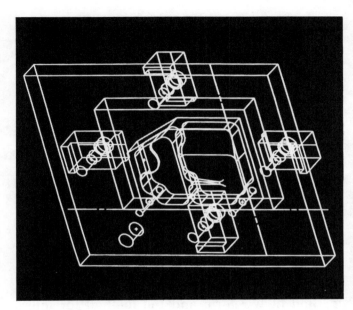

FIGURE 10-4
Fixture Check

In CAM tool display entering a parameter that impacts others automatically regenerates all affected changes. Some auxiliary functions make CAM displays compatible with most NC, CNC, or DNC configurations.

PROGRAMMING IMPROVEMENT FOR DISPLAY HARDWARE

There are a great many presentation methods for display hardware. A few examples are:

3-D presentation drawings
Detailed working drawings

Assembly drawings
Layout and design drawings
Symbolic template drafting and schematics
Isometric piping diagrams
Printed circuit board design

The ability to display the same data base in a number of ways on a variety of different display hardware is a proven aid to modern engineering graphics departments, leading to significant improvements in quality, lead time, and cost. Simplifying and improving graphic communications can be accomplished by building a universal data base (see Chapter 3) for all possible drafting and engineering documentation. This text presented a technique for the presentation of drawings ranging from details of small parts and assemblies to undimensioned drawings used as templates for fabrication of major structural components.

3-D presentation drawings. Three-dimensional representation is simple because the graphic data base is immediately available in mathematical form. The data can be used by several subprograms and can be displayed in a number of different ways, as we have seen. Some automated drafting systems must be programmed in two dimensions only, limiting the production of engineering documents in the following ways:

1. Draftspersons prepare original sketches and layouts (not needed in 3-D).
2. Graphics programmers prepare data for computer processing. (The engineer or draftsperson must communicate with the programmer for editing and revisions.)

3. Tapes are prepared for the plotting devices. (This reduces the number of direct-display devices that can be used).

This text introduced a method for streamlining 2-D systems into $2\frac{1}{2}$-D systems, and the steps necessary to prepare 3-D graphics.

Detailed working drawings. Assuming that the numerical description of the object to be detailed has been stored in three dimensions, the generation of working drawings is quite simple.

First, the user describes the object in wireform. Wireforms do not have hidden or invisible line segments. At this point all lines are represented as object lines only, which is not desired. The programmer may point to those lines that should be hidden on the CRT. A menu item especially designed to handle hidden-line representation is invoked. By touching the menu box labeled DASH, the programmer is sending a command to the host computer to recall a subprogram to erase the line segment between two inputs made earlier, and display a dashed line between these data points. This is a powerful routine because the programmer may select either wireform data points or points at random from the display line. All known cases for the technical use of a hidden line can then be represented.

Next, the programmer needs to add any special part features, such as slots, fillets, rounds, bosses, holes, and other working features. The procedure is the same as in the case of the hidden line. A menu item is selected, the display position is input, a scale for the display is entered, and the item is presented on one of the output devices shown in Chapter 5.

Now the user has finished the task of orthographic projection. Detailed drawings contain other information such as notes, dimensions, section views, and bill of materials. A detailed method for these operations was presented in Chapter 3, but it is important to mention here that steps in developing a program for detailed working drawings are sequential and follow nearly the same procedure that a detailer would use in the development of a mechanical, electrical, architectural, structural, or industrial detail drawing.

Assembly drawings. Assembly drawings are usually a combination of 3-D and working drawings. A reader who has understood both the method of wireform and the method for interactive generation of detailed drawings may proceed to the generation of an assembly drawing.

An assembly drawing is like a road map for the bill of materials. A user provides orthographic views of the object, with part features and fasteners, plus other parts related to the object in an "assembled fashion." Instead of displaying linear dimensions and notes, the user provides leaders (arrows) ending in circles. Inside each circle a number or letter is placed and cross-referenced with the bill of materials. For this reason, assembly drawings are usually programmed at the same time the bill of materials is developed.

Layout and design drawings. These types of drawings are usually not constructed by a programmer. Typically, a programmer works from design drawings to create assembly, working, and presentation drawings. Design engineers prepare design drawings and are responsible for the creation of datum references. Each datum is added to a collection called the *design data base*, from which display programs are able to generate the drawings.

Template drafting. Schematic or logic diagrams are ideally suited to menu item storage and template usage, as we saw in the familiarization program for DVST devices in Chapter 5. Anything that is prepared and manufactured as a plastic template for aid of drafting can be stored as symbols, including applications for all areas of engineering graphics. In the past this type of graphics has been produced in typical 2-D formats because the template was literally traced with an electric pen onto a graphics tablet. This type of graphics was not an improvement over plastic templates because the programming involved was extremely elementary. Recording the tracing of the pen as start- and endpoints of line segments caused local processors to become I/O bound with huge amounts of data. For example, in order to be displayed, a simple circle had to contain 60 separate X and Y locations instead of the usual center location and desired radius. Moreover, the traced circle producing the 60 data points was for a single diameter; in order to vary the diameter another function called *factoring* had to enlarge or reduce each X and Y data point.

Such procedures should be used on a limited basis only. Whenever possible, these types of programs should be converted to graphical entities and placed on a menu sheet. The menu sheet can then be placed on a data tablet, and the user can locate the particular entity by pointing to the X and Y locations on the data tablet surface. Each menu item is represented by a 3-D routine that contains internal scaling, rotation, translation, and transformation for mirrowing or windowing. By using this method, a programmer provides the draftsperson with a natural means of constructing template images. This method will be less expensive than the 2-D digitizing method described earlier and will be considerably more cost-effective than manual production.

Piping diagrams. Pictorial schematic diagrams, such as isometric riser diagrams, are now possible with the 3-D procedure just described. 3-D transformation can be used to rotate each datum into any degree relationship for viewing. Because a 3-D format is used, a pictorial presentation is as easy as an orthographic presentation.

In addition, each piping symbol may be rotated, revolved, mirrored, and placed anywhere in the isometric diagram. A viewing program then becomes a series of commands for each of the pipes to be placed and a single command for displaying all the interconnection lines that represent them. The time savings from this feature alone can reduce drawing time by 50%.

PCB design. Printed circuit board design, as shown in Figure 10-5, is one of the outstanding applications of 3-D display systems. First, the artwork itself is a 3-D entity. Second, the production of the circuit is a graphics-oriented process involving photochemical procedures and NC drilled operations.

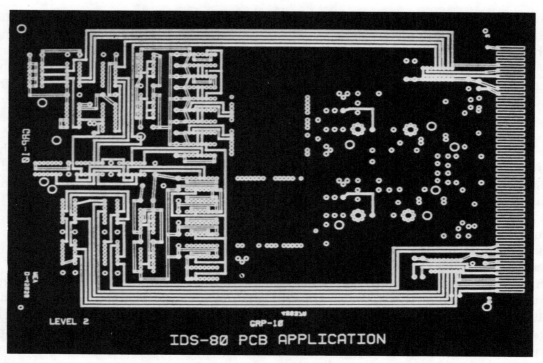

FIGURE 10-5

COMPUTER-AIDED DESIGN AND ANALYSIS

The testing programs shown in Chapter 9 are typical of the types of programs used by design engineers during the layout phase. Here objects are not coded as simple wireforms until all surfaces have been described. In this process all surfaces are considered to be a type of wireform called a *mesh network*. The network is made up of straight line segments arranged as splines. The grid may assume any shape the designer desires. Each intersection of the grid, called a *node*, is a datum that may be added to the design data base or discarded. This selection is often done manually by the design engineer during the layout stage, but later a computer program called *nodal analysis* compares each intersection and "saves" or "purges" each datum.

Three closely related computer processes are often misunderstood: nodal analysis, finite element analysis, and finite element modeling. To keep these straight in the design process, remember:

1. Nodal analysis is the selection or rejection of a single datum that was formed by the grid intersection of a plane surface. It is a plane surface, not a sculptured surface, because a spline is made up of many tiny straight-line segments. Therefore, each intersection of the grid is an intersection of two straight lines. Four intersections describe a plane surface sometimes referred to as a *patch*.

2. Finite element analysis is the selection or rejection of entire surfaces, based on the nodal analysis. Finite element analysis is almost always involved in three-dimensional objects. At the same time, remember the concept of the wireform: objects are not solid planes. To study a 3-D object, the design engineer must study each point describing the object.

3. Finite element modeling is the selection process for the entire group of surfaces that make up the object. The examples shown in this book were finite element models only.

FINAL REVIEW PROBLEMS

1. List as many applications for the programming presented in this book as you can. You may mention both strengths and weaknesses.

ANSWER The programming system described in this book is excellent for schematic drafting/design outputs from either 2-D or 3-D data bases. It is not suited for outputs such as maps, lofting problems, or landsat image processing.

2. Prepare a list of drafting functions that can be performed automatically using the programming system in this book.

ANSWER See Chapter 3 and Table 10-2.

3. Prepare a list of design functions that can be performed by using this system of programming.

ANSWER Will vary from reader to reader.

4. Prepare a list of manufacturing functions that can be aided using this system of programming.

ANSWER See Chapter 7.

5. Who are the key people in qualifying the type of programming that is needed in a company?

ANSWER Managers of drafting, design, and manufacturing.

A P P E N D I X

A.1 CUPID1

Commonly used pictorial image displays (CUPID) software programming is generally grouped into three areas:

1. 2-D usage examples
2. 3-D applications
3. Process simulation studies

In order to preform any of these types of software exercise, the user must understand the job control language (JCL) for the host processor. For example:

```
//PLOTTER JOB (ACCOUNT NUMBER, TIME, LINES)
//STEP1 EXEC FTG1CLG, PLOT = 1812
//C.SYSIN DD *
        CALL PLOTS

        / PROGRAM STATEMENTS /

        CALL PLOT(18.,0.,999)
        STOP
        END
/*
//G.SYSIN DD *

        / DATA /
/*
//
```

represents the JCL for a large host processor such as the IBM 370/3033. These statements may be punched on cards or typed from a keyboard. Their purpose is to activate an automatic spooling program, which operates at the system level. For example:

```
1     //LICHEN1 JOB (0923-2-001-00-  ,#02,1),'LIHWA BOX 22',
      //     TIME=(0000,02),REGION=256K
      ***JOBPARM Q=T
      ***JOBPARM I
      ***ROUTE PRINT TEXT
      ***JOBPARM EXCP=99999999
2     //STEP1 EXEC FTG1CLG,PLOT=0812
3     XXFTG1CLG PROC   OBJECT=DUMMY,PUNCH='SYSOUT=X',COPT=,LOPT=,
      XX    ULIB='ACS.PORT801.LOAD',SYSOUT=A,PLOT=0812,PLOTTER=CALCOMP
4     XXC       EXEC   PGM=IGIFORT,PARM='DECK,LINECNT=60&COPT'
5     XXSTEPLIB  DD    DSN=ACS.FORTG1.LOAD,DISP=SHR
6     XXSYSPRINT DD    SYSOUT=&SYSOUT,DCB=BLKSIZE=120
7     XXSYSUT1   DD    UNIT=VIO,SPACE=(CYL,(1,1)),DSN=&&UT1
8     XXSYSUT2   DD    UNIT=VIO,SPACE=(CYL,(1,1)),DSN=&&UT2
9     XXSYSLIN   DD    UNIT=SYSDA,SPACE=(CYL,(1,2)),DSN=&&OBJ,DISP=(MOD,PASS),
      XX               DCB=(LRECL=80,RECFM=FBS,BLKSIZE=400)
10    XXSYSPUNCH DD    &OBJECT,DCB=BLKSIZE=80
11    //C.SYSIN DD *
12    XXL        EXEC   PGM=IEWL,COND=(5,LT,C),PARM='LIST,MAP&LOPT'
13    XXSYSLIB   DD    DSN=ACS.MOD2.FORTLIB,DISP=(SHR,PASS)
14    XX         DD    DSN=ACS.&PLOTTER..LOAD,DISP=SHR
15    XX         DD    DSN=ACS.CALCOMP2.LOAD,DISP=SHR
16    XX         DD    DSN=&ULIB,DISP=SHR
17    XX         DD    DSN=ACS.FORTLIB.LOAD,DISP=(SHR,PASS)
18    XXSYSPRINT DD    SYSOUT=&SYSOUT
19    XXSYSUT1   DD    UNIT=VIO,SPACE=(CYL,(1,1)),DSN=&&UT1
20    XXSYSLIN   DD    DSN=&&OBJ,DISP=(MOD,DELETE),UNIT=SYSDA
21    XX         DD    DDNAME=SYSIN
22    XXSYSLMOD  DD    DSN=&&PDS(MAIN),DISP=(,PASS),UNIT=SYSDA,
      XX               SPACE=(CYL,(1,1,1),RLSE),DCB=(RECFM=U,BLKSIZE=13030)
23    XXG        EXEC   PGM=MAIN,COND=((5,LT,C),(5,LT,L)),TIME=1400
24    XXSTEPLIB DD DSN=&&PDS,DISP=(OLD,DELETE)
25    XXFT01F001 DD    DDNAME=SYSIN
```

```
26       XXFTO2FOO1 DD   &PUNCH,DCB=BLKSIZE=80
27       XXFTO3FOO1 DD   SYSOUT=&SYSOUT,DCB=(LRECL=133,RECFM=FA,BLKSIZE=133)
28       XXFTO6FOO1 DD   SYSOUT=&SYSOUT,DCB=(LRECL=133,RECFM=FA,BLKSIZE=133)
29       XXPLOTTAPE DD   SYSOUT(Y,,&PLOT)
30       XXPLOTLOG  DD   SYSOUT=&SYSOUT
31       XXVECTR1   DD   DSN=&&VECTR1,UNIT=VIO,SPACE=(TRK,(1,1)),DISP=(,PASS)
32       XXVECTR2   DD   DSN=&&VECTR2,UNIT=VIO,SPACE=(CYL,(1,1)),DISP=(,PASS)
33       //G.SYSIN DD *
         //
```

is the output from the JCL statements plus the program statements. The program statements must be included before complete processing will take place. The second page of the output from a graphics program contains any warning messages and the job statistics and appears as:

```
J E S 2   J O B   L O G

18.14.17 JOB 5908   IEF677I WARNING MESSAGE(S) FOR JOB LICHEN1  ISSUED
18.14.18 JOB 5908   $HASP373 LICHEN1  STARTED - INIT B7 - CLASS B - SYS 3033
18.14.31 JOB 5908   MVS001I LICHEN1 .C        001 IGIFORT  COND CODE 0000
18.14.59 JOB 5908   MVS001I LICHEN1 .L        002 IEWL     COND CODE 0000
18.15.05 JOB 5908   MVS001I LICHEN1 .G        003 MAIN     COND CODE 0000
18.15.06 JOB 5908   $HASP395 LICHEN1  ENDED


------ JES2 JOB STATISTICS ------

  03 DEC 80 JOB EXECUTION DATE

      45 CARDS READ

     254 SYSOUT PRINT RECORDS

      54 SYSOUT PUNCH RECORDS

    0.82 MINUTES EXECUTION TIME
```

The fourth page of the output contains the program statements. Called the MAIN program, it appears as:

```
0001          CALL PLOTS
0002          CALL TITLE(.5)
0003          CALL PLOT(18.,0.,999)
0004          STOP
0005          END
```

Any subprograms called from the main program are listed on separate pages. In this case only one subprogram, called TITLE, has been written by the graphics program. It would appear on the fifth page of the printed output as:

```
0001          SUBROUTINE TITLE(SIZE)
0002          CALL FACTOR(SIZE)
0003          CALL RECT(0.,0.,11.25,17.,0.0,3)
0004          CALL RECT(0.,0.,.750,1.,0.0,3)
0005          CALL RECT(1.,0.,.750,3.5,0.0,3)
0006          CALL RECT(4.5,0.,.375,2.5,0.0,3)
0007          CALL RECT(4.5,.375,.375,2.5,0.0,3)
0008          CALL RECT(7.0,0.,.375,3.5,0.0,3)
0009          CALL RECT(7.0,.375,.375,3.5,0.0,3)
0010          CALL RECT(10.5,.0,.750,5.25,0.0,3)
0011          CALL RECT(15.75,0.,.750,1.25,0.0,3)
0012          CALL SYMBOL(.1,.1,.08,12HDRAWING  NO.,0.,12)
0013          CALL SYMBOL(.375,.25,.25,1H1,0,1)
0014          CALL SYMBOL(1.875,.5,.09,21HENGINEERING  GRAPHICS,
              0.,21)
0015          CALL SYMBOL(1.625,.3125,.1,24HCOLLEGE  OF  ENGINEERING,
              0.,24)
0016          CALL SYMBOL(4.625,.12,.1,6HSCALE:,0.,6)
```

```
0017                CALL SYMBOL(4.625,.45,.1,5HDATE:,0.,5)
0018                CALL SYMBOL(5.25,.45,.1,6H9-6-80,0.,6)
0019                CALL SYMBOL(5.50,.12,.1,4HFULL,0.,4)
0020                CALL SYMBOL(7.125,.12,.1,7HCOURSE:,0.,7)
0021                CALL SYMBOL(8.,.12,.1,6HEG 310,0.,6)
0022                CALL SYMBOL(7.125,.45,.1,7HDR  BY:,0.,7)
0023                CALL SYMBOL(7.9,.45,.1,'LIHWA CHEN',0.,10)
0024                CALL SYMBOL(11.75,.1,.1,18HTITLE  OF  DRAWING,0.,18)
0025                CALL SYMBOL(12.5,.32,0.25,11HTITLE BLOCK,0.,11)
0026                CALL SYMBOL(16.125,.1,.1,5HDRADE,0.,5)
0027                RETURN
0028                END
```

The graphical image produced is a border line and title strip format. No drawing is produced, though one could be produced by the addition of a few program statements and another sub-program. Notice the example shown below.

```
0001                DIMENSION X(100),Y(100,IPEN(100)
0002                DATA X/2.,2*7.,2*3.,2*2.,2*5.,2*6.5,5.,2*5.,2*6.5,2*7.,
                    3*2.,3.,2.,
                    +3*3.,10.,2*13.5,12.5,11.,3*10.,13.5/
0003                DATA Y/2*2.,2*3.,2*5.,2*2.,3.,2.,3.,2*6.5,2*7.5,2*6.5,
                    2*10.,6.5,
                    +2*9.,2*7.5,10.,6.5,2*2.,4*5.,2.,2*3./
0004                DATA IPEN/3,6*2,3,2,3,2,3,8*2,3,2,3,2,3,2,3,3*2,3,2*2,
                    3,2/
0005                CALL PLOTS
0006                CALL TITLE(.5)
0007                CALL DRAW2D(X,Y,IPEN,35)
0008                CALL CIRCL(11.,5.,180.,360.,0.75,0.75,0.)
0009                CALL PLOT(18.,0.,999)
0010                STOP
0011                END
```

A prestored location in computer memory is requested by the DIMENSION statement. There are 100 possible data locations available for the subprogram DRAW2D. The data is entered by the use of the DATA statement. Finally, a system subroutine called CIRCL has been used in the image display. The subprogram DRAW2D is listed as shown here:

```
0001          SUBROUTINE DRAW2D(X,Y,IPEN,NDATA)
0002          DIMENSION X(100),Y(100),IPEN(100)
0003          DO 100 I=1,NDATA
0004     100  CALL PLOT(X(I),Y(I),IPEN(I))
0005          READ(1,4)NDASHP
0006     4    FORMAT(12)
0007          DO 5 J=1,NDASHP
0008          READ(1,*)X1,Y1,Z,W
0009          CALL PLOT(X1,Y1,3)
0010     5    CALL DASHP(Z,W,.15)
0011          RETURN
0012          END
```

This subprogram is useful for plotting any 2-D data such as a map or template figure. The graphics programmer must remember to set aside the proper amount of storage by the use of a DIMENSION statement before the CALL DRAW2D statement. If, for example, 250 X and Y data points were used to describe the graphical image, then a minimum of 250 storage locations should be provided. In this example 250 is too large for the use of DATA statements, and the introduction of a data error is probable at this point. Therefore, the data are placed after the //G.SYSIN DD * JCL statement and are read into the main program by a READ statement.

Either method of input may be used for the data. If the data base is small, it is more convenient to enter it as a DATA statement. DRAW2D is used to connect straight-line segments only. If circles or arcs are required in the 2-D image display, they are usually entered directly in the main program. An example of this type of programming would appear as:

```
0001          CALL PLOTS
0002          CALL TITLE(.5)
0003          DIMENSION X(50),Y(50),R(50),SANG(50),N(50),THETA(50)
0004          DATA X/3.,4.5,6.298,4.976,6.,2*4.5,3.,4.5,6./
```

```
0005            DATA Y/4.,6.,4.263,4.3,5.,5.5,4.1,4.,5.5,4./
0006            DATA R/3*.75,2.25,1.,1.5,1.09,.875,1.246,.875/
0007            DATA N/16,13,16,11,25,22,10,45,18,45/
0008            DATA SANG/263.,30.,134.,90.,145.,35.,240.,270.,225.,
                45./
0009            DATA THETA/3*8.,2*5.,5.,6.,3*5./
0010            CALL PLOT(0.,5.5,-3)
0011            DO 1 I=1,3
0012            X(I)=X(I)-.6
0013            Y(I)=Y(I)-2.
0014       1    CALL CIRCLE (X(I),Y(I),R(I),SANG(I),N(I),THETA(I))
0015            CALL PLOT(1.756,2.384,3)
0016            CALL PLOT(3.250,4.375,2)
0017            CALL PLOT(4.420,4.540,3)
0018            CALL PLOT(6.218,2.803,2)
0019            CALL PLOT(5.804,1.521,3)
0020            CALL PLOT(2.493,1.254,2)
0021            CALL PLOT(8.,0.,-3)
0022            DO  10 I=4,5
0023            X(I)=X(I)-1.
0024            Y(I)=Y(I)-2.5
0025      10    CALL CIRCLE (X(I),Y(I),R(I),SANG(I),N(I),THETA(I))
0026            CALL PLOT(5.,1.5,3)
0027            CALL PLOT(2.,1.5,2)
0028            CALL PLOT(-8.,-5.5,-3)
0029            DO 100 I=6,7
0030            X(I)=X(I)-.5
0031            Y(I)=Y(I)-2.
0032     100    CALL CIRCLE (X(I),Y(I),R(I),SANG(I),N(I),THETA(I))
0033            CALL PLOT(3.502,1.133,3)
0034            CALL PLOT(1.502,2.633,2)
0035            CALL PLOT(2.771,4.360,2)
0036            CALL PLOT(5.228,4.362,3)
0037            CALL PLOT(6.502,2.635,2)
0038            CALL PLOT(4.502,1.135,2)
0039            CALL PLOT(8.,0.,-3)
0040            DO 1000 I=8,10
```

```
0041              X(I)=X(I)-.6
0042              Y(I)=Y(I)-1.2
0043        1000 CALL CIRCLE (X(I),Y(I),R(I),SANG(I),N(I),THETA(I))
0044              CALL PLOT(2.402,1.925,3)
0045              CALL PLOT(5.402,1.925,2)
0046              CALL PLOT(18.,0.,999)
0047              STOP
0048              END
```

In this example DRAW2D is not used; it was replaced by CALL PLOT for straight lines and CALL CIRCLE for arcs. Note that CIRCL is a system subroutine, whereas CIRCLE must be provided as a subprogram, listed as:

```
0001              SUBROUTINE CIRCLE(X,Y,R,SANG,N,THETA)
0002              X=X-R
0003              SANG=(3.14/180.)*SANG
0004              XX=R*(1-COS(SANG))
0005              YY=R*(SIN(SANG))
0006              DX=X+XX
0007              EY=Y+YY
0008              CALL PLOT(DX,EY,3)
0009              THETA=(3.14/180.)*THETA
0010              THETA1=THETA
0011              DO 2 I=1,N
0012              FEE=SANG+THETA
0013              PX=R*(1-COS(FEE))
0014              SY=R*(SIN(FEE))
0015              DX=X+PX
0016              EY=Y+SY
0017              CALL PLOT(DX,EY,2)
0018        2     THETA=THETA+THETA1
0019              RETURN
0020              END
```

These template-type 2-D image displays are useful for single-view drawing representations but do little to represent multiview engineering drawings.

Three-dimensional data are needed to display automatic three-view type representations. The main program is modified as shown below:

```
0001                    DIMENSION X(100),Y(100),Z(100),IPEN(100)
0002                    DATA X/0.,3*0.5,3*1.5,2*3.5,3*2.,6*0.,2*3.5,4*2.,4*3.5,
                        4*0.5,1.5/
0003                    DATA Y/2*0.,4*1.5,2*0.,2*0.5,4*1.5,2*0.,1.5,2*0.,2*0.5,
                        1.5,4*0.5,
                        +4*0.,1.5,2*0./
0004                    DATA Z/3*-1.5,2*-0.5,6*-1.5,2*-0.,2*-0.,2*-1.5,7*-0.,
                        +-1.5,-0.,-1.5,-0.,-1.5,-0.,-1.5,4*-0.5/
0005                    DATA IPEN/3,16*2,3,4*2,3,2,3,2,3,2,3,2*2,3,2/
0006                    CALL PLOTS
0007                    CALL TITLE(.5)
0008                    CALL PLOT (3.5,2.5,-3)
0009                    CALL CUPID(X,Y,Z,IPEN,8.5,6.5,33,30.,1.)
0010                    CALL PLOT(18.0,0.0,999)
0011                    STOP
0012                    END
```

In this program the addition of a subprogram called CUPID displays the three-dimensional data that are contained in the DATA statements as:

```
0001                    SUBROUTINE CUPID(X,Y,Z,IPEN,XTRANS,YTRANS,NDAT,ANG,SF)
0002                    DIMENSION X(100),Y(100),Z(100),IPEN(100)XPLOT(100),
                        YPLOT(100)
0003                    COSA=COS(ANG/57.3)
0004                    SINA=SIN(ANG/57.3)
```

```
0005          DO 1 K=1,NDAT
0006          XPLOT(K)=(X(K)+Z(K)*SF*COSA)+8.2
0007          YPLOT(K)=(Y(K)+Z(K)*SF*SINA)+5.2
0008    1     CALL PLOT(XPLOT(K),YPLOT(K),IPEN(K))
0009          DO 10 J=1,NDAT
0010    10    CALL PLOT(X(J),Y(J),IPEN(J))
0011          DO 20 I=1,NDAT
0012          Z(I)=Z(I)+YTRANS
0013    20    CALL PLOT(X(I),Z(I),IPEN(I))
0014          DO 30 I=1,NDAT
0015          Z(I)=(Z(I)+XTRANS)-YTRANS
0016    30    CALL PLOT(Z(I),Y(I),IPEN(I))
0017          RETURN
0018          END
```

Notice that the three working views are located in the common view form and that a wireform pictorial is provided in the upper right-hand corner of the title sheet.

In order to use this display later, selective erase and hidden-line selection must be employed. The wireform must appear as the solid object that it represents.

```
0001          DIMENSION X(100),Y(100),Z(100),IPEN(100)
0002          DATA X/0.,3*0.5,3*1.5,2*3.5,3*2.,6*0.,2*3.5,4*2.,4*3.5,
              4*0.5,1.5/
0003          DATA Y/2*0.,4*1.5,2*0.,2*0.5,4*1.5,2*0.,1.5,2*0.,2*0.5,
              1.5,4*0.5,
              +4*0.,1.5,2*0./
0004          DATA Z/3*-1.5,2*-0.5,6*-1.5,2*-0.,2*-1.5,7*-0.,
              +-1.5,-0.,-1.5,-0.,-1.5,-0.,-1.5,4*-0.5/
0005          DATA IPEN/3,16*2,3,4*2,3,2,3,2,3,2,3,2*2,3,2/
0006          DIMENSION X1(50),Y1(50),Z1(50),DIA(50)
0007          DATA X1/2.95,2.,0.5/
```

```
0008                    DATA Y1/0.5,0.9,0.9/
0009                    DATA Z1/-0.75,-1.,-1./
0010                    DATA DIA/0.4,0.2,0.2/
0011                    CALL PLOTS
0012                    CALL TITLE(.5)
0013                    CALL PLOT (3.5,2.5,-3)
0014                    CALL CUPID(X,Y,Z,IPEN,33,30.,1.)
0015                    CALL HOLE(X1,Y1,Z1,DIA,30.,1.)
0016                    CALL PLOT(18.0,0.0,999)
0017                    STOP
0018                    END
```

The wireform pictorial was omitted by the use of the

```
CALL CUPID(X,Y,Z,IPEN,33,30.,1.)
```

statement in the main program listed above. The graphics programmer may choose to display the pictorial or work only with the three views. To more fully represent the fact of a solid machine part, three holes were displayed in the part by adding

```
CALL HOLE(X1,Y1,Z1,DIA,30.,1)
```

to the main display program. In order for the display system to respond, a subprogram for hole must be supplied by the graphics programmer:

```
0001                    SUBROUTINE HOLE(X1,Y1,Z1,DIA,ANG,SF)
0002                    DIMENSION X1(50),Y1(50),Z1(50),DIA(50),XHOLE(50),
                        YHOLE(50)
0003                    COSA=COS(ANG/57.3)
0004                    SINA=SIN(ANG/57.3)
```

```
0005                    DO 2 L=1,3
0006                    XHOLE(L)=(X1(L)+Z1(L)*SF*COSA)+8.2
0007                    YHOLE(L)=(Y1(L)+Z1(L)*SF*SINA)+5.2
0008              2     CALL CIRCL (XHOLE)L),YHOLE(L),0.,360.,DIA(L)/2.,
                        DIA(L)/2.,0.)
0009                    RETURN
0010                    END
```

Holes may be represented in the wireform pictorial or any of the three working views.

Commonly used subprograms in CUPID1 include not only DRAW2D, as listed earlier and shown as geometric objects, but also items to create a "family of parts" such as HOLE. The family of parts has been added to display useful machine elements. This concept of subpictures has been explained in detail in the text and is presented now in CUPID1-type listings. The main program appears as:

```
0001                    CALL PLOTS
0002                    CALL TITLE(1.)
0003                    DIMENSION X(10),Y(10),R(10),SANG(10),N(10),THETA(10)
0004                    DATA X/3.,4.5,6.298,4.976,6.,2*4.5,3.,4.5,6./
0005                    DATA Y/4.,6.,4.263,4.3,5.,5.5,4.1,4.,5.5,4./
0006                    DATA R/3*.75,2.25,1.,1.5,1.09,.875,1.246,.875/
0007                    DATA SANG/263.,30.,134.,90.,145.,35.,240.,270.,225.,45/
0008                    DATA N/16,13,16,11,25,22,10,45,18,45/
0009                    DATA THETA/3*8.,2*5.,5.,6.,3*5./
0010                    CALL PLOT(0.,5.5,-3)
0011                    DO 1 I=1,3
0012                    X(I)=X(I)-.6
0013                    Y(I)=Y(I)-2.
0014              1     CALL CIRCLE(X(I),Y(I),R(I),SANG(I),N(I),THETA(I))
0015                    CALL PLOT(1.756,2.384,3)
```

```
0016            CALL PLOT(3.25,4.375,2)
0017            CALL PLOT(4.42,4.54,3)
0018            CALL PLOT(6.218,2.803,2)
0019            CALL PLOT(5.804,1.521,3)
0020            CALL PLOT(2.493,1.254,2)
0021            CALL PLOT(8.,0.,-3)
0022            DO 10 I=4,5
0023            X(I)=X(I)-1.
0024            Y(I)=Y(I)-2.5
0025      10    CALL CIRCLE(X(I),Y(I),R(I),SANG(I),N(I),THETA(I))
0026            CALL PLOT(5.,1.5,3)
0027            CALL PLOT(2.,1.5,2)
0028            CALL PLOT(-8.,-5.5,-3)
0029            DO 100 I=6,7
0030            X(I)=X(I)-.5
0031            Y(I)=Y(I)-2.
0032     100    CALL CIRCLE(X)I),Y(I),R(I),SANG(I),N(I),THETA(I))
0033            CALL PLOT(3.502,1.133,3)
0034            CALL PLOT(1.502,2.633,2)
0035            CALL PLOT(2.771,4.360,2)
0036            CALL PLOT(5.228,4.362,3)
0037            CALL PLOT(6.502,2.635,2)
0038            CALL PLOT(4.502,1.135,2)
0039            CALL PLOT(8.,0.,-3)
0040            DO 1000 I=8,10
0041            X(I)=X(I)-.6
0042            Y(I)=Y(I)-1.2
0043    1000    CALL CIRCLE(X(I),Y(I),R(I),SANG(I),N(I),THETA(I))
0044            CALL PLOT(2.402,1.925,3)
0045            CALL PLOT(5.402,1.925,2)
        C       ***** ADD PART FEATURES *****
0046            CALL ZHOLE(2.45,2.76,.50)
0047            CALL ZHOLE(5.35,2.76,.50)
0048            CALL FIT(2.,7.0,2.5,9.0,3.976,9.55)
0049            CALL ZHOLE(-4.0,8.25,.7)
0050            CALL PLOT(-4.25,8.9,3)
0051            CALL PLOT(-4.25,9.05,2)
```

```
0052                    CALL  PLOT(-4.15,9.15,3)
0053                    CALL  PLOT(-3.85,9.15,2)
0054                    CALL  PLOT(-3.75,9.05,3)
0055                    CALL  PLOT(-3.75,8.9,2)
0056                    CALL  CIRCL(-2.75,8.25,0.,360.,1.25,1.25,.5)
0057                    CALL  ZHOLE(4.4,8.15,.7)
0058                    CALL  ZHOLE(-4.0,2.75,1.)
0059                    CALL  PLOT(0.,0.,999)
0060                    STOP
0061                    END
```

Where ZHOLE is a modification of the sub-program HOLE and appears as:

```
0001                    SUBROUTINE ZHOLE(XS,YS,R)
0002                    CALL  CIRCL(XS+R,YS,0.,360.,R,R,0.0)
0003                    CALL  PLOT(XS-1.2*R,YS,3)
0004                    CALL  PLOT(XS-.4*R,YS,2)
0005                    CALL  PLOT(XS-.2*R,YS,3)
0006                    CALL  PLOT(XS+.2*R,YS,2)
0007                    CALL  PLOT(XS+.4*R,YS,3)
0008                    CALL  PLOT(XS+1.2*R,YS,2)
0009                    CALL  PLOT(XS,YS+1.2*R,3)
0010                    CALL  PLOT(XS,YS+.4*R,2)
0011                    CALL  PLOT(XS,YS+.2*R,3)
0012                    CALL  PLOT(XS,YS-.2*R,2)
0013                    CALL  PLOT(XS,YS-.4*R,3)
0014                    CALL  PLOT(XS,YS-1.2*R,2)
0015                    RETURN
0016                    END
```

The ZHOLE subprogram assumes a manufactured hole in the machine part parallel to the Z axis of display. In order to create the family-of-

parts concept, part features need to be added.
Holes generally include center lines, which may
be displayed by the use of a subprogram called
CIRCNT and appear as:

```
      SUBROUTINE CIRCNT(X,Y,R,TLEN)
C     **********************************************************************
C     *   THIS SUBROUTINE DRAWS CROSSED CENTERLINES IN THE CENTER OF A   *
C     *   CIRCLE OR ANY WHERE ELSE DESIGNATED BY THE X AND Y VALUES.     *
C     *   THE LINES ARE PARALLEL AND PERPENDICULAR TO THE X AXIS. THE    *
C     *   SHORT DASH AT THE CENTER IS .1 TIMES THE RADIUS OF THE CIRCLE  *
C     *   AS IS EACH SPACE. THE LONG LINES COMPRISE THE REMAINDER OF THE *
C     *   LINE LENGTH DESIGNATED BY TLEN.                                *
C     **********************************************************************
      DSH=R*.1
      SPCE=R*.1
      ALINE=(TLEN-(DSH+2*SPCE))/2.
      CALL CNTLI(X,Y,TLEN,DSH,SPCE,ALINE,0.0)
      CALL CNTLI(X,Y,TLEN,DSH,SPCE,ALINE,90.)
      RETURN
      END


C     **********************************************************************
C     * THIS SUBROUTINE DRAWS A CENTERLINE ANY SIZE, ANY DIRECTION,      *
C     * ANYWHERE ON THE PLOTTER SURFACE. THE STARTING POINT IS THE       *
C     * CENTER OF THE LINE FOR EASE OF LOCATION. THE ARGUMENTS ARE:      *
C     *                                                                  *
C     *      X         MIDDLE OF LINE                                    *
C     *      Y         MIDDLE OF LINE                                    *
C     *    TLEN        TOTAL LENGTH OF LINE                              *
C     *    THETA       DEGREES OF ROTATION CCW                          *
C     *    DSH         LENGTH OF SHORT LINE                              *
C     *    SPCE        LENGTH OF SPACE                                   *
C     *    ALINE       LENGTH OF LONG LINE                               *
C     *                                                                  *
C     **********************************************************************
```

```
0001                    SUBROUTINE CNTLI(X,Y,TLEN,DSH,SPCE,ALINE,THETA)
0002                    THETA=3.14159/180.*THETA
0003                    TOTAL=DSH+SPCE+SPCE+ALINE+ALINE
0004                    NUM=TLEN/TOTAL
0005                    CALL PLOT(X,Y,3)
0006                    X1=X
0007                    Y1=Y
0008                    DO 3 I=1,NUM
0009                    X1=X1-DSH/2.*COS(THETA)
0010                    Y1=Y1-DSH/2.*SIN(THETA)
0011                    CALL PLOT(X1,Y1,2)
0012                    X1=X1-SPCE*COS(THETA)
0013                    Y1=Y1-SPCE*SIN(THETA)
0014                    CALL PLOT(X1,Y1,3)
0015                    X1=X1-ALINE*COS(THETA)
0016                    Y1=Y1-ALINE*SIN(THETA)
0017            3       CALL PLOT(X1,Y1,2)
0018                    X1=X
0019                    Y1=Y
0020                    CALL PLOT(X,Y,3)
0021                    DO 4 I=1,NUM
0022                    X1=X1+DSH/2.*COS(THETA)
0023                    Y1=Y1+DSH/2.*SIN(THETA)
0024                    CALL PLOT(X1,Y1,2)
0025                    X1=X1+SPCE*COS(THETA)
0026                    Y1=Y1+SPCE*SIN(THETA)
0027                    CALL PLOT(X1,Y1,3)
0028                    X1=X1+ALINE*COS(THETA)
0029                    Y1=Y1+ALINE*SIN(THETA)
0030            4       CALL PLOT(X1,Y1,2)
0031                    RETURN
0032                    END
```

The concept of special part features may include
CUPID1 views in section view.

```
      C
      C*************************************************************************
      C *    THIS PROGRAM WILL CUT AN OBJECT TO SHOW THE INTERNAL MATERIAL.    *
      C *       THOSE SOLID SECTIONS CAN THEN BE CROSSHATCHED BY CALLING       *
      C *       SHADE OR TONE.                                                 *
      C *    DRAFTING SUBROUTINES:                                            *
      C *    A: AROHD                                                         *
      C *    B: BARE                                                          *
      C *    C: CIRCL                                                         *
      C *    C: CIRCLE                                                        *
      C *    C: CENTER                                                        *
      C *    F: FIT                                                           *
      C *    P: PLOT                                                          *
      C *    P: POLY                                                          *
      C *    S: SHADE                                                         *
      C *************************************************************************
      C

      C DECLARE:
0001          DIMENSION X(50),Y(50),SANG(50),EANG(50),DIA(50)
      C
      C INPUT/OUTPUT:
0002          DATA X/1.5,12.,11.,10.25,8.45,2*10.69,2*2.,2*0.5,2*1.5/
0003          DATA Y/6.853,4*5.5,4.25,6.812,3.5,0.16,3.5,0.16,3.5,
              0.16/
0004          DATA SANG/7*0.,45.,-45.,45.,-45.,60.,-60./
0005          DATA EANG/7*360.,140.,-140.,140.,-140.,120.,-120./
0006          DATA DIA/1.,.5,.3,.1.5,3*0.90,4*0.7,2*2./
      C
      C DECLARE:
0007          DIMENSION X1(50),Y1(50),IPEN(50)
      C
      C INPUT/OUTPUT:
0008          DATA X1/0.5,1.5,2*0.,2*2.,2*0.5,2*1.5,7.,2*12.,2*10.25,
           2*8.75,
         +2*7.,2*8.25,2*10.75/
```

```
0009                    DATA Y1/2*5.,3.5,0.16,3.5,0.16,3.5,0.16,3.5,0.16,2*0.,
                 2*1.55,
                 +2*1.75,2*1.55,0.,1.55,0.,1.55,0./
0010                    DATA IPEN/3,2,3,2,3,2,3,2,3,2,3,8*2,3,2,3,2/
             C
             C DECLARE:
0011                    DIMENSION XARAY(50),YARAY(50),XXARAY(50),YYARAY(50)
             C
             C INPUT/OUTPUT:
0012                DATA XARAY/2.5,3.,4.,0.,1./
0013                DATA YARAY/1.75,2*2.618,0.,1./
0014                DATA XXARAY/3.,4.,4.5,0.,1./
0015                DATA YYARAY/2*0.875,1.75,0.,1./
             C
             C DECLARE:
0016                DIMENSION ARAY1(50),ARAY2(50),ARAY3(50),ARAY4(50)
0017                DIMENSION XLOC(50),YLOC(50),XEND(50),YEND(50)
             C
             C INPUT/OUTPUT:
0018                DATA XLOC/12.5,2*10.56,11.125,9.5,7.879,4.7,4.2,1.,2.4,
                 1.,1.6/
0019                DATA YLOC/5.5,3.75,7.31,1.75,1.95,2*1.75,4.5,8.,6.853,
                 5.4,4.5/
0020                DATA XEND/6.5,2*9.935,11.125,9.5,7.875,2.3,2.8,1.,-0.4,
                 1.,0.4/
0021                DATA YEND/5.5,4.69,6.3,3*-0.2,1.75,4.5,5.7,6.853,-0.4,
                 4.5/
             C
             C DECLARE:
0022                DIMENSION ARAYX(50),ARAYY(50),ARAYXX(50),ARAYYY(50)
             C
             C INPUT/OUTPUT:
0023                DATA ARAYX/8.25,2*8.75,2*10.25,10.75,0.,1./
0024                DATA ARAYY/2*1.55,2*1.75,2*1.55,0.,1./
0025                DATA ARAYXX/8.25,10.75,0.,1./
0026                DATA ARAYYY/2*0.,0.,1./
             C
```

```
            C CONTROL:
0027                CALL PLOTS
0028                CALL TITLE(.5)
0029                CALL PLOT(2.5,2.,-3)
0030                CALL FIT(0.5,5.,0.5,4.,0.,3.5)
0031                CALL FIT(1.5,5.,1.5,4.,2.,3.5)
            C
            C DO LOOP STATEMENT:
0032                DO 10 I=1,13
            C CONTROL:
0033                CALL CIRCL(X(I),Y(I),SANG(I),EANG(I),DIA(I)/2.,DIA(I)/
                   2.,0.0)
            C CONTROL:
0034          10    CONTINUE
            C
            C CONTROL:
0035                CALL CIRCLE(3.5,4.5,0.5,0.,30,12.,ARAY1,ARAY2,ARAY3,
                   ARAY4)
0036                CALL AROHD(6.5,5.5,6.5,6.,0.3,0.1,16)
0037                CALL AROHD(12.5,5.5,12.5,6.,0.3,0.1,16)
0038                CALL POLY(0.5,6.,1.,6.,0.0)
0039                CALL POLY(3.0,0.875,1.,6.,0.0)
            C
            C DO LOOP STATEMENTS:
0040                DO 20 I=1,23
            C    CONTROL:
0041          20    CALL PLOT(X1(I),Y1(I),IPEN(I))
            C
            C DO LOOP STATEMENTS:
0042                DO 97 I=1,12
            C
            C CONTROL:
0043          97    CALL CENTER(XLOC(I),YLOC(I),XEND(I),YEND(I))
0044                CALL BAR(7.,0.,0.,1.55,0.5,1.55,2,16)
0045                CALL BAR(11.5,0.,0.,1.55,0.5,1.55,2,16)
0046                CALL SHADE(XARAY,YARAY,XXARAY,YYARAY,0.07,73.,3,1,3,1)
0047                CALL SHADE(ARAYX,ARAYY,ARAYXX,ARAYYY,0.07,73.,6,1,2,1)
```

```
0048                CALL SHADE(ARAY1,ARAY2,ARAY3,ARAY4,0.07,73.,15,1,15,1)
0049                CALL PLOT(18.,0.,999)
           C
           C CONTROL:
0050                STOP
           C
0051                END


           C
           C ****************************************************************************
           C *   THIS SUBROUTINE GENERATES THE DATA OF THE ARRAY, IN ORDER TO      *
           C *   GET THE STARTING AND ENDING POINT OF THE CENTER LINE.             *
           C ****************************************************************************

0001                SUBROUTINE CENTER(XLOC,YLOC,XEND,YEND)
           C
           C DECLARE:
0002                DIMENSION XAR(4),YAR(4)
           C
           C ARITHMETIC:
0003                XAR(1)=XLOC
0004                XAR(2)=XEND
0005                XAR(3)=0.0
0006                XAR(4)=1.
0007                YAR(1)=YLOC
0008                YAR(2)=YEND
0009                YAR(3)=0.0
0010                YAR(4)=1.
0011                NPTS=2.
0012                INC=1
           C
           C CONTROL:
0013         95     CALL CNTRL(XAR,YAR,NPTS,INC)
           C
           C CONTROL:
0014                RETURN
           C
0015                END
```

```
       C
       C  ***********************************************************
       C  * USED THIS SUBROUTINE TO GENERATE THE COORDINATE LOCATION OF 30'S   *
       C  * POINT ON A CIRCLE.                                                 *
       C  ***********************************************************
0001          SUBROUTINE CIRCLE(X,Y,R,SANG,N,THETA,ARAY1,ARAY2,ARAY3,
              ARAY4)
       C
       C DECLARE:
0002          DIMENSION ARAY1(50),ARAY2(50),ARAY3(50),ARAY4(50)
       C
       C ARITHMETIC:
0003          X=X-R
0004          SANG=(3.14/180.)*SANG
0005          XX=R*(1-COS(SANG))
0006          YY=R*(SIN(SANG))
0007          DX=X+XX
0008          EY=Y+YY
0009          CALL PLOT(DX,EY,3)
0010          THETA=(3.14/180.)*THETA
0011          THETA1=THETA
       C
       C DO LOOP STATEMENT:
0012          DO 2 I=1,N
       C
       C ARITHMETIC:
0013          FEE=SANG+THETA
0014          PX=R*(1-COS(FEE))
0015          SY=R*(SIN(FEE))
0016          DX=X+PX
0017          EY=Y+SY
       C
       C CONTROL IF:
0018          IF(I .LE. N/2)ARAY1(I)=DX
0019          IF(I .LE. N/2)ARAY2(I)=EY
0020          IF(I .GT. N/2)ARAY3(I-N/2)=DX
```

```
0021                    IF(I .GT. N/2)ARAY4(I-N/2)=EY
            C
0022                    CALL PLOT(DX,EY,2)
            C
            C ARITHMETIC:
0023          2        THETA=THETA+THETA1
0024                    ARAY1(N/2+1)=0.
0025                    ARAY1(N/2+2)=1.
0026                    ARAY2(N/2+1)=0.
0027                    ARAY2(N/2+2)=1.
0028                    ARAY3(N/2+1)=0.
0029                    ARAY3(N/2+2)=1.
0030                    ARAY4(N/2+1)=0.
0031                    ARAY4(N/2+2)=1.
            C
            C CONTROL:
0032                    RETURN
            C
0033                    END

0001                    CALL PLOTS
            C          CALL PLOT(.75,.75,-3)
            C          ***** ADD PART FEATURES *****
0002                    CALL ZHOLE(9.55,6.2,.2)
0003                    CALL YHOLE(9.55,5.55,.2,.3)
0004                    CALL YHOLE(6.1,5.55,.2,.25)
0005                    CALL XHOLE(5.45,6.0,.2,.3)
0006                    CALL XHOLE(4.35,6.0,.2,.3)
0007                    CALL XHOLE(5.45,9.6,.2,.3)
0008                    CALL XHOLE(4.35,9.6,.2,.3)
0009                    CALL ZHOLE(6.3,10.,.2)
0010                    CALL DIMEN(4.35,5.3,4.3,0.,.6)
0011                    CALL DIMEN(9.15,5.3,1.8,0.,.6)
0012                    CALL DIMEN(4.35,8.95,.5.0.,.6)
0013                    CALL DIMEN(4.65,9.25,1.3,0.,.6)
0014                    CALL DIMEN(5.43,10.65,.5,0.,.6)
0015                    CALL DIMEN(9.,5.5,1.8,90.,.6)
```

```
0016                    CALL  DIMEN(4.2,9.4,1.35,90.,.6)
0017                    CALL  DIMEN(7.15,9.4,1.,90.,.6)
0018                    CALL  DIMEN(4.15,5.5,1.14,90.,.6)
0019                    CALL  DIMEN(7.45,10.5,1.8,270.,.6)
0020                    CALL  TITLE(1.)
0021                    CALL  FACTOR(.6)
0022                    CALL  IMAGE(42,1,0,0,1,1,0,0)
0023                    CALL  PLOT(0.,0.,999)
0024                    STOP
0025                    END
```

After the part features are chosen, the part is dimensioned for manufacture. Note that in the listing above several schemes are tried by the designer. Programming care must be given to common rules for describing 3-D objects for manufacture. Normally, the data base describing the object or image places the overall dimensions for the graphics programmer automatically around the object by the following programming technique:

```
0001                    SUBROUTINE IMAGE(NDATA,ITOP,IBOTM,ILEFT,IRITE,IFRNT,
                        IBACK,IPKTR)
0002                    DIMENSION X(100),Y(100),Z(100),IPEN(100),Z1(100),
                        XPLOT(100),
                       @YPLOT(100)
0003                    DATA X/0.,.5,.5,1.8,1.8,4.3,4.3,2.3,2.3,1.8,1.8,.5,.5,
                        0.,0.,.5,.5,
                       @.5,.5,1.8,1.8,1.8,1.8,0.,4.3,4.3,2.3,2.3,0.,0.,0.,0.,
                        0.,0.,
                       @4*2.3,4*4.3/
0004                    DATA Y/0.,5*0.,.5,.5,6*1.8,0.,0.,1.8,0.,1.8,0.,1.8,0.,
                        1.8,0.,0.,
                       @.5,.5,1.8,1.8,3*0.,4*1.8,4*.5,0.,0./
```

```
0005              DATA Z/0.,0.,1.35,1.35,6*0.,2*1.35,5*0.,4*1.35,0.,0.,
                  7*1.8,
                @0.,1.8,0.,1.8,0.,1.8,0.,1.8,0.,1.8,0.,1.8/
0006              DATA IPEN/3,14*2,3,2,3,2,3,2,3,2,3,6*2,3,2,3,2,3,2,3,
                  2,3,2,3,2/
          C*****SET   FRONT VIEW ORIGIN (LOWER LEFT HAND CORNER)*****
0007              CALL PLOT(7.25,9.2,-3)
0008              XTRANS=8.
0009              YTRANS=6.5
0010              IF(IPKTR.EQ.0)GOTO 200
0011              ANG=30.
0012              SF=1.
0013              COSA=COS(ANG/57.3)
0014              SINA=SIN(ANG/57.3)
0015              DO 1 K=1,NDATA
0016              XPLOT(K)=(X(K)+Z(K)*SF*COSA)+11.
0017              YPLOT(K)=(Y(K)+Z(K)*SF*SINA)+5.5
0018        1     CALL PLOT(XPLOT(K),YPLOT(K),IPEN(K))
          C*****   FRONT VIEW  *****
0019        200   IF(IFRNT.EQ.0)GOTO 210
0020              DO 10 J=1,NDATA
0021        10    CALL PLOT(X(J),Y(J),IPEN(J))
          C*****   TOP VIEW  *****
0022        210   IF(ITOP.EQ.0) GOTO 220
0023              DO 20 I=1,NDATA
0024              Z1(I)=Z(I)+YTRANS
0025        20    CALL PLOT(X(I),Z1(I),IPEN(I))
          C*****   RIGHT SIDE VIEW  *****
0026        220   IF(IRITE.EQ.0) GOTO 230
0027              DO 30 I=1,NDATA
0028              Z1(I)=Z(I)+XTRANS
0029        30    CALL PLOT(Z1(I),Y(I),IPEN(I))
          C*****   BOTTOM VIEW  *****
0030        230   IF(IBOTM.EQ.0) GOTO 240
0031              DO 40 I=1,NDATA
0032              Z1(I)=-1.*(Z(I)+YTRANS-4.5)
0033        40    CALL PLOT(X(I),Z1(I),IPEN(I))
          C*****   LEFT SIDE VIEW  *****
```

```
0034            240   IF(ILEFT.EQ.0) GOTO 250
0035                  DO 50 I=1,NDATA
0036                  Z1(I)=-1.*(Z(I)+2.)
0037            50    CALL PLOT(Z1(I),Y(I),IPEN(I))
                C*****   BACK VIEW   *****
0038            250   IF(IBACK.EQ.0) GOTO 100
0039                  CALL PLOT(22.,0.,-3)
0040                  DO 60 I=1,NDATA
0041                  X1=-1.*X(I)
0042            60    CALL PLOT(X1,Y(I),IPEN(I))
0043                  IF(IPKTR.EQ.1)CALL SYMBOL(13.1,5.,.2,9HPICTORIAL,0.,9)
0044                  IF(IFRNT.EQ.1)CALL SYMBOL(2.,-.5,.2,10HFRONT VIEW,0.,
                      10)
0045                  IF(ITOP.EQ.1)CALL SYMBOL(2.2,6.,.2,8HTOP VIEW,0.,8)
0046                  IF(IRITE.EQ.1)CALL SYMBOL(8.95,-.5,.2,13HRT. SIDE VIEW,
                      0.,13)
0047                  IF(IBOTM.EQ.1)CALL SYMBOL(1.9,-7.,.2,11HBOTTOM VIEW,
                      0.,11)
0048                  IF(ILEFT.EQ.1)CALL SYMBOL(-5.5,-.5,.2,13HLT. SIDE VIEW,
                      0.,13)
0049                  IF(IBACK.EQ.1)CALL SYMBOL(-3.9,-.5,.2,9HREAR VIEW,0.,9)
0050            100   RETURN
0051                  END
```

It is now left to the designer to modify, correct, or change any of the dimensions displayed in the viewing area. In most cases dimensions are added or moved, or notes are created for manufacture. This book does not treat the "art" of dimensioning, which is attained after many years of deisgn drafting. However, it does provide the science of automated data placement for sizing a machine part for manufacture.

A.2 CUPID2

The purpose of CUPID2 is the animation of 3-D objects. For example, it demonstrates an object displayed from

```
0001            CALL PLOTS
0002            DIMENSION X(100)Y(100),Z(100),R(100),SANG(100),EANG
                ( 100)
0003            CALL VANTAG(1.)
0004            DATA X/0.,.5,2.,2.5,4*3.5,2*1.,2*1.5/
0005            DATA Y/4*1.25,0.,.5,0.,.5,0.,2.,0.,2./
0006            DATA Z/4*.5,8*1./
0007            DATA R/4*.25,2*.375,2*1.,4*.5/
0008            DATA SANG/6*0.,2*270.,2*90.,2*0./
0009            DATA EANG/6*360.,2*450.,2*180.,2*90./
0010            DO 9999 I=5,12
0011            CALL YARC(X(I),Y(I),Z(I),R(I),SANG(I),EANG(I))
0012      9999  CONTINUE
          C        DO 99 I=5,12
          C        CALL ZARC(X(I),Y(I),Z(I),R(I),SANG(I),EANG(I))
          C99      CONTINUE
0013            DO 999 I=1,4
0014            CALL XARC(X(I),Y(I),Z(I),R(I),SANG(I),EANG(I))
0015      999   CONTINUE
0016            CALL PLOT(0.,0.,999)
0017            STOP
0018            END
```

Where CUPID2 subprograms are used to animate the object as a wireform, they appear as:

```
0001

                SUBROUTINE VANTAG(SIZE)
        C       ***************************************************************
        C       *                                                             *
        C       *     NP   =NO.  OF POINTS TO BE PLOTTED                       *
        C       *     NC   =NO. OF COMMANDS NECESSARY TO DRAW FIGURE           *
        C       *     NV   =NO. OF DIFFERENT VIEWS TO BE DRAWN                 *
        C       *     SPACE=SPACE ALLOWED FOR EACH VIEW                        *
        C       *     P(NP,3)=ARRAY CONTAINING X,Y, AND Z COORDINATES OF POINTS *
        C       *     IC(NC)=ARRAY CONTAINING PLOT COMMANDS                    *
        C       *     VP(NV,3)=ARRAY CONTAINING X,Y, AND Z COORDINATES OF VANTAGE*
        C       *             POINTS                                           *
        C       *                                                             *
        C       ***************************************************************

0002            DIMENSION P(100,3),IC(200),VP(100,3),PP(100,3)
0003            CALL FACTOR(SIZE)
0004            NP=24
0005            NC=36
0006            NV=39
0007            WRITE(3,10)NP,NC,NV
0008            SPACE=6.
0009            WRITE(3,101)SPACE
0010            DATA P/0.,.5,.5,1.,1.5,2.,2.,3.5,3.5,0.,0.,.5,.5,1.,
               1.5,2.0,2.0,2.
               C5,2.5,3.5,3.5,2.5,2.5,0.,76*0.,10*0.,8*2.,4*.5,2*2.,
               76*0.,2*0.,-1.
               C,2*-1.5,-1.,2*0.,2*-2.,2*0.,-1.,2*-1.5,-1.,4*0.,4*-2.,
               76*0./
0011            WRITE(3,102)
0012            WRITE(3,103)
        C        WRITE(3,104)((P(I,J),J=1,3),I=1,NP)
0013            DATA VP/0.,.083,.167,.250,.333,.417,.500,.583,.667,
               .750,.833,.917,
               C1.,87*1.,14*0.,.083,.167,.250,.333,.417,.500,.583,.667,
               .750,.833,
```

```
                        C.917,1.,74*1.,27*0.,.083,.167,.250,.333,.417,.500,.583,
                        .667,.750, 3
                        C.833,.917,1.,61*1./
0014                    WRITE(3,105)
0015                    WRITE(3,103)
              C          WRITE(3,104)((VP(I,J),J=1,3),I=1,NV)
0016                    DATA IC/-1,2,3,-4,5,-6,7,8,-9,10,1,11,12,13,-14,15,-16,
                        17,18,19,20
                        C,-21,22,23,24,11,-2,12,-7,17,-10,24,-18,23,-19,22/
0017                    WRITE(3,106)
              C          WRITE(3,107)(IC(I),I=1,NC)
0018                    DO 5 I=1,NV
0019                    A=ARTAN(VP(I,1),VP(I,3))
0020                    SA=SIN(A)
0021                    CA=COS(A)
0022                    DO 6 J=1,NP
0023                    PP(J,3)=P(J,3)*CA+P(J,1)*SA
0024                    PP(J,1)=P(J,1)*CA-P(J,3)*SA
0025          6         CONTINUE
0026                    VPP=VP(I,3)*CA+VP(I,1)*SA
0027                    A=ARTAN(VP(1,2),VPP)
0028                    SA=SIN(A)
0029                    CA=COS(A)
0030                    DO 7 J=1,NP
0031                    PP(J,2)=P(J,2)*CA-PP(J,3)*SA
0032          7         CONTINUE
0033                    DO 11 K=1,NP
0034                    PP(K,2)=PP(K,2)+6.0
0035                    PP(K,1)=PP(K,1)+SPACE*1
0036          11        CONTINUE
0037                    DO 8 J=1,NC
0038                    IF (IC(J).LT.0) GO TO 9
0039                    CALL PLOT(PP(IC(J),1),PP(IC(J),2),2)
0040                    GO TO 8
0041          9         K=-IC(J)
0042                    CALL PLOT(PP(K,1),PP(K,2),3)
0043          8         CONTINUE
```

```
0044             5      CONTINUE
0045                    XSET=(SPACE*NV)+8.
                 C      CALL PLOT(XSET,0.,999)
0046             1      FORMAT(3I5)
0047             2      FORMAT(F10.3)
0048             3      FORMAT(3F10.2)
0049             4      FORMAT(10I5)
0050             10     FORMAT('1',20X,'NUMBER OF POINTS TO BE PLOTTED=',I5,/,
                        21X,'NUMBER
                 1OF PEN MOVEMENTS REQD  =',I5,/,21X,'NUMBER OF VIEWS TO
                        BE  DRAWN
                 1=',I5)
0051             101    FORMAT('0',20X,'SPACE PROVIDED FOR EACH VIEW  =',F6.2)
0052             102    FORMAT(///,30X,'POINT COORDINATES')
0053             103    FORMAT(/,20X,'X',20X,'Y',20X,'Z')
                 C 104  FORMAT(/,F25.3,2F20.3)
0054             105    FORMAT(///,30X,'VANTAGE POINTS')
0055             106    FORMAT(/,30X,'PLOT COMMANDS')
                 C 107  FORMAT(10X,10I5)
0056                    RETURN
0057                    END


0001                    FUNCTION ARTAN(Y,X)
0002                    DATA EPS/0.001/
0003                    AX=ABS(X)
0004                    AY=ABS(Y)
0005                    IF(AX.GT.EPS.AND.AY.GT.EPS) GO TO 1
0006                    IF(AX.LT.EPS.AND.AY.LT.EPS) GO TO 3
0007                    IF(AX.LT.EPS) GO TO 2
0008             3      ARTAN=0.0
0009                    RETURN
0010             2      ARTAN=(3.14159*AY)/(Y*2.0)
0011                    RETURN
0012             1      ARTAN=ATAN2(Y,X)
0013                    RETURN
0014                    END
```

```
0001
                SUBROUTINE VANTAC(P,SIZE,N)
        C       ***********************************************************************
        C       *                                                                     *
        C       *      NP   =NO.  OF POINTS TO BE PLOTTED                              *
        C       *      NC   =NO. OF COMMANDS NECESSARY TO DRAW FIGURE                  *
        C       *      NV   =NO. OF DIFFERENT VIEWS TO BE DRAWN                        *
        C       *      SPACE=SPACE ALLOWED FOR EACH VIEW                               *
        C       *      P(NP,3)=ARRAY CONTAINING X,Y, AND Z COORDINATES OF POINTS       *
        C       *      IC(NC)=ARRAY CONTAINING PLOT COMMANDS                           *
        C       *      VP(NV,3)=ARRAY CONTAINING X,Y, ANDZ COORDINATES OF VANTAGE      *
        C       *                 POINTS                                               *
        C       *                                                                     *
        C       ***********************************************************************

0002            DIMENSION P(400,3),IC(400),VP(100,3),PP(400,3)
0003            CALL FACTOR(SIZE)
0004            NP=N
0005            NC=N
0006            NV=39
        C         WRITE(3,10)NP,NC,NV
0007            SPACE=6.
        C         WRITE(3,101)SPACE
        C         WRITE(3,102)
        C         WRITE(3,103)
        C         WRITE(3,104)((P(I,J),J=1,3),I=1,NP)
0008            DATA VP/0.,.083,.167,.250,.333,.417,.500,.583,.667,
               .750,.833,.917,
               C1.,87*1.,14*0.,.083,.167,.250,.333,.417,.500,.583,.667,
               .750,.833,
               C.917,1.,74*1.,27*0.,.083,.167,.250,.333,.417,.500,.583,
               .667,.750, 3
               C.833,.917,1.,61*1./
        C         WRITE(3,105)
        C         WRITE(3,103)
        C         WRITE(3,104)((VP(I,J),J=1,3),I=1,NV)
0009            IC(1)=-1
```

```
0010                          DO 999 I=2,NP
0011              999         IC(I)=I
                 C              WRITE(3,106)
                 C              WRITE(3,107)(IC(I),I=1,NC)
                 C              CALL PLOTS
0012                          DO 5 I=1,NV
0013                          A=ARTAN(VP(I,1),VP(I,3))
0014                          SA=SIN(A)
0015                          CA=COS(A)
0016                          DO 6 J=1,NP
0017                          PP(J,3)=P(J,3)*CA+P(J,1)*SA
0018                          PP(J,1)=P(J,1)*CA-P(J,3)*SA
0019              6           CONTINUE
0020                          VPP=VP(I,3)*CA+VP(I,1)*SA
0021                          A=ARTAN(VP(I,2),VPP)
0022                          SA=SIN(A)
0023                          CA=COS(A)
0024                          DO 7 J=1,NP
0025                          PP(J,2)=P(J,2)*CA-PP(J,3)*SA
0026              7           CONTINUE
0027                          DO 11 K=1,NP
0028                          PP(K,2)=PP(K,2)+6.0
0029                          PP(K,1)=PP(K,1)+SPACE*I
0030              11          CONTINUE
0031                          DO 8 J=1,NC
0032                          IF (IC(J).LT.0) GO TO 9
0033                          CALL PLOT(PP(IC(J),1),PP(IC(J),2),2)
0034                          GO TO 8
0035              9           K=-IC(J)
0036                          CALL PLOT(PP(K,1),PP(K,2),3)
0037              8           CONTINUE
0038              5           CONTINUE
0039                          XSET=(SPACE*NV)+8.
                 C            CALL PLOT(XSET,0.,999)
                 C 1          FORMAT(3I5)
                 C 2          FORMAT(F10.3)
                 C 3          FORMAT(3F10.2)
```

```
C 4       FORMAT(10I5)
C 10      FORMAT('1',20X,'NUMBER OF POINTS TO BE PLOTTED=',I5,/,
C         21X,'NUMBER
C         10F PEN MOVEMENTS REQD  =',I5,/,21X,'NUMBER OF VIEWS TO
C         BE DRAWN
C         1=',I5)
C 101     FORMAT('0',20X,'SPACE PROVIDED FOR EACH VIEW  =',F6.2)
C 102     FORMAT(////,30X,'POINT COORDINATES')
C 103     FORMAT(/,20X,'X',20X,'Y',20X,'Z')
C 104     FORMAT(/,F25.3,2F20.3)
C 105     FORMAT(////,30X,'VANTAGE POINTS')
C 106     FORMAT(/,30X,'PLOT COMMANDS')
C 107     FORMAT(10X,10I5)
0040      RETURN
0041      END
```

The graphics programmer has included not only straight line elements but also segments of arcs in at least three axes. The arcs are displayed as XARC, YARC, or ZARC, and are listed as:

```
0001
          SUBROUTINE XARC(XP,YP,ZP,R,SANG,EANG)
C
C         *****************************************************************
C         *                                                               *
C         *    THIS SUBROUTINE GRAPHS CIRCULAR ARCS IN THE X PLANE (IE     *
C         *    THE PLANE PERPENDICULAR TO THE X AXIS) FROM A THREE DI-     *
C         *    MENSIONAL DATA BASE IN X,Y,AND Z.                          *
C         *      XP...THE X COORDINATE OF THE CENTER OF THE ARC           *
C         *      YP...THE Y COORDINATE OF THE CENTER OF THE ARC           *
C         *      ZP...THE Z COORDINATE OF THE CENTER OF THE ARC           *
C         *       R...THE RADIUS OF THE ARC                              *
C         *    SANG...THE STARTING ANGLE OF THE ARC MEASURED IN DEGREES   *
C         *           CCW POSITIVE FROM THE POSITIVE Z AXIS              *
```

```
      C        *       EANG...THE ENDING ANGLE OF THE ARC MEASURED IN DEGREES        *
      C        *              CCW POSITIVE FROM THE POSITIVE Z AXIS                   *
      C        *                                                                      *
      C        ************************************************************************
      C
0002           DIMENSION P(400,3)
0003           PI=3.14159265
0004           N=IFIX(EANG-SANG)
0005           THETA=(EANG-SANG)/N
0006           THETAR=THETA*PI/180.
0007           SRANG=SANG*PI/180.
0008           DO 1 I=1,N
0009           DZ=R*COS(SRANG)
0010           DY=R*SIN(SRANG)
0011           P(I,1)=XP
0012           P(I,2)=YP+DY
0013           P(I,3)=-(ZP+DZ)
0014           SRANG=SRANG+THETAR
0015     1     CONTINUE
0016           CALL VANTAC(P,1.,N)
0017           RETURN
0018           END

0001
               SUBROUTINE YARC(XP,YP,ZP,R,SANG,EANG)
      C
      C        ************************************************************************
      C        *                                                                      *
      C        *    THIS SUBROUTINE GRAPHS CIRCULAR ARCS IN THE Y PLANE (IE           *
      C        *    THE PLANE PERPENDICULAR TO THE X AXIS) FROM A THREE DI-           *
      C        *    MENSIONAL DATA BASE IN X,Y,AND Z.                                 *
      C        *       XP...THE X COORDINATE OF THE CENTER OF THE ARC                 *
      C        *       YP...THE Y COORDINATE OF THE CENTER OF THE ARC                 *
      C        *       ZP...THE Z COORDINATE OF THE CENTER OF THE ARC                 *
      C        *        R...THE RADIUS OF THE ARC                                     *
      C        *     SANG...THE STARTING ANGLE OF THE ARC MEASURED IN DEGREES         *
```

```
C        *           CCW POSITIVE FROM THE POSITIVE X AXIS                *
C        *     EANG...THE ENDING ANGLE OF THE ARC MEASURED IN DEGREES     *
C        *           CCW POSITIVE FROM THE POSITIVE X AXIS                *
C        *                                                                *
C        ******************************************************************
C
0002            DIMENSION P(400,3)
0003            PI=3.14159265
0004            N=IFIX(EANG-SANG)
0005            THETA=(EANG-SANG)/N
0006            THETAR=THETA*PI/180.
0007            SRANG=SANG*PI/180.
0008            DO 1 I=1,N
0009            DX=R*COS(SRANG)
0010            DZ=R*SIN(SRANG)
0011            P(I,1)=XP+DX
0012            P(I,2)=YP
0013            P(I,3)=-(ZP+DZ)
0014            SRANG=SRANG+THETAR
0015      1     CONTINUE
0016            CALL VANTAC(P,1.,N)
0017            RETURN
0018            END


0001

                SUBROUTINE ZARC(XP,YP,ZP,R,SANG,EANG)
C
C        ******************************************************************
C        *                                                                *
C        *   THIS SUBROUTINE GRAPHS CIRCULAR ARCS IN THE Z PLANE (IE       *
C        *   THE PLANE PERPENDICULAR TO THE Z AXIS) FROM A THREE DI-       *
C        *   MENSIONAL DATA BASE IN X,Y,AND Z.                             *
C        *       XP...THE X COORDINATE OF THE CENTER OF THE ARC            *
C        *       YP...THE Y COORDINATE OF THE CENTER OF THE ARC            *
C        *       ZP...THE Z COORDINATE OF THE CENTER OF THE ARC            *
C        *        R...THE RADIUS OF THE ARC                               *
```

```
C       *      SANG...THE STARTING ANGLE OF THE ARC MEASURED IN DEGREES      *
C       *              CCW POSITIVE FROM THE POSITIVE X AXIS                  *
C       *      EANG...THE ENDING ANGLE OF THE ARC MEASURED IN DEGREES         *
C       *              CCW POSITIVE FROM THE POSITIVE X AXIS                  *
C       *                                                                     *
C       ***********************************************************************
C
```

```
0002            DIMENSION P(400,3)
0003            PI=3.14159265
0004            N=IFIX(EANG-SANG)
0005            THETA=(EANG-SANG)/N
0006            THETAR=THETA*PI/180.
0007            SRANG=SANG*PI/180.
0008            DO 1 I=1,N
0009            DX=R*COS(SRANG)
0010            DY=R*SIN(SRANG)
0011            P(I,1)=XP+DX
0012            P(I,2)=YP+DY
0013            P(I,3)=-ZP
0014            SRANG=SRANG+THETAR
0015      1     CONTINUE
0016            CALL VANTAC(P,1.,N)
0017            RETURN
0018            END
```

A.3 CUPID3

The combination of animation and analysis for the display of finite element surfaces was the concept behind the commonly used programming shown in Chapter 9. This group of subroutines was stored as CUPID3, as follows:

```
00007980 C       PROGRAM TO TEST SURF
00007990         DIMENSION X(500),Y(500),Z(500)
00008000         ICNT=0
00008010         DO 200 J=1,10
00008020         DO 300 K=1,10
00008030         ICNT=ICNT+1
00008040         Y(ICNT)=K
00008050         X(ICNT)=J
00008060   300   CONTINUE
00008070   200   CONTINUE
00008080         READ(35,*)(Z(ICNT),ICNT=1,100)
00008090         NAX=2
00008100         CALL SURF(X,Y,Z,ICNT,NAX)
00008110         CALL PLOT(0.,0.,999)
00008120         RETURN
00008130         END

00009440         SUBROUTINE SURF(A,B,C,N,NAX)
00009450         DIMENSION A(500),B(500),C(500),BUFR(500),P(20,20)
00009460         DATA AXLN/3.0/
00009470         AXLN=5.
00009480         AXLN1=AXLN+0.001
00009490         XH=0.0
00009500         YH=0.
00009510         ZH=0.
00009520         XL=100.
00009530         YL=100.
```

```
00009540          ZL=100.
00009550          NN=10
00009560          DO 1 I=1,N
00009570          IF(XH.LE.A(I))XH=A(I)
00009580          IF(YH.LE.B(I))YH=B(I)
00009590          IF(ZH.LE.C(I))ZH=C(I)
00009600          IF(XL.GE.A(I))XL=A(I)
00009610          IF(YL.GE.B(I))YL=B(I)
00009620          IF(ZL.GE.C(I))ZL=C(I)
00009630    1     CONTINUE
00009640          DO 2 I=1,N
00009650          A(I)=(A(I)-XL)/(XH-XL)*AXLN
00009660          B(I)=(B(I)-YL)/(YH-YL)*AXLN
00009670          C(I)=(C(I)-ZL)/(ZH-ZL)*AXLN
00009680    2     CONTINUE
00009690          DO 3 I=1,NN
00009700          DO 4 J=1,NN
00009710          P(I,J)=0.
00009720    4     CONTINUE
00009730    3     CONTINUE
00009740          DO 5 I=1,N
00009750          IX=A(I)/AXLN1*NN+1.
00009760          IY=B(I)/AXLN1*NN+1.
00009770          IF (C(I).GT.P(IX,IY))P(IX,IY)=C(I)
00009780    5     CONTINUE
00009790          IF(NAX.NE.1) GO TO 10
00009800          X=AXLN
00009810          Y=-YL/(YH-YL)*AXLN
00009820          Z=-ZL/(ZH-ZL)*AXLN
00009830          CALL ROTATE(X,Y,Z)
00009840          CALL PLOT(X,Y,3)
00009850          X=-XL/(XH-XL)*AXLN
00009860          Y=-YL/(YH-YL)*AXLN
00009870          CALL ROTATE(X,Y,Z)
00009880          CALL PLOT(X,Y,2)
00009890          Z=AXLN
00009900          X=-XL/(XH-XL)*AXLN
```

```
00009910           Y=-YL/(YH-YL)*AXLN
00009920           CALL ROTATE(X,Y,Z)
00009930           CALL PLOT(X,Y,1)
00009940           X=-XL/(XH-XL)*AXLN
00009950           Z=-ZL/(ZH-ZL)*AXLN
00009960           Y=-YL/(YH-YL)*AXLN
00009970           CALL ROTATE(X,Y,Z)
00009980           CALL PLOT(X,Y,3)
00009990           Y=AXLN
00010000           X=-XL/(XH-XL)*AXLN
00010010           Z=-ZL/(ZH-ZL)*AXLN
00010020           CALL ROTATE(X,Y,Z)
00010030           CALL PLOT(X,Y,2)
00010040      10   CONTINUE
00010050           DO 6 I=1,NN
00010060           X=I*AXLN/NN
00010070           SX=X
00010080           IP=3
00010090           DO 7 J=1,NN
00010100           X=SX
00010110           Y=J*AXLN/NN
00010120           Z=P(I,J)
00010130           CALL ROTATE(X,Y,Z)
00010140           CALL PLOT(X,Y,IP)
00010150           IP=2
00010160       7   CONTINUE
00010170       6   CONTINUE
00010180           DO 8 I=1,NN
00010190           Y=I*AXLN/NN
00010200           SY=Y
00010210           IP=3
00010220           DO 9 J=1,NN
00010230           Y=SY
00010240           X=J*AXLN/NN
00010250           Z=P(J,I)
00010260           CALL ROTATE(X,Y,Z)
00010270           CALL PLOT(X,Y,IP)
```

```
00010280            IP=2
00010290    9       CONTINUE
00010300    8       CONTINUE
00010310            RETURN
00010320            END
00010330            SUBROUTINE ROTATE(X,Y,Z)
00010340            DATA C1/0.707/.C2/0.808/S1/0.707/,S2/-.587/
00010350            SY=Y
00010360            Y=Z*C2+X*C1*S2+Y*S1*S2+5.
00010370            X=SY*C1-X*S1+10.
00010380            RETURN
00010390            END
```

BIBLIOGRAPHY

Appel, A., Rohlf, F., and Stein, A. Haloed line effect for hidden line elimination. *Computer Graphics 13,* 2 (Summer 1979), 151–157.

Atherton, P. Weiler, K. and Greenberg, D. Polygon shadow creation. *Computer Graphics 12, 3* (August 1978), 275–281.

Blinn, J. F. Models of light reflection for computer synthesized pictures. *Computer Graphics 11, 2* (Summer 1977), 191–198.

Blinn, J. F. Simulation of wrinkled surfaces. *Computer Graphics 12, 3* (August 1978), 286–292.

Blinn, J., and Newell, M. E. Texture and reflection in computer generated images. *Communications of the ACM 19,* 10 (October 1976), 542–546.

Catmull, E. The problems of computer-assisted animation. *Computer Graphics 12, 3* (August 1978), 348–353.

Crow, F. C. Shadow algorithms for computer graphics. *Computer Graphics 11, 2* (Summer 1977), 242–248.

Feder, A. Test Results on Computer Graphics Productivity for Aircraft Design and Fabrication. Paper No. 75–967 presented at AIAA 1975 Meeting, Los Angeles, August 4–7.

Frei, H. P., Weller, D. L., and Williams, R. A graphics-based programming support system. *Computer Graphics 12, 3* (August 1978), 43–49.

Gilioi, W. *Interactive computer graphics.* Englewood Cliffs, N.J.: Prentice-Hall, 1978.

Gonin, M. and Moffett, T. ARTES, an interactive highway design program. *Computer Graphics 10, 2* (Summer 1976), 268–274.

Keller, R. G., Reed, T. N., and Solem, A. V. An implementation of the ACM/SIGGRAPH proposed graphics standard. *Computer Graphics 12, 3* (August 1978), 308–312.

Levoy, M. A color animation system based on the multiplane technique. *Computer Graphics 11, 2* (Summer 1977), 65–71.

Lucido, A. P. Software systems for computer graphics. *Computer 9*, 8 (August 1976), 23–32.

Machover, C. Graphic displays. *IEEE Spectrum 14*, 8 (August 1977), 24–32; and *14*, 10 (October 1977), 22–27.

Mallary, R. and Ferraro, M. An application of computer-aided design to the composition of landforms for reclamation. *Computer Graphics 11*, 2 (Summer 1977), 1–7.

McCleary, L. E. Techniques for the display of ocean data on a raster-driven color CRT. *Computer Graphics 11*, 2 (Summer 1977), 98–101.

Newman, W. M. and Sproull, R. F. *Principles of interactive computer graphics.* New York: McGraw-Hill, 1973.

Orr, J. N. Computer graphics. *Mini-Micro Systems 12*, 12 (December 1977), 66–78.

Pavlidis, T. Filling algorithms for raster graphics. *Computer Graphics 12*, 3 (August 1978), 161–166.

Smith, S. G. and Sherwood, B. A. Educational uses of the PLATO computer system. Electronics: The Continuing Revolution. American Association for the Advancement of Science, Washington, D.C. (1977).

Sutherland, I. E. *Sketchpad: A man-machine graphical communications system.* Baltimore: Spartan Books, 1963.

Sutherland, I. E., Sproull, R., and Schumacker, R. A characterization of ten hidden-surface algorithms. *ACM Computering Surveys 6*, 1 (January, 1974), 1–55.

Weller, D. L., Carlson, E. D., Giddings, G. M., Palermo, F. P., Williams, R., and Zilles, S. N. Software architecture for graphics interaction. *IBM Systems Journal 19*, 3 (November, 1980), 314–330.

Williams, L. Casting curved shadows on curved surfaces. *Computer Graphics 12*, 3 (August 1978), 270–274.

INDEX

Absolute Data, 14
Absolute Point, 14
Acoustic Tablet, 14, 62
Addressable Point, 14
Address Register, 14, 75
Aiming Symbol, 14, 62
Aliasing, 14
Algorithim, 31, 259
ALLOC, 58, 60
Animation, 15, 265
  art, 232
  key-frame, 232
  3-D, 232
ANSI, 15, 36
Arithmetic, 4, 75
Area filling, 15
Arrangement of views, 15
ASCII, 15, 171
Aspect Ratio, 15
Assembly drawings, 288
ASSIGN, 63
Association for Computer Machinery
  (ACM), 16

ATTACH, 58
ATTRIBUTE, 15, 58
Auxiliary views, 15
AVAIL, 58
Axonometric projection, 15

Back view, 15
Base-line dimensioning, 15
BEGIN, 7
Bit, 15
Blink, 15, 75
Bottom view, 15
Brightness, 15

CAD (Computer-Aided Design), 39
CADD (Computer-Aided Drafting
  and Design), 33
CAG (Computer-Assisted
  Graphics), 30
Calligraphic, 15, 75, 89, 90
CAM (Computer-Aided
  Manufacturing), 285

Cathode Ray Tube (CRT), 3, 17, 42,
  63, 75, 88
CE (Create), 58
Cell-organized raster display, 16, 75
Character generator, 63, 142, 170
Character strokes, 33, 146
CIRCLE, 4, 135
  generator, 16, 62
  subroutine, 62
Clipping, 16, 170
Coding form, 10
Coherence, 16
Color display, 16, 89
Computer
  analog, 2
  digital, 2
  graphics, 16
  macro, 2
  micro, 2
  microfilm, 8, 17, 75
  mini, 2
  program, 3
  storage, 3

Conic generator, 17
Contrast, 17
Control, 4, 56, 62, 75
  CALL, 56
  CONTINUE, 56
  DO, 56
  GOTO, 56
  IF, 56
  RETURN, 4
  STOP, 56
Control ball, 17, 63
Conversion, 17
Coordinates, 3, 17, 169
CORE, 17
Cursor, 17, 63, 174
CUPID, 169
Cutting plane, 17
Cybercrud, 13

Dark trace tube, 17, 75
Data base, 2, 262, 282
  management, 6
  programming technique, 6

Data table, 2, 18, 24, 63, 88, 120
Datum, 2
Declaration, 75
    allocation, 4
    common, 4
    dimension, 4
    equivalent, 4
Deflection, 18
Delete, 58
Depth cueing, 18
Detail drawing, 18, 288
Device independent software, 18
Device driver, 18
Digital plotter, 18
Digitizer, 18, 63
Dimensioning, 71
Direct-display devices, 88
Direct memory access, 19, 63
DISPLA, 7, 42
Display
    buffer, 19, 63
    code generator, 19, 62
    controller, 19
    cycle, 19
    data, 19
    device, 19, 63
    element, 19
    file, 19
    foreground, 19
    generator, 19
    image, 19
    list, 70
    menu, 63
    order, 75
    panel, 75
    processor, 75
    screen, 19
    surface, 3, 18
    unit size, 3
Dithering, 19, 241
Dragging, 19
DRAW, 4, 263
Drawing board, 2
Drum plotter, 19
DVST, 19, 88, 96, 131, 171

Electronic pencil, 2
Electrostatic plotter, 20

ERASE, 20
ESCAPE, 20
Event primitive, 20, 62, 130
Exploded view, 20
Extension lines, 20

Familiarization program
    CRT, 91
    DVST, 99
    graphics tablet, 120
    plotters, 108
FILL, 20
Flash, 20
Flicker, 20
Flood gun, 20
Flow-charting, 32
FORMAT, 7
FORTRAN-77, 35, 55, 88
Frame buffer, 20
FREE, 58
Front view, 20
Functions, 56, 63, 172

Geometric
    constructions, 20, 129
    model, 20
Glitches, 14
Graphic
    field, 21
    language, 20, 130
    output media, 20
Grid, 21

Halftoning, 21
Haloed line, 21
Hard copy, 21, 75, 88, 124
Hardware, 87, 165, 283, 287
HASP, 21
Hedgehog, 21
Hiddenline
    elimination, 21, 257
    removal, 21, 257
Homogeneous coordinates, 169

ICON, 21, 63
If test, 4
Implicit, 56

Incremental, 21
INITT, 7
Inking, 21
Input devices, 3, 20
I/O (input/output)
    ACCEPT, 4, 56
    GET, 4, 56
    PRINT, 4, 56
    PUT, 4
    READ, 4, 56
    SEELOC, 4
    WHERE, 4
    WRITE, 4
Input primitive, 21
Insert, 56
Intensity
    linear, 241
    pixel, 240
    shading, 264
Interactive, 40, 57
Interlace scan, 21
Interpolation
    intensity, 229
    normal, 231

JCL, 21
Joystick, 21

Keyboard, 3, 21, 63, 171, 172

Layout and design drawing, 288
Light button, 21, 97
Line
    density, 22, 75
    generator, 22, 75
    weight, 22
Linear transformation, 21
Lissajous, 22
List, 58, 61
Locator, 22
LOGOFF, 58, 60
LOGON, 58, 120
LP (light pen), 4, 21, 63, 97

Mach bands, 22
Magnet, 58
Mask, 22
Matrix addressed, 22

Menu bar, 4, 41, 95, 97, 174
Microfilm, 3, 17
Mode, 22
Moire pattern, 22
Mouse, 22
MOVE, 4, 263
Multipicture system, 22

Nested subroutine, 22
NPTS, 7
Numerical control, 287

Origin, 22
Orthographic projection, 22
Output primitive, 22, 75

Pan, 23
Parameters, 23
Passive graphics, 23
PASSWD, 58
PCB design, 289
PDSLOOK, 58
Perspective, 23
PFK, 23
Pick, 23
Piping Diagrams, 289
Pitch, 232
Pixel, 23, 90
Phantom user, 57
Photographic film, 3
Plasma panel, 23
PLOT, 7
Plotter bed, 3, 20, 23, 88, 101
Pointing device, 3
Polygon, 4, 138
Primitive element, 32, 133
PROC, 58
Processor
    main, 167
    local, 168
    second, 169
PROFIL, 58
Programming technique, 2
PURGE, 58

Random scan, 23
Raster scan, 89, 90
Real time, 6, 13, 42

RECT, 4, 135
Refresh, 23
Rename, 58
Repetition, 32
Reset, 4
Roll, 234
Rotate, 23, 156, 238
RS-232, 24

SAGE, 3
SAVE, 58
Scaling, 24, 156, 237
Scissoring, 24
SCRATCH, 58
Screen, 3, 18
Scrolling, 24
Segment, 24
Selection block, 31
Selective erase, 24

Sequential job order, 57
SET, 4
Shade, 24, 159
SHOW, 7
SIGGRAPH, 16, 147
Simulation, 229, 253, 269
Solids, 160
Spline, 24
SPOOL, 58, 65
Staircassing, 24
Standalone, 24
Statements
    COMMON, 179
    DIMENSION, 177
    DO, 175
    FUNCTION, 179
    IF, 180
    I/O, 181
    NUMBERS, 177

Status, 58, 64
Stereo views, 24
Structured programming, 30, 70
Stylus, 24
Subroutines, 56
Surfaces
    multi, 229
    polygon, 229
System modularity, 281

Template drafting, 130, 289
Terminal points, 30
Thumbwheel, 24
Touch tablets, 63
TRACE, 56
Tracking, 24, 41
Transformations, 147, 231
Translation, 147, 234
Transparency, 226

TURN, 4
Turnkey, 68
TYPE, 7

USERS, 58

Vantage points, 232
Vector generator, 25, 170
Viewport, 25, 75

Wireframe, 158
Window, 25, 75, 170
Word, 25
World coordinates, 25
Wrap around, 25

Yaw, 232

Zoom, 25

DATE DUE

JA - 7 '85		
JA 31 '85		
MY 15 '85		
FE 5 '86		
AP 1 1 '86		
NO 1 1 '86		
DE 30 '86		
JA 26 '87		
FE 23 '90		
8-17-94		
GAYLORD		